THE RIGHT RELATIONSHIP

Reimagining the Implementation of Historical Treaties

The relationship between Canada's Indigenous peoples and the Canadian government is one that has increasingly come to the fore. Numerous tragic incidents, a legacy of historical negligence, and more vehement calls for action are forcing a reconsideration of the relationship between the federal government and Indigenous nations.

In *The Right Relationship*, John Borrows and Michael Coyle bring together a group of renowned scholars, both Indigenous and non-Indigenous, to cast light on the challenges Canadians face in seeking a consensus on the nature of treaty partnership in the twenty-first century. The diverse perspectives examine how Indigenous peoples' own legal and policy frameworks can be used to develop healthier attitudes between First Peoples and settler governments in Canada. While considering the existing law of Aboriginal and treaty rights, the contributors imagine what these relationships might look like if those involved pursued our highest aspirations as Canadians and Indigenous peoples. This timely and authoritative volume provides answers that will help pave the way towards good governance for all.

JOHN BORROWS is the Canada Research Chair in Indigenous Law in the Faculty of Law at the University of Victoria and is the winner of both the Canadian Political Science Association's Donald Smiley Prize (for *Recovering Canada*) and the Canadian Law and Society Association Book Prize (for *Canada's Indigenous Constitution*).

MICHAEL COYLE is an associate professor and Director of Graduate Programs in the Faculty of Law at Western University. He has over twenty-five years of experience in mediating disputes between the Crown and First Nations.

The Right Relationship

Reimagining the Implementation of Historical Treaties

EDITED BY JOHN BORROWS
AND MICHAEL COYLE

UNIVERSITY OF TORONTO PRESS
Toronto Buffalo London

Toronto Buffalo London
www.utorontopress.com
Printed in Canada

ISBN 978-1-4426-3020-8 (cloth) ISBN 978-1-4426-3021-5 (paper)

♾ Printed on acid-free, 100% post-consumer recycled paper with vegetable-based inks.

Library and Archives Canada Cataloguing in Publication

The right relationship : reimagining the implementation of historical treaties / edited by John Borrows and Michael Coyle.

Includes bibliographical references and index.
ISBN 978-1-4426-3020-8 (cloth). – ISBN 978-1-4426-3021-5 (paper)

1. Native peoples – Canada – Government relations. 2. Native peoples – Legal status, laws, etc. – Canada. I. Borrows, John, 1963–, author, editor II. Coyle, Michael, 1960–, author, editor

E92.R54 2017 971.004'97 C2016-906253-8

University of Toronto Press acknowledges the financial assistance to its publishing program of the Canada Council for the Arts and the Ontario Arts Council, an agency of the Government of Ontario.

Canada Council for the Arts Conseil des Arts du Canada

Funded by the Government of Canada Financé par le gouvernement du Canada

Canada

Contents

Acknowledgments

We would like to express our sincere thanks to the Social Sciences and Humanities Research Council of Canada for their generous support of the research reflected in this book and, in particular, for their financial support of the two national colloquiums in which the contributors to this volume were able to test and debate their theories on how the law of treaties might be reimagined. We also express our appreciation to the executive and members of the Indigenous Bar Association for providing a forum where many of these ideas were first shared. We are grateful to the JD students who helped edit the chapters of this book, Chelsea Smith and Sarah Jackson, of the Faculty of Law at Western University. Finally, we would like to acknowledge the diverse authors included in this book whose enthusiasm and collegial spirit helped create what we hope is a stimulating and intellectually interactive collection of ideas.

THE RIGHT RELATIONSHIP

Reimagining the Implementation of Historical Treaties

Introduction

MICHAEL COYLE AND JOHN BORROWS

What is the right relationship between Canada's Indigenous peoples and the modern nation that is Canada? For a growing number of Canadians, this is a question that must be tackled if Canadians are to hold their heads high when they describe the living conditions and social opportunities offered to Native people in this country. Just as pressing, reflecting on the relationship between Canada and First Peoples raises fundamental questions about Canada's legitimacy as a state and of Canadians' claims to be entitled to live where they do.

Historically, the treaty-making process was the favoured tool in Canada for assuring the future opportunities available to both the First Peoples of this land and the newly arrived settlers. Treaty-making was also the means by which colonial and, later, Canadian governments secured the legal basis of settlement within its borders. In 1764, more than 2,000 Indigenous representatives gathered for the Treaty of Niagara and were assured that settlement of land would only occur with their consent. Thus began the process by which the Senecas, the Mississaugas, the Odawa, the Potawatomis, the Saulteaux, the Dene, the Plains Cree, and many other nations entered into treaties to share their lands with settlers. For many Canadian government officials, the implications of those treaties are nicely contained within written documents drafted by Crown negotiators. However, for their Indigenous counterparts, who often spoke little English, the real importance of treaties was the relationship to which both sides had agreed. This relational aspect of the treaty-making venture is irrefutably manifested by the frequency with which, across the country, both sides' negotiators used language of kinship in describing the intended goal of the treaty process.

For much of the twentieth century, non-Indigenous Canadians and the courts viewed the historical treaties as little more than a cultural footnote in this nation's development. When it came to repatriating Canada's constitution, however, Native leaders united to ensure that at least the legal aspect of this neglect would end. The result? Section 35 of the *Constitution Act, 1982* now recognizes and affirms the treaty rights of Aboriginal peoples, which the Supreme Court of Canada has since characterized as "sacred" agreements.

Nonetheless, decades of inattention to the treaty relationship have left a legacy of confusion and disagreement about the implications of treaty-making in the modern world. Unlike New Zealand, Canada has created no effective forum to settle disputes about the meaning and modern implications of its historical treaties. Arguments have inevitably arisen about how much of a say Aboriginal people should have over proposed interferences with the environment of their homeland, or about the benefits they should receive from wealth extracted from their traditional territory. Yet when disagreements arise about whether a historical treaty allows unfettered exploitation of the resources found on treaty lands, the parties usually have nowhere to turn apart from costly and adversarial contention in the courts. In the absence of appropriate channels through which treaty disputes can be cooperatively resolved, those disagreements have repeatedly escalated into frustration and confrontation. In recent years, the inevitable result has been a constant stream of protests, blockades and, on occasion, violence and the loss of human life. This misfortune is surely inconsistent with the self-image of Canada as a pluralistic country where civic disagreements are resolved by dialogue and where the rule of law is preferred over force.

In this volume, many of Canada's leading thinkers on Indigenous issues were asked to reimagine how Canada's legal and political structures could better serve the treaty relationship that forms an inextricable part of our national story. Their common starting point for this volume was the 1764 Treaty of Niagara, one of the most important meetings of Aboriginal and settler leaders in Canadian history. Among other things, the Treaty of Niagara set the rules for new settlement in Canada, settlement that Crown officials guaranteed would come only after the Aboriginal peoples gave their consent to share their lands through treaty. To answer the question of how Canada might better address today the implications of the historical treaties that followed the Treaty of Niagara, each author in this book reflected on how disputes about those treaties should be resolved. This, in turn, required them to consider the remedies that should be available when one side claims that the other has failed to properly implement a treaty. All of the contributors are fully apprised of the existing laws of Aboriginal and treaty rights. Yet all engage the challenge of exploring what treaty relationships might look like if we pursued our highest aspirations as Canadians and Indigenous peoples.

Within this book you will find a lively and stimulating dialogue, in which the contributors grapple with basic elements of both Indigenous and non-Indigenous current law. Most of the authors gathered twice over the course of two years to discuss how treaty remedies might be reimagined. In the end, while a rich variety of views are presented here, four central questions dominate the chapters that follow: *What role should history and historical promises play in shaping modern treaty relationships? If we seek healthy treaty relationships, what should the role of the courts be in resolving disputes, and what is their role in relation to political and public dialogue? What role, if any, should be played by Indigenous values and legal traditions in informing treaty implementation? Should we look to other forums to implement treaties and to resolve treaty disputes?* These questions are not just academic concerns; they are issues that go to the heart of Canada's national identity. These questions will have to be addressed if Canada is to live in accordance with its highest aspirations as a country built on respect for the rule of law and democratic self-governance.

1. What Role Should History and Historical Promises Play in Shaping Modern Treaty Relationships?

Professor John Borrows begins this book by questioning how the Crown secured sovereignty and underlying title to lands in Canada when First Peoples never agreed to such actions. This state of domination has never been adequately explained by the Canadian courts. Such views appear to be based on assumptions that Indigenous peoples had inferior legal status to Europeans at the time of contact and assertions of sovereignty. At the same time, Borrows identifies a competing story which dates from the same era. This alternative narrative stresses the equality of peoples. In this story Canada's creation is rooted in narratives of respect, alliance, and partnership with Indigenous peoples. Borrows' chapter warns against remedies that fail to account for these complexities in Canada's history. In a practical world where historical narratives are contradictory, he calls for a more nuanced approach to treaty implementation which actively incorporates Indigenous law and legal perspectives. He posits that the goal of reconciliation as espoused by Canada's courts can be an unhealthy one *if* it asks Indigenous peoples to reconcile themselves to colonial subordination. Borrows worries that pre-contact racist and colonial narratives are integral to the Crown's culture of governance in Canada today. He argues that such views continue to undermine the courts' interpretation of treaty and Aboriginal rights. He points out ways in which these views allow federal and provincial governments to interfere with treaty-based constitutional orders which undergird the rule of law in Canada today.

Michael Coyle's chapter argues that Canadian courts have not adequately accounted for what must have been the parties' shared assumptions for the historic treaty-making process to make any rational sense. Each side was willing to enter into a formal relationship that was intended to permit both Indigenous peoples and incoming settlers to coexist long into the future ("as long as the sun shines"). In other words, they agreed to create a new and enduring normative order in this land. Historical land treaties between Indigenous peoples and the Crown were new institutions deliberately created to serve the interests of both parties, and conceivable only if they shared a number of common assumptions. For Coyle, those premises must not be ignored by the courts, regardless of the presence or dearth of surviving historical evidence in the case of individual treaties. His analysis calls for the recognition of important yet previously unrecognized implementation principles to give effect to the central intentions of the negotiators who jointly created this new institution in order to secure a healthy future for their peoples.

Kent McNeil focuses on the interaction between law and history in the adjudication of Indigenous legal claims. The Treaty of Niagara and the Royal Proclamation of 1763, which guaranteed Aboriginals rights to their lands, both offered protection for Indigenous peoples against the intrusions of local governments in matters related to their land and resources. Lately, some courts have been willing to entertain "expert evidence" that the legal implications of those protections can be undermined by proof that some colonial officials did not take them seriously in the past. As McNeil demonstrates, difficulties arise when traditional common law approaches to expert evidence are brought to bear on distant historical events. What follows is a fascinating account of legal principles that should be applied to past events.

Julie Jai draws on her experience as a former chief negotiator for the Yukon government to apply negotiation theory to understanding historical land treaties. She points out that most of those treaties were signed when Aboriginal peoples' bargaining power was at a low point and that their terms reflect this. She suggests that principles from modern treaties, beginning in 1976 in areas missed during the earlier treaty-making process, should be read into historical treaties as implied terms. In a thought-provoking analysis, she draws out common principles from contemporary Canadian treaties and urges that a proper interpretation of the older treaties would also take these common principles into account.

Francesca Allodi-Ross takes up the challenges of treaty implementation in a firmly contemporary context, exploring the question of who, individuals as well as their communities, should be entitled to articulate Indigenous treaty claims before the courts. Indigenous individuals, exercising what they believe are their peoples' treaty rights, will often be those who are the most affected by alleged violations of their treaty. Her chapter considers a recent example of the tension between individual and collective claims to treaty rights, and suggests how the courts might deal with this tension in future.

Finally, in this first section, Professor Sari Graben and Matthew Mehaffey, a negotiator for the Carcross/Tagish First Nation, examine the impact of colonial history on the interpretation of modern treaties. If the legal specificity of modern treaties purports to offer a more equitable or just approach to governing, these co-authors argue that if law is to play a role in tempering the effects of intergovernmental politics, then no matter how detailed the treaty text, courts must undertake the same task for contemporary treaties as that posed for historical treaties: develop a common legality or a narrative that does justice to right relations. They conclude that the specificity of contemporary treaties as legal documents is not able to redeem relations marked by colonialism. The authors argue here that without grounding contemporary treaties in their federalist aims, the redemptive power of law, even where painstakingly detailed, is likely to remain elusive for the courts.

2. If We Seek Healthy Treaty Relationships, What Should the Role of the Courts Be in Resolving Disputes and What Is Their Role in Relation to Political and Public Dialogue?

The Canadian courts have played an undeniably significant part in giving meaning to the rights affirmed for Aboriginal peoples in section 35 of Canada's *Constitution Act, 1982*. Indeed in its first decision on Aboriginal rights following the repatriation of the constitution, the Supreme

Court of Canada declared that the coming into effect of section 35 had renounced "the old rules of the game," under which courts had been unable to challenge Crown claims that its sovereign decisions were supreme. Since then, Canadian courts have ruled that treaties must be interpreted in accordance with the common intention of the treaty partners and that oral promises made during treaty negotiations cannot be ignored when interpreting treaty texts. Some commentators, however, including contributors to this book, argue that Canadian court procedures are ill-suited to resolving disputes about the implementation of treaties. For some, the treaties cannot be reduced to legal instruments; their scope was broader, intended to create the framework for a dynamic, political partnership between distinct societies. The treaties, after all, with their "polycentric" subject matter – ranging from regulation of land uses to relations between peoples – fall outside the usual scope of judicial experience and the borders of traditional legal remedies. Other critics argue that Canadian judges will likely be reluctant to admit claims that question the fundamental premises of their society, such as the validity of Crown assertions of sovereignty. Others, however, again including contributors to this book, argue that the courts are capable of taking up the challenge of interpreting the treaty relationship in a way that honours the expectations of both treaty partners and can help strengthen relations between Indigenous people and non-Indigenous Canadians.

Mark Walters' chapter in this volume takes us back to the foundations of the "Covenant Chain" relationship between the Indigenous peoples and the Crown memorialized in the earliest treaties entered into by the British on this continent and emphasized repeatedly in later dealings between First Nations and colonial officials. Walters highlights the importance of Indigenous world views in understanding the Covenant Chain relationship and asks whether modern Canadian courts are capable of giving meaningful effect to some of the sweeping implications imbedded in that relationship. Through a careful and cautious analysis of recent case law, he points the way towards at least one judicial remedy that might be capable of strengthening that relationship.

Aaron Mills argues passionately that, properly understood, treaties with Indigenous peoples are not even the kind of relationship capable of giving rise to a legal remedy. An emerging Indigenous scholar, Mills is deeply sceptical of the notion that Canadian courts are capable of building a body of treaty doctrine that would reflect Indigenous understandings and offer justice to Indigenous peoples. For Mills, treaties were intended to be "the total relational means" (political, social, spiritual, etc.) by which the treaty partners were to orient themselves to each other over time. To reflect this reality, Mills suggests, requires a complete rethinking of Canadian citizenship as ultimately founded on the order created by the historic treaties. The remainder of his contribution sketches out his proposed response to this challenge.

For their part, Borrows and Coyle both focus primarily on the failures and promise of Canadian law in this area. Borrows offers a troubling reflection on a recent trend in Canadian jurisprudence to depart from what he sees as the historical treaty narrative. In its place, he sees a disquieting judicial shift towards empowering local governments – the very governments most likely to find themselves in conflicts of interest with Indigenous peoples on the ground. Coyle also acknowledges and reviews some of the gaps in Canada's domestic law governing treaties. He argues that Canadian treaty law has focused immoderately on the norms accepted by non-Indigenous society. Still, he notes that, for the time being at least, Canadian courts will inevitably be drawn into legal disputes about treaty implementation. Given this fact, he suggests that the courts have a duty to take into account the values and expectations of Indigenous treaty makers and, most importantly, to expressly recognize the legal consequences of what must have been the shared assumptions of both treaty partners.

3. What Roles, If Any, Should Be Played by Indigenous Values and Legal Traditions in Informing Treaty Implementation?

It has long been recognized in the world of dispute resolution theory that, to borrow from the American scholar Frank Sander, "the forum should fit the fuss." In other words, the process used to manage or resolve disputes should be tailored to the subject matter of the dispute and the values and goals of the disputants. A process that mirrors the norms and beliefs of only one of the parties is unlikely to be seen as legitimate by the other or to produce outcomes that both will consider fair. In recent years, the Supreme Court of Canada has insisted that Indigenous law and legal perspectives should be taken into account in treaty disputes. Despite this insistence, in 2016, Canadian courts have yet to apply any specifically Indigenous perspective in identifying what a treaty is and how this intercultural institution should be interpreted. Nor have federal and provincial governments stepped up, as recommended by the Royal Commission on Aboriginal Peoples, and more recently, by the Ipperwash Inquiry in Ontario, to institute policies of engagement with Indigenous peoples about the spirit and intent of the treaties. When Indigenous law and perspectives related to treaties are ignored this creates a rising sense of frustration on both sides of the treaty table. The challenge of recognizing Indigenous agency and world views is a central preoccupation of both the Indigenous and non-Indigenous contributors to this book. How might both Indigenous and non-Indigenous perspectives on treaties be practically reconciled? The contributors to this volume offer a fascinating array of possible answers. One obvious starting point is to allow Indigenous understandings of treaty to be described in a distinctly Aboriginal voice. Aaron Mills, John Borrows, Jacinta Ruru, Sarah Morales, and Heidi Stark all offer visions of treaty relations that rely on Indigenous metaphors and values, for example, of moral commitments, gift, and right relations rather than rights.

Anishinaabe scholar Heidi Kiiwetinepinesiik Stark highlights the danger posed by fixating on the specific language used in written versions of the treaties and by the framing of rights in language familiar to the modern Canadian state. Stark suggests that the treaties' intentions can only be discerned by understanding the larger framework of Indigenous governance and legal traditions. Borrows reminds us that those Indigenous traditions were expressly recognized by Crown negotiators in building legal relationships that fostered peace and friendship over warfare and force. His contribution examines the importance of Indigenous law in developing appropriate treaty remedies. Equally, he stresses that vibrant Indigenous structures of decision-making are essential not just to treaty implementation, but also for the multigenerational well-being of Indigenous communities. Finally, Sarah Morales, a scholar from the Hul'qumi'num people in British Columbia, argues that recognition of Indigenous values in relation to "good faith" and appropriate dispute resolution are not merely worthy of attention today. For Morales, those Indigenous values must inform modern treaty-making negotiations if those negotiations are to have any chance of moving us forward on the path of reconciliation.

As noted earlier, Mark Walters' reflection on treaty rights and remedies also takes as its starting point the premise that those remedies cannot be isolated from the Indigenous legal traditions that shaped the Covenant Chain treaty relationship. Walters explores the tools available to the Canadian courts to encourage structured forms of dialogue that are consistent with Indigenous conceptions of legality. For her part, Jacinta Ruru uses a Maori perspective to describe how the flexibility of a negotiation process can allow Indigenous law to be used in unprecedented ways to address treaty disputes. Ruru describes recent innovative land settlements in Aotearoa New Zealand that could serve as examples for Canadians of the kind of creativity in building consensus across disparate world views that open-minded negotiation can make possible.

Without focusing as much on specific Indigenous legal traditions, Sara Seck and Coyle sketch out, respectively, the potential of international law and Canadian domestic law to give meaningful and equal respect to Aboriginal peoples as norm-creating and law-making agents. Expectations that Indigenous peoples in Canada will develop and use Indigenous legal interpretations of treaties are affirmed by Graben and Mehaffey. Nonetheless, they caution that, even where Indigenous legal interpretations are generated, the parties may still end up developing interim political settlements that avoid shared meaning. Finally, as mentioned, Aaron Mills is more sceptical of the courts' capacity to give effect to historic treaty understandings. Like Stark and Morales, however, he suggests that greater judicial recognition of Indigenous legal traditions would help to make space for those traditions in a way that will allow them to stand within Canada on their own terms and thus contribute to a more balanced and just treaty relationship.

4. Should We Look to Other Forums to Implement Treaties and to Resolve Treaty Disputes?

A final important question for treaty implementation in Canada is whether forums other than Canadian courts might have a unique role to play in addressing the unique challenges of treaty implementation. As Mills, Walters, Ruru, and other contributors to this volume point out, the implications of the historical treaties and the enduring relationships engendered by those treaties clearly have implications beyond the confines of the remedies traditionally available to common law courts.

The contributions to this book make clear that progress in recognizing Indigenous treaty and land rights is likely to occur in parallel in a number of separate settings. Sara Seck and Shin Imai, for example, describe the growing importance of direct dialogue between corporations and Indigenous communities in addressing those rights at the intersection of resource development and Indigenous rights. Morales describes the potential role and value of Coast Salish dispute resolution processes in confronting the obstacles at the heart of the impasse-riddled treaty negotiation process in British Columbia. Graben and Mehaffey explore how contemporary treaty governance can use ownership, program responsibility, and clear treaty entitlements to counter colonial defaults that presume centralized financial management. Finally, Jai and Ruru both explore the opportunities made available by the creation of the jointly agreed bicultural processes for managing treaty disputes. Ruru's chapter provides a comparative lens into a country on the other side of the world that was also colonized by Britain. She compares the challenges of reimagining treaties in Canada with the modern Treaty of Waitangi claims process in Aotearoa New Zealand. What is unique about that settlement process and what have been its results? Ruru's reflections on some very recent and innovative treaty settlements in Aotearoa New Zealand offer food for thought about the value of having a customized process for resolving treaty disputes.

The last section of the book focuses on the potential role of international legal norms in strengthening the treaty relationship in Canada. Leading Québécois legal scholar Jean Leclair presents a thoughtful meditation on the promulgation of law and its claims to legitimacy in guiding people's lives. His chapter weighs the arguments made by those who would defend the adjudicative authority of Canadian courts on treaties between the Crown and Indigenous peoples and the opposing claims of those who argue that the decisions of such courts will always be tainted by imperialism. Along the way, he offers a nuanced investigation of whether a middle ground is possible in the debate about the legitimacy of Canadian courts' involvement in disputes between the treaty partners.

Sara Seck focuses on an interesting evolution of international law in recent years. Her chapter describes the move from a state-centric approach in which Aboriginal treaty partners were seen only as objects of international law, to a perspective in which Aboriginal peoples have been actively involved in defining their identities, rights, and responsibilities under international law. Seck describes the growing importance, not just of Aboriginal peoples as non-state actors in international law, but also of business enterprises, which are increasingly entering into agreements with Aboriginal peoples about the conditions under which resources may be extracted from their lands. Her chapter analyses the significance of this re-energized engagement between Aboriginal peoples and businesses within the context of their involvement in shaping international law alongside of state governments.

In the book's final chapter, Imai notes that the recent United Nations Declaration on the Rights of Indigenous Peoples recognizes that

Indigenous people must consent to the exploitation of resources on their lands. The declaration is not an enforceable treaty, but many hoped that it would encourage states to voluntarily modify their conduct to comply with the declaration. Strangely, Imai argues, the declaration has not yet changed state practice, but instead has had significant uptake in corporate standards of conduct. Describing the effect of these voluntary standards of conduct, Imai discusses the possibilities for taking corporate social responsibility seriously and applying the standards in the declaration to strengthen the recognition of the need for Indigenous consent to resource extraction on Indigenous lands.

5. Conclusion

It is our hope that the diverse perspectives presented in this book cast light on the magnitude of the challenges Canadians face in seeking a consensus on the nature of treaty partnership in the twenty-first century. It becomes clear as one progresses through this book that those challenges go far beyond parsing the written words of treaties as recorded by Crown commissioners. This book suggests that Canadian law should respond in more sophisticated and nuanced ways to narratives inherent in historical treaty-making processes. Furthermore, Canadians must come to grips with the reality that treaty-making was more focused on building relationships and much less concerned with cataloguing rights. While Indigenous peoples' treaty rights are crucial parts of these agreements, this book contextualizes such rights within a broader relationship. Treaties first and foremost are concerned with right relations between First Peoples and settler governments. It is these relationships that give rights their meaning. This means that Indigenous understandings and legal traditions must be taken into account if Canada is to attain and implement a balanced approach to the treaty relationship.

This book is filled with constructive and forward-looking ideas about how Canada, its courts, and its political institutions might rethink and reform their approach to treaties. We hope that this book's orientation, looking forward rather than backward, will inspire other Canadians – lawyers, elected officials, public servants, journalists, and indeed all concerned citizens – to use their hearts and minds to engage with this issue in a similarly forward-looking way. That, after all, is what our forebears did when they strove, through treaties, to help each other navigate through a world that was changing in their midst.

PART I

Treaty Remedies – How Should History Shape the Law?

1 Canada's Colonial Constitution

JOHN BORROWS

In 1764, over two thousand Indigenous people representing twenty-two First Nations gathered at Niagara and entered into a treaty of peace, friendship, and respect between themselves and the British Crown. This agreement confirmed that Indigenous peoples would not have to deal with local colonial governments in matters of land and resource use. Instead, the Crown would empower its own representatives to deal with such matters. The Royal Proclamation of 1763 confirmed a similar policy, and subsequent treaties were often signed on this basis in many places across the land. These promises and laws created a significant check against local pressure for the development of Indigenous lands. This chapter examines how these promises and laws have been undermined in the last 140 years as the Crown has "shape shifted" in the eyes of Indigenous peoples. Canada's constitutional narratives have now placed provinces in a predominant position in relation to Indigenous peoples. This is contrary to promises made to Aboriginal peoples on whose land Canada is built. Borrows' chapter examines the importance of Indigenous law in developing treaties in the past and in constructing remedies for the challenges Indigenous peoples and Canada face today as a result of their deteriorating relationships.

... the people of the States where they are found are often their deadliest enemies.[1]

Samuel Freeman Miller, United States Supreme Court

1 *United States v Kagama*, 118 US 375 (1888) at 383.

1. Legal Fictions

There are many stories about how Canada was formed. One of those stories focuses on the dispossession and displacement of the land's first inhabitants through force. Doctrines of discovery, adverse possession, and conquest figure prominently in these accounts.[2] These doctrines imply that Canada was legally empty when Europeans arrived. "Discovering" nations claimed Indigenous peoples' lands by the sheer power of their words; through the force of "law" alone. As the Supreme Court of Canada wrote in its seminal Aboriginal rights case, "from the outset never any doubt that sovereignty and legislative power, and indeed the underlying title, to such lands vested in the Crown."[3] The Court concluded that the Crown had sovereignty and underlying title in Canada because Indigenous peoples have inferior legal status.

There are many problems with this story. It founds Canada on racist assumptions. It presumes there was a conquest when there was never any war. It assumes Indigenous peoples had imperfect claims to sovereignty and title when Europeans arrived. Indigenous peoples are pushed aside in this story because their legal status is subordinate to European power. If Canadian law flows from this view, it revolves around a loathsome core. Discrimination, coercion, and inequality lie at the roots of Canada's legal system under this view. All subsequent acts are tainted by an original sin. This story tells Canadians that our deepest political values are ultimately traceable to a denial of fairness, equality, and mutual respect. This builds Canada on a dishonorable foundation. In this view, subsequent appeals to raw force have a degree of political legitimacy because they are consistent with Canada's first principles. This story, in its unvarnished state, happens to be a lie. It does not accord with the facts. It is a legal fiction that does not take account of the complexities of Canada's formation.

2. Counter-Narratives

Of course force, deceit, fraud, inequality, and discrimination are a part of Canada's formation. There is no denying this fact. All legal systems

2 These doctrines are discussed in earlier work of mine: John Borrows, *Canada's Indigenous Constitution* (Toronto: University of Toronto Press, 2010) in chapter 1.

3 *R v Sparrow*, [1990] 1 SCR 1075.

struggle against human weakness, greed, and cruelty. Canada is no exception. But there are counterpoints to this national narrative. There are other stories which lay the heart of our nation. They appeal to a better way of living. The tensions revealed in these alternatives invite us to struggle against simplistic views when construing our constitutional foundations.

Canada's formation is not a simple horror story; nor is it the product of a gloriously pure birth. Canada is simultaneously a good and bad place with contested foundations, though severe power imbalances make it much better for some people than others. We must not romanticize our past. Nor should we misconstrue our present circumstances. We should see our country through clear eyes and celebrate its strengths *and* decry its weakness. In particular, in constitutional terms, we must avoid replacing Canada's flawed foundations with an equally problematic honourable founding myth – even if that myth places Indigenous peoples on a stronger footing. Life is more complicated than single stories would allow, and Canadian law should recognize this fact.

The truth is that Canada's formation does not just rest on racism, force, and discrimination. Canada is also rooted in doctrines of persuasion, reason, peace, friendship, and respect. While Canada's ongoing creation is deeply flawed, it also contains various positive qualities which enhance many lives. These influences mingle together in complementary and inconsistent ways throughout our legal system. For example, we can recognize that the doctrine of discovery is controversial; it does not enjoy universal acceptance. A Royal Commission called it "legally, morally and factually wrong."[4] The Supreme Court of Canada has written that "[t]he doctrine of terra nullius (that no one owned the land prior to European assertion of sovereignty) never applied in Canada."[5] While this is an overstatement which conceals how *terra nullius* continues to operate in Canada, it nevertheless presents an

---

4 See *Report of the Royal Commission on Aboriginal Peoples: Looking Forward and Looking Back*, vol. 1 (Ottawa: Supply and Services Canada, 1996) at recommendation 1.16.2 at page 696:

> Federal, provincial and territorial government further the process of renewal by: (a) acknowledging that concepts such as *terra nullius* and the doctrine of discovery are factually, legally and morally wrong.

5 *Tsilhqot'in Nation v British Columbia*, 2014 SCC 44 [*Tsilhqot'in*].

alternative view.[6] Furthermore, the Supreme Court of Canada has also attempted to repudiate this idea that Canada was built on conquest. It has written, "Put simply, Canada's Aboriginal peoples were here when Europeans came, and were never conquered."[7] These statements demonstrate that the construction of Canada's foundational facts is subject to ongoing and cross-cutting debate. We must do more to entrench the complexities of Canada's formation in our constitutional narratives.

3. Rejecting the Story of Reconciliation

The presence of alternative readings of Canada's constitutional foundations holds significant implications for taking remedial action when Indigenous peoples and the Crown find themselves embroiled in conflict. Remedies can only be implemented in real-world circumstances. A remedy which fails to consider the complexities of our nation's founding principles risks overlooking its deeply colonial nature. At the same time, a remedy which neglects the country's complex foundations also denies access to important sources of authority that challenge Canada's racism and structural inequalities. Law's remedial prospects are enhanced when decision-makers become more fully cognizant of these contradictory views and experiences.

In identifying the constitution's narrative complexities, I wish to emphasize that I am not calling for a synthesis of these differing views. This would create another kind of simplicity, which I am trying to avoid. Attending to Canada's constitutional inconsistencies is not a demand for their reconciliation. Reconciliation has problematically dominated the jurisprudence dealing with Indigenous issues and is a flawed metaphor in this field. Any compromise with colonialism causes us to be compromised by colonialism. It not enough to saw off the differences between problematic and laudatory versions of Canada's constitutional narratives. Courts and Canadians more generally must reject colonialism, and not try to reconcile Indigenous peoples and others to it. We must not harmonize racism with our higher principles. Colonialism is a

6 John Borrows, "The Durability of Terra Nullius: Tsilhqot'in v. British Columbia" (2014) *Maori Law Review* (forthcoming).

7 *Haida Nation v British Columbia*, [2004] 3 SCR 511 at para 25.

living force and it must be rejected. This would be the best remedy for constitutional conflict.

At the same time, the rejection of Canada's discriminatory constitutional principles should not be replaced with another false narrative. We should not construct an unremittingly positive, glorious past. Even positive aspects of Canada's founding narratives are partial. Life in Canada has always been horrible for many people, and this will likely be true through time. An overly bright view of our heritage of tolerance, persuasion, peace, friendship, and respect would base remedial prescriptions on false premises – on lies. It would mislead some into thinking that future harmony is possible because perfect legal guidance was found in the past. The past is not perfect, but seeing our constitutional heritage in a realistic light will reveal remedial options in the present, despite the mess in which we find ourselves. We do not have to abandon hope, even as we eschew naivety.

4. The Treaty Story

One of the dominant constitutional narratives which can be used to challenge Canada's darker colonial history is rooted in Indigenous treaty relationships. There is much to recommend in this approach. In some circles, particularly in the prairies, treaties between Indigenous peoples and the Crown are regarded as solemn, sacred covenants. In this view, treaties created Canada on a foundation of mutual regard and respect. "We are all treaty people" is part of the refrain. This perspective suggests that the country came together with the participation and consent of First Nations and Crown representatives. Since Canada was formed through agreement, this narrative demands that its ongoing formation should be forged through seeking continual consensus between Indigenous peoples and the Crown. Any departure from this arrangement is a violation of Canada's foundational laws. Sometimes this view is labelled treaty federalism. Within this view, treaties are compacts between nations. Subsequent dealings must accord with these original pacts or risk being void and of no effect.

The strength of the treaty narrative makes it difficult to develop policy with some First Nations. Any step which does not accord with the original treaty relationship is deeply suspect. This stance is understandable when we remind ourselves of the power imbalance between Indigenous peoples and governments within Canada. Invoking higher treaty principles, which are potentially constitutionally protected, provides a strong protective shield for resisting Canada's diminishment of First Nations' political power. In this respect, treaty federalism serves First Nations well if it holds back the tides of assimilatory, discriminatory, and colonial law and policy.

However, treaty principles are also invoked for reasons that are not merely strategic. In many quarters, there is a deep, sincere, and abiding belief in a purer form of constitutionalism. Elders and leaders in some circles speak of treaties in sacred terms. They are regarded as blessed by the Creator. They are seen as the product of and are viewed with profound reverence. Law is "spiritualized" in this account; it is more than the product of human action. This vision is particularly prominent in the prairies and among the numbered treaty nations. There is also much to recommend in this story, and it could be strengthened, even as we subject this narrative to critical evaluation.

When Canada was forming, First Nations were promised that their political dealings with the British settlers would be mediated by the Imperial Crown in Great Britain. There was an original agreement, and it seemed to place First Nations consent at the heart of its process. This is known as the Treaty of Niagara, which celebrated its 250th anniversary in 2014. At the gathering, 2,000 Indigenous people representing twenty-two Indigenous Nations assembled in Niagara to create a relationship with the British Crown. Indigenous leaders entered into an agreement of peace, friendship, and respect in which Indigenous peoples received promises that settler governments would not have authority over them. The Mi'kmaq, Maliseet, and Passamaquoddy of the Maritimes had created a similar process. These arrangements were confirmed by the Royal Proclamation, which pledged the Crown to respect First Nations lands and governance. Though the Royal Proclamation also contained a darker colonial vision, it nevertheless contains solemn promises to ensure that local governments ceased molesting and disturbing Indigenous peoples. Under this vision, Canada was to become a peaceful place for "Indians" and foreign settlers, based on persuasion and the rejection of force. Again, this was largely premised on the view that First Nations leaders accepted a constitutional arrangement which precluded local governments from dealing with them in matters related to their land, governance, or resources.

This framework for dealings between peoples was entrenched in subsequent constitutional arrangements. It was also a central provision in most of the treaties signed in Southern Ontario and on Vancouver Island. This view seems to have been replicated over one hundred years later at Confederation. The more distant federal government was given responsibility for dealing with "Indians and lands reserved for Indians," while the provinces were only given control over "[m]atters of a merely local or private Nature in the Province." This procedure echoed and implemented the Treaty of Niagara's arrangements – local governments (provinces) would be precluded from dealing with Indians. The English-speaking centralists with whom First Nations largely dealt reiterated this arrangement in subsequent treaties over the next fifty years. Throughout Canadian history, First Nations have largely held on to this idea. In this view, First Nations' political and legal life has been built around one central fact – colonial, and later, provincial governments were forbidden from legislating in relation to their interests. Though there are many truths in the "treaty account" of Canada which have been grossly overlooked, in its pure form, this story also dabbles in legal fiction.

5. Chronicling Colonialism through Decentralization

This is because, all the while, another colonial narrative was evolving – one which gave the colonies and provinces the upper hand. Colonies dispossessed Indigenous peoples despite the Proclamation. Subsequently, the successors to Canada's original colonies, the provinces, became a major force in the country's colonization. Indigenous peoples' constitutional arrangements stood in tension with these decentralizing political forces. Literally speaking, Indigenous peoples did not want to be "colonized" – they did not want to have to deal with the government's colonies. For many First Nations, the development of colonies meant the further development of colonialization.

On the other hand, local governments (colonies and later provinces) did not like being excluded from dealing with Indian lands. Thirteen North American colonies went to war over this issue. The American War of Independence was partially a reaction to the Crown's restrictions on local governments' authority over "Indians and lands reserved for Indians." Furthermore, when Canada was formed, the provinces acted like the American colonies before them. They wanted to get their hands on Indian lands. While they did not go to war like the colonies to the south, they did launch an offensive legal action to claim the material benefits of Indigenous peoples' lands.

Thus, while the federal government conducted the treaty process in Canada, the British Judicial Committee of the Privy Council,

Canada's highest court, vested the beneficial interest of any land surrenders in the provincial government. The Court elevated section 109 of the *Constitution Act, 1867* over other constitutional traditions which would have created a greater buffer between local governments and First Nations. The *St. Catherines Milling and Lumber Company* case held that "from beginning to end" treaties were "a transaction between the Indians and the Crown," not an agreement between the government of Canada and the Ojibway people.[8] By dividing the Crown into constituent parts, the Privy Council eroded the promises of the Proclamation and Treaty of Niagara. As a result of this decision, First Nations saw local (colonial/provincial) governments grow in strength. The provinces developed Indigenous lands; they gained the most from First Nations dispossession. While the Dominion government's actions have always been problematic, the provinces became a significant source of First Nations misery as confederation continued to decentralize across the land. This set the stage for future conflict.

Quebec and British Columbia largely refused to sign treaties through most of their history. They acted as if they owned the place despite the facts on the ground. They developed lands and harvested resources which were owned and occupied by Indigenous peoples. In other words, they stole Indigenous peoples' lands contrary to the agreement at Niagara and the high promises of the King found in the Royal Proclamation. Canada's treaty narrative was sullied in the process. The attempt to build a country on persuasion, agreement, mutual aid, participation, and consent "went off the rails." Provinces and local officials directly competed with First Nations for land. Pre-emption in British Columbia turned Native territory into provincial land.[9] In Ontario and the West, provincially backed squatters forced the repudiation or renegotiation of many treaties.[10] As provincial authority grew, courtesy of the Privy Council and other decentralizing forces, Indigenous power declined. As the treaty process waned for fifty years, beginning with the Great Depression, First Nations were pushed to the side. Provincial interests grew in strength. Canada was built at the expense of First

---

8 *St Catherines Milling and Lumber Co v The Queen*, [1888] 14 App Cas 46 (PC) at 60.

9 Paul Tennant, *Aboriginal Peoples and Politics in British Columbia: The Indian Land Question in British Columbia, 1849–1989* (Vancouver: UBC Press, 1990).

10 Sarah Carter, *Lost Harvests: Prairie Indian Reserve Farmers and Government Policy* (Montreal: McGill-Queen's University Press, 1990).

Nations. Indigenous lands and resources were redistributed from their original owners to newly settled, originally foreign governments.

6. Parliament's Complicity: Section 88 of the *Indian Act*

In the 1950s, the process of subjecting Indigenous peoples to provincial law was extended through federal legislation. The federal government further departed from its treaty and Proclamation promises and resiled from its section 91(24) responsibility to protect First Nations from provincial governments and interests. It did so through the passage of section 87 (now section 88) of the *Indian Act*. This section forces Indians to abide by all laws of general application in force within a province.[11] This makes First Nations largely subject to provincial legislation and regulates them without their consent.[12] For example, section 88 of the *Indian Act* drastically constrains jurisdictional areas over which Indigenous peoples should have had sovereign authority.[13] It does so by delegating vast fields of political activity to provincial governments by referentially incorporating, as federal law, provincial laws of general application.[14] This severely limits First Nations' political power in Canada.[15] It also creates very few incentives for the federal government to work with First Nations to pass legislation recognizing and affirming Aboriginal and treaty rights throughout the country.

---

11 Provincial laws of general application apply to Indians except if they conflict with:
existing treaty rights;
existing federal legislation;
any provisions in the *Indian Act*;
any order, rule, regulation or by-law made under the *Indian Act*.

12 Darlene Johnston, *The Taking of Indian Lands in Canada: Consent or Coercion* (Saskatoon: Native Law Center, 1989).

13 For a history and legal analysis of section 88 of the *Indian Act*, see Kerry Wilkins, "Still Crazy After All These Years: Section 88 at Fifty" (2000) 38 *Alberta Law Review* 458.

14 See *R v Dick*, [1985] 2 SCR 309 [*Dick*]; *Kitkatla Band v British Columbia (Minister of Small Business, Tourism and Culture)* [2002] 2 SCR 146 [*Kitkatla*].

15 For arguments questioning the constitutionality of section 88 of the *Indian Act*, see Leroy Little Bear, "Section 88 of the Indian Act and the Application of Provincial Laws to Indians" in J. Anthony Long and Menno Boldt, eds., *Governments in Conflict? Provinces and Indian Nations in Canada* (Toronto: University of Toronto Press, 1988); Kent McNeil, "Aboriginal Title and Section 88 of the Indian Act" (2000) 34 *University of British Columbia Law Review* 157.

The federal government's "transfer" of legislative responsibility from itself and First Nations to provincial governments is a significant derogation from a First Nations-derived constitutional narrative. It is contrary to the Treaty of Niagara and the Royal Proclamation. It does not build the country on agreement, persuasion, and consent; it constructs the country on force. Assimilation and discrimination are the hallmarks of this narrative. Section 88 does not enhance participation when it makes provincial laws applicable to "Indians." At a federal level, this allows the federal government to almost completely abandon its section 91(24) constitutional responsibility concerning "Indians and lands reserved for Indians."

By "passing the buck" to the provinces, the federal government avoids facing the consequences of its delegation of authority. First Nations must comply with provincial laws which they have no real role in crafting or administering. In fact, if provinces were to "single out" Indians in the passage of provincial legislation such action would be *ultra vires*, or unconstitutional, because acting in relation to Indians is beyond provincial authority.[16] Thus, section 88 of the *Indian Act* removes incentives from both the provincial and federal governments to work with Indians on the details of laws which most affect Indian peoples' lives. The "idea" of assimilation built into the *Indian Act* and other Canadian legislative action usurps First Nations' authority.[17] It departs from a more generous narrative concerning Canada's foundation. It is deeply colonial.

These trajectories were reinforced in 1966 and 1985 in two seminal cases from the Supreme Court of Canada. The case of *Cardinal v AG of Alberta* rejected an "enclave" theory of Indian reserves. By virtue of this case, First Nations could not claim that their lands or governance was carved out from general provincial power.[18] Contrary to the Proclamation, First Nations lands were not viewed as islands of authority free of provincial control. The Court wrote:

---

16 See *Dick, supra* note 14, and *Kitkatla, supra* note 14.

17 An innovative argument which develops First Nations autonomy in Canada along familiar constitutional lines is Bruce Ryder, "The Demise and Rise of the Classical Paradigm in Canadian Federalism: Promoting Autonomy for the Provinces and the First Nations" (1991) 36 *McGill Law Journal* 308.

18 *Cardinal v Attorney General of Alberta*, [1974] SCR 695 [*Cardinal*]; see also *Four B Manufacturing Ltd v United Garment Workers of America*, [1980] 1 SCR 1031. The Supreme Court of Canada further endorsed the rejection of the enclave theory in *Kitkatla, supra* note 14 at para 66.

> A Provincial Legislature could not enact legislation in relation to Indians, or in relation to Indian Reserves, but this is far from saying that the effect of s. 91(24) of the *British North America Act, 1867,* was to create enclaves within a Province within the boundaries of which Provincial legislation could have no application.[19]

The *Cardinal* case is significant because it rejects the spirit of the Royal Proclamation and Treaty of Niagara by enabling the provinces to "disturb" Indian interests. The holding in this case was reinforced by *R v Dick* in 1985.[20] This case held that First Nations cannot claim immunity from provincial law on the basis of their "Indianness."

If First Nations cannot function as enclaves in Canada's federation, and their authority is subject to provincial laws of general application, they will largely be subject to other peoples' authority and policy goals. This troubling legal regime, along with First Nations' smaller size and their subordination consign them to this fate. In fact, this has been a prominent theme throughout the last 100 years as Indigenous peoples were forced to comply with other government objectives. The brighter narratives of agreement gave way to the darker stories of colonialism and assimilation. This is the state of Canadian constitutional law today. Indigenous peoples are very poorly served by the present order. They are subject to the force of other people's political and legal will in most everything they do.

7. Constitutionalizing Colonialism: Section 35(1), *Tsilhqot'in* and *Grassy Narrows*

There are a few more pages to this story, however, which have recently been written by the Supreme Court of Canada. This is the story of section 35(1) of the *Constitution Act, 1982*. There are bright moments in this narrative too, despite its problems. Neither Canada nor the provinces can unilaterally extinguish existing Aboriginal and treaty rights. Aboriginal and treaty rights also cannot be infringed unless governments justify such diminishment through pressing and substantial objectives which respect and implement the honour of the Crown. Unfortunately,

19 See *Cardinal, ibid* at 703.

20 *Dick, supra* note 14.

in other respects, the post-1982 story has mostly continued the pre-1982 narrative. Colonialism remains a core Canadian activity as the state persists in vesting the "colonies" with the power to "colonize" Indians. Indigenous peoples have not been recognized as possessing governmental authority under section 35(1), at least in explicit terms. Provinces continue to have the upper hand in legislating in relation to Indians. In this respect, the Supreme Court has played the same role as the Privy Council, as abetted by Parliament, in allowing the country to be built at the expense of Indigenous rights and interests.

But there may be a brighter body of law emerging, under which still beats a very dark heart. What this growth will produce remains to be seen. A cause for hope is that Crown sovereignty is beginning to be constrained in Canada. Government power is attenuated when it encounters constitutionally protected Aboriginal and treaty rights under section 35(1) of the constitution. While it is too early to tell whether these constraints will actually restrain the provinces relative to Indigenous peoples' resources, the old framework is evolving. The repacked jurisprudential structure tantalizingly promises to subject the provinces to a justificatory process when dealing with First Nations' land.

Two cases from the Supreme Court of Canada issued in the summer of 2014 use reconciliation as their baseline principle for dealing with Aboriginal and treaty rights. The cases are *Tsilhqot'in Nation v British Columbia* and *Grassy Narrows First Nation v Ontario (Natural Resources)*.[21] They both consider the ability of provincial governments to develop resources on First Nations' territory. Despite cause for hope, in my view, section 35(1)'s conservative paradigm further diminishes the constitutional narrative built on the Proclamation and Treaty of Niagara. These decisions give the provinces an even greater role in dealing with Indigenous peoples. As such, they are the "same-old-same-old." They facilitate further provincial colonization despite their silver linings.

A. Colonialism and the Tsilhqot'in Case

The case of *Tsilhqot'in v British Columbia* recognizes Aboriginal title in British Columbia, but it empowers the provinces to pass legislation

---

21 *Tsilhqot'in*, *supra* note 5; *Grassy Narrows First Nation v Ontario (Natural Resources)*, 2014 SCC 48 [*Grassy Narrows*].

dealing with such lands as long as they are laws of general application. In coming to this conclusion, the Supreme Court of Canada applied a principle which greatly benefits the provinces at the potential expense of Indigenous interests. The Court accomplished this through judicial fiat. The Court expanded what Parliament initiated when it added section 88 to the *Indian Act* in 1951, a change which made provincial laws of general application applicable to Indians. As a result of the *Tsilhqot'in* decision, provincial laws of general applicable bind Indians even without legislative intervention. As a result, First Nations are no longer shielded from provincial control as a constitutional principle. The Court made new law to enforce older provincially beneficial practices by writing that interjurisdictional immunity does not apply when considering the application of provincial laws to Aboriginal title lands. As such, it held that "provincial laws of general application apply to lands held under Aboriginal title."[22]

The Court's rejection of First Nations' immunity from provincial action cuts against a 250-year constitutional story first outlined in the Royal Proclamation of 1763, and accepted by many First Nations in central Canada through the Treaty of Niagara in 1764. At the same time, this comment has shown how the Court's decision might also be regarded as a further endorsement of a 150-year-old counter-narrative which facilitates local dispossession of First Nations' lands to benefit the provinces. We must recognize the power imbalances created by this decision. The provinces' preferred political narrative is strengthened by the case and First Nations' political views are weakened. The Court has clearly secured a win for the provinces in this regard. First Nations' primary concerns have been severely weakened as a result of the *Tsilhqot'in* decision.

22 *Tsilhqot'in, supra* note 5 at para 101. Interjurisdictional immunity is a Canadian constitutional doctrine which prevents one level of government from encroaching on the core of the other level of government's jurisdictional grant of powers under sections 91 and 92 of the *Canada Constitution Act, 1867*. The application of this doctrine has often prevented provincial laws from applying to areas of federal authority if such application would affect the core of the federal grant of power. For example, if interjurisdictional immunity were applied to Aboriginal title (as the Court held in *Delgamuukw*), this would prevent the provinces from successfully applying any provincial power under section 92 of the constitution to the federal government's authority related to "Indians and lands reserved for Indians" under section 91(24) of the constitution.

First Nations' attempts to speak about nation-to-nation relationships have been greatly diluted by ensuring that provinces have a central role in dealing with Indigenous rights. The Proclamation and treaty principles which prevented local colonial governments from molesting or disturbing First Nations in their use and occupation of land have been largely wiped from the face of the land. Of course the Dominion government could still invoke constitutional paramountcy principles to subordinate provincial action.[23] However, if the past is any guide, this is unlikely to happen any time soon. In fact, the Dominion government argued on the side of the provinces and against the Tsilhqot'in Nation to expand the provincial sphere.[24] This does not bode well for First Nations. The federal government has all but abandoned the older constitutional narrative which was constructed with First Nations' participation, however imperfectly.

The Dominion jettisoned its treaty promises in favour of a story which strengthens the provinces' position vis-à-vis First Nations.[25] The exclusion of the provinces in dealing with First Nations was one of the few checks and balances Indigenous peoples enjoyed under Canadian law throughout history. Now that protection is gone, though it admittedly existed more in principle than in fact because of how the Dominion acted. The Court has now substituted a justificatory process which provinces,

23 *Ibid* at para 130.

24 See also Factum of the Respondent Attorney General of Canada In the Supreme Court of Canada (On Appeal from the Court of Appeal for British Columbia) between: Roger William, on his own behalf and on behalf of all other members of the Xeni Gwet'in First Nations Government and on behalf of all other members of the Tsilhqot'in Nation at para 118, http://www.scc-csc.ca/WebDocuments-DocumentsWeb/34986/FM030_Respondent_Attorney-General-of-Canada.pdf. Federal support for a provincial role in legislating in relation to Indians was also relevant in *Kitkatla, supra* note 14 at paras 72–3.

25 Provincial governments are closest to the First Nations. They have the greatest incentive to benefit from Indigenous lands; thus, they are more likely to "molest" and "disturb" Indians' interests, to use the language of the Royal Proclamation. British Columbia stands to gain the most from infringing Aboriginal title under the *Tsilhqot'in* framework; any diminishment of Aboriginal title accrues to their benefit. Therefore, the law in North America has always been that local governments were to have substantial obstacles placed in their path in dealing with First Nations. Because of this, the Royal Proclamation and 250 years of Canadian law, as affirmed in section 91(24) of the *Constitution Act, 1867*, interposed a more distant imperial or federal power between First Nations and colonial/state/local/provincial governments.

and the federal government, must follow in infringing Aboriginal title. The provinces, with all their incentives to derive benefit from indigenous lands, are now fully vested with authority to continue to colonize Indigenous peoples.

B. Colonialism and the Grassy Narrows Case

The case of *Grassy Narrows* continues Canada's colonial trajectory. It further increases provincial encroachment powers in relation to First Nations interests. The *Grassy Narrows* case permits the province to take up land under Treaty 3 without being subject to federalism's requirements. The Supreme Court held that the province is fully vested with the beneficial interest of the so-called surrendered Treaty 3 lands. The Court found that the province was unrestrained by federal authority in taking up Treaty 3 lands for settlement because the province held the beneficial interest in these lands under section 109 of the *Constitution Act, 1867*. The Aboriginal perspective is silent in this decision, despite being exceedingly prominent at trial where the Grassy Narrows Band was victorious.

The Supreme Court strengthened the province's hand despite the specific wording of the treaty, which placed the power to "take up" treaty lands in the hands of the federal government. Furthermore, the province was vindicated in its position as the Supreme Court of Canada overturned the trial judge's findings of fact, which were based on First Nations' perspectives. In the Supreme Court decision, First Nations' perspectives were subordinated to provincial views.

The Grassy Narrows people viewed the treaty relationship as having been formed with the federal government, and not with provincial authorities. Of course, this is consistent with the Royal Proclamation, Treaty of Niagara, and the broader treaty narrative. The Supreme Court would have none of this. It wrote that Treaty 3 was with the Crown, not Canada. It did not view the treaty as the Indians would naturally understand it. The Court did not resolve ambiguities in the treaty in favour of the Indians. Chief Justice McLachlin did not apply a large, liberal, and generous perspective of the agreement which interprets the treaty in their light. Section 109 prevailed over a longer 250-year narrative which would shield First Nations from the very approach taken by the Court. Provincial narratives trumped First Nations' views in the Supreme Court of Canada's narrative. The legal and political bedrock which orients First Nations' political life is savaged by this decision.

Federalism does not protect First Nations in Canada to any significant degree, not that it did so in any great degree before these decisions. First Nations have long called on the federal government to exercise jurisdiction to protect inherent Indigenous rights. The call was not heeded; the federal government failed in its obligations to protect First Nations rights. The Supreme Court of Canada has acted to enhance provincial development and control of First Nations' lands.

Unfortunately, the writing found in the *Tsilhqot'in* and *Grassy Narrows* decisions has long been on the wall: First Nations are subject to provincial interests. The shielding of First Nations from local governments has been abandoned. This hurts. It strikes against the heart of First Nations political rhetoric which claims a nation-to-nation relationship with the Crown, not a nation-to-province relationship. This is called colonialism – allowing the local colonies, now called provinces, to set the framework for Indigenous lives. In reinforcing the provincial narrative, the Supreme Court violated the Royal Proclamation and dishonoured the Treaty of Niagara as well as the historic treaties that followed it.

Canadian colonialism has further entrenched itself and placed First Nations in the very hands that most threaten their interests. The federal government may have been an exceedingly poor fiduciary, but at least that level of government did not stand to receive the direct benefits of First Nations dispossession in the same way as provincial governments. Now the very party which stands to gain the most from Indigenous deprivation has the legislative ability to directly affect Indigenous interests. The Supreme Court of Canada has killed a centuries-old constitutional narrative. It has replaced these older laws with a balancing test under section 35(1) of the constitution which allows the provinces to justifiably infringe Aboriginal and treaty rights.

8. Where Are We Now: Canada's Contemporary Constitutional Narratives

Constitutional narratives are complex; heroes and villains can sometimes play contradictory roles. Plots shift and characters change as they grow or regress through a larger story.

How might Canada's constitutional law develop as the centuries-old First Nations' narrative has diminished in strength? How will section 35(1) operate now that it has become the dominant framework for addressing First Nations' interests? The answer to this question cannot be given without considering stark political power differentials which subordinate Indigenous peoples in Canada. First Nations are likely to be subjected to further colonial encroachment within this framework. To the extent First Nations succeed in rounding out the edges of this encroachment, their interests will likely be forced to align with the provinces' interests. This is called reconciliation. Such alignment might produce some marginal economic health for First Nations. However, the beads and trinkets won through reconciliation may come at the expense of their own preferred ways of living. Reconciliation sounds nice when it is discussed in the abstract. But reconciliation, practiced in context, requires that Indigenous peoples reconcile themselves to colonialism. This is hardly a cause for celebration.

But the view being presented might contain as much fiction as the other narratives addressed in this paper. While my analysis may contain many truths, it is possible that its "pure" rendition may conceal and obscure as much as it reveals.

There is at least one positive note which might be taken from the trajectory described in this paper. It involves the removal of federal oversight in relation to Indigenous decision-making. This is probably not a bad thing. Diminishing the Dominion's role clears away some of the paternalism Indigenous peoples encounter in dealing with the federal government, though there will still be plenty of provincial paternalism to go around. The diminishment of federal authority might result in First Nations collectively sighing "goodbye and good riddance." New opportunities might present themselves as First Nations more directly advance their own interests within section 35(1)'s framework. This development potentially puts First Nations in the driver's seat; even though it is still Canada's car.

Here is what Indigenous peoples may win through this new narrative: First Nations can directly raise their concerns with responsible provincial authorities as a result of the section 35(1) test. First Nations are in charge of voicing their own views about whether provincial activities are unreasonable, cause undue hardship, or deny them the preferred means of exercising their rights. If First Nations raise a *prima facie* case of interference, the provinces must directly consult with and accommodate First Nations, if they are going to successfully infringe rights through provincial action. Furthermore, implicit in the Crown's fiduciary duty to the Aboriginal group is the requirement that the incursion is necessary to achieve the government's goal (rational connection); that the government go no further than necessary to achieve it (minimal impairment); and that the benefits that may be expected to flow from that goal are not outweighed by adverse effects on the Aboriginal interest (proportionality of impact).[26]

The direct constraint of Crown sovereignty by reference to First Nations' perspectives, rights, and interests might result in better outcomes for First Nations than federal interposition could accomplish. This narrative should not be overlooked.

But this is the end of the brighter story in its purer form. We must continue to complicate our constitutional narratives or risk accepting national myths. It is true that in some circumstances, First Nations might succeed in constraining or even stopping the Crown from acting by using section 35(1)'s framework. The result, however, might still lead First Nations into deeper colonial entanglements. This is particularly the case if the First Nation manages to minimize Crown action, but development nevertheless proceeds in a manner which infringes vital interests. For example, imagine a situation in which a mine is developed. First Nations might receive half of its profits. They may be fully employed with every available person earning a small fortune through his or her labour. If, however, the tailings ponds cause cancer and mercury and other chemicals accumulate in their food and bodies, they do not really win. Furthermore, First Nations may be worse off, rather than better off, if the mine and its effects destroy their ancient food and social and ceremonial sites. "Victories" under section 35(1) could significantly damage First Nations societies, particularly if they must reconcile themselves to the province's so-called pressing and substantial objectives.

Of course there are other views. Some might counter my critique by claiming that at least the injury to First Nations interests are minimized if Indigenous peoples have a degree of control over a development's impacts and can enjoy its results. They are getting some benefits in return.

A sceptical response to this counterargument might consider the harm of development by way of an analogy: "We are going to cut off your arm" might be the metaphorical proposal a province makes in relation to an Indigenous right. Under the section 35(1) framework, First Nations get to minimize the damage this would cause. In inflicting the harm, a First Nation could choose to have a surgeon in the hospital do the damage, as opposed to a lumberjack with a rusty chainsaw deep in

26 *Tsilhqot'in*, *supra* note 5 at para 87.

the woods. This is one version of minimal impairment. Furthermore, the province would pay handsomely for taking away a First Nation's arm. This purportedly offsets damages suffered by providing compensatory benefits. In this hypothetical, it ensures that the armless have full employment in exchange for the disability the province creates.

Of course such an example is ridiculous and open to broad ridicule. The example, however, might cut closer to the mark than we realize for some Indigenous peoples. How can you value a way of life? How can damage, such as infringement, ever be justified if it cuts down a people? First Nations who receive benefits, even significant ones, might still be endangered if their very lives were threatened or diminished through "forestry, mining, and hydroelectric power … [or] the building of infrastructure and the settlement of foreign populations to support those aims."[27]

There may nevertheless be champions of section 35(1)'s framework. They may metaphorically recognize that First Nations people still lose an arm within this framework, and consider it devastating, but they may say that at least First Nations might survive another day to eventually defeat this perverse way of dealing with their interests. In concrete terms, they may highlight black-letter law which implies that any discussion about the adequacy of the province's consultation and accommodation efforts engages the legal and political decision-making powers of First Nations, despite the limited framework within which it occurs. They may emphasize that the Supreme Court's framework implicitly recognizes First Nations governance. It is possible to conclude that, by recognizing that the province has a duty to consult and accommodate First Nations rights, the Supreme Court of Canada has implicitly recognized that First Nations possess self-government powers to respond to provincial overtures. This is surely a good thing. This argument might just allow for a back door solution to a problem First Nations have long struggled with – how to ensure their inherent rights to self-government are recognized by Canada's highest law. The Supreme Court may have now paved the way for this to occur.

While First Nations' governance powers would still be exercised within a perverse colonial framework, they may empower First Nations to take other steps to challenge the discriminatory structures

27 *Delgamuukw v British Columbia*, [1997] 3 SCR 1010 at para 65.

and outcomes they encounter. Imagine reading section 35(1) through a non-discriminatory view. Indigenous peoples can now justifiably constrain governmental authority if they have a recognized Aboriginal or treaty right and act in accordance with their own laws in advancing their interests.

Thus, we can construct plausible narratives which suggest that Indigenous peoples now have a way to expand the Court's implicit recognition of their governance power. They now have a broader array of remedies to enforce their interests which are not dependent on federal interposition. They can bring injunctions, claim damages, and secure orders for the Crown to engage if proper consultation and accommodation are not forthcoming. If Aboriginal peoples establish title, they can also bring legal suits to secure all the usual remedies for a breach of land rights, as long as they are adapted to the special nature of Aboriginal peoples' relationship to land. The Court even suggested it might cancel provincial projects if governments did not properly discharge their duties to First Nations early enough in their dealings. All the while this creates an important opportunity for First Nations to expand and develop their own powers to enforce their interests and to compel provincial, as well as federal, governments to act in accordance with their rights. The Crown's failure to properly work with First Nations governments will render federal laws and policies unconstitutional.

So, here is an interesting turn of events. Canada's constitutional narratives seem to be constantly in flux. It is true that provincial and federal Crowns can infringe Aboriginal and treaty rights if they have a pressing and substantial objective and act honourably. Yet, under this new framework, might it also be true that Indigenous governments could justifiably infringe Canadian interests under section 35(1)? Might it therefore be possible to conclude that Indigenous rights constrain and thus even deny Canadian interests under section 35(1) of the *Constitution Act, 1982*?

Perhaps so, or maybe not; the larger constitutional framework is still deeply colonial. While section 35(1) constrains Crown sovereignty, First Nations are also constrained by an even deeper colonial power imbalance. Section 35(1)'s framework may be viewed as the latest chapter in the ongoing growth of provincial power and privilege, both of which disadvantage First Nations.

Like all narratives explored in this paper, however, interpretations can only ever be partial. The view presented here is just as corruptible as the other perspectives found in this piece. Any action we take in the real world will lead to unsavoury compromises. Power and its immoral effects will never be defeated, though they may be resisted from time-to-time. Even the most optimistic section 35(1) story largely compels Aboriginal peoples to reconcile themselves to colonialism. This is not a very attractive future. Any future, however, will be like our past: impure, conflicted, sullied, and imperfect. However, my point in this paper is to illustrate that some stories are better than others. We should seek to enhance those accounts which constrain the offensive uses of power most fully. Provincial power relative to First Nations must be rolled back *and* First Nations should be empowered to reject reconciliation with colonialism. In taking this course, however, we should not lie to ourselves. We must avoid creating false myths and fictions. Nor should we leave racist, discriminatory, and colonial narratives in place. We should reject them if we can, although rejection is never easy. The world is imperfect, and theorizing that it were otherwise does not change this brute fact of life.

9. Conclusion: Questioning Constitutional Evolution

In the *Grassy Narrows* case, the Ontario Court of Appeal discussed the concept of constitutional evolution. The judges wrote that treaty rights had to be "interpreted in the light of the process of constitutional evolution from the time of the Royal Proclamation in 1763" to the present.[28] They affirmed that the special "relationship between the Crown and Canada's Aboriginal peoples remains a constant, central and defining feature" of constitutional life, but what has evolved is the allocation of legislative and administrative powers and responsibilities to different levels of government. They observed that section 35(1) rights "are not frozen in time."[29] The Court wrote:

> As the English Court of Appeal explained in *R. v. Secretary of State for Foreign and Commonwealth Affairs, ex parte Indian Association of Alberta,* in relation to a challenge to proposals for constitutional change in 1982, if treaties are to be honoured by the Crown "so long as the sun rises and river flows," treaty interpretation has to evolve along with the Constitution.[30]

28 *Grassy Narrows, supra* note 21 at para 136.
29 *Ibid* at para 137.
30 *Ibid* at para 138.

The Ontario Court of Appeal speaks as if its version of evolution is unproblematic. The Supreme Court does not use these words, but does arrive at the same conclusion and adopt the same untroubled tone. I have argued, however, that Canada's so-called evolution from the Royal Proclamation and the Treaty of Niagara has led us into a more deeply discriminatory and colonial state. The evolutionary course the Court has taken should not be endorsed. Despite the mutuality and power of First Nations political narratives, expressed over 250 years, the Canadian Courts, Parliament, and legislatures have endorsed a non-Native vision of Canada. Section 35(1)'s framework might provide some relief from the worst aspects of this dev/evolution, though I remain unconvinced.

Yet, nothing is inevitable. We must take care to ensure that the contingencies we construct do not appear to be inevitable. Darkness marks Canada's constitutional narrative, but not uniformly so. Power can be turned to either better or worse purposes. My counsel is that we take greater care to ensure that any appearance of inevitability does not defeat our active engagement with the real-world problems as they constantly shift before us. We must not speak and act in absolute terms. Canadian constitutionalism should be seen in more nuanced terms, even when it remains a dark story. Our stories are never fully true, nor do we know all the answers.

2 As Long as the Sun Shines: Recognizing That Treaties Were Intended to Last

MICHAEL COYLE

How should the history of the treaty-making process in Canada inform present understandings of the parties' relationship and reciprocal obligations? This chapter reviews the context of the historical land-sharing treaties and the shared premises that made the treaty understandings possible. The author argues that a proper understanding of the logical foundations of those treaties leads ineluctably to the recognition of certain generic obligations that form an essential element of the legal framework that constitutes this unique Canadian legal institution that is the historical land treaty.

The Queen has to think of what will come long after today. Therefore, the promises we have to make to you are not for to-day but for tomorrow, not only for you but for your children born and unborn, and the promises we make will be carried out as long as the sun shines above and the water flows in the ocean.[1]

– Alexander Morris, Crown Treaty Commissioner,
during the negotiations for Treaty 4, 1874

[C]ertainly it is good to report to each other what is for the benefit of each other. We see the good you wish to show us ... Let us join together and make the Treaty; when both join together it is very good.[2]

– Ka-ku-ish-may, a principal chief of the Crees,
on the sixth day of negotiations for Treaty 4, 1874

* I wish to thank University of Western Ontario (UWO) MLS student Matthew Glass and Professors Chi Carmody and Jean Leclair for their helpful comments on an earlier draft of this chapter. I am also grateful to UWO JD students Sarah Jackson and Chelsea Smith for their assistance in editing this chapter.

1 Hon Alexander Morris, PC, *The Treaties of Canada with the Indians of Manitoba and the North-West Territories* (Toronto: Prospero Books, 2000) at 96.

2 *Ibid* at 115.

What is the significance today of Canada's "historical" treaties?[3] At Lake Qu'Appelle, in the Northwest Territories (now Manitoba) in 1874, the answer was obvious to all involved. The newly negotiated treaty would have tremendous political, legal, and economic consequences. After all, the treaty arrangement, negotiated between federal representatives and a number of Cree and Saulteaux tribes, embraced some 75,000 square miles of territory and was clearly intended, as its negotiators attested, to create a framework that would guide the parties' relationship for the indefinite future, if not forever.

In 2016, however, some 140 years after the negotiations at Lake Qu'Appelle and more than 250 years after the Treaty of Niagara (a conference that established the protocols for all subsequent treaty-making in what is now Canada), it would be hard to find a consensus among Canadians about the enduring relevance of the historical treaties. If asked about the modern significance of those treaties, negotiated long ago in Ontario and westward, many Canadians would react with a blank expression. If pressed, some would undoubtedly suggest that the treaties are an interesting part of Canadian history, much like the travels of Samuel de Champlain. Beyond that, and I draw anecdotally from my past experience in facilitating land claims consultations in Ontario, I suspect that many of our hypothetical interviewees would have little to say about the contemporary relevance of the historical treaties.

Some Canadians (including many practising lawyers) would offer the opinion that the historical treaties contained a number of promises that were intended to be binding at the time, but whose legal and economic significance has been largely superseded by the transformation of Canadian society since they were negotiated. In stark contrast is the widely held view among First Nations people that the historical treaties

3 By "historical" I mean all of the land treaties made in what is now Canada from the time of the Treaty of Niagara in 1764 until the final adhesion was made to Treaty 9 in Ontario in 1930. As these agreements predated the entrenchment of treaty rights within Canada's *Constitution Act, 1982*, section 35, it is useful, for reasons I will make clear, to distinguish them from those negotiated after the recognition of Aboriginal title in Canadian common law and the subsequent affording of constitutional protection to Aboriginal land rights in the *Constitution Act, 1982*. Indeed, the main thrust of the argument that follows is that it is precisely because these treaties were negotiated in a very different legal context that their significance today needs to be carefully reassessed.

created a special, even sacred, bond between the first peoples of Canada and the Crown. That bond, they say, enabled the creation and settlement of this country and calls today for a fair sharing of the economic benefits that flow from the development of treaty lands. In the face of such dramatic differences in Canadians' perceptions of the treaty relationship, it is not surprising that conflicts and tension[4] have accompanied recent proposals to develop the rich chromite reserves in Ontario's Ring of Fire region and the Northern Gateway proposal to transport natural gas and diluted bitumen from Alberta to the Pacific Ocean.

Although the Crown began to enter formal treaties with Indigenous peoples on this land more than two centuries ago, Canadian law governing those treaties remains in its infancy. For much of Canada's history, its courts tended to dismiss the significance of the treaty relationship and even of treaty promises when those promises came into conflict with federal or provincial legislation. The 1982 entrenchment of Aboriginal treaty rights in Canada's constitution meant that treaty promises could no longer be ignored. Since then, the Supreme Court of Canada has provided general direction about the interpretation of treaties and, more controversially, about the circumstances in which federal and provincial governments may lawfully interfere with treaty rights. The Court has made clear that the Crown has a legal obligation to consult with its First Nations treaty partners whenever it proposes to take action that could interfere with treaty rights.[5] Nonetheless, because

4 In 2008, for example, six members of an Ontario First Nation, including five elected leaders, were imprisoned for their attempt, based on asserted treaty rights, to prevent a mineral development on their traditional lands: *Platinex v Kitchenuhmaykoosib Inninuwug*, [2008] 2 CNLR 301 (six-month sentence for contempt; members released on appeal after nine weeks in jail: see 2008 ONCA 533, 91 OR (3d) 18). Their incarceration came roughly a year after the Ontario Ipperwash Inquiry reported that between 1995 and 2007 there had been more than 100 "critical aboriginal incidents" involving police in the province. The inquiry also found that "the existence of long-standing, unresolved treaty disputes is perhaps the most important indicator of the potential for an occupation or protest." *Report of the Ipperwash Inquiry*, vol. 2 (Toronto: Ipperwash Inquiry, 2007) (Commissioner: The Honourable Sidney B. Linden) at 19, 30.

5 See, for example, *Mikisew Cree First Nation v Canada (Minister of Canadian Heritage)*, 2005 SCC 69, 3 SCR 388 and *Grassy Narrows First Nation v Ontario (Natural Resources)*, 2014 SCC 48 [*Grassy Narrows*].

treaties are considered in Canadian law to be *sui generis* agreements, not governed either by international law or the existing domestic law of Canada, huge gaps remain in our understanding of the legal principles that should be applied by Canadian courts to claims for remedies under historical treaties.

In disputes that arise under contracts between private parties, those parties can rely on well-established principles of domestic law that outline the kinds of behaviour that will give rise to one party's liability under their agreement. Further, Canadian domestic law also contains a well-developed set of principles that stipulate the kinds of recourse available to a contracting party that has been wronged. Thus, relatively clear rules of contract law govern when financial compensation will be available to the wronged party as opposed to an injunction or an order to comply with the agreement. Clear principles identify the remedies available to the innocent party when fraud, mistake, or innocent misrepresentation undermined the negotiation of the contract, and so on. By contrast, in the context of Crown-Indigenous treaties, Canadian courts have yet to set out an equivalent body of detailed principles, either about the kinds of generic obligations owed by each treaty partner or about the availability of remedies to enforce those commitments.

Some learned commentators, including several of the contributors to this book, question whether the Canadian courts should be tasked with resolving disagreements about the implementation of treaties between the state and Indigenous peoples. Others argue, as Heidi Stark and Aaron Mills so articulately do elsewhere in this book, that focusing on the parties' rights within the Canadian legal system is not the most productive way of fulfilling the treaty partnership. Whatever the undeniable merits of those arguments, there is little doubt that Canadian courts will have their say. For First Nations opposing developments on treaty lands that they think interfere with their treaty relationship, and for Indigenous peoples seeking new forms of participation and partnership with the state based on their treaty relationship, access to Canada's courts is indispensable, as is the development of a just set of rules about treaty remedies. Uncertainty about the principles that govern treaty implementation increases the likelihood of confrontation over treaty claims made by either side. Being channelled into the courts because of fundamental uncertainties in the law impairs the treaty partners' ability to work and plan together. This situation is arguably particularly unfair to the Indigenous treaty partner, the party that typically has much less money for litigation and more limited access to the ongoing legal advice necessary to develop convincing arguments about how those uncertainties about treaty responsibilities should be resolved. At the same time, the legal uncertainty over general treaty responsibilities and remedies also haunts those who would advise governments, resource companies, and municipalities who face claims that they are violating treaty promises.

This uncertainty about the legal consequences of the historical treaty relationship makes it urgent that scholars, political leaders, and judges alike turn their minds to the development of a fair framework that takes into account the historical context and purpose of treaty-making in Canada and seeks to reconcile that historical process with modern circumstances and the contemporary needs of the treaty partners. There is no template we can rely on in addressing this challenge because Canada's history and its current constitutional framework are unique. Some of Canada's leading thinkers from both sides of the treaty relationship offer thoughtful and widely differing perspectives in this book as to how the relationship might be reconceived in order to meet that challenge. One thing, at least, is clear: to be embraced by Indigenous and non-Indigenous treaty partners alike, any effective approach to the implementation of the historical treaties must be cognizable by and convincing to both treaty partners in light of their distinctive world views and legal traditions.

This chapter will focus on principles of treaty implementation that can be derived directly from the nature of the treaty-making process. Its starting point is the recognition that historical treaty-making was intended to create a new enduring normative order on lands once occupied exclusively by Indigenous peoples, but henceforth to be shared with settlers and their descendants. Looking at the historical land treaties, I will examine the particular assumptions that must be taken to have been shared by the parties for the formation of those treaties to make any sense. Finally, I will consider the treaty implementation principles that flow inevitably from those shared assumptions.

To frame our analysis of the principles that flow logically from the treaty-making process, I will begin by briefly reviewing some of the main gaps in the current Canadian case law on treaty implementation. I will then suggest a new framework for exploring the legal, political, and ethical implications of treaty-making, one that conceives of the historical treaties as significantly different in their nature and purpose than domestic contracts or international treaties, but which does not leave the parties' rights utterly contingent on their specific historical circumstances. Drawing inspiration from the work of Brian Slattery,[6] I will show that the historical treaty-making process necessarily implies the existence of certain generic principles that govern the parties' responsibilities in connection with treaty implementation. In this chapter, I will begin the project of identifying the core shared assumptions necessary for the historic treaty-making process to make sense. Those shared premises, I will argue, must be attended to in any consideration of treaty implementation, whether it be by domestic or international courts, political leaders, or Canadians at large. Respect for those principles will offer, at the very least, a secure and just starting point for Indigenous peoples and the Canadian state to work out their differences and to strengthen their treaty partnerships outside any courtroom.

1. Gaps in the Current Canadian Law

When one considers the dramatic ramifications of the historical land treaties as well as the ceremonies and formality that accompanied their negotiation, it is impossible to deny that they were intended to affect the treaty partners' rights and responsibilities towards each other. Their recognition in Canada's constitution properly reflects the importance of those rights. At the same time, there has been little political recognition in Canada of the significance of the treaty relationship. There is no equivalent in this country of New Zealand's Waitangi Day, a public holiday that memorializes the original treaty between the Maori and the British Crown. Nor is there any political forum where representatives of the original treaty partners sit down to negotiate about disagreements over the implementation of those treaties or to discuss how those treaties might be renewed to meet changing circumstances.[7] Instead, it has

---

6 For Professor Slattery's analysis of the distinction between the "specific" (community) and the "generic" (universal) rights protected by section 35 of the *Constitution Act, 1982*, see Brian Slattery's "The Generative Structure of Aboriginal Rights" (2007) 38 *Supreme Court Law Review* (2d) 595, as well as his "Making Sense of Aboriginal and Treaty Rights" (2000) 79 *Canadian Bar Review* 196.

7 Notwithstanding the recommendation of the Royal Commission on Aboriginal Peoples that Canada formally commit to a process of implementing the spirit of the historical treaties and renewing the treaty relationships: *Report of the Royal Commission on Aboriginal Peoples: Restructuring the Relationship*, vol. 2 (Ottawa: Supply and Services Canada, 1996) at 2.2.8. In a similar vein, in the 2007 report of the Ontario Ipperwash Inquiry, Justice Linden recommended the creation of an

fallen to the Canadian courts, most often in the context of Crown prosecutions of Aboriginal individuals engaged in hunting, fishing, or other harvesting, to grapple with the significance of the treaty relationship. Whether or not a court system developed by one treaty partner is the appropriate forum for resolving claims made by the other party, it is clear that the Canadian courts have yet to develop a full and rounded picture of the place of treaties in Canadian law.

There are at least three significant gaps in current Canadian law governing the interpretation and implementation of the historical treaties. The first flows from the courts' tendency to conceive of and interpret treaties in a manner not dramatically different from contracts negotiated by individuals to set out reciprocal obligations over limited periods of time. The second, related concern is that Canadian law has yet to fully acknowledge Indigenous perspectives on the treaty-making process, including the relational aspect of that encounter. The third gap is that Canada's domestic law has yet to develop a set of clear remedial principles to guide the parties, in particular the Indigenous treaty partner, if they wish to bring concerns before the courts about the implementation of treaty rights. A brief explanation of each of these gaps in the law should suffice to underscore the need for further development in the law and, at the same time, offer a helpful idea of the path that development should take.

The tendency of Canadian courts to conceive of treaties as containers of rights, akin to contracts, is an understandable one. Both treaties and contracts, after all, involve an exchange of solemn promises. Further, conceiving of treaties as creating rights, in a manner analogous to the consensual allocation of rights through contract, has allowed the courts

---

independent and impartial "Treaty Commission of Ontario" to oversee the expeditious settling of land and treaty claims. The proposed commission would promote cooperative and interest-based settlements and "undertake public education about treaties, treaty relationships, and land claims in Ontario." *Report of the Ipperwash Inquiry*, vol. 4 (Toronto: Ipperwash Inquiry, 2007) (Commissioner: The Honourable Sidney B. Linden) at 99–100. Seven years later such a commission has not yet been established. It should be noted that federal policies do exist to govern the negotiation of Aboriginal title claims and so-called specific claims. Under the latter policy, the federal government will negotiate certain treaty claims provided they involve the unlawful taking of Indigenous lands or other assets. See the federal specific claims policy, "In All Fairness" in Department of Indian Affairs and Northern Development, *In All Fairness: A Native Claims Policy* (Ottawa: Supply and Service Canada, 1981).

to shield Aboriginal persons from provincial prosecution if they were carrying on activities expressly authorized by a treaty.[8] Given the legal education of Canadian judges, contract principles are a familiar reference point. Accordingly, just as in contract law, in interpreting treaty promises, the courts have been prepared, to a limited extent, to give effect to oral assurances[9] and implied engagements.[10] Canadian law also requires that where there are doubts about the meaning of a treaty term, any ambiguity should be resolved against the Crown, just as ambiguities in contract law are construed against the party that drafted the contract.[11]

As applied to treaties, such interpretative principles are fine insofar as they go, but the doctrines of contract law did not evolve in the context of arrangements intended to endure for generations and were not formulated to resolve the kinds of disputes that are likely to arise in

---

8 See, for example *R v White and Bob* (1964), 50 DRL (2d) 613 (BCCA), affirmed (1965), 52 DLR (2d) 481 (SCC); *R v Simon*, [1985] 2 SCR 387 at 410 [*Simon*]; *R v Sioui*, [1990] 1 SCR 1025 [*Sioui*]. On treaties as analogous to contracts, see *R v Badger*, [1996] 1 SCR 771 at 793 [*Badger*].

9 *R v Taylor and Williams* (1982), 34 OR (2d) 360; *White and Bob*, *supra* note 8. For a an important example of the courts not giving effect to an alleged oral assurance made by the Crown, see *Canada v Benoit*, 2003 FCA 236, 228 DLR (4th) 1.

10 *R v Marshall (No 1)*, [1999] 3 SCR 456 [*Marshall*].

11 For decisions affirming this principle, see *Simon*, *supra* note 8 at 402, and *Sioui*, *supra* note 8 at 1036. The extent to which this principle holds sway in treaty decisions is nonetheless a matter of debate. See, for example, *R v Howard*, [1994] 2 SCR 299, which considered the effect of the so-called basket clause that reads (304):

> Now Therefore This Treaty Witnesseth that the said tribe and the Indians composing the same … do hereby cede, release, surrender and yield up to the Government of the Dominion of Canada for His Majesty the King and His Successors forever, all their right, title, interest, claim, demand and privileges whatsoever, in, to, upon, or in respect of the lands and premises described as follows, that is to say:
>
> …
>
> And Also all the right, title, interest, claim, demand and privileges whatsoever of the said Indians, in, to, upon or in respect of all other lands situate in the Province of Ontario to which they ever had, now have, or now claim to have any right, title, interest, claim, demand or privileges, except such reserves as have heretofore been set apart for them by His Majesty the King.

Although the First Nations were not represented by lawyers, and despite the fact that the treaty was negotiated to clear up potential claims in northern Ontario, far from where the First Nations signatories then resided, the Supreme Court of Canada held that the release was "clear" and extinguished not only any property rights, but also their traditional right to fish for subsistence (*ibid* at 307).

such a long-term relationship. Conceiving of treaties mainly through the principles of domestic contract law would fail to account for either the web of relational expectations that infused the treaty-making process or the necessarily unforeseeable and evolving circumstances through which the parties intended to maintain their treaty relationship. Perhaps most importantly, to adopt an approach based solely on Canada's domestic law of contracts would overlook the fundamental character of treaties, namely that they are the product of an encounter between two separate legal orders, Indigenous and non-Indigenous. Since at least 1985, with the Supreme Court of Canada's *Simon* decision, Canadian law has acknowledged that treaties between the Crown and First Nations are unique legal arrangements to be governed by a set of legal principles adapted to their unique nature.[12] This characterization of treaties and treaty law is surely correct; but the courts' reluctance so far to depart from contract-like principles in cases involving the interpretation and implementation of treaty promises means that much of the unique content of treaty law remains to be articulated. This has left a significant void in Canadian law, as enunciated so far, for those who would seek to use that law to assist in settling disputes over the substance of the parties' responsibilities today.[13]

A second, related lacuna in Canadian law is that the conception of treaties elaborated by the courts thus far has not given due attention to the relational aspect of treaty arrangements. At the heart of historical treaty-making, after all, was the need to establish formal relationships between Indigenous peoples and the Crown in such a manner as to

---

12 *Simon*, *supra* note 8 at 404: "An Indian treaty is unique; it is an agreement sui generis which is neither created nor terminated according to the rules of international law."

13 It is true that Canadian courts have developed a helpful jurisprudence around the concept of the "honour of the Crown," which requires that the Crown act honourably and avoid sharp dealing throughout the treaty process, from treaty-making to treaty implementation. See, for example, *Haida Nation v British Columbia (Minister of Forests)*, 2004 SCC 73, [2004] 3 SCR 511 [*Haida Nation*]; *Mikisew Cree First Nation v Canada (Minister of Canadian Heritage)*, 2005 SCC 69, [2005] 3 SCR 388 [*Mikisew*]; and *Manitoba Metis Federation Inc v Canada*, 2013 SCC 14 [*Manitoba Metis Federation*]. Although a requirement that one treaty partner act honourably is an important development in Canadian law, this requirement is, on its own, no substitute for a coherent set of substantive treaty principles. Arguably, reliance on the "honour of the Crown" also has certain problematic connotations in the context of the treaty relationship, as we shall see.

permit permanent, peaceful coexistence. There is abundant evidence that the negotiations leading up to the historical treaties, beginning with the landmark Treaty of Niagara in 1764, inevitably focused on the need to clarify what that new formal relationship would be. There is no doubt that other issues were at stake, such as the need to clarify governance relationships and the ability of settlers to use the treaty lands thereafter. But the metaphors used during historical treaty negotiations stand as a testament to the reality that treaties were intended to build specific and reliable forms of relationship as much as they were meant to achieve practical agreements on issues of substance, like the paying of annuities by the Crown and the circumstances in which developments could occur on the treaty lands. By 1764, Indigenous nations in North America had a long history of regulating their relationships with each other through treaty compacts.[14] Treaty negotiators for the British, and later the Canadian, Crown relied expressly on Indigenous protocols of relationship-building, starting with their use of the Covenant Chain metaphor[15] in eastern North America beginning in the 1600s to describe the strength of the treaty bond and each party's promise to attend to any ongoing concerns expressed by the other.[16] That

14 J.R. Miller, *Compact, Contract, Covenant: Aboriginal Treaty-Making in Canada* (Toronto: University of Toronto Press, 2009) at 5–8; Robert A. Williams, Jr., *Linking Arms Together: American Indian Treaty Visions of Law and Peace, 1600–1800* (Oxford: Oxford University Press, 1997) at 32–9.

15 For two interesting descriptions of the development of the Covenant Chain relationship between first the Dutch and later the British and the Haudenosaunee and their allies, see Mark Walters, "Brightening the Covenant Chain: Aboriginal Treaty Meanings in Law and History after Marshall" (2001) 24:2 *Dalhousie Law Journal* 75 and Bruce Morito, *An Ethic of Mutual Respect: The Covenant Chain and Aboriginal-Crown Relations* (Vancouver: UBC Press, 2012). For a consideration of the contemporary significance of the Covenant Chain metaphor in treaty law, see Mark Walters' chapter in this book.

16 The leaders of New France took a very similar approach in negotiating the Great Peace of Montreal in 1701. Not only did Chevalier De Callière, governor of New France, present wampum "collars" to the Wendat, Odawa, Algonquin, Abenaki, and other Indigenous delegates present, but the language of the treaty also relied heavily on metaphors of family in setting out the principles by which peace would be established. See G. Havard, *The Great Peace of Montreal of 1701: French-Native Diplomacy in the Seventeenth Century*, trans. P. Aronoff and H. Scott (Montreal: McGill-Queen's University Press, 2001) at 142–55, 210–15.

emphasis continued during the treaty discussions at Niagara in 1764, when Crown representatives presented Two Row Wampum belts to demonstrate the Crown's commitment to peaceful and respectful relations with the Indigenous peoples represented there.[17] This focus on the relational side of treaty-building continued through the negotiation of the numbered treaties, from 1871 to 1930, which reveal an emphasis by both parties on metaphors of kinship.[18]

To analyse the legal and political consequences of treaty-making by attempting only to identify a set of specific rights, crystallized for each treaty partner at a particular moment in time, would mean ignoring this central imperative of historical treaty-making in Canada, namely to establish a new structure of relationships between the parties that would endure indefinitely. Although the courts have indicated that a central task of treaty interpretation is to identify, if possible, the "common intention" of the parties, one that takes into account both parties' interests at the time of the treaty,[19] their analyses thus far have disproportionately focused on seeking to capture an often-elusive "meeting of the minds" rather than on elaborating legal norms that respond to the relational aspect of treaties. Indeed, at times, aspects of their judgments have appeared to undermine any conception of treaties as consensual

17 For an explanation of the symbolism of these wampum belts within the context of the negotiations at Niagara, see John Borrows, "Wampum at Niagara: The Royal Proclamation, Canadian Legal History, and Self-Government" in Michael Asch, ed., *Aboriginal and Treaty Rights in Canada: Essays on Law, Equality and Respect for Difference* (Vancouver: UBC Press, 1997) at 155. For an analysis of the contemporary implications of that treaty, see John Borrows' contribution in this book, "Canada's Colonial Constitution."

18 Consider, for example, the language used in the negotiation of Treaty 6 in 1876 at Fort Pitt in Saskatchewan. Toward the end of those negotiations, Wee-kas-koo-kee-say-yin (Sweet Grass), the principal Cree chief, is quoted in the Crown commissioner's account as follows: "When I hold your hand I feel as if the Great Father were looking on us both as brothers. I am thankful that I can raise up my head, and the white man and red man can stand together as long as the sun shines. When I hold your hands and touch your heart, as I do now (suiting his action to the words), let us be as one" (Morris, *supra* note 1 at 237). The Crown's negotiators took up the same language of kinship, with Lieutenant-Governor Morris, after smoking pipes of peace, quoted on the same day as referring to the Cree as the Queen's "children" and "brothers" of the Queen's representatives (*ibid* at 231).

19 See, for example, *Marshall, supra* note 10 at 491, and *Sioui, supra* note 8 at 1071–2.

relationships.[20] Rulings by the Supreme Court of Canada that only one of the treaty partners (the Crown) has the right to unilaterally amend treaty agreements[21] would seem to support such a reading.[22]

A failure of the law to properly reflect the fact that treaty-making was intended, at least in part, as a way of consensually structuring relationships between peoples would also mean disregarding Aboriginal understandings of the purpose and nature of treaty-making. The fact that Crown representatives took such pains historically to adopt relational metaphors in treaty-making is a reflection of that fact that the clarification and building of relationships were central to Indigenous perspectives on treaty-making. The responsibilities created through relationships were central to Anishinaabe social norms and laws (*inaakonigewin*) – relationships not merely among Anishinaabe individuals but also between clans and other groups and, just as importantly, between the Anishinaabe and the Creator and between the Anishinaabe and the rest of creation.[23] This broader sense of the scope of relations that matter

20 At least one Canadian appellate court has suggested in passing that a treaty may be binding even on a First Nation that was not represented in the treaty negotiations. See *Ontario (Attorney-General) v Bear Island Foundation* (1989), 68 OR (2d) 394 at 401 (CA), leave to appeal to SCC refused, [1991] 2 SCR 570. In that case, the Teme-Augama argued that they had not assented to the Robinson-Huron Treaty. In dismissing their claim, the Ontario Court of Appeal found that their ancestors were in fact represented in the treaty, but went on to say that in any event "[...] their rights were extinguished, even if the Teme-Augama were not signatories or adherents, because the treaty was at least a unilateral act of extinguishment by the sovereign authority."

21 *R v Horseman*, [1990] 1 SCR 901; *Badger*, *supra* note 8.

22 The fact that this party (the Crown) is obliged to act with honour and in consultation with its treaty partner will not necessarily mitigate this concern. I will return later to the question of whether and how the "honour of the Crown" doctrine can be fleshed out in a manner that fully respects the equality of the parties and the relational character of treaties.

23 Heidi Stark's chapter in this book offers an insightful introduction to the significance of relationships in structuring social and legal responsibilities among the Anishinaabe peoples of the Great Lakes. See also Aimée Craft, *Breathing Life into the Stone Fort Treaty: An Anishinabe Understanding of Treaty 1* (Saskatoon: Purich Publishing, 2013) at 20–36, 86–100; Miller, *supra* note 14 at 34–8; Leanne Simpson, "Looking after Gdoo-naaganinaa: Precolonial Nishnaabeg Diplomatic and Treaty Relationships" (2008) 23 *Wicazo Sa Review* 29; Johnson, *supra* note 17 at 27–33. See also John Borrows, *Canada's Indigenous Constitution* (Toronto: University of Toronto Press, 2010) at 23–58, 241–7.

was also reflected in the negotiations of the historical treaties. Smoking the pipe together before the Creator was just such a recognition, as was the affixing of *dodem* markings denoting the animal associated with the Anishinaabe signatories' clans. Such actions, combined with references to fictive familial relationships between the Indigenous and non-Indigenous treaty partners, seemed to have been conscious efforts on the part of Indigenous negotiators to educate their counterparts and introduce them to Indigenous ways of thinking about relationships and mutual responsibilities.[24] The existence of such relationships created responsibilities that included caring, loyalty, and respect. These kinds of normative expectations can be difficult at times to square with the Euro-Canadian legal tradition, but a neutral and balanced effort at elaborating the appropriate political and legal consequences of treaty-making must surely take both perspectives into account. Although the Supreme Court of Canada has repeatedly acknowledged the need to consider both perspectives in interpreting the meaning of an individual treaty term, the Court has yet to elaborate, in a concrete way, how the law concerning the implications and implementation of treaties might draw on Aboriginal conceptions of the treaty-making process.[25]

---

24 According to Niigonwedom James Sinclair, "Signing using Nindoodemag meant that Anishinaabeg were not just 'agreeing' to a set of legal arrangements over territory (and sometimes even that is questionable, considering certain barriers of language and political interests), but were also introducing Europeans to Anishinaabeg ways and introducing newcomers to the world they were entering – one full of relationships and agreements in the interests of sharing and reciprocity [...]" ("Nindoodemag Bagijiganan: A History of Anishinaabeg Narrative" [PhD diss., University of British Columbia, 2013]). For an interesting description of Anishinaabe understandings of family relations, such as those between a mother (as used, e.g., to describe the Queen) and her children, see Craft, *supra* note 22 at 86–93.

25 Indeed, the Court has been unusually reluctant, even in cases of treaty interpretation, to acknowledge any specific Aboriginal perspective on the implications of treaty-making or the meaning of a particular treaty term. For a recent example of the Court acknowledging the importance of the Aboriginal perspective without any corresponding description of that perspective (citing Elders' evidence at trial, for example) or application of the Aboriginal perspective, see *R v Marshall; R v Bernard*, 2005 SCC 43, [2005] 2 SCR 220 at 243–52. Nor, in its most recent decision on treaty interpretation, does the Court make reference to any particular Aboriginal perspective on the treaty. See *Grassy Narrows, supra* note 5, where the court dismissed First Nation objections, based on the terms of Treaty 3, to provincially authorized clear-cutting on the treaty lands.

The third area where Canadian treaty law is not yet adequately developed relates to the function of law in providing recourse in situations where one treaty partner believes that the other has not honoured its responsibilities as a treaty partner. The general need for the law to provide effective remedies in order for legal rights to be meaningful has been long recognized by Canadian and, before it, British, law as captured by the maxim *ubi jus, ibi remedium* ("where there is a right, there is a remedy").[26] When it comes to formal processes for the enforcement of treaty promises in Canada, however, one faces a dearth of general principles governing the availability of treaty remedies and the circumstances in which they may be awarded. Canada has also failed to create any unique forum for resolving treaty disputes. We certainly have no specialized framework for ascertaining whether the Crown has complied with the general intent of treaties, as exists, for example, in New Zealand. The lack of a specialized forum for addressing treaty disputes, combined with the fact that the majority of judicial pronouncements have been issued in response to the prosecution of Indigenous individuals for regulatory offences, explains in part the absence of a remedial framework for addressing treaty disputes in Canadian law. The result,

26 In the context of Indigenous peoples' claims, the state's obligation to establish effective remedies was upheld by the Inter-American Court of Human Rights in the landmark case *The Mayagna (Sumo) Awas Tingai Community v Nicaragua*, Judgment of 31 August 2001, Inter-Am Ct HR, (Ser C) No 79 (2001) (applying the American Convention on Human Rights). For a recent ruling by the Inter-American Commission of Human Rights that Canada has not provided adequate remedies for the resolution of Aboriginal title claims, see *Hul'qumi'num Treaty Group v Canada* (2009), Inter-Am Comm HR, No 105/92, Annual Report of the Inter-American Commission on Human Rights: 2009, OEA/Ser.L/V/II. To similar effect, the same principle is enshrined in Article 8 of the Universal Declaration of Human Rights: "[e]veryone has the right to an effective remedy by the competent national tribunals for acts violating the fundamental rights granted him by the constitution or by law" (Universal Declaration of Human Rights, GA Res 217(III), UNGAOR, 3d Sess, Supp No 13, UN Do A/810, [1948]). The United Nations Declaration on the Rights of Indigenous Peoples, to which Canada assented on 13 September 2007, also guarantees that the state will provide appropriate remedies for infringements of rights (United Nations Declaration on the Rights of Indigenous Peoples, UNGA Res 61/295 (13 September 2007) at Article 40). That Article reads: "Indigenous peoples have the right to access and prompt decision through just and fair procedures for the resolution of conflicts and disputes with States or other parties, as well as to effective remedies for all infringements of their individual and collective rights. Such a decision shall give due consideration to the customs, traditions, rules and legal systems of the indigenous peoples concerned and international human rights."

however, is that neither party to the treaty can properly assess its legal options when it believes that its treaty partner has failed to honour the treaty responsibilities.

What kinds of constitutional remedies, for example, should be available to a First Nation that believes Canada has not implemented its promises in the spirit of its treaty? What principles of compensation should be used in calculating the long-standing harms to First Nations if they were caused by a historical failure to implement the treaty terms? The compensation principles used in domestic law to address civil wrongs are simply not designed to address claims that stretch for decades if not centuries. How should a coherent conception of treaties and treaty remedies incorporate Indigenous perspectives about the kind of arrangement they were entering, or the reality that treaties were entered into in accordance with distinct Indigenous legal orders as well as the legal order brought by Crown negotiators? Is it conceivable and just that the majority of the disputes over treaty implementation between treaty partners be resolved through a system of negotiations, rather than through the advancement of claims and prosecutions in the courts? Should permanent forums be created to facilitate such negotiations? These are pressing questions that Canadian law has yet to address.

The conceptual and practical challenge therefore is to uncover a principled and more sophisticated framework for the enforcement of historical treaty rights that more fully reflects the shared purposes of the parties when they came together to make the treaty. Such a framework must reflect the historical fact that treaties were built across significant differences in world view, normative orders, and, undoubtedly, expectations about the future of the parties' relationship. It would also recognize that the availability of domestic legal remedies for the enforcement of treaty understandings will never be an adequate substitute for a fuller and healthier political relationship of respect and attentiveness between the treaty partners. Finally, without diminishing the diverse historical, cultural, and political contexts in which those treaties were negotiated, it should set out a common set of principles to which Indigenous peoples across the country and Crown representatives can refer when disputes arise about the parties' current responsibilities under those treaties.

2. The Implications of Treaty-Making: A Principled Approach

Any fully elaborated legal framework for the implementation and enforcement of historical treaties must reflect the central fact that those treaties were intended to create a new normative order between Indigenous peoples, the Crown, and settler governments. The fact that historical treaty partners came together and, repeatedly, signified their assent to a new framework to govern their future coexistence has powerful general implications that the courts have yet to fully explore. The very existence of such an enterprise demonstrates that both partners accepted that their negotiating counterparts represented peoples capable of creating norms and abiding by them. It also presupposes that both treaty partners, coming from societies with their own unique normative orders, nevertheless acted upon the assumption that it was possible for them to invent a new normative order through treaty that both were capable of respecting. Finally, the common enterprise of treaty-making strongly suggests that both partners believed in the presence of certain general shared norms about the intended effects of the historical treaties.

This is not to deny the extent to which the making of the historical treaties was characterized by competing claims, disagreements, and ambiguities. This would have been the case even if the treaty partners were not trying to negotiate across language and cultural differences and across legal orders that derive from fundamentally different world views.[27] One well-known historian has described treaty-making in the Great Lakes area during the seventeenth and eighteenth centuries as an encounter in which diverse peoples sought to reach consensus over "their differences through what amounts to a process of creative and often expedient" misunderstandings.[28] Nevertheless, it is possible to identify certain basic assumptions that must have been shared by the parties

27 For a fascinating description of some of the characteristics of Indigenous legal orders and their relationships to Canada's legal traditions, see Borrows, *Canada's Indigenous Constitution*. For more on the distinctiveness of Indigenous legal orders, see Val Napoleon, "Living Together: Gitksan Legal Reasoning as a Foundation for Consent" in Jeremy Webber and Colin M. Macleod, eds., *Between Consenting Peoples: Political Community and the Meaning of Consent* (Vancouver: UBC Press, 2010) at 45.

28 Richard White, *The Middle Ground: Indians, Empires, and Republics in the Great Lakes Region, 1650–1815* (New York: Cambridge University Press, 1991) at 60. On this "middle ground," according to White, "[p]eople try to persuade others who are different from themselves by appealing to what they perceive to be the values and practices of those others. They often misinterpret and distort both the values and the practices of those they deal with, but from these misunderstandings arise new meanings and through them new practices – the shared meanings and practices of the middle ground" (*ibid*).

for the treaty-making endeavour to make sense. Recognizing those necessary assumptions, I suggest, allows us to better understand historical treaties as three-dimensional institutional frameworks of coexistence. While not exhausting the political and moral implications of the historical treaty relationship, it provides a secure starting point in extrapolating the core principles that should govern treaty implementation.

Before turning to some of the parties' necessarily shared assumptions in relation to Canada's historical land treaties, it is worth dwelling on what light is shed by conceiving of treaties as evidence of the parties' shared desire to create a new institutionalized normative order. An institutional normative order is created when individuals or groups of individuals agree, expressly or implicitly, that their interactions with each other will be governed by certain general rules and expectations.[29] An institutional order may be thought of as a pattern of organizing principles that allows for the coordination of human interactions over time. As such, an institutional order is necessarily more complex than a single rule or proscription. All societies organize themselves through such sophisticated frameworks of relational ordering. Indigenous clan structures are one example of a sophisticated institutional framework for ordering expectations of care, reciprocal responsibilities, relations across communities, and an individual's sense of identity and connection with his or her human and non-human relations.[30] Socially enduring structures of government, such as the complex confederal protocols of the Haudenosaunee longhouse, also exemplify complex institutional orders.[31]

An institution, as a social or legal construct, is created to provide a framework that can guide people's interactions over time. Understood in this sense, an institutional lens seems particularly apt for conceptualizing the historical treaties. The symbolism of the Gus-Wen-Tah, or Two Row Wampum belt, documenting two peoples travelling forward beside each other in a river, can be understood as an effort to

29 For a description of the institutional theory of law, see Neil MacCormick, *Institutions of Law: An Essay in Legal Theory* (Oxford: Oxford University Press, 2007).

30 See Miller, *supra* note 14 at 7–10, 34–8.

31 For an authoritative description of the cultural foundations and historical workings of the longhouse, see William N. Fenton, *The Great Law and the Longhouse* (Oklahoma: University of Oklahoma Press, 1998) at 3–242. See also Williams, *supra* note 14 at 32–3, 63–4.

institutionalize relations between the Crown and its Indigenous allies; it is scarcely comprehensible, on the other hand, through the lens of contract theory. On the contrary, both parties' use of relational metaphors in negotiating the historical treaties is powerful evidence that both treaty partners were aware that it was impossible for them to set out all of their reciprocal obligations in advance. Both sides were aware that they could not foresee all of the challenges that would face them and allocate their shared risks far into the future. Instead, the parties' use of relational language indicates that they knew that the implementation of their treaty over time would depend upon mutual trust and that they would have to rely on their newly structured relationship to address such challenges. A central aspect of treaty-making, in other words, was the building of an institutional nexus within which the parties could "stand" securely in relation to each other or, to borrow the language of Lumbee scholar Robert Williams Jr. describing Indigenous conceptions of treaty-making, "to link arms together."[32]

One example that demonstrates the need to conceive of treaties as a sophisticated institution, rather than as a contract-like compendium of all of the parties' mutual obligations, is the interpretation of the so-called "taking-up" clause that is found in the Robinson Treaties and the numbered treaties that were negotiated between 1850 and 1930 from Ontario west to British Columbia. In the Crown's written versions of those treaties, such clauses appear to expressly permit Crown governments to interfere with hunting and fishing activities by taking up portions of the treaty lands from time to time for settlement, mining, or other purposes. The interpretation of such a clause was at the heart of the most recent treaty dispute to reach the Supreme Court of Canada, the *Grassy Narrows* case.[33] Borrows' chapter in this book analyses both the judgment of the Supreme Court of Canada and the contours of that

32 Robert A. Williams, Jr., "'The People of the States Where They are Found are Often Their Deadliest Enemies': The Indian Side of the Story of Indian Rights and Federalism" (1996) 38 *Arizona Law Review* 981 at 991. Compare Professor Williams' description of North American Indian visions of treaty diplomacy during the encounter era: "A treaty was therefore far more than just a reassuring way of blunting contradictions and conflicts of interests between societies. Indians understood a treaty as another way of reconstituting a society itself on an unstable and conflict-ridden multicultural frontier" (Williams, *supra* note 14 at 50).

33 *Grassy Narrows*, *supra* note 5.

treaty dispute in which two First Nations failed in their argument that only the federal government could approve a decision to authorize logging in their treaty territory. On its face, the taking-up clause made no provision for the Crown to consult with its Indigenous treaty partners when authorizing such developments. Nor does it require that any of the benefits of such development on treaty lands be shared with the First Nation treaty partners. A literal, contract-based approach to the clause would favour the conclusion that one party to the treaty, conscious that the treaty relationship would last "as long as the sun shines," was agreeing that the other party would ultimately have the exclusive power to eliminate, over time, their entire means of subsistence and to sever completely their social, cultural, and spiritual connection to virtually all of their traditional lands. To adopt such an interpretative approach to the treaty arrangement would be to assume that the Indigenous partners in each of these treaties were utterly irrational.[34] It would be to assume that the Indigenous treaty negotiators were not interested in protecting their traditional economy and their spiritual home.

If, on the other hand, one takes the institutional conception of treaties seriously, and if one accepts that treaty-making was only conceivable if both parties shared certain foundational premises about the purpose and implications of treaty-making, where does that leave us as we consider the appropriate framework for the implementation of treaties? In particular, does such an analysis help us to develop an appropriate normative framework to guide treaty implementation and an appropriate legal framework for addressing disputes between the treaty partners? To explore these questions, let us take the case of the historical land treaties entered into over the 150 years following the Treaty of Niagara.

Our starting point must be that treaty-making was seen by both Indigenous peoples and the Crown as a worthwhile enterprise aimed at advancing both peoples' interests through agreement, and not a meaningless charade intended only to deceive and mollify Indigenous

34 At first glance, the interpretative approach taken by the Supreme Court of Canada in *Grassy Narrows* seems consistent with just this conclusion. In the case of historical treaties, such an interpretation of the parties' intentions, as irrational as it may be, will often be difficult to rebut by the presentation of Elders' recollections of the First Nation negotiators' understanding of the treaty term. At the *Grassy Narrows* trial, for example, the First Nation was unable to locate a single Elder able to testify about negotiation of Treaty 3. See *Keewatin v Ontario (Natural Resources)*, 2013 ONCA 158, 114 OR (3d) 401 at para 37.

peoples.[35] If both parties shared the assumption that treaty-making was worthwhile, this suggests that they accepted certain other common premises. First, that both sets of negotiators were capable of committing their peoples to the terms of any agreement that might be reached. This may seem like a mundane conclusion, given the solemnity that accompanied both sides' assent to each treaty, a solemnity mirrored by the formal and legalistic language used by Crown representatives to memorialize the treaty. But it has further implications. It implies a shared understanding that both sets of negotiators were supported by legal orders that authorized them to ratify the new treaty framework and the legal, or what we would now call constitutional, authority to make decisions of enormous importance on behalf of their peoples. Finally, for treaty-making to be capable of proving worthwhile after the negotiations ended, both parties must have shared the assumption that both were legally capable of ensuring that their respective peoples complied with the new treaty arrangement.

Certain principles flow from these premises and must be considered part of the new normative order that the parties intended to create through the treaties. First, *both treaty partners possess an inherent and historically recognized right to make governance decisions in connection with, at the very least, the subject matter of the treaties*. Second, both parties intended to create a normative order under which both parties would be accountable and which both would be entitled to enforce. In other words, the new normative order must include the principle that *both parties would cooperate to ensure that there would be effective recourse should disputes arise about what had been agreed or what actions would amount to full compliance with the spirit of the treaty relationship*. Because none of the historical treaties appear to specify how disputes were to be resolved, it is possible to debate which forum (political, judicial, or even international) is most appropriate to address implementation concerns.[36] The

35 The fact that treaty rights have been recognized and affirmed in Canada's constitution, combined with the constitutional jurisprudence indicating that sharp dealing is not to be countenanced in the treaty context, indicate that the latter interpretation is no longer open for argument.

36 Persuasive arguments can be made that a permanent specialized treaty forum, designed to account for the unique nature of treaty disputes, would be the most effective vehicle for addressing and managing treaty disagreements within the treaty relationship. A carefully structured, assisted negotiation process may be the best avenue for resolving specific and pressing treaty disputes. For the potential

nature of the treaty-making enterprise and the stakes involved for both treaty partners, however, make it inconceivable that they intended to create a new normative order that lacked effective remedial mechanisms accessible to both parties and appropriate to the treaty relationship.[37] The failure to create any comprehensive remedial framework for resolving treaty disputes would seem, then, to violate the normative order created by treaty-making.

A further set of principles flows from the context of the historical land-sharing treaties. A fundamental premise of these treaties was that the Crown, and through it Canadian legislatures, would have the power to regulate the arrival of settlers to the lands agreed to be shared under the treaty. The Crown would also have the ability to regulate the extent to which settlers and companies would be permitted to use resources on the shared lands and potentially, therefore, to interfere with existing Indigenous economies. Thus, in a very real sense, it was known not only that circumstances on the ground would inevitably change over the life of the treaty relationship, but also that one party to the treaty would have the capacity to determine precisely how those circumstances would change. In fact, non-Indigenous governments subsequently enacted "homestead laws" to encourage migration of settlers onto treaty lands and authorized forestry, mining, and hydroelectric projects that would dramatically affect the face of those lands. It can be debated, particularly in relation to the early land treaties, how quickly the parties expected such encroachments to occur, but a shared

---

advantages of negotiation to resolve disputes in the treaty context, see Michael Coyle, "Transcending Colonialism? Power and the Resolution of Indigenous Treaty Claims in Canada and New Zealand" (2011) 24:4 *New Zealand Universities Law Review* 596; see also Kent Roach, *Constitutional Remedies in Canada* (Aurora, ON: Canada Law Book, 2005) at 15.80–90 and 15.330–336; Shin Imai, "Sound Science, Careful Policy Analysis, and Ongoing Relationships: Integrating Litigation and Negotiation in Aboriginal Lands and Resources Disputes" (2003) 41 *Osgoode Hall Law Journal* 587. For an example of the Supreme Court of Canada exhorting the parties to address treaty and other section 35 rights issues through negotiation, see *Delgamuukw v British Columbia*, [1997] 3 SCR 1010 at 1123–4 [*Delgamuukw*].

37 Certainly this was the understanding of Indigenous leaders, like the Reverend Peter Jones, also called Kahkewaquonaby, who travelled to England in 1838 on behalf of the Mississaugas to petition the Queen for the protection of his people's land rights guaranteed by treaty.

assumption of all of the historical land treaties was that after the treaty, there would be changes in the uses of the lands agreed to be shared.

This reality suggests that two further principles are an inherent part of the new institutional order created by the land treaties. First, some way must be found to reconcile the fact that while the treaties themselves were clearly intended to endure indefinitely amidst inevitable changes on the ground, the written texts of the land treaties in Canada were framed in very narrow and precise terms. For example, the written text of Treaty 4, described at the outset of this chapter, provides that each "head man" will be provided with fifteen dollars in cash and a coat. Further, the document promises that annually thereafter each chief and headman will receive powder, shot, ball, and twine not to exceed a value of $750. The written text also provides for the delivery of "suitable" suits of clothing to the headmen and for each band that takes up agriculture, "two hoes, one spade, one scythe and one axe for every family so actually cultivating."[38] Every one of the written texts of the historical land treaties describes the benefits to be provided by the Crown in similarly specific terms, tied to the context and circumstances prevailing at the time of the treaty.

Further, although the historical land treaties were negotiated for the purpose of facilitating significant changes on the treaty lands, the written treaty texts include no provision for resolving disputes about the implementation of the treaty. And, although the language of the treaty documents and the records of their negotiation make clear that they were intended to endure indefinitely, those texts fail to identify any process for renegotiating the treaty terms to address future changes in circumstances. Until 1982, it was theoretically possible in Canada to argue that those circumstances on treaty lands have changed so dramatically over time as to render the historical treaties legally and practically obsolete,[39] although I would argue that this was an inappropriate conclusion

38 Morris, *supra* note 1 at 332.

39 For just such an argument, based on the international law principle *rebus non sic stantibus*, see Jeremy Waldron, "F.W. Guest Memorial Lecture: August 22nd, 2005: The Half-Life of Treaties: Waitangi, Rebus Sic Stantibus" (2006) 11:2 *Otago Law Review* 161. For spirited rebuttals of Waldron's conclusion, see Douglas Sanderson, "Against Supersession" (2011) 24 *Canadian Journal of Law and Jurisprudence* 155 and Claire Charters, "Responding to Waldron's Defence of Legislatures: Why New Zealand's Parliament Does Not Protect Rights in Hard Cases" (2006) 4 *New Zealand Law Review* 621.

given the parties' shared expectation that such changes would occur. With the constitutional protection of treaty rights in 1982, that conclusion of invalidity is no longer possible in Canada. The historical treaties did create enforceable rights, at least from the perspective of Canadian constitutional law, and our challenge is how to make sense of, and give contemporary meaning to, those treaty understandings. If, as we have seen, the historical land treaties were intended to provide for the long-term future of both treaty partners, how can this be reconciled with the narrow written terms of those treaties in the absence of expressed provisions for renegotiation? The inescapable context of every historical land treaty in what is now Canada is that both treaty partners needed an arrangement under which the future of their peoples could be secured in the face of inevitable changes to come. And, in every case, what the parties sought was a consensual arrangement for coexistence, one based on reciprocal commitments and understandings. Accepting these premises means that a third principle must inevitably form part of the normative order created by the historical land treaties. That is, in entering into a relationship expected to endure indefinitely, *the historical treaty partners would be prepared, in the face of significant changes in circumstances over time, to negotiate, in good faith, a new consensus as to how their treaty understandings should be renewed to address both sides' contemporary needs and interests in relation to the treaty lands.*[40]

40 Such a principle is, of course, consistent with the early understandings of the Crown and its Indigenous partners in regard to the Covenant Chain treaties according to which the strength of the chain that binds the parties can be maintained only by the parties regularly coming together to "polish" the chain. See Mark Walters, "Brightening the Covenant Chain: Aboriginal Treaty Meanings in Law and History after *Marshall*" (2001) 24 *Dalhousie Law Journal* 75 as well as Walters' chapter in this book analysing the modern day implications of the Covenant Chain for Canadian law. For an example of the importance of constructing and reconstructing consensus within Indigenous legal traditions, see Val Napoleon, "Living Together: Gitksan Legal Reasoning as a Foundation for Consent" in Jeremy Webber and Colin M. MacLeod, eds., *Between Consenting Peoples: Political Community and the Meaning of Consent* (Vancouver: UBC Press, 2010) at 46. Professor Napoleon argues that Gitksan law is founded on a "dialogic construction of consent," that is a "process of discussion, disagreement, affirmation and reconciliation, performed at intervals whenever important actions or decisions were required." A similar commitment to ongoing dialogue underlies the constant process of constitutional contestation and renewal between federal and provincial governments, on issues of resource sharing and jurisdiction, that characterizes contemporary "cooperative federalism" in Canada.

This obligation to renew the treaty arrangement is an ongoing one, just as the treaty partnership is ongoing and further changes in circumstances are inevitable.

The responsibility to renegotiate raises some important questions. What is the appropriate forum for such discussions? What should be the particular responsibilities of federal and provincial representatives? What would be the consequences if one treaty partner refuses to come to the table or refuses to address what the other side identifies as key issues for negotiation? To what extent should Canadian courts support, oversee, and guide those negotiations? These are matters that ideally should be left for the treaty partners themselves to resolve. There is little doubt that political dialogue between the treaty partners offers greater potential for strengthening the treaty relationship than adversarial encounters in the courts or at blockades. Aaron Mills' chapter in this book describes the importance of taking the treaty relationship seriously at the level of political structures and citizenship. In Mills' view, "the work of law is to coordinate right relationships, not to resolve rights claims." At the same time, it cannot be denied that law currently plays an important role in guiding the resolution of disputes over the implementation of treaties and the law's treatment of that relationship can scarcely ignore the shared premises that shaped that relationship.

What particular norms might guide the parties as they come together to renegotiate the specific commitments of the historical land treaties? A foundational principle here, I suggest, is that *the treaty shall not be interpreted or implemented in such a way as to render it an improvident arrangement for either side*. To do so would, of course, directly contradict repeated representations by Crown negotiators that entering the historical land treaties would benefit the Aboriginal treaty partners.[41] But an equally compelling reason to recognize that this principle must form part of the new order created by the historical land treaties is that it is inconceivable that those treaties would have been agreed upon unless

41 For only one example, see Alexander Morris' account of his statement in the negotiation of the Treaty 6: "We are not here as traders, I do not come as to buy or sell horses or goods, I come to you, children of the Queen, to try to help you" (Morris, *supra* note 1 at 201). So too, his comment during the negotiation of Treaty 3, "I hope … that I can go back and report that I left my Indian friends contented and that I put into their hands the means of providing for themselves and their families at home" (*ibid* at 866). Similar assurances were made by the Crown representatives at all of the numbered treaty negotiations.

both partners adhered to this principle. Because the historical land treaty was an institution established for the purpose of permitting the coexistence of two sets of peoples on treaty lands, it cannot be rationally interpreted as effecting an entirely improvident arrangement for one of the treaty parties. As rational beings, each party's negotiators cannot be taken as having intended that the treaty have such an effect from the very beginning, on the basis that the treaty partners intended to provide one party with a monopoly of all the resource benefits to be obtained from the Aboriginal partner's traditional lands. Nor, given the parties' knowledge that the Crown would have decision-making power over the use of the treaty lands after the treaty was made, can the treaty arrangement be rationally conceived as giving one party, the Crown, untrammelled discretion to render the arrangement improvident in the future.[42]

This last principle is not just a necessary implication of the historical treaty-making process. It is also consistent with Aboriginal views of the additional responsibilities of treaty partners that derive from their having cemented a more intimate form of kinship between them.[43] Further, it builds naturally on existing Canadian jurisprudence that requires the Crown to act honourably in its dealings with Aboriginal peoples. The duty to act honourably goes beyond a mere procedural obligation to consult with Aboriginal peoples when the Crown proposes to act in a way that might infringe treaty or Aboriginal rights.[44] As mentioned above, the jurisprudence makes clear that the Crown's duty requires

42 For a similar conclusion anchored in historical evidence about the parties' intentions in negotiating Treaty 3, see *Keewatin v Ontario (Minister of Natural Resources)*, 2011 ONSC 4801, [2012] 1 CNLR 13 at para 1293 per Justice Sanderson: "I reject the submission of Ontario that the Ojibway understood that unlimited development was 'the tangible and anticipated manifestation' of the Treaty agreement."

43 See, for example, Robert A. Williams, Jr., "Linking Arms Together: Multicultural Constitutionalism in a North American Indigenous Vision of Law and Peace" (1994) 82 *California Law Review* 981 at 1047: "In the Iroquois vision of law and peace, a treaty relationship meant that the two sides agreed to enter into a continuing and binding compact, encapsulated by a network of special relations with each other. Each side is to treat the other as if they were related, and the sharp dealings that might occur between strangers are replaced by the customary norms governing kinship and relations."

44 For the landmark case establishing this duty, see *Haida Nation*, *supra* note 13. For an application of the consultation principles in the context of a historical treaty, see *Mikisew*, *supra* note 13.

it to avoid "sharp dealing" in the making and implementation of treaties. The Canadian courts have yet to fully flesh out the substantive implications of this duty to avoid sharp dealing. It is clear, however, that the honour of the Crown requires it "to act diligently in pursuit of its solemn obligations and the honourable reconciliation of Crown and Aboriginal interests."[45] The duty also requires Crown servants to perform their treaty obligations in a manner that, to use the language of the Supreme Court of Canada, "pursues the purpose behind the promise."[46] It is reasonable to conclude that the duty of the Crown to act honourably in the making and implementation of treaties requires it to be accountable to its Aboriginal partners in the historical land treaties to demonstrate that it has not in its dealings with the treaty lands rendered the treaty an improvident arrangement for the Aboriginal side.[47]

Recognizing that the historical land treaties were intended to create an enduring relationship that would not lead to the impoverishment of either party seems relatively straightforward. In practice, however, it would force federal and provincial governments to comprehensively re-examine the sharing of the benefits obtained from treaty lands.[48] Further, while this conclusion builds on existing jurisprudence on the

---

45 *Manitoba Metis Federation*, *supra* note 13 at para 78.

46 *Ibid* at para 80. See also *Marshall*, *supra* note 10 at para 52.

47 In addition, it would incidentally address an apparent double standard in Canada's treatment of treaty-making. That is, those Aboriginal peoples who by an accident of history encountered settlers and negotiated treaties in the historical era received much less value, even in relative terms, in exchange for their promises than is reflected in modern treaty negotiations and settlements. Addressing this apparent injustice is perhaps not a sufficient reason for the enforcement of a legal principle, but all things being equal, an interpretation of the law that avoids such a double standard is surely to be preferred.

48 The historical marginalization of Aboriginal peoples in Canada in relation to the benefits derived by others from treaty lands is an important basis of grievance today. A general economic study of the situation would make an important contribution to promoting understanding between Aboriginal peoples and other Canadians on the need for change here. One writer has reported that the negotiation of Treaty 9 in northern Ontario called for an initial payment of $40,000, while silver mining alone in the area generated more than 200 million dollars over the following eighteen years. See Sebastian Grammond, *Terms of Existence: Indigenous Peoples and Canadian Law* (Toronto: Carswell, 2013) at 108, citing E. Brian Titley, *A Narrow Vision: Duncan Campbell Scott and the Administration of Indian Affairs in Canada* (Vancouver: UBC Press, 1986) at 73.

honour of the Crown, the Crown's responsibility here is more appropriately anchored in the fundamental premises of the treaty-making process rather than in a hierarchical view of Crown sovereignty and connotations of *noblesse oblige*. It would be helpful if the courts expressly acknowledged that this responsibility flows from the foundational premises of historical land treaties, and did so within a more comprehensive review of the general remedial principles that necessarily flow from the historical treaty-making process.[49]

Recognizing such a responsibility to provide proportionate benefits from the use of treaty lands would address only one, albeit important, aspect of the treaty relationship. Thus far, from the shared assumptions that must be taken to have informed the making of the historical land treaties, we have drawn out the following principles:

1. *Both treaty partners possess an inherent and historically recognized right to make governance decisions in connection with, at the very least, the subject matter of the treaties;*
2. *Both treaty partners would cooperate to ensure that there would be effective recourse should disputes arise about what had been agreed or what actions would amount to full compliance with the spirit of the treaty relationship;*
3. *Both historical treaty partners to the historical land treaties are required to sit down in the face of significant changes in circumstances over time to negotiate, in good faith, a new consensus as to how their treaty understandings should be renewed to address both sides' contemporary needs and interests in relation to the treaty lands*; and
4. *The historical land treaties shall not be interpreted or implemented in such a way as to render them an improvident arrangement for either treaty partner.*

These four principles are foundational elements of the new institutional legal order that was created through the historical land treaties. They do not depend for their validity on the evidentiary details of a particular treaty negotiation any more than the general principles

---

49 In the recent *Grassy Narrows* decision referred to earlier (*supra* note 5), the Supreme Court of Canada declined even to state expressly that the compensation from the Crown was the logical corollary of an exercise of Crown authority on treaty lands (here the approval of clear-cutting) that would interfere with treaty hunting and fishing rights.

of contract law, such as like the need for mutual consideration in the absence of a seal, depend on the subjective understandings of two particular contracting parties, or than the general responsibilities of Anishinaabe *ogiima* varied with the colour of their hair. Instead, these implementation principles should apply in every case where a historical treaty covered a significant amount of the land that supported an Aboriginal peoples' traditional economy. To acknowledge the generic principles I have described means that they are not subject to being displaced by argument based on the literal reading of a treaty text drafted by the Crown in accordance with current canons of treaty interpretation. They are principles derived from the inherent nature of the historical treaties, just as at common law, fiduciary obligations and shared liability flowed from the inherent nature of commercial partnerships.[50] As such, just as common law partnership principles once did, the treaty principles described here overlay the written treaty texts and logically precede the interpretive process.

Recognizing these principles in Canadian law does not amount to disregarding the actual agreement of the treaty parties. On the contrary, it gives effect to the shared assumptions that must rationally be taken to have undergirded the reaching of those historical agreements. Treaties were an effort to establish a new point of reference – not some abstract, objective reference point, but one that could nevertheless be understood, embraced, and committed to by both sides.

3. Conclusion

Acknowledging remedial principles that are based on the foundational norms of the treaty institution is consistent with the honour of the Crown principle as elucidated by the Supreme Court of Canada. At the same time, for several reasons, expressly recognizing those principles

50 Before the law governing commercial partnerships was codified in England, the obligations of partners were derived from English and international customary norms shared by merchants. In the words of Harvard Law professor Philip Thayer, the law merchant was "a system of law that does not rest exclusively on the institutions and local customs of any particular country, but consists of certain principles of equity and usages of trade which general convenience and a common sense of justice have established to regulate the dealings of merchants and mariners in all the commercial countries of the civilized world." See Philip W. Thayer, "Comparative Law and the Law Merchant" (1936) 6 *Brooklyn Law Review* 139.

offers a more appropriately nuanced basis for addressing issues of treaty implementation. First, it focuses on both treaty partners and their expectations and relational obligations, not solely on the perspective and obligations of one party. Second, it offers a rational and balanced basis for the development of remedial norms in the treaty context, including norms relating to the substance of the parties' mutual obligations. Further, it offers the prospect of developing a clearer and more certain legal framework for determining the parties' obligations under treaties than can the general concept of "honour" on its own. Finally, by focusing on the parties' overriding substantive commitment to ensure that the implementation of historical land treaties remains a provident arrangement for both treaty partners, this approach offers the hope, not just of greater consistency with the rule of the law,[51] but also of reducing the number of conflicts on the ground over proposed developments on treaty lands.

What does this institutional approach to treaties mean in practice? Among other things, as noted above, it requires both levels of the Crown to regularly review the distribution of benefits derived from treaty lands and resources between non-Aboriginal persons and communities and the Aboriginal peoples represented in the treaty. For a community like Grassy Narrows, that has already suffered tragically from mercury poisoning caused by forestry operations on their traditional lands,[52] it means they have more than a right to participate as a treaty partner in occasional provincial decisions to "take up" unoccupied treaty lands. They have a treaty right to share meaningfully in any benefits that are derived from their traditional lands. This suggests that the Supreme Court of Canada will eventually need to examine the Crown's obligations in more depth than the Court did in the recent *Grassy Narrows* case, when it wrote: "if the taking up leaves the Ojibway

51 In the sense of offering a predictable normative framework that allows citizens to plan their interactions securely; see *Re Manitoba Language Rights*, [1985] 1 SCR 721, 19 DLR (4th) 1. For a famous argument that for a set of rules to count as "law," they must be general, prospective, stable and intelligible, see Lon L. Fuller, *The Morality of Law* (New Haven: Yale University Press, 1964).

52 For a powerful and moving description of the devastating effects on the Grassy Narrows community caused by one particular taking up of their treaty lands, see Anastasia M. Shkilnyk, *A Poison Stronger Than Love: The Destruction of an Ojibwa Community* (New Haven: Yale University Press, 1985).

with no meaningful right to hunt, fish or trap in relation to the territories over which they traditionally hunted, fished, and trapped, a potential action for treaty infringement will arise."[53] The rights of the Aboriginal treaty partner are engaged well before they are left with no meaningful ability to use their traditional lands; the historical treaty arrangement must be implemented *in a mutually beneficial manner* long before it comes to that point.

Acknowledging the four implementation principles set out in this chapter offers a secure starting point for further refinement of the reciprocal responsibilities owed by the partners to the historical land treaties. To be sure, the four principles examined here are not an exhaustive list of the remedial implications of the historical treaty-making process. We have not tried, for example, to tease out in detail the implications of treaty-making on the Indigenous treaty partner's rights of self-governance. It might be argued that a list of minimal, binding legal norms cannot ensure a fully balanced, healthy, and prosperous relationship between Canada's historical treaty partners. The principles identified in this chapter, grimly focused as they are on minimum standards for the implementation of historical treaties, do not capture the web of ethical responsibilities and moral connections that should also guide the treaty partners' relationship. Few legal theorists, if any, have ever suggested that a body of legal obligations should be designed to, or could be capable of, providing a template that ensures "virtuous" citizenship or good governance. The fact that legal norms, like the rules enforced by Canada's domestic courts, do not provide such an all-encompassing guide to the good life is not in itself a ground for criticizing those legal norms.

On the other hand, what the remedial principles laid out above do offer is an important nuancing of the treaty implementation principles that have been developed thus far by the Canadian courts. Expressly acknowledging those basic principles makes clearer the substantive legal accountability of the Crown to take into account its historical treaties in its dealings with the lands covered by those treaties. To the extent that these principles delineate the economic obligations of the Crown to its Aboriginal treaty partners, they leave appropriate *political* space for both treaty partners to negotiate an appropriate contemporary recognition of

53 *Grassy Narrows*, *supra* note 5, at para 52.

the premises of the historical treaty-making process. On the foundation of the remedial principles described above, the treaty partners will be required to negotiate understandings that take into account both sides' cultures and world views. Outside of that political space, the Crown is legally accountable to show, at a minimum, that it has acted in good faith to ensure an honourable allocation of benefits from treaty lands to its historical treaty partners. To be sure, the role of the Canadian courts in monitoring that accountability will need to be exercised with discretion, respecting the polycentric nature of government decision-making. Governments, after all, must respect other interests than those of Indigenous peoples. But the Supreme Court of Canada has long since proved its ability to be creative in promoting principled negotiation to address Aboriginal rights.[54]

Finally, it would be an impoverished vision of the treaty relationship, or indeed of any human relationship, that looked only at the parties' legal or economic obligations and rights. Political partnership and the ethics of caring, mutual respect, and trust were clearly intended to be integral to the new order created by the historical treaties. Indigenous scholars like John Borrows, Aaron Mills, and Heidi Stark, all contributors to this book, have rightly emphasized that these kinds of responsibilities seem to be inherent in the treaty relationship. Any proper account of the implications of the historical land treaties must respect the norms of both treaty partners who created them. Finally, attending to the legal norms that flow from the treaty-making process should enhance, not undermine, the treaty partners' political and ethical responsibilities to each other.

54 The Court famously urged the use of negotiation to address Aboriginal title claims in *Delgamuukw, supra* note 37 at 1123–4, Chief Justice Lamer. In its more recent decision in *Manitoba Metis Federation*, the majority of the Court expressly noted, in issuing a declaration, that the Crown had not fulfilled its obligations as required by the Crown's honour, that the Metis were seeking "in order to assist them in extra-judicial negotiations with the Crown in pursuit of the overarching constitutional goal of reconciliation that is reflected in s. 35 of the *Constitution Act, 1982*" (*Manitoba Metis Federation, supra* note 13 at para 137).

3 Indigenous Rights Litigation, Legal History, and the Role of Experts

KENT MCNEIL*

How should history be treated by modern courts when they address treaty disputes? This chapter discusses the role of legal historians as expert witnesses in litigation involving Indigenous rights. It emphasizes that their testimony needs to be limited to historical matters and avoid opinions on the law that the court must apply in reaching a decision. While not addressing treaty litigation specifically, the analysis of the role of these experts applies equally to litigation involving treaty rights. In every such case, the distinction between legal history and current law must be kept carefully in mind.

Litigation involving the rights of the Indigenous peoples of Canada usually involves historical facts and events from a long time ago, sometimes as far back as 400 years.[1] This reality presents significant challenges for proving the facts upon which these rights are based. In addition to historical documents, the parties have to rely on testimony by Indigenous witnesses who are able to present the oral histories and traditions of

* This chapter first appeared in the (2014) 77 *Saskatchewan Law Review*, 173. A version of the chapter was presented at the SSHRC/Indigenous Bar Association Annual Conference, Rama, Ontario, 8 October 2013, and at the Intensive Program in Aboriginal Lands, Resources and Governments at Osgoode Hall Law School, Toronto, 2 April 2014. I am very grateful for helpful feedback on drafts of this paper generously provided by Allan Beever, Benjamin Berger, Amar Bhatia, Andrée Boisselle, David Dyzenhaus, Hamar Foster, Philip Girard, Douglas Hay, Allan Hutchinson, Shin Imai, Jim Miller, Arthur Ray, Kathy Simo, Mark Walters, and Kerry Wilkins. The opinions and any errors in this chapter are nonetheless my own.

1 See e.g., *R v Adams*, [1996] 3 SCR 101, where the accused had to prove that fishing for food in Lake St. Francis in what is now Quebec had been a practice, custom, or tradition integral to the Mohawks' distinctive culture at the time of contact with the French in 1603.

their people, as well as on the opinion evidence of experts, such as archaeologists, anthropologists, linguists, historians, ethnohistorians, and legal historians. In this chapter, I examine the role of legal historians in Indigenous rights cases, using the example of one academic in particular as an illustration. But first, it is necessary to distinguish between law and history because, as a general rule, expert witnesses cannot testify and offer opinions on applicable domestic law because, in the common law system, domestic law is within the purview of judges and is not a matter of evidence.[2] So where is the line between law and history to be drawn in the context of legal proceedings involving Indigenous rights?

In attempting to answer this question, one needs to take account of a debate, originating mainly in New Zealand and Australia, over the place and appropriate use of history in Indigenous claims,[3] especially, but not limited to,[4] claims involving lands and resources.[5] Although this debate has not yet had the same impact in Canada,[6]

---

2 Domestic law is the law of the jurisdiction where the case is being tried. See Ron Delisle, Don Stuart, and David Tanovich, *Evidence: Principles and Problems*, 9th ed. (Toronto: Carswell, 2010) at 387–9; David M. Paciocco and Lee Stuesser, *The Law of Evidence*, 6th ed. (Toronto: Irwin Law, 2011) at 186. Foreign law and local custom (including the laws and customs of Indigenous peoples) are not part of the domestic law that a judge is assumed to know, and so, they generally do have to be proven by expert testimony: see Adrian Keane, James Griffiths, and Paul McKeown, *The Modern Law of Evidence*, 8th ed. (Oxford: Oxford University Press, 2010) at 33, 526–7. I am grateful to my colleague, Benjamin Berger, for helping me understand the role of expert witnesses and the distinction between current domestic law and law that belongs to the legal history of a particular jurisdiction.

3 In Australia, this debate arose mainly out of *Mabo v Queensland [No 2]* (1992), 175 CLR 1 [*Mabo*], in which the High Court decided that the denial of non-statutory Indigenous land rights by Australian governments and courts for 200 years was legally wrong and no longer acceptable.

4 Another context for this debate concerns the "stolen generations" of Indigenous children who were taken from their families in Australia: see e.g. Peter Read, *The Stolen Generations: The Removal of Aboriginal Children in New South Wales 1883 to 1969* (Sydney: New South Wales Ministry of Aboriginal Affairs, 1982); Robert van Krieken, "The Barbarism of Civilization: Cultural Genocide and the 'Stolen Generations'" (1999) 50 *British Journal of Sociology* 297; A. Dirk Moses, ed., *Genocide and Settler Society: Frontier Violence and Stolen Indigenous Children in Australian History* (New York: Berghahn Books, 2004); Bain Attwood, "In the Age of Testimony: The Stolen Generations Narrative, 'Distance,' and Public History" (2008) 20 *Public Culture* 75; Alexander Reilly, "Sovereign Apologies" in Julie Evans, Ann Genovese, Alexander Reilly, and Patrick Wolfe, eds., *Sovereignty: Frontiers of Possibility* (Honolulu: University of Hawai'i Press, 2013) at 196.

5 For a sampling of the extensive literature, see Henry Reynolds, *The Law of the Land* (Ringwood, AU: Penguin, 1987); Andrew Sharp, *Justice and the Maori: The Philosophy*

Paul McHugh, a prominent academic from New Zealand who teaches at Cambridge University, is attempting to give it more traction here through his published work and, more significantly, as an expert witness for the Crown as a legal historian in Indigenous rights cases in Canada. Because I am concerned about the way in which McHugh is attempting to influence the development of Canadian law in relation to Indigenous rights, I have structured this paper around an analysis and critique of his views on the use of history in this context.[7] In so doing, I hope to shed light on the distinction between history and law and the proper role of legal historians in Indigenous rights cases.

1. The Distinction between History and Law

It is trite to observe that historians and lawyers approach and use history in different ways. Historians are generally interested in history for its own sake – they study and try to understand and illuminate the past.

---

and Practice of Maori Claims in New Zealand since the 1970s, 2nd ed. (Oxford: Oxford University Press, 1997); Alex Reilly and Ann Genovese, "Claiming the Past: Historical Understanding in Australian Native Title Jurisprudence" (2004) 3 *Indigenous Law Journal* 19; Bain Attwood, "*The Law of the Land* or the Law of the Land? History, Law and Narrative in a Settler Society" (2004) 2 *History Compass* 1 [Attwood, "History, Law and Narrative"]; Ian Hunter, "Natural Law, Historiography, and Aboriginal Sovereignty" (2007) 11 *Legal History* 137; Ann Curthoys, Ann Genovese, and Alexander Reilly, *Rights and Redemption: History, Law and Indigenous People* (Sydney: UNSW Press, 2008).

6 But see Alain Beaulieu, "An Instrumentalized History: Reflections on the Use of the Past in Aboriginal Claims," http://www.academia.edu/5129408/An_Instrumentalized_History_Reflections_on_the_Use_of_the_Past_in_Aboriginal_Claims, a translation of « Une histoire instrumentalisée. Réflexions sur l'usage du passé dans les revendications autochtones » in *Vert, le droit ? Conférence des juristes de l'État 2009* (Cowansville, QC: Éditions Yvon Blais, 2009) at 349; Janna Promislow, "Treaties in History and Law" (2014) 47 *University of British Columbia Law Review* 1085. In Canada, the role of Indigenous oral histories in proving Aboriginal and treaty rights has received more attention: see e.g., Lori Ann Roness and Kent McNeil, "Legalizing Oral History: Proving Aboriginal Title in Canadian Courts" (2000) 39:3 *Journal of the West* 66; John Borrows, "Listening for a Change: The Courts and Oral Tradition" (2001) 39 *Osgoode Hall Law Journal* 2; Val Napoleon, "*Delgamuukw*: A Legal Straightjacket for Oral Histories?" (2005) 20 *Canadian Journal of Law and Society* 123; Bruce Granville Miller, *Oral Histories on Trial: Recognizing Aboriginal Narratives in the Courts* (Vancouver: UBC Press, 2011).

7 My criticisms of Paul McHugh's views are intellectual and academic. I have known him since 1980 when we were both at the University of Saskatchewan, and respect him as a person and a scholar, while disagreeing with him fundamentally on some issues.

McHugh describes this as the "scientific" or "disinterested" approach to history.[8] Legal historians likewise seek to shed light on the past, specifically by revealing the place of the law and the role of legal practitioners in given social and political contexts. McHugh describes the legal historian's task as involving "the disinterested retrieval and recounting of a past that is specifically or, rather, primarily legal in character. Basically, it is an enquiry into how law has operated in the past."[9]

Of course one can dispute the degree to which historians in general and legal historians in particular are truly disinterested, given that no one, in my opinion, can be entirely disengaged from political perspective, cultural world view, and personal bias.[10] In theory, however, the role of the historian is to shine an objective light on the past.[11]

Lawyers, on the other hand, take a more instrumental approach – they are interested in using history to help resolve present-day disputes. To do this, they tend to search the past selectively for facts and precedents that can be used and applied to the legal problems they are trying to solve. McHugh refers to this practical use of the past as "presentism," which he defines as the "use of the past for present purposes":

---

8 Paul G. McHugh, *Aboriginal Title: The Modern Jurisprudence of Tribal Land Rights* (Oxford: Oxford University Press, 2011) at 274–6 [McHugh, *Aboriginal Title*]. See also Paul G. McHugh, "The Politics of Historiography and the Taxonomies of the Colonial Past: Law, History and the Tribes" in Anthony Musson and Chantal Stebbings, eds., *Making Legal History: Approaches and Methodologies* (Cambridge: Cambridge University Press, 2012) at 164 [McHugh, "Politics of Historiography"].

9 McHugh, *Aboriginal Title*, *supra* note 8 at 274. See also Frederick Bernays Wiener, *Uses and Abuses of Legal History: A Practitioner's View*, published lecture delivered 29 March 1962 for the Selden Society (London: Bernard Quaritch, 1962) at 16: "legal history itself is essentially a record of changing rules and doctrines."

10 For the "history wars" that have raged during the past twenty-five years over the proper interpretation of Australia's past, in particular in regard to the treatment of Indigenous peoples, see the works cited in *supra* note 5, as well as Bain Attwood, *Telling the Truth About Aboriginal History* (Crows Nest, AU: Allen & Unwin, 2005); Lorenzo Veracini, "A Prehistory of Australia's History Wars: The Evolution of Aboriginal History during the 1970s and 1980s" (2006) 52 *Australian Journal of History and Politics* 439; Bain Attwood and Tom Griffiths, eds., *Frontier, Race, and Nation: Henry Reynolds and Australian History* (Melbourne: Australian Scholarly Publishing, 2009).

11 See Attwood, *supra* note 5 at 20: "With works of history, the author undertakes to represent the past as truthfully to that time as he or she can." On the attainability of this goal, see William Twining, "Some Scepticism about Some Scepticisms" in *Rethinking Evidence: Explanatory Essays* (Oxford: Basil Blackwell, 1990) at 103–12. For detailed discussion of the distinction between history and law in the context of Indigenous peoples' rights, see Promislow, *supra* note 6.

> The common lawyer's use of the past is, therefore, seen through the lens of the present, which renders the questions and issues for the resolution of which the past is the primary resource. The report of that past is marshalled around the demands presently being made of the law.[12]

Now, I agree with McHugh that lawyers make practical use of the past by "seeing [it] in terms of the requirements of the present,"[13] but I think he fails to distinguish adequately between the use lawyers make of history and the use they make of law. These are entirely different inquiries. As stated by F.W. Maitland in a passage McHugh quotes, one has to be very careful not "to mix up two different logics, the logic of authority, and the logic of evidence."[14] Maitland was distinguishing here between the logic employed by lawyers who look to the past for precedents to resolve contemporary legal disputes and the logic used by legal historians who are interested in evidence of how the law was understood and applied in the past. Immediately after quoting this statement, McHugh observes that Maitland (along with A.V. Dicey[15]) was "sure that the historian required evidence and was concerned with questions of origin and what 'was,' matters that did not strictly concern the lawyer."[16] Now if McHugh means by this that lawyers, unlike legal historians, are generally not concerned with how law operated in the past, but only with how it applies in the present, I think he is right. But regarding the facts of history, as opposed to "legal" history, lawyers are just as concerned as historians with what "was," as every case must have a factual basis that depends on what actually happened in the past.[17]

---

12 McHugh, *Aboriginal Title, supra* note 8 at 275.

13 *Ibid* at 276. See also Allan C. Hutchinson, *Evolution and the Common Law* (Cambridge: Cambridge University Press, 2005) at 6.

14 "Why the History of English Law is not Written," in H.A.L. Fisher, ed., *The Collected Papers of Frederic William Maitland,* vol. 1 (Cambridge: Cambridge University Press, 1911) at 491, quoted in McHugh, *Aboriginal Title, supra* note 8 at 274.

15 A.V. Dicey, *Introduction to the Study of the Law of the Constitution*, 10th ed. [1885] (London: Macmillan & Co., 1959) at 22.

16 McHugh, *Aboriginal Title, supra* note 8 at 274.

17 Paraphrasing Maitland in the sentence immediately before the one quoted at *supra* note 14, McHugh writes that "Maitland saw the common lawyer's interest in the past as no more than a trawling for the authority of precedent" (274). But it seems to me that this trawling exercise relates to the "logic of authority," not to the "logic of evidence" which relates to relevant historical facts that are of equal interest to lawyers.

In a courtroom, history is a matter of fact – part of Maitland's "logic of evidence" – that has to be either proven by testimony and documentary sources or accepted through judicial notice.[18] Lawyers will, of course, search the past for historical evidence that supports their client's case: this is part of their professional obligation.[19] But they can also expect their opponent to do the same. Neither side intends to present an entirely disinterested historical account to the court; instead, both are advocates trying to convince the court that history (i.e., the facts) favours their client's case. Judges, however, are in a different position. They are supposed to be disinterested and impartial, and, in the absence of a jury, make findings of historical fact to the best of their ability based on the evidence presented by both sides.[20]

McHugh contends that, given their goal of seeking certain solutions for current legal problems, lawyers tend to decontextualize and oversimplify history.[21] He also accuses them of failing to distinguish adequately between legal argument supporting Aboriginal title today and the historical foundations for that title. In a particularly sarcastic passage, he writes,

> Those unable to apprehend the distinction between the legal and historical foundation of aboriginal title have tended to be lawyers, wedded (blinkered, more like) to the declaratory theory's belief that contemporary doctrine articulates eternal verities as available to past (though, of course, less clever) actors as themselves – re-educating the dead, as Bartleson [*sic*] put it.[22]

18 Judges can take judicial notice of undisputed historical facts and, more controversially, conduct their own historical research in relation to the case before them: see *Read v Bishop of Lincoln*, [1892] AC 644 at 652–4 (Lord Halsbury); *Monarch Steamship Co v Karlshamns Oljefabriker (A/B)*, [1949] AC 196 at 234 (Lord du Parcq); *R v Sioui*, [1990] 1 SCR 1025 at 1050 (Lamer J).

19 See Wiener, *supra* note 9 at 31–2; Richard Boast, "Lawyers, Historians, Ethics, and the Judicial Process" (1998) 28 *Victoria University of Wellington Law Review* 87.

20 See *R v Marshall*, [1999] 3 SCR 456 at para 37 (Binnie J).

21 "Lawyers seek to allay anxiety about the contingency of the present, and the future, and do so by removing it from their account of the past" (McHugh, *Aboriginal Title, supra* note 8 at 284).

22 *Ibid* at 283. The reference is to Jens Bartelson, *A Genealogy of Sovereignty* (Cambridge: Cambridge University Press, 1995) at 57.

But I think McHugh himself fails to take sufficient account of the distinction between law and historical fact, or, as Maitland put it, "the logic of authority, and the logic of evidence." In formulating a common law doctrine of Aboriginal title, lawyers have sought legal precedents (authority) from the past that would support Indigenous land claims today. These precedents are part of the historical development of the common law itself – they are not "eternal verities" that lawyers discover in the present and inappropriately apply to the past.

To better understand the nature of my disagreement with McHugh, we need to examine the declaratory theory more carefully. Simplistically stated, the theory is that common law judges do not make law – they just "discover" and declare it.[23] In *Parker v British Airways Board*, Lord Donaldson put it this way: "As a matter of legal theory, the common law has a ready made solution for every problem and it is only for the judges, as legal technicians, to find it."[24] But, as he went on to observe,

> [t]he reality is somewhat different. Take the present case. The conflicting rights of finder and occupier have indeed been considered by various courts in the past. But under the rules of English jurisprudence, none of their decisions binds this court. We therefore have both the right and the duty to extend and adapt the common law in the light of established principles and the current needs of the community. This is not to say that we start with a clean sheet. In doing so, we should draw from the experience of the past as revealed by the previous decisions of the courts.[25]

So while the view that the declaratory theory is a "fiction" is not entirely incorrect,[26] the theory does not depend on, as McHugh put

---

23 See Peter Wesley-Smith, "Theories of Adjudication and the Status of *Stare Decisis*," in Laurence Goldstein, ed., *Precedent in Law* (Oxford: Clarendon Press, 1987) at 73–82.

24 [1982] 2 WLR 503 at 505 (CA) [*Parker*].

25 *Ibid* at 505–6. The *Parker* case involved a dispute over entitlement to a gold bracelet between the finder of it (Parker) and the occupier of the premises where it had been found (British Airways).

26 However, classifying the theory as a fiction does not mean it has no legitimate place in the common law, as fictions are very much a part – in some instances a necessary part – of our legal tradition. On the development and role of legal fictions, see Sir Henry Sumner Maine, *Ancient Law: Its Connection with the Early History of Society and its Relation to Modern Ideas* [1861] (New York: Dorset Press, 1986) at 17–36; Peter Birks, "Fictions Ancient and Modern" in Neil MacCormick and Peter Birks, eds.,

it, a "belief that contemporary doctrine articulates eternal verities."[27] Common law methodology is much more nuanced than that. In deciding cases where the law is still uncertain, which is usually the situation in appeal courts, judges do, as Lord Donaldson stated, properly consider "previous decisions," "established principles," and "the current needs of the community."[28] The common law is neither divorced from nor rigidly tied to the past.[29] These observations apply as much to the doctrine of Aboriginal title as to the rest of the common law.

And yet McHugh seems to think that the articulation in the 1990s of the common law doctrine of Aboriginal title by the highest courts in Australia and Canada in particular was "presentist" and ahistorical in the sense that the judges constructed new law and then applied it backwards to a time when Indigenous peoples had no legal rights to their traditional lands. He states,

> [...] throughout the nineteenth century and most of the twentieth, the legal position had been that technically the tribes' land was vested in the Crown

---

The Legal Mind: Essays in Honour of Tony Honoré (Oxford: Clarendon Press, 1986) at 83; J.H. Baker, *The Law's Two Bodies: Some Evidential Problems in Legal History* (Oxford: Oxford University Press, 2001) at 33–57.

27 McHugh, *Aboriginal Title, supra* note 8 at 282–3. See also McHugh, *Aboriginal Societies and the Common Law: A History of Sovereignty, Status, and Self-Determination* (Oxford: Oxford University Press, 2004) at 18 [McHugh, *Aboriginal Societies*]. For a review of *Aboriginal Societies* that raises some of the concerns that I express in this paper, see Mark D. Walters, "Histories of Colonialism, Legality, and Aboriginality" (2007) 57 *University of Toronto Law Journal* 819.

28 See also *Harrison v Carswell*, [1976] 2 SCR 200 at 218 [*Harrison*], per Dickson J: "The duty of the Court, as I envisage it, is to proceed in the discharge of its adjudicative function in a reasoned way from principled decision and established concepts."

29 See Sir Carleton Kemp Allen, *Law in the Making*, 7th ed. (Oxford: Clarendon Press, 1964) at 307: "A judge, in laying down a rule to meet these situations [where there is no precedent to guide the decision of the court], is certainly making a new contribution to our law, but only within limits, usually well defined. If he has to decide upon the authority of natural justice, or simply 'the common sense of the thing' [*Pearce v Gardner*, [1897] 1 QB 688 (CA) at 690 (Lord Esher MR)], he employs that kind of natural justice or common sense which he has absorbed from the study of law and which he believes to be consistent with the general principles of English jurisprudence." See also Benjamin N. Cardozo, *The Nature of the Judicial Process* (New Haven: Yale University Press, 1921); Wiener, *supra* note 9 at 16; Frederic Reynold, *The Judge as Lawmaker* (London: MacGibbon and Kee, 1967); Louis L. Jaffe, *English and American Judges as Lawmakers* (Oxford: Clarendon Press, 1969).

> as sovereign and that any aboriginal interest was protected by and through the Crown. This was an expression of the feudal doctrine of tenures according to which all enforceable legal title to land derived from a Crown grant [...] The reasoning ran that since tribal occupation did not rest upon a Crown-derived basis and remained un-granted land, the tribe had no land rights of which a common law court might take cognizance.[30]

While this feudal basis for denying Indigenous land rights in the Crown's settled colonies did indeed have resonance in Australia prior to the High Court's 1992 decision in *Mabo v Queensland*[31] and was relied upon by Justice Blackburn of the Northern Territory Supreme Court in 1971 in *Milirrpum v Nabalco Pty*,[32] the legal status of Indigenous land rights in Canada remained an open question[33] until all doubt was removed in 1973 by the Supreme Court's acknowledgment of the legality of these rights in *Calder v Attorney-General of British Columbia*.[34]

---

30 McHugh, *Aboriginal Title*, *supra* note 8 at 111. In reality, however, even in England it was recognized early on that the doctrine of tenures does not have a factual basis; the fiction of Crown grants was a "supposition in law" invented to explain and support the feudal doctrine of tenures: Anonymous, *Considerations on the Law of Forfeitures, for High Treason*, 4th ed. (London: J. Williams, 1775) at 64–5. See also William Blackstone, *Commentaries on the Laws of England*, vol. 2 (Oxford: Clarendon Press, 1765–9) at 51; Joseph Chitty, *A Treatise on the Law of the Prerogatives of the Crown: And the Relative Duties and Rights of the Subject* (London: Joseph Butterworth & Son, 1820) at 211.

31 *Mabo*, *supra* note 3.

32 (1971), 17 FLR 141. For an argument, based on English precedent and legal principle predating British colonization (see, e.g., works cited in *supra* note 26), that the Australian courts prior to *Mabo*, *supra* note 3, misunderstood the fictional nature and colonial relevance of the doctrine of tenures, see Kent McNeil, "A Question of Title: Has the Common Law Been Misapplied to Dispossess the Aboriginals?" (1990) 16 *Monash University Law Review* 91 [McNeil, "Question of Title"].

33 See, for example, the differences in opinion and the inconclusive pronouncements on Aboriginal title expressed by the judges of the Supreme Court of Canada and Privy Council in *St Catharines Milling and Lumber Company v The Queen* (1887), 13 SCR 577, *St Catherine's [sic] Milling and Lumber Company v The Queen* (1888), 14 App Cas 46 (PC) [*St Catherine's Milling*].

34 [1973] SCR 313 [*Calder*]. Importantly, the majority of the Supreme Court in *Calder* decided that, although Aboriginal title entailed legal rights, it was not justiciable because the plaintiffs had not obtained permission from the Crown to bring legal action against it.

But beyond pointing out that the law in relation to Indigenous land rights in the nineteenth and most of the twentieth centuries was not as settled as McHugh seems to think,[35] the argument I want to make is broader, going to the very nature of judicial decision-making and the vital distinction between fact and law. If I understand him correctly, McHugh is suggesting that, in the context of Indigenous land rights, common law doctrine did not exist until the latter part of the twentieth century when it was created by judges who ignored the historical context and applied the doctrine retroactively to an earlier time. In my opinion, this is not the way the common law works. Rather, when cases involving unresolved legal questions come before the courts, judges are obliged to say what the law is, but, as Lord Donaldson explained in the *Parker* decision, they are not working in a legal vacuum.[36] Just because a legal issue has not yet been resolved by a court does not mean there is no law in relation thereto.[37] On the contrary, the matter may not have gone to court because legal practitioners were in no doubt about the relevant law. Or, as where Indigenous land rights are concerned, the people who might have asserted the rights in court were unable to do so because they did not understand the legal system,[38] did not have the financial resources to hire lawyers, or were legally prevented from

35 See Hamar Foster, "Letting Go the Bone: The Idea of Indian Title in British Columbia, 1849–1927" in Hamar Foster and John McLaren, eds., *Essays in the History of Canadian Law*, vol. 6, *British Columbia and the Yukon* (Toronto: The Osgoode Society for Canadian Legal History, 1995) at 28; Foster, "We Are Not O'Meara's Children: Law, Lawyers, and the First Campaign for Aboriginal Title in British Columbia, 1908–28" [Foster, "Not O'Meara's Children"] in Hamar Foster, Heather Raven, and Jeremy Webber, eds., *Let Right Be Done: Aboriginal Title, the* Calder *Case, and the Future of Indigenous Rights* (Vancouver: UBC Press, 2007); and Foster, "One Good Thing: Law, Elevator Etiquette, and Litigating Aboriginal Rights in Canada" (2010) 37 *Advocates' Quarterly* 66 [Foster, "One Good Thing"].

36 McHugh acknowledges that the late twentieth century Indigenous land rights decisions were not made "in a legal vacuum," but nonetheless maintains that "they represented a paradigm shift and the assertion by the courts of a new role in what until then had been the mostly non-justiciable" (*Aboriginal Title*, *supra* note 8 at 31).

37 See Baker, *Law's Two Bodies*, *supra* note 26 at 59–90.

38 See *Manitoba Métis Federation v Canada (Attorney General)*, 2013 SCC 14, [2013] 2 CNLR 281 at paras 147–9. Compare McHugh, "Politics of Historiography," *supra* note 9 at 190: "By the mid nineteenth century, tribes were becoming better versed in the ways of Anglo-settler polity and had they been able to enforce a common law aboriginal title against the Crown, then surely that would have happened."

litigating, either by Crown immunity from suit[39] or by discriminatory laws such as the section of the Canadian *Indian Act* enacted in 1927 that made it an offence, absent written permission from the Superintendent General of Indian Affairs, for anyone to solicit or receive funds from Indians to pursue any of their claims.[40] Or, as in the case of the *Milirrpum* decision in Australia, a trial judge may have misapplied the common law,[41] though this did not become apparent until the High Court overruled that decision in *Mabo*.

This brings me back to the distinction between fact and law. In a common law court, history is a matter of fact. In cases involving Indigenous rights, lawyers and judges treat it as such: in Aboriginal title and treaty claims in Canada, for example, lawyers often spend huge amounts of time presenting historical evidence to the court through witnesses, and trial judges devote large portions of their judgments to outlining their

---

39 In the common law, the Crown could not be sued in its own courts without its consent, which is why the Nisga'a Nation's claim to Aboriginal title in *Calder*, *supra* note 34, was dismissed by the majority of the Supreme Court of Canada. See Foster, *supra* note 35 at 70–9. This Crown immunity has been removed by statute in the United Kingdom and Canada by the *Crown Proceedings Act* (UK), 1947, 10 & 11 Geo VI, c 44; *Petition of Right Amendment Act*, SC 1951, c 33; and *Crown Proceedings Act*, SBC 1974, c 24. See Walter Clode, *The Law and Practice of Petition of Right under the Petitions of Right Act, 1860* (London: William Clowes and Sons, 1887); H. Street, *Governmental Liability: A Comparative Study* (Cambridge: Cambridge University Press, 1953) at 1–7; Peter W. Hogg, Patrick J. Monahan, and Wade K. Wright, *Liability of the Crown*, 4th ed. (Toronto: Carswell, 2011) at 5, 8–10.

40 *An Act to Amend the Indian Act*, SC 1926–7, c 32, s 6, continued in *Indian Act*, RSC 1927, c 98, s 141, repealed by *Indian Act*, SC 1951, c 29, s 123(2). If the Crown's legal advisers in early twentieth century Canada were so sure that Indigenous peoples had no legal rights to their traditional lands, why did the Parliament of Canada bother to enact this provision? Professor Paul Tennant, in his book *Aboriginal Peoples and Politics: The Indian Land Question in British Columbia, 1849–1989* (Vancouver: UBC Press, 1990) at 112, provides this answer, referring to the sponsors of the amendment after detailing the history leading up to it: "their intent was to prevent all land claims activity and, above all, to block the British Columbia claim from getting to the Judicial Committee of the Privy Council." The timing of the amendment was significant: the Privy Council, in *Amodu Tijani v Secretary, Southern Nigeria*, [1921] 2 AC 399, had decided that the land rights of the Africans in the British colony of Southern Nigeria continued after Crown acquisition of sovereignty, and the Allied Tribes in British Columbia planned to rely on this decision in legal action. See Foster, "Not O'Meara's Children," *supra* note 35 at 79–84.

41 See McNeil, "Question of Title," *supra* note 32.

factual findings.[42] The lawyers and judges are also completely aware that legal argument about the applicable law is distinct from factual evidence about history. They understand that the relevant domestic law is not a matter of history that has to be proven by evidence, but depends instead on Maitland's "logic of authority." This is not to say that the common law has a ready-made solution to every novel issue that arises in the context of Indigenous claims. But the common law, along with equity, does contain principles and precedents honed over centuries of development that are relevant to Indigenous claims. For example, in applying to Aboriginal title claims the common law rule that a person in occupation of land has a title derived from the occupation, the Supreme Court in *Delgamuukw v British Columbia*[43] simply acknowledged the relevance to these claims of a long-standing common law rule that predated European colonization of North America.[44] Similarly, when the Supreme Court in *Guerin v The Queen*[45] decided that the Crown owes fiduciary duties to First Nations in relation to reserve lands held by the Crown for their benefit, the judges were adapting and applying principles of equity that for centuries had governed the dealings of trustees with land held in trust for beneficiaries.[46] In these cases, the Supreme Court was doing exactly what Lord Donaldson in *Parker* said judges have both the right and duty to do, namely "to extend and adapt the common law [equity in *Guerin*] in the light of established principles and the current needs of the community." In the context of Indigenous rights, "current needs" identified by the Supreme Court include the present-day need to reconcile the prior presence of Indigenous peoples in North America with the assertion of sovereignty

42 See, e.g., *Tsilhqot'in Nation v British Columbia*, [2008] 1 CNLR 112 (BCSC); *Keewatin v Minister of Natural Resources*, [2012] 1 CNLR 13 (Ont Sup Ct J). These cases were subsequently appealed to the Supreme Court of Canada: *Tsilhqot'in Nation v British Columbia*, [2014] 2 SCR 257; *Grassy Narrows First Nation v Ontario (Natural Resources)*, [2014] 2 SCR 447.

43 [1997] 3 SCR 1010 at paras 114, 149 (Chief Justice Lamer) [*Delgamuukw*].

44 On the common law origins of this rule, see Kent McNeil, *Common Law Aboriginal Title* (Oxford: Clarendon Press, 1989) at 6–78.

45 [1984] 2 SCR 335 [*Guerin*].

46 In my view, Justice Dickson, delivering the principal judgment in *Guerin*, consistently followed the description of the adjudicative function that he had provided in *Harrison*, *supra* note 28.

by the Crown.[47] The Court has also taken account of the need to adapt existing law to the unique circumstances of the Indigenous peoples. In *Guerin*, Justice Dickson (as he then was) held that the Crown's obligation to First Nations is trust-like, but the relationship is not a true trust. This permitted him to apply fiduciary principles from trust law to the Crown–First Nation relationship, while at the same time acknowledging that "the fiduciary obligation which is owed to the Indians by the Crown is *sui generis*," given "the unique character both of the Indians' interest in land and of their historical relationship with the Crown."[48]

I think McHugh would contend that *Guerin*, for example, changed the law by replacing the discretionary, non-justiciable authority that government officials in the past had exercised over First Nation lands with legally enforceable obligations because, in his view, the dealings of representatives of the Crown with Indigenous peoples prior to what he calls "the breakthrough cases" of the 1970s through the 1990s were political rather than legal.[49] In reality, however, the case is an illustration of one reason why the Crown had not been held legally accountable for wrongful dealings with First Nation lands in the past. In the 1950s, officials of the Department of Indian Affairs negotiated a long-term lease of Musqueam reserve lands to a golf club. The Musqueam were induced to surrender the lands to the Crown for this purpose, but were misled by those government officials over the terms of the lease and were unable to obtain a copy of it from Indian Affairs until 1970, after which they commenced their legal action against the Crown.[50] The Supreme Court decided that the Crown owes fiduciary obligations to First Nations in the context of surrenders of reserve lands, and that the Indian Affairs officials had breached these obligations almost thirty years earlier by not providing the Musqueam with accurate information and by proceeding with a lease that was not in their best interests.

In the *Guerin* decision, the Supreme Court did not purport to create "new law" in 1984 and apply it retroactively to actions of the Crown

---

47 See *R v Van der Peet*, [1996] 2 SCR 507; *Delgamuukw*, *supra* note 43; *Haida Nation v British Columbia*, [2004] 3 SCR 511.

48 *Guerin*, *supra* note 45 at 387.

49 McHugh, *Aboriginal Title*, *supra* note 8 at 20–4, 27–31, 107, and quotation accompanying *infra* note 67.

50 For an illuminating account of the history leading up to the legal proceedings and detailed analysis of the judgments, see James I. Reynolds, *A Breach of Duty: Fiduciary Obligations and Aboriginal Peoples* (Saskatoon: Purich Publishing, 2005) at 25–125.

in the 1950s. Instead, the Court ruled that the relevant fiduciary principles already existed in the 1950s and then applied them to surrenders of reserve lands. So it was not an absence of law that prevented the Musqueam from suing the Crown earlier, but rather a lack of access to justice caused in large part by the wrongful actions of government officials acting on behalf of the Crown, actions which also led the Court to hold that the legal proceedings were not barred by limitation periods. Moreover, the fact that the government officials seem to have *thought* they had discretion that was unfettered by law, as the Crown argued in *Guerin*,[51] was irrelevant, as it must be in a constitutional monarchy governed by the rule of law where it is up to the courts – not the executive branch of government – to determine what the law is.[52]

2. Legal Historians as Expert Witnesses

As mentioned above, McHugh has not limited his expression of opinion on the absence of earlier law in relation to Aboriginal title and on Crown discretion to his academic publications; he has been saying the same thing even more forcefully as an expert witness for the Crown in Canadian cases. The tenor of his testimony in *Chippewas of Sarnia Band v Canada (Attorney General)*,[53] for example, was summarized by the Ontario Court of Appeal:

> [...] one Crown expert, Dr. Paul Gerald McHugh, posits that the government of the day did not regard the Royal Proclamation [of 1763] as being operative even before the passage of the *Quebec Act* [1774]. According to his evidence, it would appear that instructions as to the treatment of Indians, including the formalities for the surrender of Indian lands, were treated as an ongoing exercise of the royal prerogative. He further asserted that while the spirit of the Royal Proclamation was respected in that all surrender procedures were to be of a public nature, the specific procedure

51 *Guerin*, *supra* note 45 at 384.

52 See *Entick v Carrington* (1765), 19 St Tr 1029 (CP); *Roncarelli v Duplessis*, [1959] SCR 121. The classic work on the rule of law is Dicey, *supra* note 15, first published in 1885 during the period when McHugh contends that there was no "law" governing Crown–Indigenous relations in North America.

53 [1999] 40 RPR (3d) 49 (Ont Sup Ct J).

in each case was a matter to be determined on a case-by-case basis by the Governor in Council.[54]

In that case, the Court of Appeal declined to express an opinion on the legal status of the Royal Proclamation,[55] while observing that "[t]here can be little doubt that from the Aboriginal perspective, the Royal Proclamation was perceived as an authoritative and enduring statement of the principles governing their relationship with the Crown."[56]

More recently, McHugh was an expert witness in *Ross River Dena Council v Canada (Attorney General)*,[57] decided by the Yukon Supreme Court in 2012 but overturned by the Yukon Court of Appeal in May 2013.[58] The case involves the legal status and application of the following undertaking by the Parliament of Canada in relation to the transfer of Rupert's Land and the North-Western Territory to Canada in 1870:

---

54 [2001] 1 CNLR 56 at para 200 [*Chippewas of Sarnia*], leave to appeal to SCC refused, [2001] SCCA No 63. See also McHugh, "Politics of Historiography," *supra* note 9, commenting on this case. Compare Brian Slattery, *The Land Rights of Indigenous Canadian Peoples* (Saskatoon: University of Saskatchewan Native Law Centre, 1979); Walters, *supra* note 27 at 826, 831.

55 The Court nonetheless held, on the authority of its own decision in *Ontario (Attorney General) v Bear Island Foundation*, [1989] 2 CNLR 73, aff'd on other grounds [1991] 2 SCR 570, that "the surrender provisions of the Royal Proclamation were revoked by the *Quebec Act*, 1774, RSC 1985, App. II, No. 2": *Chippewas of Sarnia*, *supra* note 54 at paras 19, 206–19. With all due respect, this is doubtful: see Kent McNeil, "The High Cost of Accepting Benefits from the Crown: A Comment on the Temagami Indian Land Case," [1992] 1 CNLR 40, reprinted in McNeil, *Emerging Justice? Essays on Indigenous Rights in Canada and Australia* (Saskatoon: University of Saskatchewan Native Law Centre, 2001) 25 at 42–4 [McNeil, *Emerging Justice?*].

56 *Chippewas of Sarnia*, *supra* note 54 at para 201. See also Alain Beaulieu, "'An Equitable Right to Be Compensated': The Dispossession of the Aboriginal Peoples of Quebec and the Emergence of a New Legal Rationale (1760–1860)" (2013) 94 *Canadian Historical Review* 1.

57 [2012] 2 CNLR 276 [*Ross River* YSC].

58 [2013] 4 CNLR 355 [*Ross River* YCA]. The Court of Appeal decided that the trial judge should not have severed the issue of the justiciability of Canada's undertakings in the context of the *Rupert's Land and North-Western Territory Order*, 23 June 1870, in RSC 1985, App II, No 9 [*Rupert's Land Order*], from the other issues in the case, and so sent the matter back to be tried as a whole. The case has been retried, but judgment was suspended until after the trial of a related case: *Ross River Dena Council v Canada (Attorney General)*, 2015 YKSC 33.

> And furthermore, that, upon the transference of the territories in question to the Canadian Government, the claims of the Indian tribes to compensation for lands required for purposes of settlement will be considered and settled in conformity with the equitable principles which have uniformly governed the British Crown in its dealings with the aborigines.[59]

This undertaking (hereinafter the "equitable principles undertaking") was one of the terms and conditions under which the Queen transferred these territories to the newly created Dominion of Canada by the *Rupert's Land and North-Western Territory Order* of 1870, which due to section 146 of the *Constitution Act, 1867*,[60] has the force and effect of an imperial statute and forms part of the constitution of Canada.[61] Justice Gower stated the following threshold question to be addressed in this context: "Were the terms and conditions referred to in the *Rupert's Land and North-Western Territory Order* of June 23, 1870 concerning 'the claims of the Indian tribes to compensation for lands required for purposes of settlement' intended to have legal force and effect and give rise to obligations capable of being enforced by this Court?"[62] It was in regard to this question, and in particular on the legislative intention and executive understanding at the time regarding the legal enforceability of this undertaking, that McHugh acted as an expert witness.[63]

During cross-examination, McHugh was asked whether he agreed with the Ontario Court of Appeal in *Chippewas of Sarnia* that the Royal Proclamation of 1763 "has been consistently cited in the case law from the earliest times as the defining source of the principles governing the Crown in its dealing with the Aboriginal people of Canada."[64] He responded,

---

59 Address to Her Majesty the Queen from the Senate and House of Commons of the Dominion of Canada, 16 and 17 December 1867, Schedule A to the *Rupert's Land Order*, *supra* note 58 at 8.

60 (UK), 30 & 31 Vict, c 3, reprinted in RSC 1985, Appendix II, No 5.

61 See Schedule to the *Constitution Act, 1982*, listing the documents acknowledged by s 52(2)(b) to be part of the Constitution of Canada.

62 *Ross River* YSC, *supra* note 57 at para 6.

63 "Dr. McHugh was asked by Canada to provide an expert opinion on the historical context of the 1870 Order to assist this Court in determining the intention of Parliament in including terms about Aboriginal peoples. He was also asked to address the legal understanding of the Crown's role at the time of the 1870 Order and to provide an account of how the Order would have been understood as a legal instrument at that time." *Ibid* at para 81.

64 *Ibid* at para 44, citing *Chippewas of Sarnia*, *supra* note 54 at para 201.

> [...] the word is principles. [...] Principles are not rules. Principles – you see, we're getting into an argument here about – I'm resisting the suggestion that you're making it historically. There was a perception that they were externally enforceable standards that could be brought to bear against the Crown for the conduct of its relations with First Nations. That is a suggestion you are making, it seems to me, and that I'm resisting, in the period that we're looking at, because *historically there was no perception that there were externally enforceable standards that could be brought to bear against the Crown.*[65]

In his judgment at trial, Justice Gower observed that "the evidence of Dr. McHugh on this point, which I discuss below and find to be credible, casts doubt on the current justiciability of the Royal Proclamation, notwithstanding its inclusion in the Constitution of Canada, at s.25."[66]

In his expert report, McHugh addressed the issue of the justiciability of Aboriginal title claims generally prior to the decisions of the Supreme Court of Canada in the late twentieth century:

> In the late-nineteenth century (and for most of the twentieth), the Crown's relations with tribes in respect of their land "rights" were conceived as a matter of non-justiciable executive grace in the sense that the "trust" and "guardianship" duties avowed by the Crown, including the practice of obtaining formal cessions of their land, were regarded as having a high moral character not enforceable directly through court process. It was not until the courts developed the common law doctrine of Aboriginal title from the 1970s onwards that those collective land rights and associated Crown obligations became justiciable [...]
>
> The Crown recognized the land rights of tribes and negotiated for their cession but these practices were undertaken as a matter of executive

65 *Ibid* at para 45 (my emphasis).

66 *Ibid* at para 47. The reference is to s 25 of the *Constitution Act, 1982*, being Schedule B to the *Canada Act 1982*, (UK) 1982, c11. Compare *R v Marshall; R v Bernard*, [2005] 2 SCR 220 (not cited in *Ross River* YSC, *supra* note 57) at para 86, where Chief Justice McLachlin stated that "the Royal Proclamation must be interpreted in light of its status as the 'Magna Carta' of Indian rights in North America and Indian 'Bill of Rights': *R v Secretary of State for Foreign and Commonwealth Affairs*, [1982] 1 Q.B. 892 (C.A.), at p. 912." How, one might ask, can the Royal Proclamation be the Magna Carta of Indian "rights" if its provisions are not legal? See also *Campbell v Hall* (1774), Lofft 655, 1 Cowp 204 (KB), on the constitutional impact of other provisions in the Proclamation.

> grace rather than from any legal imperative compelling this treaty-making. These relations engaged Crown beneficence and guardianship but they were never regarded as justiciable or enforceable by legal process – a possibility that the state of legal art could not admit (until the late-twentieth century).[67]

McHugh apparently thinks that, because, in his view, Crown officials from the time of the Royal Proclamation of 1763 to long after the issuance of the *Rupert's Land Order* did not regard Aboriginal title claims as justiciable,[68] the Parliament of Canada, in formulating its address in

67 Paul McHugh, Expert Report, 21 September 2011, paras 9–10, as quoted in *Ross River* YSC, *supra* note 57 at paras 84–5 [McHugh's Report]. See also para 20 of McHugh's Report. Compare *Connolly v Woolrich* (1867), 17 RJRQ 75 at 87 (Que SC), aff'd sub nom *Johnstone v Connolly* (1869), 17 RJRQ 266 (Que CA), where Justice Monk stated that, after French and British assertions of sovereignty in the interior of North America, "the Indian political and *territorial right*, laws, and usages remained in full force" (emphasis mine): see discussion in Royal Commission on Aboriginal Peoples, *Partners in Confederation: Aboriginal Peoples, Self-Government, and the Constitution* (Ottawa: Minister of Supply and Services Canada, 1993) at 5–8. See also a speech given by the Earl of Dufferin, Governor General of Canada, at Government House, Victoria, British Columbia, 20 September 1876: "[T]here has been an initial error ever since Sir James Douglass [sic] quitted office [in 1864], in the Government of British Columbia neglecting to recognize what is known as the Indian title. In Canada this has always been done: no Government, whether provincial or central, has failed to acknowledge that the original title to the land existed in the Indian tribes and communities that hunted or wandered over them. Before we touch an acre we make a treaty with the chiefs representing the bands we are dealing with, and having agreed upon and paid the stipulated price, oftentimes arrived at after a great deal of haggling and difficulty, we enter into possession, but not until then do we consider that we are entitled to deal with a single acre." Henry Milton, ed., *Speeches and Addresses of the Right Honourable Frederick Temple Hamilton, Earl of Dufferin* (London: John Murray, 1882) at 209 [Earl of Dufferin's Speech].

68 Contrast Earl of Dufferin's Speech, *ibid* at 210: "I consider that our Indian fellow-subjects are entitled to exactly the same civil rights under the law as are possessed by the white population, and that if an Indian can prove a prescriptive right of way to a fishing station, or a right of any other kind, that that right should no more be ignored than if it were the case of a white man." McHugh might contend that this statement applies only to the private rights of *individual* Indians, not to *communal* Indian land rights (see McHugh, *Aboriginal Societies*, *supra* note 27 at 155, where this kind of distinction is made), but in fact the context makes clear that the Governor General had the communal rights of the Indigenous peoples of British Columbia in mind. See the passage from the previous page of his speech quoted in *supra* note 67.

1867 and the Queen in approving the terms and conditions contained therein in 1870, cannot have intended the equitable principles undertaking to have legal force.[69]

One can dispute McHugh's opinion on the views of Crown officials at the time on this issue of the legal status of Indigenous land rights and the equitable principles undertaking.[70] But even if one agrees with

---

69 At one level, McHugh is right when he asserts that Crown undertakings in the Royal Proclamation and the *Rupert's Land Order* were not justiciable in the sense that they were not enforceable in the Crown's courts. This is because, prior to the enactment of Crown liability statutes in the United Kingdom and Canada from the middle of the 20th century, no one's rights were enforceable in court against the Crown without the Crown's consent (see *supra* note 39). However, from his academic writing and expert testimony, McHugh's position seems to be that Aboriginal land rights and Crown promises in regard thereto were non-justiciable, not just because there were jurisdictional barriers preventing their enforcement in court, but because *they were not legal* (I think this is apparent from his reliance on the royal prerogative and his use of terms such as "executive grace": see text accompanying *supra* notes 54 and 67). I am grateful to Hamar Foster for reminding me of the important point that rights can be legal without being justiciable. For example, some statutes of limitation bar an owner of personal property from going to court to recover for wrongful taking (e.g., conversion) after the limitation period has passed, but do not extinguish the owner's legal title: see *Miller v Dell*, [1891] 1 QB 468 (CA); *Barberree v Bilo* (1991), 84 Alta LR (2d) 216 (QB); Eileen E. Gillese, *Property Law: Cases, Text and Materials*, 2nd ed. (Toronto: Emond Montgomery, 1990) at 3:38–3:39. More generally, see Lorne Sossin, *Boundaries of Judicial Review: The Law of Justiciability in Canada*, 2nd ed. (Toronto: Carswell, 2012).

70 See e.g., Frank J. Tough, "Aboriginal Rights Versus the Deed of Surrender: The Legal Rights of Native Peoples and Canada's Acquisition of the Hudson's Bay Company Territory" (1992) 17:2 *Prairie Forum* 225. See also a Report of the Minister and Deputy Minister of Justice for Canada to the Governor General, dated 19 January 1875, in which the authors expressed their "duty to assert such a legal or equitable claim as may be found to exist on the part of the Indians" in British Columbia where, apart from the Vancouver Island treaties entered into in the 1850s, land cessions had not been obtained. On their recommendation, Canada disallowed a provincial statute, *An Act to Amend and Consolidate the Laws Affecting Crown Lands in British Columbia*, because it did not respect Indian rights. See *Ross River* YSC, *supra* note 57 at paras 53–8, where the report is quoted and discussed. In cross-examination on this report, McHugh is recorded in the judgment as opining that, "notwithstanding the language used by the two law officers, there was no pattern of matters of Aboriginal title being enforced in courts at that time and that this particular Report was 'not indicative of a general understanding' in that regard": *ibid* at para 57. But how could a "pattern of matters of Aboriginal title being enforced in courts" emerge when Indigenous peoples had no knowledge of such a possibility and no capacity to commence legal action? Even in the first

him on this issue, which I do not,[71] the question remains: why are the views of Crown officials even relevant to this issue of legal status? To answer this, we have to know whose opinions are being considered. While this is not clear from the extensive references to McHugh's testimony by Justice Gower in his judgment in the *Ross River* case, McHugh's Report reveals that he relies largely on a dispatch in relation to the Rupert's Land transfer dated 10 April 1869, from the Colonial Secretary, Earl Granville, to Sir John Young, the Governor General of Canada, in which Granville referred to the "uncertain rights" of the Indian tribes and the "obligations" of Canada to protect them in face of "the advance of civilized man."[72] Beyond this "evidence" of the perception of Crown officials in his report,[73] in McHugh's oral testimony as explicitly relied upon by Justice Gower one finds only vague statements,

---

important case involving Aboriginal title in Canada, *St Catherine's Milling*, *supra* note 33, in the 1880s, there were no Indigenous parties or witnesses. Nonetheless, despite McHugh's opinion to the contrary (see *Ross River* YSC at paras 120–6), the *St Catherine's Milling* case confirms the legal uncertainty over Indian land rights expressed by the law officers of the Crown in their 1875 report. In that case, Canada argued that, "inasmuch as the proclamation [of 1763] recites that the territories thereby reserved for Indians had never 'been ceded to or purchased by' the Crown, the entire property of the land remained with them" (*St Catherine's Milling*, *supra* note 33 at 54). Although the Privy Council rejected that argument while declining to express an opinion on the exact nature of Indian title, the fact Canada would make such an argument reveals that there was sufficient doubt in the 1880s over the legal nature of Aboriginal land rights for Crown counsel to think the argument was worth making and might be accepted. Indeed, Lord Watson observed that "[t]here was a great deal of learned discussion at the Bar with respect to the precise quality of the Indian right" (at 55), confirming that the Indians did have a right to the land but revealing disagreement over the nature thereof.

71 See Kent McNeil, *Native Claims in Rupert's Land and the North-Western Territory: Canada's Constitutional Obligations* (Saskatoon: University of Saskatchewan Native Law Centre, 1982) [McNeil, *Canada's Constitutional Obligations*], and "Fiduciary Obligations and Federal Responsibility for the Aboriginal Peoples" in McNeil, *Emerging Justice? supra* note 55, 309 at 326–40 [McNeil, "Fiduciary Obligations"].

72 McHugh's Report, *supra* note 67 at paras 22–5. Glanville's dispatch can be found in Canada, *Sessional Papers*, vol. 2:5, No 25 of 1869 (32 Vict) at 37–8.

73 Compare my perspective on this dispatch in McNeil, "Fiduciary Obligations," *supra* note 71 at 329–30: "Earl Granville thus foresaw the dangers to the Indian tribes inherent in the transfer of the two territories to Canada, and impressed on the Governor General that Canada would have an obligation to protect them against these dangers." I then present reasons why this obligation is not just legal – it is constitutional. See also McNeil, *Canada's Constitutional Obligations*, *supra* note 71.

such as "historically there was no perception that there were externally enforceable standards that could be brought to bear against the Crown" and "the Crown's relations with tribes in respect of their land 'rights' were conceived as a matter of non-justiciable executive grace."[74]

These statements raise the questions of whose "perception" is being referred to and who, besides Earl Granville as questionably interpreted by McHugh, "conceived" of the matter in this way. McHugh evidently does not have Indigenous people in mind, despite the fact that they seem to have generally regarded promises made to them by the Crown as binding.[75] Nor does he seem to have judges in mind, as he points out that the issue of the justiciability of Indigenous land rights was not judicially determined in Canada until the latter part of the twentieth century,[76] in decisions that reveal that the perception upon which he relies

74 *Ross River* YSC, *supra* note 57 at paras 45, 85: see text accompanying *supra* notes 65 and 67 for quotations containing these phrases. In his report, McHugh does provide a couple of specific examples of opinions expressed by executive officers in the 1830s that relations with the Indian tribes in British North America were a matter of royal prerogative. See McHugh's Report, *supra* note 67 at paras 37, 51.

75 See the statement by the Ontario Court of Appeal in *Chippewas of Sarnia*, *supra* note 54, quoted in text accompanying that note. Regarding Crown promises in treaties, see Treaty 7 Elders and Tribal Council, *The True Spirit and Original Intent of Treaty 7* (Montreal: McGill-Queen's University Press, 1996); John Borrows, "Wampum at Niagara: The Royal Proclamation, Canadian Legal History and Self-Government" in Michael Asch, ed., *Aboriginal and Treaty Rights in Canada: Essays on Law, Equality and Respect for Difference* (Vancouver: UBC Press, 1997) at 155; Harold Cardinal and Walter Hildebrandt, *Treaty Elders of Saskatchewan: Our Dream Is That Our Peoples Will One Day Be Clearly Recognized as Nations* (Calgary: University of Calgary Press, 2000); James (Sa'ke'j) Youngblood Henderson, *Treaty Rights in the Constitution of Canada* (Toronto: Carswell, 2007); Michael Asch, *On Being Here to Stay: Treaties and Aboriginal Rights in Canada* (Toronto: University of Toronto Press, 2014) especially at 73–99.

76 See quotation from McHugh's Report accompanying *supra* note 67. See also *Ross River* YSC, *supra* note 57 at para 57, quoted in *supra* note 70. In his report at paras 48–9, McHugh does give one example of a decision by Chief Justice Robinson of the Upper Canada Queen's Bench in *Doe d Sheldon v Ramsey* (1852), 9 UCQB 105, holding that the Haldimand Grant to the Six Nations in 1784 did not create a legal right to the granted land, but that decision involved the court's assessment of Governor Haldimand's authority and intention in making the grant, not a judicial determination of Aboriginal rights (see Walters, *supra* note 27 at 831n40). Surprisingly, in his report, McHugh does not mention *Connolly v Woolrich*, a well-known and directly relevant case decided just *five months before* the Parliament of Canada included the equitable principles undertaking in its Address to the Queen, where Justice Monk expressed the view that the "territorial right" of the Indian tribes in Rupert's Land

was legally erroneous.[77] Nor does McHugh point to legislation as the source of this perception, as he apparently uses the alleged perception to determine the intention of the Imperial and Canadian Parliaments between 1867 and 1870, rather than the other way around. In other words, he concludes that it cannot have been the intention of these Parliaments for the equitable principles undertaking to be legally enforceable because the perception at the time was that the land rights of the Indigenous peoples were "a matter of non-justiciable executive grace."[78] So the perception McHugh alleges to be present in the historical record is the perception, not of the judicial or legislative branches of the imperial and Canadian governments, but mainly of Earl Granville and other members of the executive branch, as clairvoyantly revealed by McHugh.[79]

---

remained in full force after Crown assertion of sovereignty (*supra* note 67 at 87). Justice Monk also held that Indigenous laws, including laws relating to marriage, remained in full force in Rupert's Land in 1803 (133 years after the Hudson's Bay Company Charter) and were a source of rights enforceable in Canadian courts.

77 See *Calder*, *supra* note 34; *Guerin*, *supra* note 45; *Delgamuukw*, *supra* note 43.

78 McHugh's Report, *supra* note 67 at paras 9–10, as quoted in *Ross River* YSC, *supra* note 57 at paras 85. See text accompanying *supra* note 67.

79 Even if McHugh is right (which is highly questionable: see *supra* notes 68–71) that there was a consensus among Crown officials in the nineteenth century that Indigenous peoples in Canada had no legal land rights, one needs to keep in mind the cautionary words of Justice Hall, dissenting on other grounds, in *Calder*, *supra* note 34 at 346: "The assessment and interpretation of the historical documents and enactments tendered in evidence must be approached in the light of present-day research and knowledge disregarding ancient concepts formulated when understanding of the customs and culture of our original people was rudimentary and incomplete and when they were thought to be wholly without cohesion, laws or culture, in effect a subhuman species." In other words, to the extent that past perceptions of Indigenous peoples' rights were based on erroneous factual assumptions, they can have no validity. For a stark example, consider Chancellor Boyd's trial decision in the *St Catharines* case, where he described Indigenous people not living on reserves variously as "wild," "primitive," "untaught," "uncivilized," "rude," and "degraded," apparently without evidence being presented in court to substantiate this assessment: *R v St Catharines* [spelled *Catherine's* in the Privy Council decision, *supra* note 33] *Milling and Lumbering Company* (1885), 10 OR 196 at 211, 227–8. After admitting that "little is known of the people in this remote region" (the area of Treaty 3, entered into in 1873), he nonetheless concluded that most of them were "a more than usually degraded Indian type" (*ibid* at 227). For discussion connecting his judgment with discredited nineteenth century theories of the evolution of human societies from "barbarism to civilization" (Boyd C's words, *ibid* at 228), see Kent McNeil, "Social Darwinism and Judicial Conceptions of Indian Title in Canada in the 1880s" (1999) 38:1 *Journal of the West* 68.

This takes us back to the rule of law: from the constitutional crisis in England in the 17th century, Parliament and the common law courts emerged supreme over the executive. As Chief Justice Coke had decided in 1610 in the *Proclamations Case*,[80] the Crown, acting executively (i.e., without the authorization of Parliament), does not have the constitutional authority to change or make law.[81] Consequently, the rights of British subjects, including their land rights, are protected by the common law against executive action, or, to put it another way, against the prerogative of the Crown.[82] And yet, McHugh seems to think that Crown dealing with the communally held lands of the Indigenous peoples was a matter of royal prerogative, not governed by law.[83] He bases this conclusion, not on a denial that Indigenous people were British subjects[84] and therefore not protected by the common law at the relevant time (1867–70 in the context of the *Rupert's Land Order*), but rather on the perception that they had no legal rights to these lands.[85] This, on McHugh's own admission, was not the result of judicial determination or legislative enactment; rather, he opines that it was the view of the executive, whose officers did not conceive that the Indians could have legal rights.[86] But since when does the perception of the executive in relation to legal rights determine the law? While this may have been the attitude of the seventeenth century Stuart kings of England, it was also a major reason why one was beheaded in 1649 and another deposed in

---

80 12 Co R 74 (KB).

81 See also Herbert Broom, *Constitutional Law Viewed in Relation to Common Law*, 2nd ed. by George L. Denman (London: W. Maxwell & Son, 1885) at 245, 386–8. On the development of the rule of law as a constitutional principle, see William Huse Dunham, "Regal Power and the Rule of Law: A Tudor Paradox" (1964) 3:2 *Journal of British Studies* 24.

82 See *Field v Boethsby* (1657), 1 Sid 137 at 139 (KB): "The prerogative of the King will not destroy or prejudice the property of the subject." See also *Nichols v Nichols* (1677), 2 Plow 477 at 487 (CP); *Attorney-General v De Keyser's Royal Hotel*, [1920] AC 508 at 569 (HL); *Eshugbayi Eleko v Government of Nigeria*, [1931] AC 662 at 670 (PC).

83 *Ross River* YSC, *supra* note 57 at paras 57, 150; McHugh, "Politics of Historiography," *supra* note 9 especially at 189–95.

84 McHugh, *ibid* at 189, 193. For confirmation that Indigenous people living within the Dominions of the Crown were regarded as British subjects at the time, see Earl of Dufferin's Speech, *supra* note 67 at 210, quoted in *supra* note 68.

85 See also McHugh, *Aboriginal Societies*, *supra* note 27 especially at 155–6.

86 See McHugh, "Politics of Historiography," *supra* note 9.

1688: their views of kingship and prerogative power were out of touch with the constitutional monarchy that England had become.[87]

So whatever the views of executive officers of the Crown on the land rights of Indigenous peoples in British North America, those views, to the extent they can be ascertained from the historical record, are matters of fact, not law. However, McHugh did extrapolate from those views and arrive at legal conclusions in relation to two issues in particular. First, as we have seen he testified that there was no intention at the time of the Rupert's Land transfer that the equitable principles undertaking would be legally enforceable.[88] Justice Gower accepted this opinion, stating that on "the intention of the Canadian Parliament when the 1867 Address was drafted and the intention of the Imperial Parliament when the 1870 Order was enacted,"[89] he "generally accepted Dr. McHugh's expert opinion evidence that the relevant provision [the equitable principles undertaking] was not intended to have justiciable legal force and effect."[90] Second, McHugh stated repeatedly that there was no law in relation to Indigenous land rights in what is now Canada during the

87 See Theodore F.T. Plucknett, *Taswell-Langmead's English Constitutional History* (1875), 11th ed. (Boston: Houghton Mifflin Company, 1960) at 328–460. As discussed in Dicey, *supra* note 15, parliamentary sovereignty and the rule of law prevailed over prerogative power. See also Blackstone, *supra* note 30, vol. 1 at 136–7, 226–32; Chitty, *supra* note 30 at 7–9. Compare McHugh's Report, *supra* note 67 at para 54, stating that, at the time of the Rupert's Land transfer in 1870, "the idea of a constitution as a substantive normative constraint upon governmental authority had not taken hold." Nor can it be argued that the constitutional protections of the rights of British subjects did not apply in the colonies, for in settled colonies, and conquered and ceded colonies where the common law had been introduced or a legislative assembly had been promised or created (see *Campbell v Hall*, *supra* note 66), the royal prerogative was subject to the same constitutional constraints as in England. See Chitty, *supra* note 30 at 25–39, stating at 32–3 that, if the charter granted to the subjects of a colony "be silent on the subject it cannot be doubted, but that the King's prerogatives in the colony are precisely those prerogatives which he may exercise in the mother country ... Where the colonial charters afford no criterion, the common law of England, with respect to the royal prerogative, is the common law of the plantations."

88 See *Ross River* YSC, *supra* note 57 at paras 94–106.

89 *Ibid* at para 136. Note, however, that the *Rupert's Land Order* was issued by the Queen, not enacted by Parliament, though the order had effect as if it "had been enacted by the Parliament of the United Kingdom" (*Constitution Act, 1867*, *supra* note 60, s 146).

90 *Ross River* YSC, *supra* note 57 at para 139.

period under consideration.[91] On both these issues, one needs to ask whether his testimony went beyond the permissible scope of expert testimony, as legislative intention and the existence of domestic law are legal, not factual, matters.[92] If McHugh's testimony as a legal historian related only to a matter of domestic law as it existed in the past, arguably it would come within Maitland's "logic of evidence" as historical "fact." If the law in the past, however, *is the law that the court is being asked to apply in the present* to the case before it, then testimony on that law could cross over into Maitland's "logic of authority," taking it outside the scope of expert testimony. If, for example, the question before the court involves the interpretation of legislation that is still in force and that relates to the matter before the court, the legislative intent is a matter of domestic law that is up to the judge to determine, regardless of when the statute was enacted.[93]

---

91 *Ibid* at paras 45, 57, 84–6, 107, 129, 132–3. See also McHugh's Report, *supra* note 67, especially para 55.

92 On the duty of judges to ascertain legislative intent, see P. St. J. Langan, *Maxwell on the Interpretation of Statutes*, 12th ed. (London: Sweet and Maxwell, 1969) at 1; F.A.R. Bennion, *Bennion on Statutory Interpretation*, 5th ed. (London: LexisNexis, 2008) at 123; Pierre-André Côté, *The Interpretation of Legislation in Canada*, 4th ed. (Toronto: Carswell, 2011) at 5–6, 13–14, 315–24. On domestic law, see references in *supra* note 2.

93 In *Willick v Willick*, [1994] 3 SCR 670 at para 42, L'Heureux-Dubé J, in relation to interpretation of provisions of the *Divorce Act*, RSC 1985, c 3 (2nd Supp), stated: "The task of statutory interpretation requires that courts discover the intention of Parliament"; see also per Justice Sopinka at paras 1–2. Legislative intent is ascertained from the context, purpose, and text of a statute (including the grammatical and ordinary sense of the language used), and from the application of rules of statutory interpretation, not from trying to determine the factual, subjective intent of the members of the legislature. See Randal N. Graham, *Statutory Interpretation: Theory and Practice* (Toronto: Emond Montgomery Publications, 2001) at 18–20; Ruth Sullivan, *Statutory Interpretation*, 2nd ed. (Toronto: Irwin Law, 2007) at 32–3, 37–42; *Rizzo & Rizzo Shoes Ltd (Re)*, [1998] 1 SCR 27; *Bell ExpressVu Limited Partnership v Rex*, [2002] 2 SCR 559. Judges can, however, take judicial notice of and receive expert testimony on facts pertaining to the context and purpose of a statute (known as "legislative facts"), but legislative *intent* is still a legal question. See Sullivan at especially 159–60; *R v Gladue*, [1999] 1 SCR 688; *Canada 3000 Inc (Re)*, [2006] 1 SCR 865 at paras 36–40. On judicial notice of legislative facts, see *R v Spence*, [2005] 3 SCR 458 at paras 57–68.

3. The Common Law Tradition

Of course McHugh is entitled to express an opinion as an academic (though probably not as an expert witness) on the existence of Canadian law in relation to Indigenous land rights – as we have seen, he has done this in his published work, denying that there was any such law prior to what he calls "the breakthrough cases" in the last forty-five years or so.[94] His conclusion that there were no legal rights follows from his opinion that there was no law. But how do we know there was no law? McHugh says this was the perception of the Crown's executive officers, but as we have seen, they do not have the constitutional authority to determine whether law and rights exist – they can only express opinions on the matter. Since McHugh must be aware of this fundamental limitation on executive authority arising from the constitutional separation of powers,[95] I think his conclusion that there was no law on the matter until recently necessarily rests on his cursory dismissal of the declaratory theory of law, as he seems to think there was no law in relation to Indigenous land rights until a court decision or competent legislature acknowledged those rights and gave them legal force. He regards those who hold a contrary view as "wedded (or blinkered, more likely) to the declaratory theory" of law.[96]

As discussed above, one does not have to adhere to a Platonic conception of the declaratory theory to realize that non-statutory law can exist before judges articulate it in particular cases.[97] Nor does one need to resort to natural law theories or Dworkinian conceptions of fundamental rights, though these are relevant and can influence judicial

94 See McHugh, *Aboriginal Title, supra* note 8 at 29–31, 111 (quotation accompanying *supra* note 30). Note that this denial applies to the law of the Canadian state; McHugh is not denying that Indigenous peoples have land rights under their own laws.

95 See McHugh, "Politics of Historiography," *supra* note 9 at 173.

96 McHugh, *Aboriginal Title, supra* note 8 at 283, quoted in text accompanying *supra* note 22; see also *ibid* at 282, 310, and McHugh, *Aboriginal Societies, supra* note 27 at 18, where he says that this "notion of immanence according to which all law is already and previously 'made'" stems from a "whiggish or presentist technique."

97 One can also point to local custom that must have been in existence long before declared by judges to be legally enforceable, presumably from the time Richard I became king in 1189. See Allen, *supra* note 29 at 129–46, especially 130: "if a custom is proved in an English court by satisfactory evidence to exist and to be observed, the function of the court is merely to declare the custom operative law."

decision-making.[98] The common law itself is a rich body of principles and precedents that can be and are adapted and applied in new contexts virtually every time an appeal court makes a decision. Moreover, as the influential English legal historian Brian Simpson has pointed out, it is often impossible to identify the case in which a particular principle or rule was first articulated.[99] Rather, like the English language, the common law developed out of custom and usage, with authority to formulate the law on an ongoing basis assigned to the judiciary:

> Formulations of the common law are to be conceived of as similar to grammarians' rules, which both describe linguistic practices and attempt to systematize and order them; such rules serve as guides to proper practice since the proper practice is in part the normal practice; such formulations are inherently corrigible, for it is always possible that they may be improved upon, or require modification as what they describe changes.[100]

Though McHugh might deny it,[101] I think his argument that Indigenous land claims were not legal before the latter part of the twentieth century is an extreme positivist position that is contrary to the common

---

98 See e.g., John Finnis, *Natural Law and Natural Rights* (Oxford: Clarendon Press, 1980) [Finnis, *Natural Rights*]; John Finnis, ed, *Natural Law*, 2 vols. (Aldershot, UK: Dartmouth Publishing, 1991); Ronald Dworkin, *Law's Empire* (London: Fontana Press, 1986). As William Geldart observed, "In the absence of clear precedents which might govern a question, we find judges relying on such considerations as the opinions of legal writers, the practice of conveyancers, the law of other modern countries, the Roman law, principles of 'natural justice,' or public policy": W.M. Geldart, *Elements of English Law* (London: Williams and Norgate, 1911) at 23. To the same effect, see Neil Duxbury, *The Nature and Authority of Precedent* (Cambridge: Cambridge University Press, 2008) at 41.

99 Sir Matthew Hale made the same point three centuries earlier in *The History of the Common Law of England* (London: J. Nutt, 1713) at 59–60. See also Baker, *Law's Two Bodies, supra* note 26 at 1–31.

100 See A.W.B. Simpson, "The Common Law and Legal Theory" in A.W.B. Simpson, ed., *Oxford Essays in Jurisprudence*, 2nd series (Oxford: Clarendon Press, 1973) 75 at 96. See also Gerald J. Postema, *Bentham and the Common Law Tradition* (Oxford: Clarendon Press, 1986) at 9–11.

101 See McHugh, *Aboriginal Societies, supra* note 27 at 18–20, where he links whiggish thinking, the declaratory theory, and positivism, apparently disapproving of each of them.

law tradition.[102] For him, it seems that law does not exist until made by a legislature or court, that is, by command of the legislative or judicial arm of the sovereign state. Jeremy Bentham, whose forceful positivism has influenced generations of legal theorists in England from John Austin[103] to H.L.A. Hart[104] and beyond, was of like mind, leading him to question the very existence of the common law "as a system of general rules," since for him, there could be no law in relation to a particular matter until created by a judge or legislature.[105] Bentham concluded that the exercise of judicial power in England is arbitrary.[106] After asserting that judges "make the common law," he used an extreme analogy to describe the judicial process:

> Do you know how they make it? Just as a man makes laws for his dog. When your dog does anything you want to break him of, you wait till he does it, and then beat him for it. This is the way you make laws for your dog: and this is the way the judges make law for you and me.[107]

While Bentham's scepticism about the common law may seem excessive, he does have a point: if no law exists before a judge decides a case on a particular matter, the judge's decision is necessarily retroactive to the facts of the case that transpired previously,[108] and in that sense the decision can be regarded as arbitrary. One can view the declaratory theory of law as an answer to Bentham, though of course the theory

102 On the rejection of the declaratory theory by positivists, see Wesley-Smith, *supra* note 23 at 74–5.

103 See John Austin, *Lectures on Jurisprudence*, vol. 2 (1861; New York: Burt Franklin, 1970) at 216: "there can be no law without a legislative act" ("legislative act" taken here to include judicial decision; see Simpson, *supra* note 100 at 84), though Austin describes "judicial law" as "improper legislation" (*ibid* at 321–2).

104 H.L.A. Hart, *The Concept of Law* (Oxford: Clarendon Press, 1961).

105 Jeremy Bentham, *A Comment on the Commentaries: A Criticism of William Blackstone's Commentaries on the Laws of England*, ed. Charles Warren Everett (Oxford: Clarendon Press, 1928) at 125: "As a system of general rules, the common law is a thing merely imaginary." See Postema, *supra* note 100 at 286–301.

106 John Bowring, ed., *The Works of Jeremy Bentham*, vol. 4 (1838–43; New York: Russell & Russell, 1962) at 460.

107 *Ibid*, vol. 5 at 235.

108 See Postema, *supra* note 100 at 207–10, 275–8; Neil MacCormick, *Rhetoric and the Rule of Law: A Theory of Legal Reasoning* (Oxford: Oxford University Press, 2005) at 160–1, 262–6.

predates the writings of the famous positivist.[109] But if one discards the theory entirely, one does have to confront the problem of the retrospective nature of judicial law-making,[110] which Bentham did by proposing the codification of English law, as happened with French private law during his lifetime when the Napoleonic Civil Code was created, largely out of Roman law.

Short of replacing the common law with an English equivalent of the civil code, jurisdictions that adhere to the common law tradition are obliged to accept the reality that judicial decisions can have retroactive effect for the litigants in the case before the court.[111] This does not mean that judges, even in cases where they overrule previous decisions, are making new law out of whole cloth.[112] As Brian Simpson suggests, it is not a matter of choosing between the two extremes posed by John Austin, "either agreeing that the common law was laid down by judges, or believing in the childish fiction (as he [Austin] called it) that the common law was 'a miraculous something made by nobody, existing, I suppose, from eternity, and merely *declared* from time to time by the judges.'"[113] Judges have to make decisions based on law, and when the law in relation to the matter before them is in dispute (as it often is), they "must of course choose between incompatible views, selecting one or other as the law, and the fiction that the common law provides a unique solution is only a way of expressing this necessity."[114]

In a recent article, "The Declaratory Theory of Law," Allan Beever argues convincingly that the scorn heaped upon the theory by some critics stems from a misunderstanding, not only of the theory itself, but of the conception of law that prevailed in England before the advent of positivism and that is of continuing relevance today.[115] As an example

109 See Hale, *supra* note 99 at 68–70; Blackstone, *supra* note 30, vol. 1 at 68–71.

110 See Rupert Cross and J.W. Harris, *Precedent in English Law*, 4th ed. (Oxford: Clarendon Press, 1991) at 30–3; R.H.S. Tur, "Time and the Law" (2002) 22 *Oxford Journal of Legal Studies* 463.

111 See discussion of *Donoghue v Stevenson*, [1932] AC 562 (HL), in Cross and Harris, *supra* note 110 at 31–3.

112 See the quotation from *Parker*, *supra* note 24, accompanying *supra* note 25.

113 Simpson, *supra* note 100 at 84, quoting John Austin, *Lectures on Jurisprudence, or the Philosophy of Positive Law*, vol. 2, 4th ed. by R. Campbell (London: John Murray, 1879), at 634 (emphasis in original).

114 Simpson, *ibid* at 97.

115 Allan Beever, "The Declaratory Theory of Law" (2013) 33 *Oxford Journal of Legal Studies* 421 [Beever, "Declaratory Theory"].

of that earlier understanding, he refers to Lord Coke's judgment in *Calvin's Case*, where the chief justice, in answer to the defendant's objection that a judgment for the plaintiff would be a dangerous innovation in the law, stated,

> [T]his judgment was rather a renovation of the judgments and censures of the reverend Judges and Sages of the law in so many ages past, than any innovation, as it appeareth by the books and book cases before recited: neither have Judges power to judge according to that which they think fit, but that which out of the laws they know to be right and consonant to law.[116]

Beever contends that earlier judges and jurists, including Coke, Hale, and Blackstone, distinguished positive laws, consisting of rules laid down by statute or stemming from particular cases, from the reason of the law and fundamental principles (sometimes stated as legal maxims): the former are subject to change whereas the latter generally are not. Another way of putting this is that the letter of the law can change, whereas the spirit of the law, based as it is on reason and underlying values, is much more enduring.[117] Moreover, Beever argues that the modern common law adheres more closely to the pre-positivist conception of the declaratory theory than most commentators, and even some judges, are willing to admit.[118] To avoid accusations that judges violate the separation of powers and improperly legislate retroactively,[119] one needs to distinguish between judicial development of the positive law in conformity with underlying principles and legislative alteration of

---

116 *Calvin's Case* (1608), 7 Co R 1 at 27a. See also J.H. Baker, *An Introduction to English Legal History*, 4th ed. (London: Butterworths, 2002) at 195: "Common lawyers before the nineteenth century liked to think of their law as an unchanging body of common sense and reasoning which was part of the heritage of the English people."

117 This is not to say that the underlying values of a society do not change, as we have seen in the past fifty years in Canada, during which time equality, especially gender and racial equality, have become fundamental values of Canadian society and law.

118 Beever, "Declaratory Theory," *supra* note 115, analysing Lord Reid, "The Judge as Lawmaker" (1972–3) 12 *Journal of the Society of Public Teachers of Law* 22, and Lord Goff's judgment in *Kleinwort Benson Ltd v Lincoln City Council*, [1999] 2 AC 349 (HL). For another perspective on the *Kleinwort* decision, see MacCormick, *supra* note 108 at 262–6.

119 For an American perspective, see Fred V Cahill, Jr., *Judicial Legislation: A Study in American Legal History* (New York: Ronald Press Company, 1952).

it through the political process.[120] "In reality," Beever asserts, "change in the positive law is perfectly consistent with the declaratory theory as long as that change can be seen to accord with more abstract legal principles."[121] He concludes that these principles, forming as they do the basis of the common law, are as much a part of it – indeed, are more fundamental to it – than the evolving rules of positive law.[122] I think Beever would agree, if the word "permanent" were qualified or deleted,[123] with Sir Carleton Kemp Allen's observation that "underneath the whole elaborate structure of precedents in our courts lies a permanent foundation of fundamental legal doctrine."[124]

Beever's deeper understanding of the intimate connection between the declaratory theory and common law methodology can be contrasted with McHugh's dismissive attitude towards "the declaratory theory's

---

120 See Allen, *supra* note 29 at 307–10, distinguishing the law-making authority of judges from that of legislatures. At 309–10, Allen utilizes this analogy: "A man who chops a tree into logs has in a sense 'made' the logs [...]. Mankind, with all its resource and inventiveness, is limited in its creative power by the physical material vouchsafed to it. Similarly, the creative power of courts is limited by existing legal material at their command. They find the material and shape it. The legislature may manufacture entirely new material." See also Geldart, *supra* note 98 at 23–7; Dennis Lloyd, *The Idea of Law* (Harmondsworth: Penguin Books, 1964) at 256–73. Likewise, John Finnis, in "The Fairy Tale's Moral" (1999) 115 *Law Quarterly Review* 170, republished as "Adjudication and Legal Change" in his *Collected Essays*, vol. 4, *Philosophy of Law* (Oxford: Oxford University Press, 2011) at 400, points out that the declaratory theory is "a way of stating an important element in judicial duty," namely, "the duty of judges to differentiate their authority and responsibility, and thus their practical reasoning, from that of legislatures."

121 Beever, "Declaratory Theory," *supra* note 115 at 440.

122 See also Allan Beever, "Formalism in Music and Law" (2011) 61 *University of Toronto Law Journal* 213 at 228–9. Beever's point can be supported by many concrete examples. To take just one, a murderer cannot inherit from the victim by will or intestacy, nor benefit as survivor from a joint tenancy held with the victim. In these instances, the positive law rules of inheritance and survivorship are overridden by legal principle, expressed in the maxim, *nullus commodum capere potest de injuria sua propria* (no one can obtain an advantage by his own wrong). See *Lundy v Lundy* (1895), 24 SCR 650; *Nordstrom v Baumann*, [1962] SCR 147; *Schobelt v Barber*, [1967] 1 OR 349 (HC); *Singh Estate v Bajrangie-Singh* (1999), 29 ETR (2d) 302 (Ont SCJ).

123 See Beever, "Declaratory Theory," *supra* note 115 at 441, where he states that he "would not wish to defend precisely" the version of the theory that "these principles are unalterable."

124 Allen, *supra* note 29 at 293. With the same deletion, I would also agree with Allen.

belief that contemporary doctrine articulates eternal verities"[125] and his apparent conviction that legal principles are not law.[126] Like Austin, McHugh seems to regard all law as positive law that has no existence until brought into being by a court decision or legislative enactment. This positivist viewpoint stems from a legal theory that has strong critics, especially in its extreme Austinian form,[127] and, as Simpson and others have pointed out, is also at odds with the common law tradition.[128] Yet as an expert witness McHugh implicitly relies on this controversial legal theory and purports to present as "evidence" questionable opinions on the (non)existence of law – opinions that to some extent seem to involve the content of applicable domestic law, which is beyond the permissible scope of expert testimony.

As mentioned earlier, it is important to distinguish between a legal academic's role as a scholar and the role he or she may choose to play as an expert witness in litigation. The limitations on what is permissible in a courtroom do not apply in the academic realm. Indeed, a major aspect of a law professor's job is to describe, analyse, and critique the law. In so doing, however, one still has to keep in mind Maitland's caution against mixing the "logic of evidence" and the "logic of authority." In effect, McHugh tends to treat the existence of law in the past as a matter of historical fact that fits into the logic of evidence. However, while a legal historian can probe and seek to illuminate the existence and content of law in the past, in doing so, the logic of evidence necessarily mingles with the logic of authority. As John Finnis has pointed out,

125 McHugh, *Aboriginal Title*, *supra* note 8 at 283, quoted more fully in text accompanying *supra* note 22.

126 See quotation from his testimony in *Ross River* YSC, *supra* note 57 at para 45, accompanying *supra* note 65.

127 See, e.g., Lon L. Fuller, *The Morality of Law* (New Haven: Yale University Press, 1964); Patrick Devlin, *The Enforcement of Morals* (Oxford: Oxford University Press, 1965); Lloyd, *supra* note 120 at 95–115; Finnis, *Natural Rights*, *supra* note 98; Dworkin, *supra* note 98 and *Taking Rights Seriously* (Cambridge, MA: Harvard University Press, 1978); Foster, "One Good Thing," *supra* note 35 at 83–6. For a historical overview, see J.M. Kelly, *A Short History of Western Legal Theory* (Oxford: Clarendon Press, 1992) at ch 8–10.

128 See also Geldart, *supra* note 98 at 23–7; Allen, *supra* note 29, at especially 1–8; Hutchinson, *supra* note 13.

> Law has a double life. It is *in force* as a matter of fact; historians and contemporary observers can describe – and make predictions about – its content and effect by attending to the opinions and practices prevalent among certain persons and groups, especially courts and their officers. But it *has its force* by directing the practical reasoning of those persons and groups.[129]

Judges have to make decisions based on the force of law as a normative system of principles and rules, not on law as an evidential matter of historical fact. In so doing, they are not "falsifying history," but instead are determining the legal norms that apply to the historical facts that have been ascertained by evidence.[130] When a case before a court presents novel legal issues, as is often the situation in appeals, the judges still have to say what the law is – they cannot throw up their hands and exclaim that the case cannot be decided because there is no applicable law.[131] This is as true in cases involving Indigenous rights as it is in other cases. The main difference is that the historical facts giving rise to Indigenous cases are usually much further back in the past, often decades or centuries, for a variety of reasons, including Indigenous people's lack of knowledge of the common law system and lack of access to the courts to have their claims adjudicated. But this difference does not change the role of the judges or the nature of adjudication, nor does it cause history to be rewritten – as in all cases, judges rely on the historical record presented in court as evidence,[132] and have to determine and apply the law as they understand it.[133]

---

129 Finnis, "Adjudication," *supra* note 98 at 397 (emphasis mine).

130 See *ibid* at 401–2.

131 See Postema, *supra* note 100 at 11: "strictly novel cases call for judicial resolution." Postema cites Lord Ellesmere in "The Speech of the Lord Chancellor of England, in the Eschequer [*sic*] Chamber, Touching on the *Post-Nati*" (1608) [*Calvin's Case*, *supra* note 116], in Louis A. Knafla, *Law and Politics in Jacobean England: The Tracts of Lord Chancellor Ellesmere* (Cambridge: Cambridge University Press, 1977), 202 at 219: "There is a Rule in the Common Law, That *in novo casu remedium est apponendum*."

132 See Wiener, *supra* note 9 at 26: "The truth of historical assertions depends on facts and facts alone," as established by evidence.

133 See Paul Roberts and Adrian Zuckerman, *Criminal Evidence* (Oxford: Oxford University Press, 2004) at 132–3.

4. Conclusion

This chapter challenges Paul McHugh's position, expressed in his published work and on the witness stand, that there was no law in relation to Indigenous land rights in Canada prior to decisions of the Supreme Court in cases such as *Calder*, *Guerin*, and *Delgamuukw*.[134] In my opinion, the Crown was bound by the common law and constitutional documents, in particular the Royal Proclamation of 1763 and the *Rupert's Land Order* of 1870, to acknowledge the land rights of the Indigenous peoples and to settle those rights through established practices in accordance with legal principles. In other words, the Crown's dealings with the Indigenous peoples were not a matter of royal prerogative and executive grace, but rather were governed by law. The reason why Indigenous peoples did not go to court to assert their land rights prior to the latter half of the twentieth century was not because they had no legal rights, but rather because they were denied access to justice by a variety of factors, including lack of knowledge of Canadian law, inability to hire lawyers, and Crown immunity from suit.

My intention in this chapter, however, is not just to challenge McHugh's opinion on the historical existence of Indigenous land rights. Beyond that, I hope to clarify the distinction between law and history, as well as the role of legal historians in relation thereto. History is a matter of fact, provable in court through the testimony of witnesses who have firsthand experience with the relevant events and qualified experts who have studied the past and can provide opinions in relation thereto. Every case that goes to court involves history, in the sense that the events forming the basis for the claim necessarily happened in the past. Most cases, however, involve fairly recent events that are within the living memory of the participants and observers. Indigenous claims, however, often involve events that happened decades or centuries before. As witnesses with direct experience of the events are no longer available, courts have to rely on the testimony of experts, including Indigenous Elders, who are authorities on the oral histories of their people, and trained historians, who have studied and written about the people and period in question.

In the common law system, the opinions of experts are admissible insofar as they relate to factual matters. Experts cannot offer opinions

134 *Supra* notes 34, 45, and 43.

on the domestic law to be applied in deciding a case, as judges are expected to know that law and should not accept expert testimony on it, as that would permit experts to impinge on the judicial role and duty.[135] This distinction between questions of fact that are provable though witnesses and questions of law that are within the purview of judges is fundamental.[136] It is as applicable in Indigenous rights cases as it is in other cases, with the above-mentioned difference that in cases involving Indigenous rights opinions of experts on the historical facts are often needed because the events usually took place before living memory.

I do not think there is any controversy over this distinction between historical fact and applicable domestic law, and the proper role of historians as such in the courtroom. The distinction becomes murky, however, when the expert is a *legal* historian because legal history obviously involves both history and law. So where is the line between these to be drawn when a legal historian testifies as an expert? Clearly, a legal historian cannot testify and offer opinions on the domestic law that the judge will have to apply in deciding the case. There would not seem to be any problem, however, with a legal historian offering an opinion on what the law was at some time in the past, *as long as that is not the law that the judge will have to apply*, because the existence of law in the past can be viewed as historical fact.[137] But if the law in the past *is* the law that the judge will have to apply, it is a different matter; in that situation, it seems to me that the existence and content of that law is for the judge to determine, and the opinion of a legal historian on those issues is both irrelevant and inadmissible.

---

135 On the judicial duty to determine the applicable law, see the quotation from Lord Donaldson's judgment in *Parker* at *supra* note 25. However, the domestic law judges are expected to know does not include local custom (in England, at least) or Indigenous law (in Canada), which can be proven by expert testimony: see *supra* note 2.

136 See Keane, Griffiths, and McKeown, *supra* note 2 at 524–32; Delisle, Stuart, and Tanovich, *supra* note 2 at 858–929.

137 See the quotation from Finnis accompanying *supra* note 129.

4 Bargains Made in Bad Times: How Principles from Modern Treaties Can Reinvigorate Historic Treaties

JULIE JAI[1]

This chapter argues that treaties made in Canada in the modern era (from 1973 on) provide a principled basis for reinterpreting the written text of historic treaties negotiated when First Nations were at a bargaining power disadvantage. It shows how principles from modern treaties – in particular, notions of mutual benefit, the honour of the Crown, and mutually agreed upon dispute resolution processes – could be used to revitalize historic treaties and provide a basis for fair dealing. In doing so, it addresses questions about how treaties from different historical periods can be brought into alignment to achieve healthy treaty relationships.

1. Introduction

Treaties between Indigenous peoples and the Crown establish the terms for coexistence between Indigenous peoples and the European and other settlers who came later. They are generally divided into "historic treaties," negotiated prior to 1921, and "modern treaties," negotiated after 1973. The historic treaties can be further subdivided into the early "peace and friendship" treaties, culminating in the Royal Proclamation of 1763/Treaty of Niagara 1764, and "land cession" treaties that were largely a product of the mid-nineteenth to early twentieth centuries. In the written text of the historic treaties surrendering land, the terms are significantly less favourable to the Indigenous parties than those of the modern treaties. In this chapter, I argue that these substantive differences relate directly to when the treaties were made and how strong the bargaining power of the Indigenous parties was relative to the Crown's at the time the particular treaty was negotiated.

I approach this analysis of Crown–First Nations treaties from a negotiator's perspective.[2] Looking at these agreements through a negotiator's lens means understanding that the negotiating process matters; that who sits at the table matters; that the location and duration of the negotiations matter; that parties learn about each other's perspectives, cultures, and interests through the negotiating process; that a good negotiating process results in an agreement which meets most of the parties' key interests; that timing matters; that motivation matters; that each party's view of its fallback position, or "best alternative to a negotiated agreement," matters; that relationships matter; and that relative bargaining power matters.[3] Cumulatively, all of these factors become part of the negotiating context and they influence not just the process and perceptions of legitimacy but also the substantive outcomes.

The next two parts of this chapter seek to establish the following points as a factual backdrop to the understanding of treaties and treaty-making in Canada:

1. The relationship and relative power between Indigenous peoples and Europeans has changed significantly over the last 400 years. The bargaining power dynamics can be divided into roughly three periods: relatively equal bargaining power; unequal bargaining power; and a gradual return to greater balance in the negotiating environment.
2. The degree to which a treaty meets the needs of its Indigenous signatories is directly related to the relative bargaining power of the parties when the treaties were negotiated.

---

1 The author would like to thank Michael Coyle for the stimulating discussions which led to the idea for this chapter. Thanks also to Colleen Parrish, David Trick, Richard Ogden, Charles Pryce, and two anonymous reviewers for their helpful suggestions on earlier drafts of this paper.

2 I was the Yukon's Chief Negotiator on Administration of Justice Negotiations with the Teslin Tlingit Council as well as legal counsel on several comprehensive land claim and self-government negotiations between 1996 and 2002.

3 These views are my own but are not controversial and are consistent with the interest-based negotiation process used in modern land claim negotiations and with the principled negotiation approach developed at the Harvard Negotiation Project, set out in Roger Fisher, William Ury, and Bruce Patton, *Getting to Yes*, 3rd ed. (London: Penguin Books, 2011), which many modern land claim negotiations follow.

3. Historic land cession treaties were negotiated at the demographic low point for Indigenous peoples, which coincided with the relative lack of Indigenous economic, military, and legal power.
4. The written texts of historic land cession treaties appear to surrender vast amounts of land but provide fewer benefits to Indigenous peoples than treaties negotiated later, failing to include verbal promises.[4]
5. Modern treaties were and are negotiated during a period of increasing demographic, legal, and economic power for Indigenous peoples and, as a result, meet their needs much better than historic treaties.
6. Some First Nations have more favourable treaty terms than others simply because of when they signed their agreements. This suggests that the relative benefits of treaties to Indigenous peoples depend to a significant extent on when they were signed.

After reviewing how the context of treaty negotiations affects the outcomes, the last part of this chapter develops approaches to remedy the disparity between historic and modern treaties. While governments in the past have taken positions based on a literal reading of the written treaty text, it is not in keeping with the honour of the Crown for governments to rely on the strict wording of historic treaties negotiated in bad times, taking advantage of unequal bargaining power. There is much evidence to indicate that the written text of historic treaties does not reflect the intent or the understanding of the Indigenous signatories. This chapter suggests a new approach to interpreting historic treaties, based on the principle of fair dealing and applying mechanisms developed through modern treaty negotiations. The honour of the Crown,

4 Some Indigenous leaders and citizens argue that the modern treaties are less favourable to Indigenous peoples than the historic treaties because the modern treaties, in very detailed and explicit language, surrender Aboriginal rights and title, whereas it is arguable that based on the oral understandings of the Indigenous parties, the historic treaties did not. They also argue that the modern treaty process is not fair and balanced, as the federal government sets certain non-negotiable conditions. See Russell Diabo, "Harper Launches Major First Nation Termination Plan" in The Kino-nda-niimi Collective, *The Winter We Danced, Voices from the Past, the Future, and the Idle No More Movement* (Winnipeg: ARP Books, 2014) at 51–8.

Supreme Court of Canada decisions, and contract law[5] all provide a principled basis for saying that we need to go beyond the written text to properly interpret and implement historic treaties. There is also widespread support from a policy and political perspective for re-examining historic treaties.[6] However, there is also understandable concern about re-visiting constitutionally protected documents. Consistent principles are essential to assist the parties in reinvigorating historic treaties.

The modern treaty negotiation process, with its more inclusive process and greater safeguards for ensuring that the intentions of all parties are fairly reflected in the agreement, has so far led to twenty-seven agreements with remarkably consistent principles. Interestingly, these principles are similar to some of the principles in the Royal Proclamation of 1763 and the 1764 Treaty of Niagara, and reflect many of the principles which treaty elders[7] say that their ancestors understood to be part of the historic treaties but which did not make their way into the written text. So, a principled solution to the inequity between historic and modern treaties may lie in the terms of the modern treaties themselves.

There are both policy and legal reasons for looking to principles from modern treaties as a basis for reinvigorating historic treaties. The

---

5 For an analysis of how the contract law doctrines of duress and undue influence could usefully be applied to historic treaties, see Michael Coyle, "Marginalized by Sui Generis? Duress, Undue Influence and Crown-Aboriginal Treaties" (2007) 32:2 *Manitoba Law Journal* 34.

6 For example, at a 2012 Crown–First Nation Gathering, the Government of Canada and First Nations committed "to respect and honour our treaty relationship and advance approaches to find common ground on Treaty implementation." Office of the Prime Minister, News Release, "Crown–First Nations Gathering Outcome Statement" (24 January 2012), http://acelebrationofwomen.org/2012/01/pmo-crown-first-nations-gathering-outcome-statement/. The 1996 report of the Royal Commission on Aboriginal Peoples also recommended the establishment of a treaty renewal process to address historic treaties. See *Report of the Royal Commission on Aboriginal Peoples: Renewal: A Twenty Year Commitment*, vol. 5 (Ottawa: Supply and Services Canada, 1996). The Idle No More movement calls on the government to honour the spirit and intent of historic treaties. See "Calls for Change," Idle No More, http://www.idlenomore.ca/.

7 Sharon Venne explains the role of elders in passing on their understanding of the treaties, and the reasons why these accounts are likely to be accurate. See Sharon Venne, "Understanding Treaty 6: An Indigenous Perspective" in Michael Asch, ed., *Aboriginal and Treaty Rights in Canada: Essays on Law, Equality and Respect for Difference* (Vancouver: UBC Press, 1997) 173 at 174–7. Several books have gathered the testimony of elders with respect to specific treaties – some of these are cited in this chapter.

legitimacy of these principles flows from the fact that these were the terms which Indigenous and non-Indigenous parties agreed to when they were negotiating under more balanced conditions. These modern treaties were also ratified by the Indigenous communities and all of their terms are set out in the written agreement, further reinforcing their legitimacy. I propose that principles from modern treaties be read into historic treaties as implied terms based on the Crown's legal obligation to act honourably. In the conclusion to this chapter, I suggest three specific principles underlying modern treaties that could be used as the starting point for reinvigorating historic treaties. I also outline specific mechanisms that give meaning to these principles and could be applied to historic treaties.

2. Bargaining Power Dynamics: Three Periods in Indigenous–Crown Relationships

In this section, I examine how demographics, bargaining power dynamics and changing economic and political factors affected the relationships between Indigenous and non-Indigenous people in Canada during three distinct periods.

A. First Period: Early Contact to Late 1700s – Relative Strength in Numbers and Relatively Equal Bargaining Power

When Europeans first arrived in Canada, they were in a relatively weak position and needed the help of Indigenous people simply to survive. As time went by, they began to profit from trade, particularly the lucrative fur trade and later the trade in bison. The European newcomers also needed help militarily. They were concerned about the safety of small settler populations and, by the late 1700s, about incursion from the United States, a fear realized in the War of 1812. In the early days, Indigenous people greatly outnumbered non-Indigenous people, and even though this relative share of the total population was diminishing, by 1763, the Indigenous population was still larger than the settler population by a factor of two to one.[8]

8 The author estimates the Indigenous population in 1763 was approximately 200,000, based on data from "Canada Native Peoples 1823," *The National Atlas of Canada*, 5th ed. (Ottawa: Canada Centre for Mapping, Energy, Mines and Resources, 1990).

During this first period, both France and Britain were keen to conclude treaties to secure the assistance and friendship of Indigenous peoples. The French, who developed trading relationships with Indigenous peoples prior to the arrival of the British, were careful to observe Indigenous diplomatic protocol, such as the exchange of gifts and smoking the ceremonial pipe to formalize agreements. The French were so keen to maintain the fur trade that they were in greater fear of offending the Indigenous peoples than vice versa.[9] This illustrates the relatively strong bargaining power that Indigenous peoples held in this early period.

In addition to their value as trading partners, Indigenous peoples were also useful to the French and British in their political and military conflicts – primarily the fight between France and Britain for control of North America. The European powers entered into agreements with various First Nations to secure their support. These early treaties are often referred to as peace and friendship treaties because they did not require land to be surrendered but were primarily focused on relationship-building for both trade and military purposes.

In 1763, the Indigenous population of what is now Canada is estimated to have been about 200,000, while the non-Indigenous population of Canada at the time was about 100,000.[10] The relative numbers of Indigenous people in the 1600s and 1700s and their ability to provide desired trade goods gave them bargaining power. This bargaining power is reflected in the terms of the early treaties as well as the terms of the Royal Proclamation and the Treaty of Niagara in 1764, both of which were relatively favourable to Indigenous people compared to the treaties that followed.

However, even by 1763, the number of Indigenous people was diminishing, and their share of the total population was shrinking even more sharply as a result of the increasing number of non-Indigenous settlers. As described by *The National Atlas of Canada*,

---

This data is on the back of the large map which forms the *National Atlas*. The author estimates the non-Indigenous population of Canada in 1763 as approximately 100,000 based on combining census data from different regions at different times, taken from Statistics Canada, *Estimated Population of Canada, 1605 to Present*, http://www.statcan.gc.ca/pub/98-187-x/4151287-eng.htm. These are estimates only.

9 This is recounted by Olive Dickason and David McNab, referencing reports from Friar Sagard in the early 1600s, in Olive Dickason and David McNab, *Canada's First Nations: A History of Founding Peoples from Earliest Times* (Don Mills, ON: Oxford University Press, 2009) at 80.

10 *Supra* note 8.

> In the early 1820s, the native population of what is now Canada stood at about 150,000, a significant drop from the 200,000 estimated for the 1740s, and 250,000 estimated for the early 1630s. Up to the late 18th century, this decline was largely due to epidemic diseases and to a lesser extent, warfare. As the 19th century progressed, disease continued to take a dreadful toll across Canada, but starvation increasingly manifested itself in the eastern parts of the country, where the spread of European settlement, overhunting and overtrapping were changing the native subsistence base.[11]

The brief advantage in numbers and bargaining power which Indigenous people had enjoyed in the early years of contact was ending and demographics and power relationships were rapidly shifting in favour of the European powers.

B. Second Period: Late 1700s to 1973 – Declining Indigenous Share of Relative Population – Unequal Bargaining Power

In this second period, the numbers of European and American settlers increased rapidly while Indigenous communities were further decimated by new diseases and the economic basis of their way of life was eroded by overharvesting and other changes brought on by pressures from European trade.[12] The relative proportion of Indigenous people as a percentage of total population fell sharply. The drop in population was directly linked to the arrival of the Europeans, as noted even in official documents at the time.[13]

---

11 *The National Atlas of Canada*, *supra* note 8, text taken from the back of this large map which forms the *National Atlas*. Similar data and trends are noted in Geoffrey J. Matthews, cartographer, *Historical Atlas of Canada*, vol. 1, ed. R. Cole Harris (Toronto: University of Toronto Press, 1987) Plate 69: Native Canada, ca 1820.

12 Game was depleted by the fur trade, trading and harvesting patterns amongst First Nation groups were changed, and natural cycles of scarcity and plenty were intensified, "making glaringly evident the fundamental conflict between the requirements of the fur trade and the needs for subsistence," Dickason and McNab, *supra* note 9 at 116.

13 An 1876 review of census data patronizingly but revealingly concluded "that Indian populations, keeping to the habits of the hunting tribes, diminish in number in the ratio of the extent and frequency of their relations with civilized nations, by the destruction of their primitive means of existence, and the introduction of vices and diseases, or by absorption, in the creation of a half-breed race." Statistics Canada, *Censuses of Canada 1665 to 1871* (1876) at 2, http://www.statcan.gc.ca/pub/98-187-x/4151278-eng.htm. A note indicates that the views in the 1876 report "in no way reflect the views of Statistics Canada."

The bargaining power of Indigenous peoples was also reduced by changes in the economic interests of the French and the English. Reduced European demand for the trade goods supplied by Indigenous people reinforced the power disparities as demand for furs declined and the bison, which had been the subject of robust trade, had become virtually extinct by the 1870s,[14] leading to widespread starvation and the loss of a way of life that had endured for 10,000 years.[15]

Political and military interests also shifted over time. In 1760, Britain conquered New France, and the 1763 Treaty of Paris formally transferred New France to Great Britain, reducing the need for First Nation military allies. While incursions from the United States were a threat in the late eighteenth and early nineteenth centuries, the War of 1812 and the gradual peaceful resolution of the boundary between the United States and British North America ended the need for First Nation military assistance. In addition, increasing settlement in what is now Canada, including significant immigration from the United States, increased the demand for land. Britain's interests turned to securing and settling its colonies and developing an agrarian economy in North America that would make the colonies self-sustaining. Thus, economic and political forces combined with demographics to reduce the relative bargaining power of Indigenous people during this second period.

This is significant because most of the historic treaties which allegedly surrendered land were signed during this second period when Indigenous populations had been decimated by European diseases, wars, loss of wildlife which they relied upon, and settler pressures for the best agricultural land. The Aboriginal share of the total population of Canada slid from an estimated 67 per cent in 1763 to only 1.3 per cent by 1921;[16] so the land cession treaties were signed during a demographic low point, on terms which, based on the written text, were not very favourable to the First Nation signatories. This demographic history is summarized in Figure 4.1, which shows the Aboriginal population of

14 Gerald Friesen, *The Canadian Prairies: A History* (Toronto: University of Toronto Press, 1984) at 92.

15 James Daschuk, *Clearing the Plains – Disease, Politics of Starvation, and the Loss of Aboriginal Life* (Regina: University of Regina Press, 2013) at 183.

16 Author's calculation, based on Statistics Canada, *Historical Statistics of Canada*, Table A125–163: Origins of the population, census dates, 1871 to 1971, http://www.statcan.gc.ca/pub/11-516-x/sectiona/4147436-eng.htm.

Figure 4.1. Aboriginal population of Canada, and Aboriginal share of population of Canada, from early contact to 2011[17]

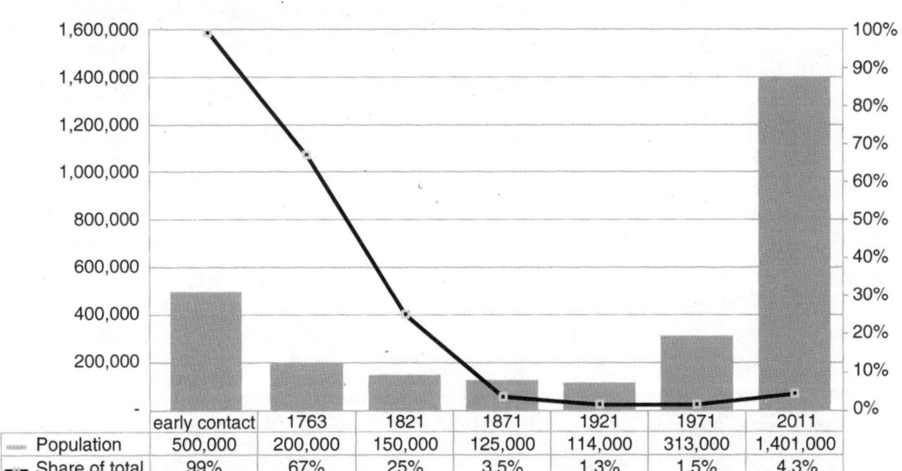

	early contact	1763	1821	1871	1921	1971	2011
Population	500,000	200,000	150,000	125,000	114,000	313,000	1,401,000
Share of total	99%	67%	25%	3.5%	1.3%	1.5%	4.3%

Canada in absolute numbers and as a share of the total population from early contact to 2011. The bars represent the Aboriginal population in numbers, which are set out on the left hand side, while the line represents the Aboriginal population as a percentage of the total population of Canada.

Treaties 1 to 11, whose written terms collectively surrendered almost half of Canada's land mass, were signed between 1871 and 1921, when

17 Sources for the data in Figure 4.1 are as follows: Aboriginal population at early contact, Dickason and McNab, *supra* note 9 at 40; I estimate the Aboriginal populations in 1763 and 1821 based on *The National Atlas of Canada*, *supra* note 8; I estimate the Aboriginal population in 1871 based on the Aboriginal population in the 1881 Census.

For the Aboriginal population from 1901 to 2001, see Statistics Canada, "Population reporting Aboriginal ancestry (origin), Canada, 1901–2001," http://www12.statcan.ca/English/census01/products/analytic/companion/abor/canada.cfm (first chart). For Aboriginal population in 2011, see Statistics Canada, 2011 Census of Canada.

Population of Canada 1763 and 1821 are estimated by the author based on Statistics Canada, "Estimated population of Canada, 1605 to present," http://www.statcan.gc.ca/pub/98-187-x/4151287-eng.htm. The population of Canada in 1871 and later are from the Census of Canada.

the Indigenous population was in absolute as well as relative decline. These key historic treaties were negotiated and signed at the point in time when economic, political, and demographic forces had combined to bring those treaty First Nations to their lowest ebb in terms of relative population and bargaining power.

C. Third Period: 1973 to Present – Increasing Indigenous Population and Bargaining Power, and the Game-Changing Calder Decision

By 1971, the Indigenous population was on the upswing after a long period of decline with census data revealing an increase in absolute numbers to 313,000 (up from 114,000 in 1921) and a small percentage increase to 1.5 per cent of the total Canadian population (up from 1.3 per cent in 1921). This gradual recovery in population coincided with an increase in awareness and activism by Indigenous people throughout North America, exemplified by the birth of the American Indian Movement in 1968 and the Native People's Caravan, which travelled across Canada in 1974 to raise awareness of broken treaty promises and other grievances against the government.[18] The share of the population who identify themselves as Aboriginal has continued to rise since 1971 and is currently the fastest growing segment of the population. According to the 2011 National Household Survey, 4.3 per cent of the Canadian population is Aboriginal, continuing an upward trajectory from 1.5 per cent in 1971 and 2.8 per cent in 1996.[19]

In 1973, the Supreme Court of Canada released its decision in the game-changing *Calder* case. In this decision, the Court found that Aboriginal title to land continues to exist unless validly extinguished by the Crown. The Court stated, "[T]he fact is that when the settlers came, the Indians were there, organized in societies and occupying the land as their forefathers had done for centuries. This is what Indian title means."[20]

---

18 See Vern Harper's account in Vern Harper, *Following the Red Path: The Native People's Caravan, 1974* (Toronto: NC Press, 1979) at 83–7.

19 Statistics Canada, *2011 Census, Aboriginal Peoples in Canada*, https://www12.statcan.gc.ca/nhs-enm/2011/as-sa/99-011-x/99-011-x2011001-eng.cfm.

20 *Calder v AG British Columbia*, [1973] SCR 313 at 328 [*Calder*], Justice Judson speaking for three members of the Court in what is considered the majority decision. The decision was split 3:3:1 and the actual declaration of Aboriginal title which the Nisga'a sought was denied on the basis of a technicality by Justice Pigeon who held

The court in *Calder* was split on the issue of whether the Nisga'a Nation's title to land had been extinguished by certain proclamations, but the decision was significant in foreclosing the argument that Aboriginal title had never existed. It was now clear that unless there had been a surrender of land rights in a treaty, or other valid extinguishment, Aboriginal title continued to exist.[21]

Aboriginal and treaty rights received further protection in 1982, when section 35 of the *Constitution Act, 1982* came into effect, which "recognized and affirmed existing Aboriginal and treaty rights." Since "existing Aboriginal and treaty rights" were not defined in the Constitution or by subsequent constitutional conferences that were held for this purpose, the courts have played a major role in defining the scope and limits of these rights. It is clear that since the enactment of section 35, legislatures can no longer unilaterally "extinguish" Aboriginal or treaty rights, although these rights can be "infringed" based on a test set out by the Supreme Court of Canada.[22]

The increased bargaining power for First Nations that flowed from the *Calder* decision and from the 1982 constitutional provisions has been reinforced in a series of subsequent Supreme Court of Canada decisions, notably: the 1990 *Sparrow*[23] decision recognizing Aboriginal rights to fish in traditional territories; the 1997 *Delgamuukw*[24] decision setting out a test for Aboriginal title to land; the 1999 *Marshall*[25] decision

---

the deciding vote. The judgment changed the law, however, as both the majority and the minority decisions recognized that Aboriginal title flows from the original use and occupation of the land, not from some grant or recognition by European powers, and that without a clear act of extinguishment such as a treaty, Aboriginal title to the land continues to be enforceable at common law.

21 The Supreme Court of Canada later clarified in *R v Sparrow*, [1990] 1 SCR 1075 [*Sparrow*] and *Delgamuukw v British Columbia*, [1997] 3 SCR 1010 [*Delgamuukw*] that Aboriginal title could only have been extinguished through a treaty or through clear and plain federal legislation. Since the enactment of the *Constitution Act, 1982*, unilateral extinguishment of Aboriginal or treaty rights, even by clear federal legislation, is no longer possible, although these rights may be infringed or affected in accordance with criteria set out by the Supreme Court of Canada in cases such as *Sparrow*.

22 The Supreme Court of Canada set out the framework for justifying infringements of Aboriginal rights in *Sparrow, supra* note 21.

23 *Ibid.*

24 *Delgamuukw, supra* note 21.

25 *R v Marshall*, [1999] 3 SCR 456 [*Marshall*].

declaring that a historic treaty granted a limited right to fish for trading purposes and articulating interpretative principles for historic treaties; the 2004 *Haida*[26] decision establishing an independent Crown duty to consult with and, in some cases, accommodate Aboriginal peoples where there is a credibly asserted Aboriginal right and a Crown decision that has the potential to adversely affect that right; the 2005 decision in *Mikisew Cree*[27] applying the Crown's duty to consult to situations in which treaty rights might be affected; the 2010 *Beckman*[28] decision extending the duty to consult to govern modern as well as historic treaties; the 2013 *Manitoba Metis*[29] decision expanding on what the honour of the Crown requires; and the 2014 *Tsilhqot'in Nation*[30] decision finding that the Tsilhqot'in Nation had Aboriginal title to areas which it had regularly used for hunting and fishing. These Supreme Court of Canada decisions have changed the law significantly and have provided substantial leverage to First Nations.

In addition, there are now a growing number of Indigenous people who have become lawyers, and the field of Aboriginal law has developed as a specialized discipline. There are professional negotiators and lawyers representing First Nations, and there is greater scrutiny of government actions and litigation positions by specialists in Aboriginal law. First Nations have successfully used the courts to challenge government and third-party actions. The availability and use of court challenges has significantly improved First Nations' bargaining positions. Government officials and lawyers also have an increased understanding of their obligation to ensure that the Crown behaves honourably in its relations with Indigenous peoples.

While Indigenous people are still subject to a bargaining power disadvantage as compared with governments, the playing field is more level than in the past. In addition, there are tools that First Nations can deploy now that were not available in the second period to assist in overcoming the bargaining power disparity. In addition to having a good fallback position or BATNA (best alternative to a negotiated agreement), there are other sources of negotiating power:

26 *Haida Nation v BC (Minister of Forests)*, [2004] 3 SCR 511 [*Haida Nation*].
27 *Mikisew Cree v Canada (Minister of Canadian Heritage)*, [2005] 3 SCR 388 [*Mikisew Cree*].
28 *Beckman v Little Salmon Carmacks First Nation*, [2010] 3 SCR 103.
29 *Manitoba Metis Federation Inc v Canada*, [2013] 1 SCR 623.
30 *Tsilhqot'in Nation v British Columbia*, 2014 SCC 44.

- developing a good working relationship with the people you are negotiating with – the slow pace of modern claims negotiations can provide the time for good relationships to develop;
- effective communication – this is much easier when all parties are speaking the same language, and when First Nations have the resources to hire professional negotiators and lawyers and the time to engage their communities in the discussion;
- elegant or creative options or solutions – the creation of a new territory with a public government model for Nunavut is one example of a creative solution. Another example is creative wording, which has been developed to move away from extinguishment of rights language towards a non-assertion of rights model, which still gives government the certainty it requires but retains Aboriginal title and rights to the extent possible; and
- using external standards of legitimacy – international standards, such as those set out in instruments such as the United Nations Declaration on the Rights of Indigenous Peoples, Supreme Court of Canada decisions, or influential reports such as the Royal Commission on Aboriginal Peoples or the Truth and Reconciliation Commission can be helpful references to support Indigenous claims.[31]

All of these techniques to overcome bargaining power disparities have been applied by First Nations negotiators in modern treaty negotiations.

In my experience as a former government negotiator and lawyer, I have found that governments are very conscious of their BATNA. In an environment of increasing court recognition of Aboriginal rights, as well as the growing population, influence, and assertiveness of Indigenous people, governments carefully assess the risks of protracted litigation which they might ultimately lose, as well as the risk of direct action by Indigenous people. In fact, developments in Aboriginal jurisprudence have been gradually expanding the rights of Indigenous people, making governments aware that delaying treaty negotiations could result in an even worse court-imposed alternative to a negotiated agreement. These alternatives make a negotiated agreement more attractive from the government's perspective, making the Crown more willing to negotiate

31 These four sources of bargaining power are drawn from Fisher, Ury, and Patton, *supra* note 3 at 183–93.

treaties on terms that are agreeable to First Nations. Court decisions have played a significant role in putting the negotiating parties on a more equal level.

In fact, it was the 1973 *Calder* decision that motivated the federal government to develop its first policy on comprehensive land claims in 1973.[32] After many years of ignoring Indigenous claims in vast areas of Canada where Indigenous people had not surrendered title to land, Canada began negotiating modern treaties under this policy to try to achieve greater legal certainty over rights to land. This approach to negotiating comprehensive claims is a policy-based approach and does not require proof of legal title to land by the Indigenous party before negotiations can begin. Significant resources have been put into negotiating modern treaties, and as of January 2016, twenty-six modern treaties[33] have been reached. There are also approximately ninety ongoing comprehensive claims negotiations[34] with First Nations across Canada in which Indigenous people have not surrendered their title to land.[35] Modern treaties include the James Bay and Northern Quebec Agreement, the Nunavut Land Claims Agreement, agreements covering much of the Yukon and Northwest Territories, and a few agreements in British Columbia, such as the Nisga'a Final Agreement. These modern treaties were all negotiated during this third period of increasing Aboriginal population and improved bargaining power.

---

32 Department of Indian Affairs and Northern Development, "Statement Made by the Honourable Jean Chrétien, Minister of Indian Affairs and Northern Development on Claims of Indian and Inuit People," Communiqué (8 August 1973). The policy was reaffirmed in *In All Fairness: A Native Claims Policy – Comprehensive Claims* (Ottawa: Department of Indian Affairs and Northern Development, 1981).

33 A map showing areas covered by modern treaties can be found at http://www.aadnc-aandc.gc.ca/DAM/DAM-INTER-HQ-AI/STAGING/texte-text/mprm_pdf_modrn-treaty_1383144351646_eng.pdf.

34 For details of current comprehensive land claim negotiations, see Department of Indian Affairs and Northern Development, "General Briefing Note on Canada's Self-government and Comprehensive Land Claims Policies and the Status of Negotiations," https://www.aadnc-aandc.gc.ca/eng/1373385502190/1373385561540#s2-18.

35 In Christopher Alcantara, *Negotiating the Deal: Comprehensive Land Claims Agreements in Canada* (Toronto: University of Toronto Press, 2013) at 56, Alcantara argues that certain factors make it more likely that a First Nation will successfully negotiate a modern treaty, including compatibility of government and Aboriginal goals, minimal use of confrontational tactics, strong Aboriginal group cohesion, and positive government perceptions of the Aboriginal group's capacity.

3. First Nation–Crown Treaties: Three Types of Treaties from the Three Periods

A. Early Peace and Friendship Treaties, the 1763 Royal Proclamation and the Treaty of Niagara (Early Contact to Late 1700s)

Early treaties between European powers and Indigenous peoples in Canada reflected the relatively strong position of Indigenous people at the time. They gained bargaining power from their large population, their greater understanding of how to live off the land, their strategic relationships with the British and the French, which they sometimes played against each other, and the strong desire of the French and English for furs. In these early days, the Indigenous parties were also dominant militarily at times, and were sometimes able to dictate the terms of peace.[36] Europeans adopted Indigenous diplomatic protocols in order to establish commercial trading relationships and peace and friendship treaties because they needed their help much more than Indigenous people needed them.[37]

The 1664 Treaty of Albany established the first formal alliance between the British and Aboriginal people in North America. Through this treaty, the British sought to ally themselves with the Iroquois, who were more powerful and numerous than they were, and to strengthen their position against other European nations in North America. The text of the Treaty of Albany was written by the British on parchment. For their part, the Iroquois presented the British with a Two Row Wampum belt, symbolizing the two parallel paths that each nation would take, neither party trying to steer the other's vessel but travelling in peace, friendship, and mutual respect.[38]

In the Maritimes, a series of peace and friendship treaties were signed between the British and the Mi'kmaq and Maliseet between 1713 and

36 Dickason and McNab in *Canada's First Nations* describe a failed invasion by the French in 1684, when the Iroquois found the French disease-ridden and running out of food, allowing Chief Otreouti to dictate the terms of settlement, which the French had no option but to accept (*supra* note 9 at 126).

37 See J.R. Miller, *Compact, Contract, Covenant: Aboriginal Treaty-Making in Canada* (Toronto: University of Toronto Press, 2009) at 285.

38 John Borrows and Leonard Rotman, *Aboriginal Legal Issues: Cases, Materials and Commentary*, 3rd ed. (Markham, ON: LexisNexis Canada, 2007) at 14–16.

1762, providing for an end to hostilities and continued hunting, fishing, and trading rights for the Mi'kmaq and Maliseet. As with all of the treaties prior to 1763, these pre-Royal Proclamation treaties, accurately described as peace and friendship treaties, did not involve the surrender of any land rights.[39]

In 1763, following the cession of New France to Britain, King George III issued the Royal Proclamation to establish a basis for administering the recently acquired territory and setting out protocols for dealing with Indigenous people. The Royal Proclamation recognized that land was held collectively by Indigenous nations, and provided that only the Crown could purchase land from First Nations. There had been increased pressure for land from settlers, and the Royal Proclamation was intended to "provide a solution to the problems created by the greed which hitherto some of the English had all too often demonstrated in buying up Indian land at low prices."[40]

The Royal Proclamation defined the land west of the established colonies as "Indian Territories," where First Nations people "should not be molested or disturbed" by settlers, and led to the Indian Department being interposed as the primary liaison between the Crown and First Nations. In order to prevent any future abuse, the proclamation prohibited colonial governors from making any grants or taking any land cessions from First Nations people, and established a set of protocols and procedures for the purchasing of First Nations land.[41] In this way, the Royal Proclamation recognized prior Indigenous occupation and rights to land and provided the basis for subsequent treaties, which from this point on included land surrender provisions in the written text.

Although the Royal Proclamation was a unilateral declaration by the British monarch, in 1764, a gathering of approximately 2,000 chiefs from as far east as Nova Scotia and as far west as Mississippi was convened at Niagara to meet with Sir William Johnson on behalf of the British Crown. At this gathering, speeches were made, copies of the Royal Proclamation were distributed, and Two Row Wampum belts were

---

39 Thomas Isaac, *Aboriginal Law Commentary and Analysis* (Saskatoon: Purich Publishing, 2012) at 144–5. See also Indigenous and Northern Affairs Canada's website at https://www.aadnc-aandc.gc.ca/eng/1100100028589/1100100028591.

40 As stated by Justice Lamer in *R v Sioui*, [1990] 1 SCR 1025 at 1064.

41 See Indigenous and Northern Affairs Canada, "250th Anniversary of the Royal Proclamation of 1763," https://www.aadnc-aandc.gc.ca/eng/1370355181092/1370355203645.

exchanged in accordance with Indigenous diplomatic protocol. The effect of this was to create what is known as the 1764 Treaty of Niagara. The Royal Proclamation and the Treaty of Niagara collectively set out the terms of a historic treaty between First Nations and the Crown.[42]

The Royal Proclamation of 1763 recognized Indigenous peoples as "Nations" with rights to their lands and the right to not be disturbed in pursuing their way of life.[43] The Two Row Wampum belt exchanged at Niagara conveys the Indigenous understanding of a mutual relationship of peace and non-interference in each other's way of life. While many of the promises made at Niagara were oral, subsequent written documents by British officials confirm that First Nations did not surrender land or sovereignty but in fact viewed the agreement as affirming their powers of self-government and land rights.[44]

The Royal Proclamation and Treaty of Niagara collectively provide for:

- the preservation of First Nations' sovereignty or right to self-government
- an alliance between sovereign nations
- free and open trade and passage between the Crown and First Nations
- permission needed for settlement of First Nations territory
- a relationship of mutual peace, friendship, and respect

42 For a detailed exposition of this argument, see John Borrows, "Wampum at Niagara: The Royal Proclamation, Canadian Legal History and Self-Government" in Michael Asch, ed., *Aboriginal and Treaty Rights in Canada: Essays on Law, Equality and Respect for Difference* (Vancouver: UBC Press, 1997) at 155. See also Indigenous and Northern Affairs Canada, "250th Anniversary of the Royal Proclamation of 1763" (Crown–First Nation Relationship), https://www.aadnc-aandc.gc.ca/eng/370355181092/1370355203645#a5.

43 The Royal Proclamation states, "And whereas it is just and reasonable, and essential to Our Interest and the Security of Our Colonies, that the several Nations or Tribes of Indians, with whom We are connected, and who live under Our Protection, should not be molested or disturbed in the Possession of such Parts of Our Dominions and Territories as, not having been ceded to, or purchased by Us, are reserved to them, or any of them, as their Hunting Grounds." Indigenous and Northern Affairs Canada, "250th Anniversary of the Royal Proclamation of 1763" (Royal Proclamation of 1763), https://www.aadnc-aandc.gc.ca/eng/1370355181092/1370355203645#a6.

44 Borrows, *supra* note 42 at 164–8.

- presents from and protection by the Crown to First Nations
- non-interference with the Indigenous way of life, including harvesting rights. [45]

The relatively balanced provisions of the Royal Proclamation and the Treaty of Niagara reflect the strong bargaining position of Indigenous people at the time – a position that gradually changed after 1763.

B. The Historic Treaties which Allegedly Surrendered Land (Late 1700s to 1973)

It is not as though the Treaty 8 First Nations did not pay dearly for their entitlement to honourable conduct on the part of the Crown; surrender of the aboriginal interest in an area larger than France is a hefty purchase price.[46]

We made an agreement, but land was never mentioned … a person must be crazy to accept five dollars to give up his land.[47]

After the Royal Proclamation of 1763, and even more so after the end of the War of 1812, political interests shifted for the British, who had conquered the French in North America, settled with the Americans, and were now the dominant power in the world. By the early 1800s, British focus had shifted from trade and military alliances with Indigenous people to the expansion of colonies, obtaining land for settlers, and creating markets for British manufactured goods. After Confederation, Canada's focus was on acquiring access to resources, including access to waterways and access to land on which to build a railway to open up Western Canada. Government perception of Indigenous peoples shifted from being necessary allies to obstacles in the acquisition of land and resources needed for settlement. As this shift was occurring, Indigenous people became more interested in treaty-making because their lands were being taken without their permission; the fur-bearing animals that were essential to their sustenance and way of life were disappearing;

45 *Ibid* at 167–9.

46 Justice Binnie, speaking for the Court in *Mikisew Cree, supra* note 27 at para 52.

47 Chief Jimmy Bruneau describing Treaty 11 in a 1968 interview, as quoted in René Fumoleau, *As Long As This Land Shall Last: A History of Treaty 8 and Treaty 11, 1870–1939*, rev. ed. (Calgary: University of Calgary Press, 2004) at 248.

European-borne diseases such as smallpox were decimating their populations; and starvation was becoming more prevalent.[48]

The focus of governments during this period was to obtain land, so the text of all of the treaties made during this period included land surrenders. This includes thirty land cessions in what is now Southern Ontario between 1764 and 1862,[49] mostly gained in exchange for one-time cash payments. In 1850, the Robinson-Superior Treaty and the Robinson-Huron Treaty were negotiated in the Lake Superior and Lake Huron areas by William Robinson for the Crown. These treaties surrendered land in exchange for the continued right to hunt and fish, the creation of reserve lands, a one-time payment, and annuities.

The "numbered treaties," made between 1871 and 1921, followed the pattern of the Robinson treaties, and collectively purported to surrender a vast area of Central and Western Canada.

Treaty 1 was negotiated over nine days in 1871 with the Saulteaux of Manitoba, and its oral and written terms reflected both Saulteaux and government objectives. The Saulteaux wanted assistance in transitioning to agriculture, since they could no longer sustain themselves from hunting. The government's commissioner agreed to this orally, but not in writing, as he did not have the mandate to agree to this type of assistance. The government implemented only the written text of the treaty, leaving out the key oral provisions required by the Saulteaux. As a result, the government had great difficulty getting other First Nations to agree to treaty terms until they agreed to provide the promised agricultural assistance to the Saulteaux. They did so "as a matter of benevolence" rather than acknowledging that it was part of the treaty terms, in order to quell unrest and facilitate the negotiation of further treaties.[50]

Treaty 3, covering land in what is now Ontario and Manitoba, contained more generous written terms than Treaties 1 and 2, in part because of the difficulties with the unfulfilled oral promises of those earlier treaties. Treaty 3 benefits included reserve land; hunting and fishing rights

---

48 These motivations are summarized in an 1871 petition from the Cree Chiefs along the North Saskatchewan River, represented by Sweet Grass, to Lieutenant-Governor Archibald, set out in Alexander Morris, *The Treaties of Canada with the Indians of Manitoba and the North-West Territories* (1880; reprint, Saskatoon: Fifth House, 1991), 170–1.

49 See Indigenous and Northern Affairs Canada, "Summaries of Pre-1975 Treaties," at https://www.aadnc-aandc.gc.ca/eng/1370362690208/1370362747827.

50 Miller, *supra* note 37 at 163–6. See also Morris, *supra* note 48 at 126–7.

throughout the surrendered territories subject to tracts taken up by the Crown for settlement, forestry, mining, or other purposes; an annuity of $5 per person; agricultural implements and livestock; a $25 annual salary for the chief, as well as a suit of clothing, a flag, and a medal; $1,500 per year for ammunition and twine; and schools on the reserve.[51] Treaty 4, covering southern Saskatchewan and parts of Alberta and Manitoba, contained similar terms.[52] James Daschuk writes that "hunger played a role in the completion of Treaty 4"[53] and, in some cases, "rations were used as a means of coercing Indians into submitting to [the] Treaty."[54] Several chiefs who were not present at the original negotiations later signed on through adhesion, meaning that they had to accept the terms of the treaty without further negotiation – a "take it or leave it" proposition.[55] The terms of Treaty 5, covering much of Manitoba, were similar to those of Treaty 4.

Treaty 6, signed in 1876, provided that the Indigenous parties cede, release, and surrender forever all rights to 121,000 square miles in what is now Alberta and Saskatchewan in exchange for reserves, hunting rights throughout the territory subject to tracts taken up, an annuity of $5 per person, as well as the agricultural assistance and other items set out in the earlier treaties. The Plains Cree, who still posed a military threat, which gave them some bargaining power, pressed for the provision of a medicine chest and assistance in the event of pestilence or famine in Treaty 6, as they had seen the devastation resulting from smallpox.[56] Treaty 6 Elders maintain that their ancestors could not have agreed to surrender the land, as they only had the authority to share the

---

51 Miller, *supra* note 37 at 169. See also the text of Treaty 3 at Indigenous and Northern Affairs Canada, http://www.aadnc-aandc.gc.ca/eng/1100100028675/1100100028679.

52 See the text of Treaty 4 at Indigenous and Northern Affairs Canada, https://www.aadnc-aandc.gc.ca/eng/1100100028689/1100100028690.

53 James Daschuk, *Clearing the Plains: Disease, Politics of Starvation, and the Loss of Aboriginal Life* (Regina: University of Regina Press, 2013) at 95.

54 *Ibid* at 114.

55 Miller, *supra* note 37 at 173, where he also states, "Over time, the number of adhesions increased as conditions worsened and the bands became more eager for the assistance treaty represented."

56 Daschuk, *supra* note 53 at 97, quotes Cree chief Mistawassis when arguing in favour of signing Treaty 6 as saying, "We are few in numbers compared to former times, by wars and the terrible ravages of smallpox … Even if it were possible to gather all the tribes together, to throw away the hand that is offered to help us, we would be too weak to make our demands heard." They were aware of their diminishing

land according to the Cree, Saulteaux, Assiniboine, and Dene laws.[57] Not all chiefs were satisfied, even at the time, with the terms of Treaty 6, and Chief Big Bear resisted for several years until desperate straits and starvation forced him into signing an adhesion.[58] Treaty 7, covering southern Alberta, was also signed during increasingly difficult times. Tsuu T'ina Elder Lucy Big Plume has said that the Tsuu T'ina entered into the treaty "because the buffalo were getting smaller and people were starving. They had to do something to keep people living."[59]

By the 1880s, the Canadian government no longer saw Indigenous peoples as partners. Negative attitudes towards Indigenous people were heightened by the 1869 and 1885 rebellions in Western Canada (the first and second Riel Rebellions), which caused fear and hostility, particularly in Protestant Ontario, towards the Catholic Métis and their Indian allies. In 1878 the Canadian government announced a National Policy that focused on western expansion and east–west trade, combined with high tariffs for foreign goods and, later, the building of the railroad.[60] Canada's political, territorial and trade ambitions combined with the diminishing Indigenous population to create the perfect storm of low bargaining power and low government interest in seeking fair arrangements with Indigenous peoples. Treaties were no longer viewed by government as agreements based on a relationship of equality and mutual respect.

---

bargaining power – Chief Ahtahkakoop states, "We are weak and my brother Mista-wa-sis I think is right that the buffalo will be gone before many snows. What then will be left us with which to bargain?" (98).

57 Venne, *supra* note 7 at 192–3. She also states that it is the women who owned the land, and as they did not participate in the treaty-making, they could not possibly have signed away possession of the land (191–2).

58 "Chief Big Bear … was displeased with the agreed terms of the Treaty 6 and did not adhere to it. Refusing to sign the treaty for another seven years, Big Bear and his followers moved freely across the Prairie in an attempt to pressure the Crown to renegotiate the treaties with terms more favourable for First Nation signatories. After years of hardship due to disappearing buffalo, living off Northwest Mounted Police rations and the numbers of his followers dwindling, Big Bear finally agreed to sign an adhesion to Treaty 6 in August 1883 and settle on a reserve." Indigenous and Northern Affairs Canada, "The Numbered Treaties," http://www.aadnc-aandc.gc.ca/eng/1360948213124/1360948312708.

59 Treaty 7 Elders and Tribal Council with Walter Hildebrandt, Dorothy First Rider and Sarah Carter, *The True Spirit and Original Intent of Treaty 7* (Montreal: McGill-Queen's University Press, 1996) at 81.

60 See *The Canadian Encyclopedia*, "National Policy," http://www.thecanadianencyclopedia.ca/en/article/national-policy/

The 1876 *Indian Act* established more of a trustee–ward relationship between the Crown and Indigenous people, replacing what First Nations had considered to be a relationship of equal kinship, like that between brother and sister, with a parent–child model. By this time, the Crown had received what it needed from Indigenous people, who now had very limited bargaining power. Treaty commitments were not fulfilled and any oral promises not set out in the written text were ignored.[61] The government now had peaceful access to western resources, and Indigenous populations were on the decline, with the collapse of the bison and the deterioration of the traditional way of life.[62] The government no longer needed good relationships with Indigenous peoples and had little incentive to implement the treaties fairly. Treaties 8, 9, 10, and 11 in Northern Ontario, Saskatchewan, Alberta, BC, and the Northwest Territories were negotiated during this particularly challenging period, often on the initiative of the Indigenous people who found themselves in difficult straits, with the government agreeing only when material incentives such as the discovery of gold in the Yukon or oil in the Northwest Territories made it worth their while.[63] These treaties were particularly unbalanced in their terms.[64] Oral promises that

---

61 Michael Asch points out that Alexander Morris, who negotiated most of the numbered treaties on behalf of the Crown, intended that the treaties be implemented in accordance with their spirit and intent, including oral promises: "During his tenure as lieutenant governor of Manitoba, Morris advocated tirelessly for the faithful implementation of the spirit of the treaties, arguing that oral promises, from specific agricultural implements to general principles of reciprocity and mutual assistance, should be honoured." Michael Asch, *On Being Here to Stay: Treaties and Aboriginal Rights in Canada* (Toronto: University of Toronto Press, 2014) at 161.

62 Miller, *supra* note 37 at 190–1.

63 See Fumoleau, *supra* note 47. He quotes Bishop Breynat's diary regarding the impetus for Treaty 8: "Worrying about the news of rich gold mines having been discovered on Great Slave Lake, and desiring to assure its rights to the greatest part of the loot, the Government prudently hurried to send a treaty commission to deal with the Indians and to purchase from them a complete surrender of their land rights in exchange for a perpetual yearly rent and other gifts" (*ibid* at 37). Fumoleau states, "Later, when the discovery of oil outside of the Treaty 8 area made it highly desirable to 'extinguish the Indian title' a new treaty was needed: Treaty 11" (*ibid* at 128).

64 Miller, *supra* note 37 at 211–21. Regarding Treaty 9, Miller states, "When it came to locating reserves, the commissioners were particularly ungenerous. Requests for long sections of river shoreline were rebuffed, and of course, no band that wanted a reserve where the waterways held potential for hydroelectric power generation had its request granted" (*ibid* at 211–12). See also the text of Treaties 9, 10 and 11 at http://www.aadnc-aandc.gc.ca/eng/1370373165583/1370373202340.

the First Nations' way of life would not be affected did not make their way into the written text; however, the text was clear on the surrender of land and extinguishment of rights.[65]

The Dene interpretation of Treaties 8 and 11 is based on oral history from their Elders, not on the written text. In the 1973 *Paulette* case, Elders who were present at the time the treaties were made testified that they never intended to surrender the land, only to share it. Justice Morrow of the Supreme Court of the Northwest Territories found that there was sufficient doubt as to whether Aboriginal title had been extinguished to justify the filing of a caveat on certain lands.[66] Not long after, the federal government decided to negotiate modern treaties in the Northwest Territories, and modern treaties now cover some of the same land covered by Treaties 8 and 11.

How can we assess whether these historic treaties were successful? From a negotiator's perspective, a negotiated agreement is not successful if the parties leave with differing understandings of what has been agreed to. It is also problematic if the written text does not include all of the key terms of the agreement, as this will make it harder to implement the agreement, as well as to establish the precise terms of the agreement after the fact. Finally, an agreement is unlikely to be successful in the long term if it does not appear to address the key underlying interests of both parties. All three concerns (lack of success indicators) are present with the historic treaties.

For example, the written texts of these historic treaties do not appear to meet what the treaty elders say were their key objectives: continuation of their way of life, peaceful coexistence and mutual sharing, mutual respect, recognition, protection from starvation, and tools to adapt to the new realities resulting from the influx of newcomers.[67]

---

65 See Fumoleau, *supra* note 47 at 79–80, where an interpreter for the "Chipewyans" states that the treaty he read to the Indians did not say anything about regulating hunting, but the copy later sent back to them included a new clause regarding obeying hunting regulations. Also, a witness to the 1921 signing of Treaty 11 testified in a court proceeding, "There was a 3-day meeting but, as far as I know, the land and the country never was sold or surrendered to the white man" (*ibid* at 448).

66 See Government of the Northwest Territories, *Aboriginal Peoples and the Crown – A Changing Relationship*, page 6, http://caid.ca/NWTAboSelGovBk1.pdf

67 See Harold Cardinal and Walter Hildebrandt, *Treaty Elders of Saskatchewan: Our Dream Is that Our Peoples Will One Day Be Clearly Recognized as Nations* (Calgary: University of Calgary Press, 2000) at 25–47.

If these were in fact the underlying interests and objectives of the Indigenous parties, it seems unlikely that they would have agreed to the terms of the treaties as set out in the written text of the agreement unless they did so under duress. There were arguably aspects of duress, given that many Indigenous peoples were dealing with starvation, disease, diminishing populations, settler pressures for land, and loss of their way of life at the time that these treaties were being negotiated. However, many of the stories passed on from those present at the time the treaties were negotiated to current Elders indicate that the leaders negotiating on behalf of the Indigenous people were skilled negotiators who would not have agreed to a bad bargain. This oral evidence also indicates that it would have been inconceivable for the Indigenous leaders at the time to have surrendered title to their traditional territories, as this concept did not exist – under their own laws, they could only share the land.[68]

Historian J.R. Miller, describing the clause in Treaty 4 that surrendered and extinguished all Aboriginal rights to land, states that "it is doubtful the oral version of the agreement had such a sweeping provision."[69] An alternative explanation, which has been consistently related by the Elders, is that the written text of the treaty does not represent what the Indigenous leaders thought they were agreeing to, and that the true agreement includes the oral representations made to them. Anthropologist Michael Asch concludes that the description of Treaty 4 as recounted by Indigenous people provides a more accurate reflection of the agreement than the written text of the treaty.[70] Arguing from first principles, Michael Coyle points out elsewhere in this book that based on the shared assumptions that must be taken to have informed the making of historical treaties, historic treaties should not be interpreted in such a way as to render them an improvident arrangement for either side.

According to the treaty Elders, who are remarkably consistent in their accounts of the numbered treaty negotiations that were passed down to them by their Elders, the principles set out in the historic treaties are:

- mutual respect between peoples;
- a relationship of peace;

---

68 See Venne, *supra* note 7 at 192–3.
69 Miller, *supra* note 37 at 172.
70 Asch, *supra* note 61 at 96–7.

- understanding that the treaty was a sacred covenant with the other government and the Creator and all parties recognize the divine sovereignty;[71]
- recognition of First Nations' right to maintain their relationship with the Creator, including the laws given by the Creator, which include the right to self-government, the right to use the lands and resources, harvesting rights and the right to maintain their way of life;
- ongoing familial relationship – according to Indigenous traditions, entering into a treaty means entering into relationship with your treaty partner and bringing them into a relationship of kinship;
- mutual sharing of resources;
- continued right to livelihood and way of life; and
- sharing – not surrender – of land.[72]

The Elders' believe that this was what the Indigenous parties were agreeing to at the time the historic treaties were made. From a negotiator's perspective, an agreement embodying these principles, while also meeting the underlying interests of the European parties for access to land for settlement, would be a successful agreement – the normal outcome from a negotiation between two parties of roughly equal bargaining power. However, we know that at the time, the Indigenous parties did not have equal bargaining power. This would have prevented them from ensuring that the oral representations upon which they relied were ultimately included in the written texts of the treaties, and could also have caused them to agree to terms that did not meet their interests. So it is likely that there were two factors at play which disadvantaged the Indigenous parties to the historic treaties: unequal bargaining power meant that the treaties were a "bad deal" from the perspective of the Indigenous parties, and the treaty texts did not include the oral understandings, and so did not reflect the "real deal" that

71 Regarding the smoking of the pipe to conclude the treaty, Venne states, "It was more than a pipe ceremony: it was a solemn undertaking by both sides before the Creator that this agreement would last into the future. Often, the Elders speak of a third party at the negotiations. They are speaking of the Creator, who was a witness to the process" (Venne, *supra* note 7 at 168).

72 Cardinal and Hildebrandt, *supra* note 67 at 25–38. See also Venne, *supra* note 7, regarding Treaty 6.

the Indigenous parties thought they were agreeing to.[73] Compounding these disadvantages was the failure of government to fully implement even the meagre provisions of the written treaty text.

The principles, which the treaty Elders believe underlie the historic treaties, are significant for several reasons. First, they help to explain why the Indigenous parties would have signed these treaties in the first place. The principles also shed light on why many First Nations who are signatories to historic treaties continue to be proud of those treaties – because they understand the treaty based not on the narrow wording of the written text but on the information passed down to their Elders, including their ancestors' views of what was included in the treaty and the relationship established by the treaty. Finally, the principles are significant because they are consistent with the principles set out in the Royal Proclamation and Treaty of Niagara (negotiated in the first period) and the principles set out in modern treaties (negotiated during the third period). They provide insight into what the Indigenous parties' underlying interests were when the treaties were made and what might be required to accommodate those interests.

C. *Modern Treaties (1973 to Present)*

Modern treaties were negotiated in the post-*Calder* period of improved First Nation bargaining power. The very first modern treaty, the 1975 James Bay and Northern Quebec Agreement, was negotiated because the government wanted to build the massive James Bay hydroelectric project. The James Bay Cree actively resisted this by seeking a court injunction to stop the development, eventually forcing the government to the negotiating table. The treaty provided $225 million in compensation to the James Bay Cree and the Inuit of Northern Quebec, defined land rights and harvesting rights, and established new local First Nation governments as well as joint consultative bodies with First Nation and government officials to advise on environmental and resource management issues.[74]

---

73 For an excellent and succinct analysis of historic treaties and whether they reflect the real deal, a fair deal, or no deal, see Nancy Kleer and Judith Rae, "Divided We Fall: Tsilhqot'in and the Historic Treaties," 11 July 2014, Olthuis Kleer Townshend – LLP [Blog], at http://www.oktlaw.com/blog/divided-we-fall-tsilhqotin-and-the-historic-treaties/.

74 For more details, see the Makivik Corporation website at http://www.makivik.org/history/jbnqa/; also *Quebec (Attorney General) v Moses*, [2010] 1 SCR 557.

The James Bay Treaty has been one of the most litigated modern treaties.[75] It was negotiated quickly as a result of hydroelectric development pressures and, as the first modern treaty, it did not have the benefit of precedents. The James Bay Treaty has been amended more than twenty times to address implementation issues, to resolve differences of interpretation, and to provide for further hydroelectric developments.[76]

The Nunavut Land Claims Agreement covers the largest land mass of any modern treaty. It is unique in that it uses a public governance model and resulted in the 1999 creation of a new territory, Nunavut, from land formerly in the Northwest Territories. In Nunavut, which has a land mass of 1.9 million square kilometres, the Inuit represent 86 per cent of the total population of about 32,000 people.[77] Under the agreement, the Inuit exchange Aboriginal title to all their traditional land in the Nunavut Settlement Area for rights and benefits, including:

- ownership of about 18 per cent of the land in Nunavut, including mineral rights to 2 per cent of these lands;
- the creation of the territory of Nunavut, with an elected government to represent the interests of all Nunavut residents, while respecting Inuit values;
- capital transfer payments of $1.148 billion over 14 years and a $13 million Training Trust Fund for the establishment of the Government of Nunavut;
- equal representation of Inuit and government representatives on wildlife management, resource management and environmental boards, allowing for joint management and planning;
- harvesting rights throughout the Nunavut Settlement Area;

---

75 In addition to litigation, the James Bay Cree also fought a public relations campaign against another proposed hydro megaproject, the Great Whale project, and were successful in turning public opinion in the northeastern United States against the project. This caused the Quebec government to ultimately abandon the project. See Miller, *supra* note 37 at 281–2.

76 Isaac, *supra* note 39 at 174.

77 Statistics Canada, *National Household Survey, 2011*, "Table 2: Number and distribution of the population reporting an Aboriginal identity and percentage of Aboriginal people in the population, Canada, provinces and territories," http://www12.statcan.gc.ca/nhs-enm/2011/as-sa/99-011-x/2011001/tbl/tbl02-eng.cfm [Statistics Canada, 2011 Census Table 2]; Statistics Canada, "Focus on Geography Series, 2011 Census," http://www12.statcan.gc.ca/census-recensement/2011/as-sa/fogs-spg/Facts-pr-eng.cfm?Lang=eng&GC=62.

- a share of federal government royalties from oil, gas, and mineral development on Crown lands;
- the right to negotiate with industry for economic and social benefits from the development of non-renewable resources on Inuit Owned Lands;
- the right of first refusal on the sporting use or commercial development of renewable resources in the Nunavut Settlement Area; and
- the creation of three federally funded national parks.[78]

By creating Nunavut from the eastern part of the North West Territories, the Inuit found an imaginative solution to address their desire for control over a separate territory. The public government model fits within the existing constitutional structure, while relying on the majority Inuit population to maintain links to Inuit culture and traditions in governance.

One of the primary goals of modern treaties from the government's perspective is clarity about rights to lands and resources in order to facilitate investment and economic development. This can be achieved by defining categories of land that the First Nation "owns," as well as other lands within its traditional territory where hunting and fishing rights may be exercised. From a First Nation perspective, self-government, economic development, and a relationship of mutual respect are critical objectives. Some modern treaties include self-government agreements, while others deal only with land-related issues. The Nisga'a Final Agreement, involving the First Nation which brought the 1973 *Calder* case to the Supreme Court of Canada, is an example of a modern treaty encompassing both land claim and self-government provisions in a province where Indigenous people are a small percentage of the population (5.4 per cent), but may form a large percentage within their respective traditional territories.

In the Yukon, eleven modern land claim and self-government agreements have been reached.[79] These settle the majority of claims in the Yukon and bring much greater certainty for governments and resource

78 Much of this summary is taken from the Kitikmeot Inuit Association website at https://kitia.ca/node/23.

79 The Yukon negotiations began in 1973, prior to the federal government's development of its comprehensive claims policy or its policy on the inherent right to self-government. As a result, while the land claim agreements are treaties, the Yukon

development companies as to respective rights over lands and resources. The result has been greater economic development, increased prosperity for all Yukoners, and self-government for eleven out of fourteen Yukon First Nations.[80]

The Yukon agreements provide that Yukon First Nations, which make up 23 per cent of the Yukon's population,[81] receive title to a total of 44,000 square kilometres of land as Settlement Land (approximately 9 per cent of the Yukon's total land), over which they have ownership rights. The First Nations also have equal participation in a number of Yukon-wide management bodies, such as the Fish and Wildlife Management Board, the Land Use Planning Council, and the Heritage Resources Board. Yukon First Nation members retain hunting and fishing rights over the rest of the Yukon within their traditional territories other than on privately owned land.[82] The agreements also provide for compensation of $260 million; the creation of several large special management areas, which are protected from development; forestry harvesting rights; protection of cultural and heritage resources; resource revenue sharing; and economic opportunities, including training. The self-government agreements recognize traditional forms of decision-making and provide for broad self-government powers similar in scope to the powers of provinces.[83]

The Yukon agreements embody a number of important principles: the need for reconciliation, which is the understanding that collectively, all parties need to work together to reconcile their differing needs and interests and build a new kind of society; mutual consultation; recognition of co-management and reciprocity as a means to ensure that both

---

self-government agreements are separate agreements that do not have the status of section 35 constitutionally protected treaties, although they have been given the force of law through legislation and prevail over other legislation.

80 Three Yukon First Nations have not reached modern land claim settlements, despite years of negotiations. These are the White River First Nation, Ross River Dena Council, and the Liard First Nation.

81 Based on Statistics Canada, 2011 Census Table 2, *supra* note 77.

82 *Umbrella Final Agreement*, signed 29 May 1993 (Ottawa: Ministry of Supply and Services, 1993) at sections 6.2.1 and 16.4.2.

83 For more details on the Yukon agreements, including the benefits to all Yukoners arising from the agreements, see Julie Jai, "The Interpretation of Modern Treaties and the Honour of the Crown: Why Modern Treaties Deserve Judicial Deference" (2009) 26 *National Journal of Constitutional Law* 25.

First Nation and non-First Nation perspectives are considered; conservation; sustainable development; respect for all living things; the interdependency of all things; and the spiritual and economic relationship of Indigenous people with the land, reflecting a holistic world view. First Nation laws apply to non-First Nation people on First Nation land and vice-versa, an example of the reciprocity in the agreements. Also, cooperative arrangements have been worked out, for example between conservation officers acting to enforce Yukon and First Nation wildlife laws.

The co-management boards are tools for managing the ongoing relationships and provide a forum to encourage dialogue as a foundation for ongoing reconciliation. The agreements recognize and respect a government-to-government relationship, and recognize the right to self-government and the right of First Nations to govern themselves according to Indigenous values, culture, traditions and laws.

The process for implementing the agreements allows the First Nations gradually to draw on self-government powers as they build capacity, and recognizes that First Nation societies are not frozen in time: their political institutions, economic and cultural activities may change over time, just as the institutions and practices in non-Indigenous societies change. First Nation societies are distinct and the treaties recognize that this Indigenous difference is a valuable thing that should be protected and preserved, not assimilated. Finally, the agreements provide that Yukon First Nation citizens have a right to similar levels of public services as other Yukoners at similar levels of taxation.[84]

The process and timing of the negotiation of modern treaties meant that these agreements, unlike historic treaties, were written down in detail, drafted, and carefully reviewed by counsel and negotiators for all parties, and therefore are much less likely to give rise to vastly differing views of what was agreed. Modern treaties must also be ratified by a majority, sometimes a two-thirds majority, of community members, which generally follows a long period of community consultation and engagement. This helps to increase the acceptance and legitimacy of the treaty, and reduces the risks of subsequent misunderstandings or repudiation of the treaty. Unlike historic treaties, modern treaties contain

---

84 Much of this text describing the Yukon and Nisga'a agreements is taken from Julie Jai, "The Journey of Reconciliation: Understanding our Treaty Past, Present and Future" (January 2014), Caledon Institute of Social Policy, http://www.caledoninst.org/Publications/Detail/?ID=1032&IsBack=0.

amending provisions and recognize the need for ongoing discussion and dialogue in a rapidly changing world. As one of the parties stated, "[T]he Nunavut Land Claims Agreement will be a living document. It will grow with time. It is a foundation on which Inuit can build their future."[85]

There are still, of course, disagreements relating to whether the Crown is adequately implementing the terms of modern treaties, some of which are currently being litigated or discussed before dispute resolution tribunals.[86] There are also some who argue that modern treaties create First Nation bureaucracies that mirror government bureaucracies and force Indigenous people to frame issues using the language and conceptual frameworks of Euro-Canadian society, thereby undermining their own culture.[87] Some members and leaders of First Nations with historic treaties argue that modern treaties are actually worse than historic treaties because they clearly state that the First Nation surrenders Aboriginal title to the land, whereas it is arguable that historic treaties, despite their written text, were intended to share rather than surrender land. While I acknowledge these concerns, from a negotiator's perspective, it appears that modern treaties have been much more successful than historic treaties in three significant ways. First, once the treaty has been concluded, all parties have a similar understanding of what has been agreed to. Second, the written text accurately reflects all the key terms of the agreement. Third, the substantive content of the treaty provides benefits that come closer to meeting the underlying interests of both the Indigenous and non-Indigenous parties to the

---

85 From *A Plain Language Guide to the Nunavut Land Claims Agreement,* prepared by the Nunavut Tunngavik Inc., http://www.tunngavik.com/documents/publications/2004-00-00-A-Plain-Language-Guide-to-the-Nunavut-Land-Claims-Agreement-English.pdf.

86 The Land Claims Agreement Coalition brings together all First Nations with modern treaties. It has identified a number of implementation issues, which have been echoed in Senate reports. See the Land Claims Agreement Coalition website at http://www.landclaimscoalition.ca/implementation-issues/, and Standing Senate Committee on Aboriginal Peoples, *Interim Report on the Special Study on the Implementation of Comprehensive Land Claims Agreements in Canada: Honouring the Spirit of Modern Treaties: Closing the Loopholes* (May 2008) (Chair: Honourable Gerry St. Germain, PC), http://www.parl.gc.ca/Content/SEN/Committee/392/abor/rep/rep05may08-e.pdf.

87 See, in particular, Paul Nadasdy, *Hunters and Bureaucrats: Power, Knowledge and Aboriginal-State Relations in the Southwest Yukon* (Vancouver: UBC Press, 2003) at 7–8, 263.

agreement. Finally, on a practical level, studies show that community well-being is better for those who are governed by modern rather than historic treaties.[88]

In the previous section, I discussed the principles underlying historic treaties from the perspective of the treaty Elders, who say that the historic treaties represent a sacred commitment to a relationship of equality and mutual respect among nations. Chief Joseph Gosnell, describing the modern Nisga'a treaty, states, "To us, a treaty is a sacred instrument. It represents an understanding between distinct cultures and shows respect for each other's way of life. We know we are here for a long time together."[89] He could have been describing a historic treaty from the second period, or a peace and friendship treaty made in the first period. From the Indigenous perspective, the underlying objectives and principles for treaty-making have remained the same over the last four centuries.

While modern treaties are hundreds of pages long, go into far more detail than the historic treaties or the Royal Proclamation, and are negotiated over years rather than days, they are based on very similar underlying principles. The following principles from modern treaties are entirely consistent with the principles underlying the early peace and friendship treaties and the Royal Proclamation in the first period, and are also consistent with the elders' views of the principles underlying the land cession treaties of the second period:

- a government-to-government relationship of mutual respect;
- recognition of treaties as a solemn covenant between governments;
- sharing of lands and resources, with specific rules to clarify the parties' respective rights in order to facilitate mutual coexistence;

88 See Joseph Quesnell, "All Treaties Aren't Created Equal," *Winnipeg Sun*, 4 July 2014, http://www.winnipegsun.com/2014/07/04/all-treaties-arent-created-equal, and AANDC Strategic Research Directorate, *Community Well-Being and Treaties*, available http://www.aadnc-aandc.gc.ca/DAM/DAM-INTER-HQ-AI/STAGING/texte-text/rs_re_pubs_cwb-treaties_PDF_1358355905129_eng.pdf. See also C.D. Howe Institute Report, "The Effect of First Nations Modern Treaties on Local Income," 28 October 2015, https://www.cdhowe.org/sites/default/files/attachments/research_papers/mixed/e-brief_218_0.pdf, in which author Fernando M. Aragón demonstrates that real income in First Nation communities with modern treaties has increased by 17 per cent compared to communities without modern treaties.

89 Chief Joseph Gosnell on the Nisga'a Treaty, quoted in Joseph Gosnell, "Speech to the British Columbia Legislature, December 2, 1998," (1998) 120 *BC Studies* 5 at 9.

- recognition and protection for the Indigenous way of life, including the relationship with the land;
- tools to facilitate economic development and employment by Indigenous people;
- right to self-government within certain parameters;
- co-management and consultation on matters affecting the other party;
- the treaty is not frozen in time. It is a relationship which must be nurtured, reviewed and revisited (like the polishing of the Covenant Chain,[90] or the annual meetings and ceremonies which were used to renew historic treaties). However, the degree to which a treaty is open to change varies depending on one's perspective. It is still the case that governments seek certainty and perceive the treaties as "full and final settlements" whereas the Indigenous parties see the treaties as the basis for ongoing good relationships, the details of which may evolve over time.

While there are similar principles underlying both historic and modern treaties (at least from the perspective of the Indigenous parties), modern treaties differ from historic treaties by more clearly reflecting these principles in their written text, and giving them life through specific mechanisms.

4. Borrowing Principles and Mechanisms from Modern Treaties to Reinvigorate Historic Treaties

As demonstrated in the previous section, the principles underlying treaties from the Indigenous perspective have been consistent over the three periods of Indigenous–Crown relationships. However, the modern treaties have been much more successful in establishing treaty relationships in at least three ways: (1) ensuring that all parties have a

90 The Covenant Chain was a military, political, social, and economic alliance between the British and the Iroquois Confederacy, founded on the Treaty of Albany. While it was intended as a permanent alliance, "it was expected that the nations would regularly renew their respective undertakings. This process of renewal – which was often described as 'polishing the chain' – was designed to remind the parties of the solemn compact that they had entered into." From Borrows and Rotman, *supra* note 38 at 16–17.

common understanding as to what was agreed to; (2) setting out the whole agreement in the written text; and (3) providing substantive benefits which meet both parties' key interests. These modern agreements were negotiated during the third period when Indigenous parties had greater leverage, as well as the benefits of speaking the same language, having the assistance of legal counsel and time to involve, consult with, and win the support of their communities for the treaty. Modern treaties provide better substantive benefits, have more legitimacy, and come about through a fairer, more balanced process than historic treaties. The result is a much fairer agreement for all parties.

A major challenge for governments and First Nations today is to reinvigorate historic treaties and find ways to implement them with respect to their spirit and intent, moving away from the rigid and literal interpretation of the text – like the $5 annuities that have never been adjusted for inflation – to a principled discussion of how the treaty can form the basis of a contemporary relationship of mutual respect and coexistence. I propose applying principles from modern treaties to establish a principled basis for reinterpreting historic treaties. This section examines three principles drawn from modern treaties and specific mechanisms to implement them that could be applied to assist in the renewal of historic treaties.

A. PRINCIPLE: Treaties Provide a Framework for an Ongoing Relationship of Mutual Respect and Mutual Benefit[91]

Modern treaties contain clauses which recognize that the treaty is not just a static agreement but a framework for maintaining relationships of mutual respect and mutual benefit on an ongoing basis. To meet this objective, modern treaties have mechanisms for fostering ongoing relationships of cooperation and communication, such as co-management bodies, where representatives of the parties meet to jointly manage resources and make decisions about issues such as harvesting, land use planning, or protection of historical sites.

91 Aaron Mills outlines his vision of treaties as a framework for relationships in chap. 8 of this book. Michael Coyle, in chap. 2 of this book, concludes that the shared assumptions that would have informed treaty-making have led to the principle that historic treaties should not be interpreted in such a way as to make them an improvident arrangement for either side.

MODERN TREATY MECHANISM

An example of a successful co-management or public government body set up under a modern treaty is the Nunavut Impact Review Board. The Nunavut Impact Review Board consists of four members appointed by Inuit organizations, two members appointed by the federal government, two members appointed by the Nunavut government, and a chair appointed by the federal government from nominations provided by the board. The board makes recommendations and decisions about which development proposals may proceed.[92]

Looking back, historic treaties also contained mechanisms to support an ongoing relationship, such as annual exchanges of gifts, meetings and ceremonies, and the exchange and display of symbols such as the Two Row Wampum. These all illustrate that treaties, both modern and historic, were intended to create an ongoing relationship of cooperation and communication, which requires regular meetings, discussions, and other activities to address issues that arise.

The provisions that establish co-management bodies illustrate that a treaty can be both an agreement intended to define and clarify rights, as well as a means of creating ongoing mechanisms for harmonious relationships. The government's need for "certainty" as to respective rights and responsibilities does not mean that modern treaties do not anticipate the need for ongoing dialogue to deal with change. Modern treaties are relationship-building instruments as well as rights-defining instruments. They include amendment provisions and review provisions. Historic treaties were also intended to build relationships as well as define rights, and broadly worded commitments provided flexibility to respond to changing circumstances.[93] Treaties can define rights while

---

92 See the board's website at http://www.nirb.ca/mandate-and-mission.

93 For example, Treaty 6 provides "that in the event hereafter of the Indians comprised within this treaty being overtaken by any pestilence, or by a general famine, the Queen, on being satisfied and certified thereof by Her Indian Agent or Agents, will grant to the Indians assistance of such character and to such extent as Her Chief Superintendent of Indian Affairs shall deem necessary and sufficient to relieve the Indians from the calamity that shall have befallen them." "Treaty Texts – Treaty No. 6," Indigenous and Northern Affairs Canada, https://www.aadnc-aandc.gc.ca/eng/1100100028710/1100100028783.

also providing a framework for ongoing dialogue and evolution. In the same way, the solemnity of historic agreements can be respected, while also recognizing that they were intended to evolve through dialogue over time, relying on the Crown's duty to behave with honour.

APPLICATION TO HISTORIC TREATIES

This approach of co-management or cooperative management could be applied to wildlife management in the traditional territories of First Nations with historic treaties. A standing committee or board with joint First Nation–Crown representation could provide a ready mechanism for mediating, advising, or making decisions (depending on its mandate) on activities affecting First Nation harvesting rights in its traditional territory. This would also be consistent with the evolving jurisprudence that imposes a duty to consult on governments when Aboriginal or treaty rights could be affected by an activity. From a government perspective, it provides a legitimate mechanism for such consultation as part of its normal way of operating, creating greater predictability and stability.

MODERN TREATY MECHANISM

Another mechanism from modern treaties that reflects the principle of mutual respect and mutual benefit is the requirement for an impact benefit agreement (IBA) in the Labrador Innu Agreement in Principle for any major projects on Labrador Innu lands.[94] This respects Innu rights and recognizes that development should benefit both treaty partners. This IBA requirement also reflects what is happening on the ground as a result of the Supreme Court of Canada's jurisprudence on the duty to consult[95] – private sector project proponents now routinely negotiate IBA's with First Nations as part of their consultation process. In the current legal environment, it would not be unreasonable to read a requirement for impact benefit agreements into historic treaties.

94 See chapter 21, Part 21.5 of the Labrador Innu Land Claims Agreement-in-Principle, available at http://www.aadnc-aandc.gc.ca/eng/1331657507074/1331657630719#chp21.

95 *Haida Nation*, *supra* note 26, *Mikisew Cree*, *supra* note 27.

B. PRINCIPLE: Fair Dealing – the Crown Should Behave Honourably and Not Disadvantage a First Nation Because of When They Signed Their Treaty

Why should some First Nations, who signed treaties in bad times when they had neither bargaining power nor the benefit of lawyers, professional negotiators, and more favourable jurisprudence, have less favourable treaty terms than those who signed in more propitious times? The honour of the Crown requires fair dealing. Arguably, First Nations who signed historic treaties should have the benefit of provisions negotiated more recently by First Nations who were able to understand the agreements they were signing, and who had the benefit of more equal bargaining power. This approach reflects the principle and obligation of fair dealing and can be supported on both policy and legal grounds. Applying it would be an example of the Crown behaving honourably towards First Nations.

MODERN TREATY MECHANISM

Yukon self-government agreements contain what is called a "most favoured nation clause" stating that if in a future negotiation, another First Nation gets a better deal, First Nations who have already signed off on their agreements can open up their agreements and get the benefit of this more favourable provision. The Council for Yukon First Nations pushed for this early on in the negotiations because it did not trust Canada to be fair and because its members were concerned that earlier-signing First Nations might be shortchanged.[96] This type of provision has also been used in international trade negotiations and even between the Yukon and Canada in respect of devolution agreements.[97]

---

96 Dave Joe, legal counsel for the Council for Yukon First Nations, email discussion with the author, 30 September 2013.

97 When the Yukon government found out that the Northwest Territories had just negotiated a more favourable resource revenue-sharing deal with the federal government in its devolution agreement, it successfully pushed the federal government to amend its agreement from a decade earlier to provide the same deal. An agreement was signed between the Yukon government and the Government of Canada on 21 August 2012, amending the original Yukon Northern Affairs Program Devolution Transfer Agreement of 29 October 2001 to revise the global resource revenue formula to provide the benefits negotiated by the Northwest Territories.

Interestingly, the concept was also applied to historic treaties dating back to the 1870s, as the signing of Treaty 3 forced the government to revise the terms of Treaties 1 and 2 to provide the same benefits.[98] This clause reflects the honour of the Crown: it is not fair to disadvantage earlier parties who reached an agreement with the Crown.

APPLICATION TO HISTORIC TREATIES

In Ontario, the 1923 Williams Treaty was an anomaly in that, unlike other historic treaties, it included the surrender of harvesting rights for the Indigenous signatories in their traditional territories. The Supreme Court of Canada in 1994 confirmed that the seven Williams Treaty First Nations lost their right to fish for food, as well as to hunt or trap.[99] In response, the Ontario government made efforts to redress this inequity and developed Aboriginal Communal Fishing Licenses in conjunction with the federal government, with the goal of providing the Williams Treaty First Nations with the same harvesting rights as other Ontario First Nations. The licensing regime required the First Nation to provide a conservation framework for their community's harvest – thereby involving the First Nation in meeting the province's conservation goals, while also involving them in regulating their harvest.[100] This is an illustration of how an approach of fair dealing has been applied to help remedy a deficiency in a historic treaty. It adopts a most favoured nation type of approach by looking back to previous historic treaties that retained harvesting rights, and by looking forward to provisions in modern treaties in which conservation goals are managed alongside increased Indigenous involvement and control.

---

98 Wayne E. Daugherty, "Treaty Research Report - Treaty Three (1873)" (1986) , at Indigenous and Northern Affairs Canada, http://www.aadnc-aandc.gc.ca/eng/1100100028671/1100100028673. See also Morris, *supra* note 48 at 126–7, where he notes changes that were made to Treaties 1 and 2 to include items promised verbally, as well as an offer to increase the annuities from $3 to $5, which is the amount provided in Treaty 3.

99 *R v Howard*, [1994] 2 SCR 299.

100 Isaac, *supra* note 39 at 160. The Aboriginal Communal Fishing License regime was cancelled soon after the Conservative government led by Premier Mike Harris was elected in 1995. Litigation initiated by the Williams Treaty First Nations against the federal and Ontario governments is currently underway in the federal court system.

The most favoured nation approach reinforces the view that a treaty is not an immutable instrument carved in stone, but a living document which can be amended to take into account subsequent improvements. A treaty renewal process would enable First Nations to articulate their view of what was originally agreed and negotiate amendments to bring the treaty terms more in line with their understanding of the agreement, including oral representations. Not all modern treaties contain a "most favoured nation" clause, but all modern treaties contain amendment provisions enabling the treaty to be reviewed and modified based on the agreement of the parties. Amending clauses should be read into historic treaties and the Crown should be required to deal honourably with First Nations in amending these treaties.

C. PRINCIPLE: *Treaties Should Include a Fair Process for Resolving Disputes*

Treaties can be viewed as negotiated agreements to resolve disputes, including those that may arise in the future. In chapter 2 of this book, Michael Coyle concludes that both parties to a treaty would have wanted to cooperate to ensure that there would be effective recourse should disputes arise as to what had been agreed or what actions would be required to comply with the spirit of the treaty relationship. Both historic and modern treaties are expected to last forever, and therefore, it is to be expected that disputes will arise. The critical issue is what processes will be engaged to resolve these disputes, and to what extent will they involve both treaty partners.

MODERN TREATY MECHANISMS

In all modern treaties, a mutually agreed-upon process has been established whereby disputes are mediated or arbitrated by a body that is jointly selected by First Nations and government, and whose members have an understanding of First Nation cultural values. For example, under the Yukon Final Agreements, the Dispute Resolution Board consists of three people jointly appointed by the government and by Yukon First Nations. The Inuvialuit Arbitration Board, which arbitrates disputes between the Inuvialuit and the governments of Canada, the Northwest Territories, or Yukon, as well as between the Inuvialuit and industry, consists of members appointed by the government, by the Inuvialuit and by industry, with a neutral chair acceptable to all parties.

APPLICATION TO HISTORIC TREATIES

The concept of a specialized dispute resolution body, whose members are jointly selected by the Indigenous and government parties to resolve disputes that arise with respect to modern treaties also has relevance for historic treaties. First Nations have long complained that they have had to use processes established by one party (e.g., the Specific Claims Process established by the federal government) or processes based on one party's legal system (the courts) to challenge the interpretation or implementation of historic treaties. The example set out in modern treaties, of a jointly appointed, specialized dispute resolution body could be applied to historic treaties to establish a more neutral body to resolve disputes where negotiations do not succeed.

Many commentators, including the Royal Commission on Aboriginal Peoples, have argued that a specialized treaty tribunal should be established to help resolve issues relating to historic treaties. Such a body could encourage negotiations between the parties, bring the historic treaty rights into a modern form that recognizes the ongoing treaty relationship and the need for static provisions to evolve, and more accurately reflect the spirit and intent of the treaty.

The Supreme Court of Canada's jurisprudence on the duty to consult reinforces the view that treaties involve ongoing processes that require an ongoing reconciliation of Indigenous and Crown sovereignties.[101] The Supreme Court of Canada's decision in *Beckman* makes it clear that this ongoing process applies to modern treaties as well as to historic ones. This duty to consult jurisprudence mandates dialogue between the treaty partners to resolve conflicts and provides judicial support for the view that treaties create ongoing relationships and are not just static contracts.

MODERN TREATY MECHANISMS

Treaties can be challenged by third parties and provisions may be found to be invalid. Modern treaties usually contain a provision to deal with this possibility, providing that if one treaty provision is found to be invalid, the parties will work together to amend the agreement and replace the invalid provision.[102] This provision clarifies that one invalid provision will not void the entire treaty and commits both parties to

101 See *Mikisew Cree*, *supra* note 27.

102 See, for example, clause 2.8.3 of the Teslin Tlingit Council Final Agreement, at https://www.aadnc-aandc.gc.ca/eng/1297212747034/1297212802068#chp2.

work together to amend the treaty. This provision could be read into historic treaties so that the entire treaty will not be voided by a finding that one clause is invalid, for example, because there was no *consensus ad idem*. This would encourage the parties to work together to revise treaty provisions that are of questionable legal validity.

5. Conclusion: Breathing Life into Historic Treaties – Fulfilling the Honour of the Crown

The honour of the Crown also infuses the processes of treaty-making and treaty interpretation.[103]

A review of the history of treaties and treaty-making in Canada makes clear the extent to which First Nations have borne the burden of dramatic changes in the political, demographic, and economic environment. While the relationship sought by First Nations over time has remained founded on consistent principles, the capacity to recognize and implement such principles was unrealized until recently. The burden has been particularly heavy for those First Nation parties to historic treaties that faced the hostile treaty-making environment of the nineteenth and early twentieth centuries.

In my view, it is now recognized that the text of historic treaties does not accurately reflect the understandings of both treaty parties, and these treaties are not being implemented fairly.[104] Based on their written text, many historic treaties were a bad deal for the Indigenous parties, and the written text did not reflect the actual agreement which had been orally agreed to. There have been many calls to review the historic treaties, to look at their spirit and intent from the Indigenous perspective and to reinvigorate them in a way which fulfils their promise as agreements intended to facilitate mutual respect and coexistence.

---

103 *Haida Nation*, *supra* note 26 at para 19.

104 For example, many provisions of historic treaties have not being implemented fairly. None of the dollar amounts have been adjusted for inflation, and promises of education have not resulted in equal amounts of funding for schools on reserve as compared with their off-reserve counterparts. Even following a strict literal interpretation of the texts, there have been delays and issues with respect to the creation of some promised reserves. A striking example of a delay in creating a promised reserve is the situation of the Lubicon Lake Cree, described in Asch, *supra* note 61 at 148–9.

In this treaty-renewal process, evidence of the oral commitments made at the time should be considered, including oral history evidence from Indigenous Elders. In addition, key principles from modern treaties should be used to breathe life into historic treaties, and in this way, fulfil the honour of the Crown.

As a negotiator struck by the disparities in treaties negotiated at different times, I have suggested several mechanisms used in modern treaties that could be applied to invigorate historic treaties. Each of these mechanisms is founded on an important underlying principle that has proven durable over time and resulted in positive treaty negotiation outcomes. These principles – that treaties provide a framework for a relationship of mutual benefit and respect; that the Crown should behave honourably and deal fairly with First Nations; and that treaties create ongoing relationships that require jointly agreed-upon dispute resolution mechanisms – find support in other chapters of this book as well as in the jurisprudence of the Supreme Court of Canada. These principles have been implemented through specific mechanisms in modern treaties that could also be applied to historic treaties.

The first mechanism, the creation of co-management bodies, embodies a key principle: the commitment to an ongoing relationship of mutual respect and mutual benefit. A co-management body with members jointly selected by the parties creates an ongoing forum for dialogue, education, and the opportunity to see issues from multiple perspectives. It requires representatives of all parties to sit down together, listen to each other's views, and come to a decision, ideally by consensus. It does not privilege one party's views over another's. The ongoing mandate of such bodies, whether to manage wildlife resources or socio-economic and environmental issues, recognizes that the need for discussion and relationship building never ends.

The second mechanism discussed, the negotiation of impact benefit agreements, flows from the same principle as the co-management mechanism, that is, that treaties are intended to create an ongoing relationship of mutual respect and mutual benefit.

The third mechanism discussed, the most favoured nation approach, flows from the duty of the Crown to behave honourably in its dealings with Indigenous people. Applying this approach would give all First Nations access to the most favourable provisions negotiated in other treaties, often the more recent treaties. The principle underlying this mechanism is one of relative parity and fair dealing – to the extent practical, all First Nations should receive the same treatment, regardless of when they negotiated their treaty. This principle is consistent with upholding the honour of the Crown: it would not be fair for the Crown to take advantage of the adverse circumstances of the nineteenth century to hold First Nations to the written text (which does not reflect the whole agreement) of historic treaties signed during those difficult times. A shared government–First Nation objective of moving towards greater parity and fairness could result in benefits not just to the affected First Nation but to society at large, creating social license for developments which hitherto have been stalled.

The fourth mechanism discussed is the creation of dispute resolution processes within the modern treaties themselves. These dispute resolution processes recognize that in any relationship, disputes will arise and that a fair process for resolving disputes should be jointly agreed upon in advance in order to optimize the relationship. A process that is established by all parties will have greater credibility than a process imposed by one party. Thus, the dispute resolution mechanisms in modern treaties embody the principle that a fair process for resolving disputes must be a jointly agreed-upon process that treats each party as an equal partner. Unilateral government processes, and even the court system, do not meet this standard of a jointly agreed upon process. The fifth mechanism, committing both parties to work together to amend the treaty if a provision is found to be void, also reflects this principle by ensuring that when issues arise, the parties will work together to resolve them through a jointly agreed-upon process.

The principles from modern treaties are consistent with the principles set out in the peace and friendship treaties and the Royal Proclamation in the first period, which emphasized a relationship of mutual peace, friendship, equality, and respect. The modern treaties provide concrete mechanisms to accommodate both Crown and First Nation interests, giving life to the principles of committing to an ongoing relationship of mutual respect and mutual benefit; fulfilling the honour of the Crown by providing for relative parity between First Nations; and preserving the ongoing relationship by anticipating disputes and giving each party equal weight in a dispute resolution process.

These mechanisms, derived from modern treaties but stemming from timeless principles of mutual respect and fair dealing, can help in the process of renewing historic treaties and bringing about greater fairness for First Nations who negotiated treaties during the dark days when Indigenous bargaining power was at its lowest. Bad timing should not disadvantage some First Nations over others, nor would it be honourable for the Crown to take advantage of a narrow reading of bargains made in hard times.

Treaties made at times when bargaining power was more equal, both before and after the numbered treaties and other treaties allegedly ceding land were made, offer mechanisms to reinvigorate these historic treaties. Modern treaties provide a principled basis to support a new approach to the interpretation of historic treaties, one which respects the spirit and intent of the treaties and meets the Crown's obligation to act honourably. Principles from modern treaties should be read into historic treaties as implied terms based on the obligation of the Crown to act honourably and based on the oral promises which were made at the time. This is desirable as a matter of fairness and good public policy. It remains to be seen whether the law will develop in such a way as to make this a legal requirement and further work will be required to fully develop this argument. However, even under current law there is potential legal liability to the Crown for its failure to fulfil historic treaty promises, which the Supreme Court requires be given a large and liberal interpretation,[105] especially if oral promises are included. Recognizing this legal risk, the Crown should do the honourable thing and initiate a process to provide for the fair interpretation and implementation of historic treaties. This would not be without precedent. The federal government proactively developed its 1973 comprehensive land claims negotiation policy after the *Calder* decision signalled upcoming changes in the law and authorized negotiations based on asserted rather than proven rights.[106] The Supreme Court of Canada used a similar approach in the *Haida Nation* decision by requiring consultation when an Aboriginal right is asserted rather than proven.[107] The Crown's duty to behave honourably was reinforced once again in the *Manitoba Metis Federation* decision.[108]

Finally, a jointly appointed Crown–First Nation dispute resolution body should be created to oversee the renewal of historic treaties, building on the principles and mechanisms established in modern treaties. In this way, the long overdue process of reinvigorating historic treaties can move forward, and the legal and policy imperatives for the Crown to act with honour can finally be met.

105 See *Marshall*, *supra* note 25 at 511–13.

106 *Supra* note 32.

107 *Supra* note 26 at 513.

108 *Supra* note 29.

5 Who Calls the Shots? Balancing Individual and Collective Interests in the Assertion of Aboriginal and Treaty Harvesting Rights

FRANCESCA ALLODI-ROSS

The other chapters in this book deal mainly with treaty disputes between Indigenous communities and the Crown. Treaty disputes, however, can also occur within Indigenous communities, as when the rights of the collective are in tension with the individual rights of members of the collective. This chapter considers a recent example of such a tension, the case of Behn v Moulton Contracting Ltd., and suggests how the courts might deal with this in future.

1. Introduction

In May 2013, the Supreme Court of Canada released its decision in *Behn v Moulton Contracting Ltd.*, in which it stated explicitly for the first time that Aboriginal rights, though collective in nature, may have individual aspects.[1] It wrote this in the context of considering whether an individual member of an Aboriginal band needs permission from the collective to assert a breach of a treaty harvesting right. The Court ultimately decided the case on other grounds but signalled this as an area for future development in the jurisprudence.

In this chapter, I will consider the tension between group and individual interests that arises in the context of Aboriginal and treaty rights and describe what an appropriate balance would look like in a situation like the one that arose in *Behn*. Specifically, I will argue that courts should generally require individuals wishing to assert an Aboriginal

1 2013 SCC 26 at para 33, [2013] SCJ No 26, [*Behn*].

or treaty harvesting right to seek authorization from the right-holding collective; however, when the individual has been charged with a regulatory or criminal offence or is being sued, the court should not require that person to get authorization from the collective to assert that right as a defence.

While harvesting rights are not the only rights where issues of authorization from the right-holding community have and will come up, different rules may apply to different rights. For example, requiring authorization for an assertion of the right to be consulted seems more reasonable than requiring authorization to assert a treaty right to a personal annuity.[2] Given these differences and the limited scope of this chapter, I will analyse only one type of right: harvesting rights. This is an important example, as it is one of the most heavily litigated types of rights.[3]

This chapter focuses on how courts should address the assertion of an Aboriginal or treaty right by an individual, not how communities themselves should resolve those tensions. Those are important discussions, however, and other chapters in this collection may offer guidance. Sarah Morales, for example, describes traditional Indigenous dispute resolution mechanisms that she recommends be used in the BC treaty process between Aboriginal communities and government, but that might also be a resource for communities struggling with questions about when and how to put forward their rights for consideration by Canadian courts.

Many of the chapters in this book propose radical alternative arrangements for more just relationships between settlers and Indigenous peoples. This chapter is decidedly more modest in ambition. It advocates for a small development of Aboriginal law, one that fits comfortably within the existing judicial system and political framework. In working for major social change, both types of proposals are valuable. Clarifying when a band's permission is necessary to litigate a treaty right will do

2 The Grand Council of the Crees and Cree Regional Authority, interveners in *Behn*, argued that there are three categories of rights: rights that are exclusively collective (e.g., the right to be consulted, Aboriginal title to lands and resources, and self-government), rights that are predominantly individual (e.g., treaty rights to health and education and specific individual payments), and rights that are mixed (e.g., treaty harvesting rights). The Supreme Court did not endorse this classification, but it did note it as an "interesting suggestion." *Ibid* at para 34.

3 *Ibid* at para 34.

little, if anything, to address the important systemic problems articulated by other authors in this book, such as the disregard for Indigenous legal traditions in treaty interpretation. It will, however, affect Aboriginal people trying to assert their treaty rights within the system that we currently have. There are no doubt interesting ways in which these tensions between individual and collective rights could be explored and resolved that push the boundaries of the existing Canadian legal system (e.g., using the intercultural dispute resolution processes described by Sarah Morales); however, these are beyond the scope of this chapter. This proposal recognizes that most legal assertions of Aboriginal and treaty rights originate when a person is charged with a criminal or regulatory offence, and explores the ways in which individual lives are deeply affected when that happens. Therefore, while the scope of reform imagined in this chapter is more limited than in others in the book, it shares with them an appreciation of the importance of the current realities of Indigenous life in Canada.

2. *Behn v Moulton Contracting Ltd.*

Behn began as a suit brought by a logging company, Moulton Contracting Ltd., who had been authorized by the Government of British Columbia to harvest timber on the territory of the Fort Nelson First Nation (FNFN). The logging sites were on land that was traditionally used by the Behn family of the FNFN for trapping, and they opposed the logging. Members of the family set up a camp on the road to the logging sites, preventing Moulton from accessing one of them. As a result, the company filed a tort action against eight members of the Behn family. In their defence, the Behns argued that the licences were void, because they were issued in violation of the Crown's duty to consult and because they violated the members' treaty harvesting rights. The company brought a motion to strike these two defences.

Moulton alleged, among other things, that the Behns did not have standing to argue a treaty right as a defence, because Aboriginal rights are collective and cannot be asserted by individuals on their own behalf. The trial court and the BC Court of Appeal found in favour of the logging company, and the Supreme Court upheld those decisions; however, the Supreme Court did so on the basis of the doctrine of abuse of process and did not decide on the standing issue. Nevertheless, it wrote a few paragraphs on the topic and marked it as an area for future consideration:

> The Crown argues that claims in relation to treaty rights must be brought by, or on behalf of, the Aboriginal community. This general proposition is too narrow. It is true that Aboriginal and treaty rights are collective in nature: see *R. v. Sparrow*, [1990] 1 S.C.R. 1075, at p. 1112; *Delgamuukẁ*, at para. 115; *R. v. Sundown*, [1999] 1 S.C.R. 393, at para. 36; *R. v. Marshall*, [1999] 3 S.C.R. 533, at para. 17 and 37; *R. v. Sappier*, 2006 SCC 54, [2006] 2 S.C.R. 686, at para. 31; *Beckman*, at para. 35. However, certain rights, despite being held by the Aboriginal community, are nonetheless exercised by individual members or assigned to them. These rights may therefore have both collective and individual aspects. Individual members of a community may have a vested interest in the protection of these rights. It may well be that in appropriate circumstances individual members can assert certain Aboriginal or treaty rights, as some of the interveners have proposed ...
>
> [D]espite the critical importance of the collective aspect of Aboriginal and treaty rights, rights may sometimes be assigned to or exercised by individual members of Aboriginal communities, and entitlements may sometimes be created in their favour. In a broad sense, it could be said that these rights might belong to them or that they have an individual aspect regardless of their collective nature. Nothing more need be said at this time.[4]

3. Tensions between Individual and Collective Rights

Behn brings to light tensions that can arise within Aboriginal communities regarding treaty and Aboriginal rights. In *Behn*, Moulton sued eight members of a community, who then sought to assert their individual rights to, among other things, make full answer and defence by invoking a collective treaty right to hunt. The Behns' decision to do so invited the Supreme Court to consider that right, and the FNFN could have been impacted by the Court's decision. Should the Court have allowed the Behns to argue, without explicit permission from the FNFN, that their treaty right had been violated? Or should it have forbidden this in favour of the FNFN's right to choose how and when its collective rights might be brought before the courts, for example, through the careful selection of a test case? How should Canadian courts balance individual and collective interests in similar situations?

4 *Ibid* at paras 33, 35.

4. The SCC on Collective Rights and Collective Authorization

Given that the issue of authorization arises because courts have defined Aboriginal and treaty rights as collective in nature (no one else's permission is needed to assert individual rights), it is relevant to consider what the Supreme Court said about collective rights. As noted in the above passage, the Court has consistently characterized Aboriginal and treaty rights as being "communal" or "collective" in nature.[5] It has said that these rights are enjoyed by "Aboriginal people in common with other Aboriginal people" and that the rights belong to the group and not to any individual member.[6]

The Court has said relatively little about the *implications* of Aboriginal and treaty rights being collective. Some guidance may be taken from *R v Marshall* ("*Marshall No 2*"), where the Court found that the right to gather and trade certain goods was limited by, among other things, "the communal nature of a treaty right."[7] The Court seemed to be saying that the communal nature of a treaty right meant that communities had the authority to create rules around the exercise of treaty rights, which would limit an individual member's ability to hunt or fish as much as they wanted.

Given that the Court has suggested that Aboriginal groups can limit the individual exercise of collective rights, it would make sense that the group can decide how and when an individual raises a collective right in court. The Court has not stated this explicitly, but it has suggested as much by holding that the issue of authority to bring a claim as an individual member regarding a collective right is a question of fact or mixed fact and law.[8] The Court, however, has never required proof that

---

5 *R v Sparrow*, [1990] 1 SCR 1075, 70 DLR (4th) 385 [*Sparrow*]; *Delgamuukw v British Columbia*, [1997] SCR 1010 at para 115, 153 DLR (4th) 193; *R v Sappier; R v Gray*, 2006 SCC 43 at para 31, [2006] 2 SCR 686 [*Sappier*]; *R v Kapp*, 2008 SCC 41 at para 41, [2008] 2 SCR 483.

6 *R v Sundown*, [1999] 1 SCR 393 at paras 35–6, 170 DLR (4th) 385 [*Sundown*]; *R v Marshall*, [1999] 3 SCR 456 at paras 17, 177 DLR (4th) 513.

7 [1999] 3 SCR 533 at para 38, 179 DLR (4th) 193 [*Marshall No 2*].

8 *Oregon Jack Creek Indian Band v Canadian National Railway Co.*, [1989] 2 SCR 1069.

the collective has authorized an individual to assert an Aboriginal or treaty right as a defence in a prosecution.[9]

5. When Is Authorization Necessary?

A. The Rationale for Collective Rights

Given the lack of guidance from the courts on the issue of when authorization from the collective is needed to assert an Aboriginal or treaty right, it may be helpful to consider why the courts have defined them as collective in nature. The rationale for defining Aboriginal and treaty rights as collective is related to the purpose of section 35 of the *Constitution Act, 1982*, which the Court has stated is to "assist in ensuring the continued existence of these particular Aboriginal societies."[10] The Court claims to place great weight on the fact that Aboriginal peoples lived in organized societies before the arrival of Europeans and seems to define Aboriginal rights as collective in order to protect those societies.[11]

The logic of characterizing Aboriginal and treaty rights as collective in order to protect Aboriginal culture is supported by at least some group rights theorists. Denise Réaume posits that participatory goods, such as living in a cultured society, if they are rights, must be group rights.[12] Leighton McDonald suggests that rights to engage in Aboriginal practices are collective because of the role they play in the reproduction and development of culture, which cannot be fully captured in the language

9 *R v Sioui*, [1990] 1 SCR 1025, 70 DLR (4th) 427; *Sparrow*, *supra* note 5; *R v Badger*, [1996] 1 SCR 771, 133 DLR (4th) 324; *R v Adams*, [1996] 3 SCR 101, 138 DLR (4th) 657; *R v Côté*, [1996] 3 SCR 139, 138 DLR (4th) 385 [*Côté*]; *Sundown*, *supra* note 6; *Sappier*, *supra* note 5.

10 *Sappier*, *supra* note 5 at para 26.

11 *R v Van der Peet*, [1996] 2 SCR 507 at para 31, 137 DLR (4th) 289 [*Van der Peet*]; *Sappier*, *supra* note 5 at para 26; *Côté*, *supra* note 8 at para 67; *Mitchell v MNR*, 2001 SCC 33 at para 9, [2001] 1 SCR 911.

12 Réaume's paradigmatic examples of participatory goods are friendship and team sports, because these necessarily require other individuals. Hunting can be practised alone, and some might argue that it is not a participatory good; however, I would argue that hunting would receive protection as an Aboriginal right only if it were "integral to a distinctive culture," making it incidental to living in a cultured society and therefore a participatory good according to Réaume's schema. Denise Réaume, "Individuals, Groups, and Rights to Public Goods" (1988) 38 *University ofToronto Law Journal* 1 at 12–13.

of individual rights.[13] The right to hunt, for example, has no significance without reference to the collective; its significance comes from the role it plays in perpetuating and defining the group's culture.

Defining rights as collective may also allow the group to overcome classic problems of collective action. For example, the fact that reserve lands are collective means that Indigenous peoples have not been able to sell off parts of reserves, which benefits the band as a whole, as well as future generations.[14] In terms of harvesting rights, defining them as collective allows the community to regulate individual use (at least as suggested in *Marshall No 2*) and can prevent individuals from overharvesting, allowing the community to prioritize long-term interests such as conservation.

B. Tensions with Individual Rights

It is this emphasis on the value of collective interests described above that grounded the position taken in the *Behn* case by the Moose Cree First Nation (MCFN) on the issue of authorization. They submitted that Aboriginal and treaty harvesting rights could be asserted only with the authority of the collective, whether the individual asserting the claim is a plaintiff or a defendant.[15]

While some deference to the will of the collective in choosing whether or not its members can bring claims with respect to Aboriginal and treaty harvesting rights is appropriate, the position taken by the MCFN does not do enough to protect the interests of individual members of Aboriginal communities. A common concern in group rights discourse is that when groups are granted rights, the members of the group will have their individual rights restricted.[16] In the context of authorization,

---

13 Leighton McDonald, "Can Collective and Individual Rights Coexist?" (1998) 22 *Melbourne University Law Review* 310 at 318.

14 Will Kymlicka, *Multicultural Citizenship* (Oxford: Oxford University Press, 1996) at 43.

15 FI-MCFN, *supra* note 9 at para 24.

16 See for example Andrew Vincent, "Can Groups Be Persons?" (1989) 42:4 *Review of Metaphysics* 687 at 713–14. See also Thomas Isaac, "Individual Versus Collective Rights: Aboriginal People and the Significance of *Thomas v. Norris*" (1991) 21 *Manitoba Law Journal* 618, which discusses the case of an Aboriginal man who sued others in his community for assault, battery, and unlawful imprisonment. The defendants argued that the events were part of an initiation ceremony for spirit dancing, that this was an Aboriginal right protected by section 35, and that the common law infringed on that right by restricting their ability to engage in spirit dancing.

conflict arises when the group does not want to assert a right that an individual does. This might happen as a result of corruption (the group leadership is receiving a benefit in exchange for not asserting their right), risk aversion (the group does not want to bear the financial risk, for example, of asserting their rights in court), or simply a difference in opinion about the merit of asserting the claim (the group may prefer to exchange this right for a benefit from the government or a third party).[17]

Disputes between the group and its members may be more likely when different members of the collective enjoy the harvesting right to different extents. This was the case in *Behn* and was the basis for their challenge to Moulton's motion to strike their defences. They argued that they had a differential interest in the FNFN's treaty right to hunt as a result of the band's customary laws, which granted the Behns a trapline in the area where Moulton planned to log.[18]

C. *A Balanced Approach*

On the issue of authorization, I would advocate for an approach that was proposed by an intervener in *Behn*, the Grand Council of the Crees and Cree Regional Authority (GCCEI/CRA) and that strikes an appropriate balance between collective and individual interests.[19] The

17 For example, after the blockade at issue in *Behn*, the FNFN entered into the Economic Benefits Agreement with the British Colombia government whereby the FNFN receives certain benefits in exchange for agreeing to certain obligations. Notably, the FNFN agreed to (1) abide by certain consultation protocols, (2) that allegations of failure in the duty to consult would be addressed by way of judicial review, (3) not to support or participate in acts of individual members that interfere with conduct authorized by the Crown, and (4) not to support any legal proceeding in which an individual member of the FNFN raised a defence based on an alleged infringement of an Aboriginal or treaty right, unless that person was authorized by the FNFN to do so on behalf of the FNFN, or where the individual raised it as a defence to a charge of a regulatory or criminal offence. See "Economic Benefits Agreement," dated 8 June 2012, between British Columbia and the Fort Nelson First Nation, http://www2.gov.bc.ca/assets/gov/environment/natural-resource-stewardship/consulting-with-first-nations/agreements/eba_fort_nelson.pdf.

18 *Behn v Moulton Contracting Ltd.*, 2013 SCC 26, [2013] SCJ No 26 (Factum of the Appellant at para 71).

19 *Behn v Moulton Contracting Ltd.*, 2013 SCC 26, [2013] SCJ No 26 (Factum of the Intervener, Grand Council of the Crees and Cree Regional Authority, at para 18).

proposal is that in cases in which an individual wants to bring a claim based on a right on their own behalf or that of the collective, the person would ordinarily need authorization from the collective; however, when the right is being asserted as a defence in regulatory or criminal proceedings, no such authorization would be necessary. Furthermore, even when authorization is generally required, an individual would be able to get authorization from the court if he or she could show that the collective's refusal to grant permission was unreasonable. Though the invocation of Aboriginal or treaty rights in defence of civil claims is less common, in theory, authorization would also be unnecessary there.[20] In *Behn*, a civil suit, the Court held that the assertion of a treaty right as a defence was an abuse of process, since the Behns did not directly challenge the government's issuance of the permits to Moulton.

This proposal is most in line with what the Court has said and done up to this point, which in the common law is a virtue. It accords with what the Court said in *Behn*, which is that treaty rights are collective but claims related to those rights do not need to be brought by or on behalf of the collective in all circumstances. It is also consistent with the many prosecutions mentioned above in which Aboriginal or treaty rights were successfully raised as defences for which the court did not require authorization.[21]

Making an exception to the authorization requirement when rights are raised as part of a defence addresses some concerns about judicial procedural fairness, as pointed out by the GCCEI/CRA.[22] Persons accused in criminal proceedings have a right to make full answer and defence, and denying them the ability to raise Aboriginal or treaty rights as part of that defence would seem to violate this procedural right.[23] Even potentially barring persons from raising Aboriginal or treaty rights in a civil defence would seem to violate constitutional principles, such as the right to be heard, the right to a fair hearing, and the right to

20 In *Behn*, the Court rejected the Behns' treaty right defence not because they failed to get authorization to raise it but because raising it was an abuse of process. See the discussion below.

21 *Supra* note 8.

22 *Behn v Moulton Contracting Ltd.*, 2013 SCC 26, [2013] SCJ No 26 (Factum of the Intervener, Grand Council of the Crees and Cree Regional Authority).

23 *Wu v The King*, [1934] SCR 609 at 616, 1934 CanLII 28 (SCC); *R v Rose*, [1998] 3 SCR 262 at paras 103, 166 DLR (4th) 385; *R v Ahmad*, 2011 SCC 6 at para 2, [2011] 1 SCR 110.

a remedy.[24] In either the criminal or civil context, it could violate principles in the United Nations Declaration on the Rights of Indigenous Peoples, such as the right to the full enjoyment of all human rights and the right to equality.[25] Bringing modern principles of justice into the interpretation of historical treaties is not anachronistic. It is in keeping with the understanding of treaties, advocated elsewhere in this book, as establishing relationships rather than being static agreements whose power lies only in the original spirit and intent of the signatories. Julie Jai argues that borrowing principles from modern treaties to interpret historical treaties fulfils the "honour of the Crown."[26] Here, the honour of the Crown is fulfilled when governments and courts interpret historical treaties in accordance with modern understandings of procedural fairness.

It seems particularly problematic to require an individual charged with an offence to get permission from the right-bearing collective when there is no guarantee that the collective even has the institutional capacity to grant that permission. The Supreme Court recently held that Aboriginal rights can be vested not only in bands, but in whole nations, when it declared that the Tsilhqot'in Nation, a group of six bands, had Aboriginal title.[27] If the right belongs to the band, it will very likely have a decision-making structure in place to decide whether or not to grant authorization to this person, but if it is a right owing to a nation, it is possible there will be no such mechanism. While this could pose a problem for *any* Aboriginal person who wants to assert a right, there is an urgency in criminal and regulatory prosecutions that suggests requiring authorization would be unacceptable.

One concern about individuals unilaterally raising an Aboriginal or treaty right as a defence is that the facts may not be ideal for a test case, increasing the likelihood of a decision that limits the right for the entire community. This was a major issue in *Howard*, for example, where the defendant's arguments, after a trial in which a former chief had taken the stand for the Crown to argue that the community had given

24 *R v Big M Drug Mart Ltd.*, [1985] 1 SCR 295, 18 DLR (4th) 321; *R v Marshall; R v Bernard*, 2005 SCC 43 at paras 142–4, [2005] 2 SCR 220.

25 *United Nations Declaration on the Rights of Indigenous Peoples*, GA Res 61/295, UNGA, 2007, art 1, 2.

26 See Julie Jai's chapter in this volume.

27 *Tsilhqot'in Nation v British Columbia*, 2014 SCC 44.

up harvesting rights throughout the province in a treaty covering only northern Ontario, led to all of the signatories to the Williams Treaty losing their previously recognized harvesting rights.[28] While classical legal thinking is that the facts will not affect the principles articulated by courts, from a legal realist perspective, the facts of a case and the way a case is litigated play an important role in the evolution of legal principles. Allowing individuals to assert an Aboriginal or treaty right as a defence without the community's formal approval does potentially weaken the community's power to make strategic decisions about how to advance its legal interests. Though this is a valid concern, there may be practical considerations that mitigate this threat to collective power. Courts do not currently require authorization to raise an Aboriginal or treaty right as a defence, and yet it appears that defendants often do have the support of their communities. As the Moose Cree First Nation (MCFN), who intervened in *Behn*, pointed out, without the social and financial backing of their communities, defendants are unlikely to be able to make it to Canada's highest court.[29] The MCFN was arguing that the Supreme Court should have codified this pattern of unofficial consent by always requiring formal authorization. I would argue the opposite – that this pattern of unofficial consent means that the threat to collective authority posed by allowing the unilateral assertion of an Aboriginal or treaty right as a defence may be exaggerated.

Even with community support, courts may make decisions that hurt more than the individual who raised the argument.[30] Take *Pamajewon*, for example, a case in which two men charged with gambling-related offences argued unsuccessfully that this was part of their right to self-government, the effect of which has been to make it more difficult for any Aboriginal community to establish a right to self-government. One of the defendants was chief of his band and the other was a councillor, which makes it likely they would have been given community approval to proceed with the case, had it been required.

The MCFN, as noted above, argued that Aboriginal and treaty harvesting rights should be asserted only after the collective authorizes it. The MCFN had a number of concerns grounding this position. One was

28 *R v Howard*, [1994] 2 SCR 299.

29 *Behn v Moulton Contracting Ltd.*, 2013 SCC 26, [2013] SCJ No 26 (Oral argument, Intervener, Moose Cree First Nation) [*Behn* Oral Argument].

30 See for example, *R v Pamajewon*, [1996] 2 SCR 821.

that allowing individuals to assert claims without authorization would undermine the governance of Aboriginal communities, "allowing the sub-group to dictate to the collective how rights and benefits will be defined, used and shared within the collective."[31]

Allowing an individual to assert a harvesting right in court does not necessarily affect the collective's ability to regulate the exercise of that right by community members. Even if a harvesting right is found, the court has stated repeatedly that the right is communal, and the statement in *Marshall No 2* suggests that Aboriginal communities have the authority to limit the exercise of that right by individuals.[32] All the individual would be doing is establishing that such a legal right exists for the community to enjoy if it chooses to do so. Although the Behns' assertion of their treaty right to hunt, if successful, would have impacted the collective in that logging companies might have been less willing to invest in projects associated with that community in future, it is important to note that this defence was not successful. The Court struck down the Behns' defence as an abuse of process, because it held that the Behns could have and should have sought judicial review of the permits that the province had issued to Moulton. A judicial review of logging permits is one type of action that, under this proposal, the Behns would have needed to seek permission from their First Nation to undertake. The threat to the authority of the collective is therefore not as great as it may have seemed to the MCFN when it intervened in *Behn* and before the Court issued its decision.

A second concern of the intervenor, MCFN, was that not requiring authorization would undermine the ability of the collective's leadership to represent the group in consultation with the Crown.[33] I agree that it would be problematic if, for example, the province had engaged in meaningful consultation with the FNFN regarding logging on their traditional territory and the courts had then allowed the Behns, on their own, to challenge the permits through judicial review. The province would have had less incentive to engage in consultation, since there would have been less finality. Under this proposal, however, the Behns would not have been allowed to seek judicial review without the permission of the collective. And while it is true that the collective's

31 See FI-MCFN, *supra* note 9 at para 25 and *Behn* Oral Argument, *supra* note 10.

32 *Marshall No 2*, *supra* note 7.

33 FI-MCFN, *supra* note 9 at para 26.

authority might be undermined in cases where an individual raises a harvesting right as a defence in a prosecution, I submit that it is worth the potential cost to the authority of the collective to protect the individual rights at stake.

A third concern of the MCFN centred on the implications for the administration of justice, in terms of uncertainty around res judicata if the Aboriginal group is itself not a party to the claim.[34] Given that the courts have not yet required authorization from the collective to raise Aboriginal or treaty rights as a defence in prosecutions, and that uncertainty has generally not been an issue, it is unlikely to become one under the current proposal.

Nor is requiring authorization in some circumstances discriminatory against Aboriginal persons, as one might argue based on a comparison with how non-Aboriginal collective rights are asserted. It is true that alleged violations of what are generally considered to be group rights, such as freedom of religion and language rights, can be challenged by individuals without authorization. For example, a Catholic alleging a violation of his or her Charter right to freedom of religion is not required to seek authorization from the Vatican to make this claim in court. One might argue that it is unfair to make it more difficult for people to assert Aboriginal collective rights in court than it is to pursue non-Aboriginal collective rights. The usefulness of this comparison is limited, however, by the Court's emphatic differentiation between Aboriginal rights and other rights, the latter belonging to everyone in Canada in recognition of their human dignity and the former belonging only to Aboriginals out of recognition of their important role in the origins of this country.[35] That the process for asserting those rights is different is therefore not necessarily discriminatory.

The final proviso of the proposal is to allow courts to grant authorization where the court finds the community's decision to be unreasonable. This will likely bring unwanted attention to governance processes and politics within Aboriginal communities and may be seen as patronizing and meddling. However, I would argue it is a reasonable restriction on the power of the collective in favour of individual freedoms.

---

34 *Ibid* at para 27.

35 *Van der Peet, supra* note 12 at para 18.

Furthermore, it would be possible only in positive rights claims, since authorization in the context of a defence would not be required.

6. Conclusion

This chapter has sought to answer the question raised but not resolved in *Behn* about whether authorization from the right-holding group is needed before an individual can assert an Aboriginal or treaty harvesting right in court. In trying to balance the individual and collective interests of Aboriginal communities, I suggested that authorization generally be required, except when the right is raised as a defence, and that courts be allowed to grant authorization when the court finds that the group's decision to deny permission was unreasonable. The chapter's scope may appear narrow, but consideration of this one scenario will help further analysis about whether authorization should be required for other types of rights, and about the collective nature of Aboriginal and treaty rights more broadly. The issue of how and by whom collective rights can be asserted has relevance in a variety of Aboriginal contexts, including child adoption, religious freedom, and the control of knowledge held by Aboriginal groups.[36]

While concerns about requiring community authorization deserve attention – their resolution will in some cases have a meaningful impact on the lives of Aboriginal persons – they also miss an important point. As a number of chapters in this book have argued, historical treaties should be understood as agreements between nations, as a way of furthering justice and improving relations between settlers and Indigenous peoples. Limiting individual freedom for the sake of collective freedom is more easily justified when it is the collective itself or its members making this decision, not one nation deciding for another. Here, the decisions will be made by the Canadian judiciary, in which Aboriginal people are grossly underrepresented, and it is likely that the decisive principles will be articulated by the nine members of the Supreme Court of Canada, none of whom are Aboriginal. For our courts to limit the individual freedom of Aboriginal persons for the

36 Dwight G. Newman, "Theorizing Collective Indigenous Rights" (2006) 31 *American Indian Law Review* 273; Thomas Isaac, "Individual versus Collective Rights: Aboriginal People and the Significance of *Thomas v. Norris*" (1991) 21 *Manitoba Law Journal* 618.

sake of the continued existence of their societies, when our own legal system is built on liberal Enlightenment principles that undeniably prioritize individual freedom, is patronizing. If we truly want to respect the fact that Aboriginal people lived in organized societies before the arrival of Europeans, we should recognize their inherent right to self-government and allow them to decide for themselves how to strike this difficult balance between personal and communal interests.

6 Negotiating Self-Government Over & Over & Over Again: Interpreting Contemporary Treaties

SARI GRABEN AND MATTHEW MEHAFFEY

In this chapter, the authors question what role colonial history plays in the interpretation of modern or contemporary treaties when there is ambiguity. Using an account of funding negotiations with the Carcross/Tagish First Nation (CTFN) under the Yukon Self-Government Agreement the authors find that the specificity of contemporary treaties is not in and of itself able to rectify relations marked by colonialism. Instead, the role of courts in defining treaty terms and judging conformity remains essential to implementation. Consequently, those using law to make rights, right relations, or obligations certain under contemporary treaties eventually face the same questions as those under historic treaties: what interpretive tools will the courts use to determine the political rights and obligations of treaty parties?

1. Introduction

To a bureaucrat in the federal or a provincial government, historical treaties are perhaps most clearly understood as intergovernmental agreements that clarify the proprietary and governing rights of the federal, provincial, and Aboriginal governments of Canada. They are poorly drafted, fail to reference any relevant details about government, use opaque language, and contain terms that are deeply contested. Despite this, these historical treaties are still used to rationalize federal and provincial power over Aboriginal governments and their traditional territories. In fact, a bureaucrat can treat the terms of historical treaties as so clear that they obviate any legal requirement to negotiate the political rights of Aboriginal governments or any need to negotiate the proprietary rights to the lands detailed in them. This is because, to a bureaucrat, treaties evidence the exercise by Aboriginal peoples of a pre-contact political sovereignty in a one-time agreement that subordinated Aboriginal governmental authority to the Crown and surrendered ownership of lands.[1]

As may be imagined, this interpretation of historical treaties is often criticized as failing to do justice to the political relationship of the parties and their rights to ownership, as conceived by Aboriginal peoples.[2] Instead of abdicating ownership and authority, Aboriginal peoples instead maintain that they retained their political sovereignty and thus the legislative and executive authority needed to govern through treaties. Rather than subordinate governments, treaties evidence the federal government's responsibility to recognize Aboriginal authority as distinct within the Canadian federation.[3]

Contributors to this book reflect on the relevance of history to these interpretations of treaties.[4] Most advocate a prominent role for the courts, advocating interpretations that give primary weight to the intention of the treaties' framers. Following in the same vein, we question what role colonial history plays in the interpretation of modern or contemporary treaties. As highly technical and detailed documents, contemporary treaties have been crafted to avoid colonial defaults. Contemporary treaties purport to reflect agreement on authority, jurisdiction, intergovernmental relations, and ownership. They therefore represent a highly legal solution to long-standing political conflict. However, contemporary

---

1 For a mapping of the various views on treaties, see J.R. Miller, *Compact, Contract, Covenant: Aboriginal Treaty-Making in Canada* (Toronto: University of Toronto Press, 2009) at 283–309.

2 Aaron Mills, "What Is a Treaty? On Contract and Mutual Aid," in this volume. Mills rejects the argument that the Treaty of Niagara legally authorized the federal and provincial governments to subordinate Aboriginal governments.

3 James Sákéj Youngblood Henderson, "Empowering Treaty Federalism" (1994) 58 *Saskatchewan Law Review*, 241–329.

4 Advocacy for treaties as political compacts that can be redeemed through law is shared by many of the authors in this book. See Michael Coyle, "As Long as The Sun Shines: Recognizing that Treaties Were Intended to Last," which favours a principled implementation in line with the core premises of the treaty-making process; Mark Walters, "Rights and Remedies within Common Law and Indigenous Legal Traditions: Can the Covenant Chain Be Judicially Enforced Today?" which favours a robust understanding of remedy that does justice to Indigenous understandings of treaty; and Jean Leclair, "Nanabush, Lon Fuller, and Historical Treaties: The Potentialities and Limits of Adjudication," which favours reform based on a "community of purpose."

treaties are also mired in interpretive difficulties, especially when sections of the treaties related to funding are being interpreted.[5] Ambiguity about the obligations of the federal government has fuelled continuing disagreement over what it means to be an Aboriginal government in Canada. In this legal vacuum, the federal government still attempts to retain the mantle of financial management and First Nations look for leverage to counteract it.[6]

It is unclear what role law plays in mediating this legal ambiguity in contemporary treaties. Do bureaucrats on all sides rely on the shared interpretation of contemporary treaties when determining obligations? In those circumstances where there are interpretive differences or blatant disregard for the treaty, how should the parties proceed? When law is uncertain, will the parties resort to the courts for clarity or will they develop interim legal arrangements for the purposes of governing? More tellingly, are those interim arrangements legal solutions if they are imposed through power or force, rather than shared treaty interpretation? If it is instead more accurate to identify those interpretations as political settlement, what implications will their adoption have on future negotiations and litigation about treaty meaning?

Using an account of funding negotiations with the CTFN under the Yukon Self-Government Agreement, we reflect upon a circumstance in which funding remains uncertain and the parties must renegotiate agreement. We find that while contemporary treaties purport to use law to create certainty, it is inaccurate to presume bureaucrats on either side will rely on shared interpretations when determining their obligations. While parties do generate interpretations, the parties are likely to develop interim arrangements for the purposes of governing that avoid

5 For example, see the issues raised in: *Nunavut Tunngavik Incorporated v Canada (Attorney General)*, [2014] NUCA 2 (treaty implementation); *Tlicho Government v Canada (Attorney General)*, [2015] NWTJ 14 (fair dealing and consultation). For further discussion, see reports of the Land Claims Coalition, http://www.landclaimscoalition.ca/external-reports/.

6 For an overview of implementation issues, see Land Claims Coalition, "Honouring the Spirit of Modern Treaties: Closing the Loopholes," *Interim Report to the Standing Senate Committee on Aboriginal Peoples*, May 2008, http://www.landclaimscoalition.ca/assets/080515-Senate_Cttee_Report.pdf. For specific discussion of funding disputes, see Land Claims Coalition, *Fiscal Harmonization Initiative Background Brief*, http://www.landclaimscoalition.ca/coalition-documents/.

shared meaning. Moreover, path dependencies that have enabled the federal government to control and direct Aboriginal governments for 150 years and an aversion to governmental growth cause Aboriginal governments under contemporary treaties to experience similar impediments to achieving a principled basis for intergovernmental relations as those governments under the *Indian Act*. Instead of resolution based on law, negotiations are defined by political power, resistance, and limited political choice.

Nonetheless, we find that bargaining in the shadow of law does have some effect on political negotiations. Strategic positions taken by the CTFN illustrate that contemporary treaty governments can use ownership, program responsibility, and clear treaty entitlements to counter colonial defaults that presume centralized financial management. This leads us to conclude that deep and long-term investments in lobbying, lawyering, and legislating remain key to the success of Aboriginal governments under contemporary treaties. However, this requires vigorous effort by the Aboriginal treaty party, draining resources and capacity from communities and the transformative exercise of nation-building.

Ultimately, we conclude that the specificity of contemporary treaties as legal documents is not able to rectify relations marked by colonialism. Instead, the role of courts in defining treaty terms and judging conformity remains essential to implementation. Yet, in order to avoid the same pitfalls that have turned historic treaties into instruments of management and control, courts must develop an understanding of treaties that reflects the parties' political intentions. If law is to play a role in tempering the effects of intergovernmental politics, then courts must undertake the same task for contemporary treaties as that posed for historical treaties, no matter how detailed the treaty text: develop a common legality or a narrative that does justice to right relations. The authors argue here that without grounding contemporary treaties in their federalist aims, the redemptive power of law, even where painstakingly detailed, is likely to remain elusive.

2. An Overview of Self-Government and Funding in the Yukon

The Carcross/Tagish First Nation (CTFN), which sits in the southwest Yukon, was instrumental in the revitalization of the First Nation political movement in the early 1970s. However, the CTFN was one of the last Yukon First Nations to enter the modern treaty process and sign a self-government agreement, a procedure the First Nation completed in

2005. Nonetheless, the CTFN's negotiations with Canada over programs and services and financial transfers were deeply impacted by earlier self-government agreements between Yukon First Nations and Canada.

There are eleven self-governing First Nations in the Yukon. The first self-government agreements came into effect in February 1995. The land claim agreements, officially called final agreements (FAs) are treaties pursuant to section 35 of the Canadian constitution. The self-government agreements, though not explicitly constitutional documents like the FAs, were negotiated pursuant to chapter 26 of the treaty. They are by their nature a "constitutional document."

The Yukon self-government agreements (SGAs) recognize the respective First Nations as governments with a wide range of powers. These powers are divided into five categories:

(1) exclusive jurisdiction over internal affairs matters and the management and administration of FA rights and benefits;
(2) jurisdiction over citizens within the Yukon, generally with regard to programs and services;
(3) local or private matters, which includes a wide range of matters with respect to the management of affairs within settlement land;
(4) concurrent jurisdiction with respect to taxation; and
(5) emergency powers.

Where the First Nations' jurisdiction is recognized, it is almost always paramount to that of the Yukon government. The SGA states that where a Yukon First Nation passes a law, the Yukon law of general application shall be rendered inoperative to the extent that it deals with any matter dealt with under the First Nation law.[7] The SGA does not explicitly address paramountcy with respect to Canada and the First Nation. However, it is clearly contemplated by all parties that there would be areas in which Yukon First Nation legislation would prevail as evidenced by the requirement for the First Nation and Canada to negotiate those areas where the First Nation law would prevail.[8] This is important in the fiscal context, as it provides a glimpse into the minds

7 Carcross/Tagish First Nation Self-Government Agreement ["CTFN SGA"] 2005 s. 13.5.3.
8 CTFN SGA s. 13.5.2.

of the negotiators and parties at the time the agreements were concluded. It clearly demonstrates the level and scope of government being recognized by the SGA.

When the "First Four" SGAs[9] came into effect in 1995, the parties implemented a Financial Transfer Agreement (FTA). The FTA was to be negotiated every five years pursuant to section 16.0 of the SGAs. Section 16.0 is perhaps the most debated section of the SGAs and contains key elements for consideration when concluding a financial agreement. Perhaps the most important section from a financial standpoint is section 16.1. It states that Canada and the First Nation *shall negotiate* an agreement "[...] with the objective of providing the [...] First Nation with resources to allow the [...] First Nation to provide public services at levels reasonably comparable to those generally prevailing in Yukon, at reasonably comparable levels of taxation."

This wording was key for two reasons:[10]

(1) It imported the concept of comparability from section 36 of the *Constitution Act, 1982*, and
(2) It made clear that the comparability test is the capacity of the particular First Nation government to deliver comparable programs and services.

The objective of the FTA is to allow the First Nation to provide comparable levels of service to its citizens at comparable levels of taxation. Beyond that objective, there is a list of factors that the parties will take into account in seeking to achieve that objective, including: economics and diseconomies of scale, effectiveness and efficiency, existing federal policies, and existing federal transfers to other Aboriginal governments. The overarching goal set out in the SGAs, however, is to ensure not simply that Yukon First Nations citizens have comparable access to

9 The "First Four" Yukon First Nations refers to the Vuntut Gwitchin First Nation, the First Nation of Na-Cho Nyak Dun, Champagne and Aishihik First Nations, and the Teslin Tlingit Council, each of which signed their FA and SGA in 1993.

10 Report of the Parties to Seven of the Self-Government Financial Transfer Agreements to the Senior Financial Arrangements Committee to the Yukon First Nation Financial Transfers Agreements, "First Nation Financial Transfer Agreement Review: Final Consolidated Report," vol. 3 (2007) 5 (a copy on file with the authors) ["Financial Transfer Agreement Review"].

programs and services, but that the First Nation, as a government, has the resources to provide those services at comparable levels.

3. The Review

At the time the initial Yukon FTAs were concluded, the parties had no shared basis for determining how much a new self-government initiative should cost. While Canada did not provide any justification for its initial FTA offer, its primary purpose was to combine the existing funding of the predecessor Indian Band with funding for treaty implementation into a single block grant to provide to the First Nation. The Yukon First Nations did not think the funding on offer from Canada met the objectives of 16.1 of the SGA. Nevertheless, the "First Four" Yukon First Nations signed the FTA based on an all-party commitment to undertake reviews of the implementation plans, the FTA, and the SGA, including the adequacy of funding.[11] These reviews were expected to provide a valuable look back and an opportunity for the parties to assess matters once some experience had been gained.

The reviews began in May 2003 and a report was submitted to the parties in October 2007.[12] The process concluded with the CTFN FTA renewal effective as of April 2014.[13] The process had two parts: (1) the implementation review undertaken by the Implementation Review Group and (2) the Self Government Financial Transfer Agreement Review.[14] The Implementation Review Group process consolidated a number of reviews including those set out in the implementation plans, section 6.6 of the SGA, and the *Umbrella Final Agreement*. The review looked at a broad range of matters, many of which had fiscal implications for

---

11 Report of the Parties to the Yukon Self-Government Implementation Review Group, "Yukon First Nation Final and Self-Government Agreement Implementation Reviews" Appendix B – Funding Adequacy Review: The Interim Report of the Adequacy Work Group (3 October 2007) ["IRG Report"] (copy on file with authors).

12 *Ibid* at 5.

13 Carcross/Tagish First Nation Financial Transfer Agreement between her Majesty the Queen in the Right of Canada and Carcross/Tagish First Nation, Effective Date 1 April 2014 (a copy on file with the authors).

14 The Yukon review process primarily involved seven Yukon First Nations, the Council of Yukon First Nations, Canada, and the Yukon; although, at times, other First Nations and boards, committees and councils established under the *Umbrella Final Agreement* were included.

First Nations and other organizations from the Council of Yukon First Nations, land use planning councils, and other boards and committees. The Self Government Financial Transfer Agreement Review documented the history of the FTAs and the foundational flaws with the self-government fiscal process. It examined a broad range of underlying problems with funding up until that point, including various issues with taxation and own source revenue. Most importantly for the purposes of transfers, however, the review identified that rather than use the factors in 16.1 to determine funding, the federal government was using the pre-existing transfers provided as "current dollar offloads" for status Indians under the *Indian Act* as the primary basis for calculating funding levels. In short, the government was treating the various First Nations as *Indian Act* bands, despite the fact that First Nations have greater responsibilities and jurisdiction than bands.[15]

While parties to the Yukon agreements recognized that it could not be demonstrated that the objective of section 16.1 of the SGA had been met, Canada argued it was also impossible to conclude it had not been met, as there was no way to measure comparability.[16] In an effort to develop a measure for self-government funding, Canada hired Richard Zuker, former long-time Department of Finance employee and one of the architects of the first-generation financial transfer agreements, to undertake a scoping exercise. Zuker's report outlined how subnational governments in various areas around the world were funded and proposed a methodology for costing self-government.[17] As a result of this report, the parties agreed to begin the costing process on a pilot project basis to determine whether the methodology proposed worked and was acceptable to the parties. Zuker's exercise led to the conclusion that general governance costs alone would eat up most, if not all, of the current transfers.[18]

15 This history and its broader implications are set out with precision and detail in the Financial Transfer Agreement Review, *supra* note 10.

16 *Ibid* at iv.

17 Richard C. Zuker, "Scoping Out the Measurements of Expenditure Need and Revenue Means for Yukon First Nation Governments," report prepared for Indian and Northern Affairs Canada, 23 May 2006.

18 Richard C. Zuker and David Janoff, "Study on Yukon First Nations Governments Expenditure Needs for General Government Functions," prepared for Implementation Planning and Negotiations Directorate Implementation Branch, Indian and Northern Affairs Canada, December 2006.

In short, existing transfers were insufficient to achieve comparability with those prevailing in the Yukon, as required by the treaty.

While it was unwilling to use the report Zuker submitted, the federal government did agree to compare funds for self-government against funds provided to the Yukon Government for similar services. When the process finally concluded, the results again showed a stark gap between the funding provided and the resources needed to reach a measure of comparability. While the gap was different depending on whether Canada's numbers or the First Nations' numbers were used, even Canada's approach showed a gap in excess of 50 per cent for most First Nations.[19] The question was how this would translate into a funding mandate.

4. Translating Findings into a Negotiation Mandate

In 2009, Canada and seven Yukon First Nations began negotiating the third generation of Yukon financial transfer agreements. These negotiations included an increase in funding for the governance functions of the Yukon First Nations and made an interim funding increase permanent.[20] While the new funding provided a short-term benefit to the Yukon First Nations, the federal government's approach would ultimately prove problematic for some Yukon First Nations and lead to a protracted dispute between the CTFN and the federal government.

The Carcross/Tagish is the latest of the Yukon First Nations to conclude final and self-government agreements. The CTFN Final Agreement came into effect in 2006. However, by the time the CTFN agreements were concluded, the process related to funding was firmly entrenched. Despite the obligation to negotiate, the government would only offer an amount based on a funding formula that it had unilaterally developed.[21] What the predecessor Indian band was spending would be transferred to the self-governing First Nation along with whatever had been

---

19 Yukon Self-Government Implementation Working Group, "An Examination of the Gross Expenditure Base of Self-Governing Yukon First Nations," 14 July 2008 (a copy is on file with the authors).

20 On 31 March 2007, the FTAs of seven Yukon First Nations would have expired. The parties agreed to amend the FTAs to extend them and to provide each of the seven First Nations with additional funding equal to 12.5 per cent of the FTA.

21 Reported by members of the CTFN's original negotiation team, Mark Wedge and Beverly Sembsmoen.

determined years earlier by others to be their portion of the indirect funding and of the SGA and FA funding envelopes.[22]

Because of this formula, the CTFN and several other Yukon First Nations received less funding than other signatories. This was exacerbated by a few factors. Most importantly, from a fiscal standpoint, the FTA negotiations did not account for the fact that Indian band funding had been frozen for over a decade and the funding for many programs and services had been flat for much longer.[23] Meanwhile, self-government funding for those already under agreements, while inadequate, had been growing, as it was adjusted annually for inflation and a 3 per cent population escalator. This resulted in an average increase in funding of over 5 per cent for early signatories. This meant that when the CTFN became self-governing in 2006, it did not receive the same funding as those already under agreements.

The earlier review reports concluded that Yukon First Nations were not funded at levels sufficient to provide comparable programs and services to their citizens.[24] The CTFN did not even reach comparability with other Yukon First Nations. When it came time to "re-negotiate" FTAs in 2009, however, Canada explained how it had concluded new agreements with the seven other new signatory First Nations, explained how that would work for the CTFN, and made it clear that it had no mandate to discuss anything different. Moreover, as the discussion, or lack thereof, moved ever closer to the expiration of the FTA term, Canada turned up the financial pressure. As time ticked away, the CTFN and the three other First Nations in negotiations were informed that if they did not reach an agreement by a specified time, the funding increase Canada had offered for that fiscal year would be lost.

With the pressure turned up, the three other First Nations concluded new agreements based on the terms offered, but the CTFN held firm. The inability of Canada's negotiator to address historic issues, coupled with substantial changes to the manner in which funding was adjusted

22 Richard Zuker and David Janoff, "Study on Yukon First Nations Governments Expenditure Needs for General Government Functions," prepared for Implementation Planning and Negotiations Directorate Implementation Branch, Indian and Northern Affairs, December 2006 at 3 (a copy is on file with the authors).

23 Matthew Mehaffey, "Analysis of 'First Four' Versus CTFN Source Agreements" (2010) (on file with the authors).

24 IRG Report, *supra* note 11.

and sweeping changes to the calculation of own source revenue,[25] meant that the First Nation was simply unable to agree to what was tabled. The agreement continued the "haves and have nots" system of funding Yukon First Nations. While the system may not have been put in place intentionally, the refusal to undertake actual negotiations with the objectives set out in SGA 16.1 meant it would continue.

As the CTFN continued to push Canada for meaningful negotiations, Canada informed the First Nation that any new money on offer for the fiscal year in which the negotiations were occurring was now off the table. The First Nation should sign the new FTA or lose the increased governance funding for the upcoming fiscal year – a cost of over $1.8 million. This was followed by a more pressing threat that as of 1 April 2011, Canada would stop funding the CTFN altogether if the First Nation did not accept the offer being provided. With the fiscal year coming to a close, the federal position was that not only would the FTA be allowed to expire, but the obligation to provide funding to the First Nation for programs and services would also cease to exist. If the CTFN did not sign the agreement presented by Canada, it would become the first self-governing First Nation in Canada to be defunded. Essentially, by de-funding the CTFN government, the federal government expected that it would step in as a manager and govern in the place of the First Nation.

The impasse in negotiations led to a two-pronged approach by the CTFN. First the litigation firm Pape Salter Teillet was retained to argue the illegality of the government's position, and second intense political lobbying took place. Much of this lobbying focused on the distinctive character of the self-government agreements. The treaties obligate the federal government to provide funding. While the amounts are to be negotiated on the basis of comparability, the federal government cannot disavow the responsibility as it could under the *Indian Act*. Similarly, in threatening to defund the CTFN, the federal government assumed that it could assign managers who would operate as though the CTFN were an Indian band. However, the federal government was not in a

25 Own source revenue is revenue generated by the First Nation from non-governmental sources that is then taken into account for the purpose of reducing Canada's grant to the First Nation. For every dollar of eligible own source revenue, Canada reduces its transfer by fifty cents. The primary change to own source revenue in 2015 was the removal of most of the exclusions that had been provided to Yukon First Nations. See the CTFN FTA (2006) versus CTFN FTA (2015).

position to undertake the task. It had no operational capacity or legal authority to manage in place of the First Nation. Unlike its position under the *Indian Act*, the federal government does not own any of the infrastructure or operational property of the CTFN. It has no ownership rights over the land, the buildings, the snowplows, the garbage trucks, etc. The lobbying around making this point clear was enhanced by the work of the law firm and eventually, with the assistance of MP Ryan Leef, a six-month extension was secured. At the end of the extension, Canada informed the CTFN of its intention to pursue mediation.

The formal mediation process was simple and short. Although only two formal sessions were held, numerous informal discussions took place at the legal and political level. While the ultimate goal was a breakthrough on the issue of comparability, the pragmatic goal was to obtain the funds identified and endorsed by the CTFN executive council at the outset of negotiations. The eventual solution allowed the CTFN to be reclassified as a large First Nation within the formula Canada had applied in the Yukon. This resulted in additional funding for the First Nation without going outside the federal mandate. This meant that the CTFN met its dollar target. Moreover, Canada had told the First Nation throughout the process that each year a new FTA was not signed, that money would be lost. However, the CTFN made it a condition that any solution included any "lost money" being put back on the table. While Canada could not agree to retroactive funding, the CTFN was provided a supplementary funding grant of $4 million as part of their new FTA, slightly more than the $3.6 million in lost money. Ultimately, the CTFN achieved, through mediation, the goal its executive had set for funding and therefore accepted the subsequent offer made by the federal government. At no point, however, did the parties achieve any shared understanding of federal obligations under the treaty terms or agree on a formula for determining funding that would address treaty obligations.

5. Insights into Implementation

What insights about the role of law under contemporary treaties can be taken from this account of treaty implementation? The main insight is that while contemporary treaties purport to use law to create certainty, it is inaccurate to presume that bureaucrats of any government party will rely on shared legal meaning when determining obligations. Instead, where there are interpretive differences, the parties are likely to develop interim arrangements for the purposes of governing that avoid shared treaty interpretation. Moreover, these arrangements are more properly understood as political, rather than legal, agreements. Even if it is more accurate to identify those interpretations as political or strategic, however, their very adoption is still likely to have implications on future negotiations and litigation over treaty meaning. What are these implications?

One of the first insights is that negotiations attempt to place First Nations back in the familiar territory of the *Indian Act*. Policies that replace negotiated self-government fiscal financing arrangements with formula financing that is unilaterally determined by the federal government are interpreted as a policy choice by the federal government, but are a threat to the very essence of what was negotiated by treaty governments under contemporary treaties.[26] Policies that attempt to prompt settlement, such as the federal government's threats to hold back funding to those governments that do not accept these unilateral offers, are perhaps not in themselves neocolonial. Responding to advocacy for resources is part of being a government and federal opportunism that redirects those resources elsewhere is part and parcel of intergovernmental relations. However, much like governments under historic treaties, contemporary treaty governments do not have the same levers to encourage settlement as other levels of government in Canada. They do not possess a large electoral base that makes the federal government accountable to the populace. Nor, at the time being, can they derive financial independence from a large or diverse source of taxation.

If, however, Aboriginal parties must anticipate power-based negotiations as inevitable and, for the foreseeable future, neocolonial, they are not without their strategic defenses under contemporary agreements. The activities of the CTFN illustrate that contemporary treaty governments can use land ownership, program responsibility, and clear treaty entitlements to counter colonial strategies employed by the federal government. Historical treaties are understood in law to vest ownership of land in the federal Crown and a beneficial interest in the First Nation. Based on this relationship, the federal government trustee is authorized

26 Land Claim Coalition Agreement, "Modern Treaty Organizations Oppose Federal Government Formula," 3 May 2012, online: http://www.landclaimscoalition.ca/modern-treaty-organizations-oppose-federal-government-formula-financing-proposal/.

to step in as manager of that interest at any time. While defenses under contemporary treaties are limited, they do alter the powers of the federal government and force it to abandon practices that assume management authority without legal right.

For example, the Yukon final and self-government agreements made three fundamental alterations to the legal powers of the federal government to manage and therefore control the CTFN. First, contemporary treaties severed the managing authority of the Minister of Aboriginal and Northern Affairs, as outlined under the *Indian Act*, leaving the Canadian government with no statutory right to manage the assets of the CTFN government that are used to effect governance and provide services. The CTFN's land, capital, and monies are no longer held in trust by the Crown and therefore cannot be seized for the purposes of effecting its obligations to its beneficiaries as it does under the *Indian Act*.[27] Second, the federal government has no knowledge of the CTFN's programs or services necessary for program delivery. As the treaties established, the federal government has no approval authority, oversight, or knowledge about the complex of programs and services provided by the CTFN. Lastly, the federal government is constitutionally obligated under contemporary treaties to fund treaty parties. This changes the dynamic between those negotiating. The CTFN is not just a stubborn Indian band having a dispute with a government over a funding contract that flows from federal constitutional authority. The federal government now has a constitutional obligation. While parties may dispute the dollar amount of that obligation, contemporary treaties constitutionally preclude the federal government from defunding the First Nation treaty party. It is the combination of these powers that prevented the federal government from merely leaving the CTFN unfunded and managing the CTFN peoples directly through Ottawa.

A second insight of this account is that a deep investment in lobbying, lawyering, and legislating is key to the efficacy of Aboriginal governments under contemporary treaties. Claiming and maintaining jurisdiction are seen in this account as an integral part of contemporary government in Canada. While exhausting and expensive, contemporary treaties require Aboriginal governments to vigilantly and strategically defend what legal rights they believe they obtained through the agreements. In short, for

27 *Indian Act*, RSC 1985 c. I–5 s. 62–9

the foreseeable future, they must anticipate and plan for the negotiation of self-government over and over and over again.

Again, to some degree, intergovernmental negotiation is a reality for all levels of government in Canada. Consistent litigation over jurisdiction between Aboriginal governments and federal and provincial governments since 1867 bears witness to this reality, as does the portion of their budgets allocated to intergovernmental relations. However, its implications for contemporary treaty governments, which operate under significantly more restrictive budgets will be different and will require different strategies. First, it requires economic plans that recognize and save for the foreseeable and unforeseeable litigation that contemporary treaties create. Second, it requires governments to pool their resources and energies so that the burden of advocacy does not fall on only a handful of contemporary treaty governments. Efforts of the Land Claims Agreement Coalition, an association of Aboriginal governments under contemporary treaties, reflect this effort.[28] Third, it requires the multiple communities governed by one treaty to exercise significant unity for the purposes of intergovernmental advocacy. The support of the CTFN communities for greater funding allocations was key to maintaining a consistent position throughout negotiations.

If, however, this account represents one reality of treaty implementation, a strategic approach to treaties carries with it numerous concerns. A first concern is that a strategic approach departs from a narrative of treaties as ideal or sacred documents. Instead of representing the essence of self-determination that the parties ideally realize through negotiation, pragmatism can debase these values. Rather than negotiate mutual growth and nation-building, the treaty partners negotiate funding as a zero-sum game. Compelling the federal government to meet the obligations of the agreement, however, requires vigorous effort by the Aboriginal treaty party, draining resources and capacity from communities and the transformative exercise of nation-building.

A second and related concern is that seeing treaties as strategic instruments risks reinforcing colonial systems rather than challenging them. As the case study illustrates, a "win" for a treaty government is unlikely to involve a revolutionary recognition of shared interpretations or a revision of destabilizing systems. Instead, the parties will often settle

28 For the activities of the LCAC, see online: http://www.landclaimscoalition.ca.

for a remedy that meets the essential but more mundane needs of government: money. Naturally, settlement is not inherently neocolonial. Incremental financial settlement represents the realities of intergovernmental negotiation. Again, for this reason, federal and provincial or territorial negotiations over transfer payments can be equally fraught with the use of fiscal power. First Nations, however, face a different hurdle than other levels of government.

Because First Nation governments are funded as a cost of the federal government, their funding has become subject to budget allocations made to the Ministry of Aboriginal and Northern Affairs. Rather than negotiate the determination of expected costs, as contemplated by provisions like section16.1 of the SGA, First Nations negotiate with a ministry on the basis of its budgetary allocation – not the cost of government. The Ministry of Aboriginal and Northern Affairs operates with a strict and certain financial mandate for negotiation linked to budget. Moreover, the ministry has institutional incentives to offer random amounts and threats to First Nations that have had their funding pulled in order to keep costs down. Consequently, much like band governments, self-governing First Nations must still contemplate simply accepting what is offered, rather than negotiating. Contemporary treaty governments must therefore still engage with federal bureaucrats that use similar policies, methods, and rationalizations as they do for bands under the *Indian Act*. Any "win" that does not address these path dependencies reinforces the view of government that funding is a contingent and not-guaranteed part of constitutional negotiation.

Lastly, and perhaps most importantly for the themes discussed in this book, understanding treaties as strategic instruments may encourage courts to subjugate the law contained within them to the realities of politics. Insofar as contemporary treaties require regular negotiation, one could foresee the reluctance of courts to intervene. In fact, it seems entirely predictable that the courts will see negotiation as an essential component of intergovernmental relations. This is not an erroneous interpretation. The courts, however, must be cautious not to abdicate their power to enforce what the parties have negotiated and thereby require First Nations to defend and negotiate self-government over and over again.

Ultimately, the courts must decide whether contemporary treaty implementation operates outside of law or within its ambiguities. If it is the former, then we can anticipate that the common law, through neglect, might reify treaties as political documents that legitimize a deeply strategic approach to intergovernmental relations. If it is the latter, then the law must address the question of whether legal ambiguities create a vacuum in which only politics, and therefore power, will determine outcome, or whether a contextual understanding of treaties allows the inference of purpose and therefore meaning. Should the courts seek to ascribe meaning that does justice to treaties as constitutional compacts, rather than contracts, then they must still undertake the task posed by the authors of this text for historical treaties: develop a common legality or a narrative that does justice to right relations.

6. Interpreting a Common Federal Legality

If contemporary agreements require the courts to adopt principles that aid in interpretation, what concept of right relations should the courts use to interpret contemporary treaties? As mentioned at the beginning of the chapter, courts have generally ignored the argument of Aboriginal peoples that historic treaties are political compacts. Rejecting the relevance of treaty federalism through the adoption of contractual interpretation,[29] Canadian federalism has so far been treated in law as an arrangement between the central government and the provinces alone.[30] As Canadians have come to expect, fiscal relations between the federal and provincial governments are defined by their origins in the financial settlement between the new Dominion and the provinces at Confederation.[31] Although the early settlement focused on higher levels of federal revenue and expenditure, the increased responsibilities and powers of the provinces has resulted in a greater transfer of revenue to match expenditures.[32]

---

29 For the concept of treaty federalism, see James Sákéj Youngblood Henderson, "Empowering Treaty Federalism" (1994) 58 *Saskatchewan Law Review* 241.

30 *Constitution Act, 1867* (U.K.) 30 and 31 Vict., c. 3, reprinted in R.S.C. 1985, App II, No. 5 [*Constitution Act, 1867*]. The powers of the two governments are also defined in sections 93–101. The jurisprudence has supported the legislative competence of the federal and provincial orders. See *Hodge v. The Queen* (1883), 9 App. Cas. 117 (P.C.) [*Hodge*] and *Liquidators of the Maritime Bank v. Receiver General of N.B.*, [1892] A.C. 437 (P.C.) [*Liquidators*].

31 Michael J. Prince and Frances Abele, "Paying for Self-Determination: Aboriginal Peoples, Self-Government and Fiscal Relations in Canada" in Michael Murphy, ed., *Canada: The State of the Federation 2003; Reconfiguring Aboriginal-State Relations* (Kingston: McGill-Queen's University Press, 2005) 237 at 240.

32 *Ibid* at 242.

In contrast to federal fiscal relations, the history of federal/Aboriginal fiscal relations is marked by non-participation in Confederation and the assumption of control over Aboriginal governance through Crown sovereignty. Because "Indian people played no part in negotiating Confederation, or in drafting the British North America Act of 1867,"[33] key political communities were left out of negotiating a set of relationships that would determine their future fiscal affairs. As such, no expenditure functions, legislative powers, or taxing powers were assigned or recognized. Most importantly, the Crown replaced Aboriginal self-government with a successive series of *Indian Acts* that leaves real decision-making power, including budget control and policy choices, to the Department of Indian Affairs.[34] When compared with fiscal federalism, federal/Aboriginal fiscal relations have differed in a manner that underscores the absence of a comparable federal relationship.[35]

It should therefore be significant to courts that contemporary treaties depart from traditional federal/Aboriginal fiscal relations and focus on a future relationship marked by federalism.[36] Contemporary treaties that establish a new order of government have redefined the traditional configuration to actively include Aboriginal peoples as constituent entities of the federal state and alter the rights and obligations of governments.[37] Fiscal provisions that outline the constitutional division of powers in contemporary treaties clarify independent revenue raising powers, requirements for tax harmonization, the value of transfer payments, requirements for comparability, and especially requirements to

---

33 *Ibid* at 243, quoting House of Commons, *Indian Self-Government in Canada: Report of the Special Committee* (Ottawa: Supply and Services Canada, 1983) at 39.

34 *Ibid.*

35 Frances Abele and Michael J. Prince, "Counsel for Canadian Federalism: Aboriginal Governments and the Council of the Federation" in *Constructive and Cooperative Federalism? A Series of Commentaries on the Council of the Federation*, vol. 11 (Institute of Intergovernmental Relations and Institute for Research on Public Policy, 2003).

36 For discussion, see Sari Graben, "Contemporary Treaties: Negotiating a New Federal Arrangement" (2007) 6:2 *Indigenous Law Journal* 2–32, 17–21.

37 Assumptions of a "third order of government" range from highly general pronouncements on Aboriginal nationalism coexisting within the Canadian federal state to specific statements on the effect of the NFA. For the former approach see Will Kymlika, *Finding Our Way: Rethinking Ethnocultural Relations in Canada* (Toronto: Oxford University Press, 1998) and Jean Leclair, "Federal Constitutionalism and Aboriginal Difference" (2007) 31:2 *Queen's Law Journal* 521. Also see *Campbell v British Columbia (A.G.)* (2000), 189 D.L.R. (4th) 333.

negotiate. These provisions indicate that financing is not to be interpreted as discretionary or as a unilateral power of the federal government. Expenditure functions, as well as legislative and taxing powers, have been recognized through constitutional settlements that mirror the federal-provincial relationship. There may not be absolute clarity as to what type of federal relationship has been created, but the courts will have to exercise a particular kind of blindness to ignore the purposeful use of the legal, institutional, and consensual elements of federalism that contemporary treaties contain.[38]

Here, participation in constitutional federalism takes on a legal meaning insofar as it permits or forbids certain legislative or executive behaviour. Instead of contractual interpretations, it is incumbent upon courts to recognize that contemporary treaties use the institutions and hallmarks of federalism to invoke an intellectual approach to treaties that upsets the law's acceptance of political dominance historically exercised by the federal government over Aboriginal peoples.[39] For the CTFN, language that requires *negotiation* over the relevance of factors that determine comparability under section 16.1 of the *Yukon Final Agreement* references a version of fiscal federalism that recognizes the independent powers and jurisdiction of Yukon First Nations. The requirement for agreement prevents the presumption of unilateral determination of need or entitlement by the federal government and the concomitant expectation of unprincipled acceptance by First Nations.

In the context of fiscal negotiations, the CTFN account shows that a minimal role for law is to prevent the use of executive or legislative authority that contravenes treaty terms. The *Yukon Final Agreement* uses treaty terms that preclude the presumption of authority to dominate through unilateral policy or legislation that contravenes the treaties. Yet

38 Sari Graben, "Contemporary Treaties: Negotiating a New Federal Arrangement" (2007) 6:2 *Indigenous Law Journal* 2–32. For further discussion, see Kiera L. Ladner, "Treaty Federalism: An Indigenous Vision of Canadian Federalisms" in Francois Rocher and Miriam Smith, eds., *New Trends in Canadian Federalism* (Toronto: University of Toronto Press, 2003); Dwight Newman, "Contractual and Covenantal Conceptions of Modern Treaty Interpretation" (2011) 54 *Supreme Court Law Review* (2d) 475–91; James Tully, *Strange Multiplicity: Constitutionalism in an Age of Diversity* (Cambridge: Cambridge University Press, 1995); Alain-G. Gagnon, ed., *Contemporary Canadian Federalism: Foundations, Traditions, Institutions* (Toronto: University of Toronto Press, 2009).

39 *Ibid.*

the account here also foreshadows what powers the federal government might try to exercise, even if exercising these powers contravenes the language, spirit, and intent of the treaties. Could a future government that is unable to financially manage First Nations under the *Indian Act* introduce new legislation that would grant it new management authority over contemporary treaty governments in exigent circumstances? It is not unfathomable. That the federal government has already attempted to unilaterally alter resource management regimes in the Northwest Territories presumably protected by contemporary treaties illustrates its current willingness to contravene treaty terms and wait for the courts to prevent it.[40] Looking forward, the clear establishment of treaties as constitutional compacts that implement inviolable federal arrangements could go some distance in achieving such prevention.

7. Conclusion

This chapter's account of negotiations over funding allocations highlights some of what has changed and not changed under contemporary treaties and also illustrates the role of law in treaty implementation. This one intergovernmental negotiation reveals that practices of contemporary treaty implementation by all parties can be deeply strategic, rather than principled or legal. Moreover, path dependencies that have enabled the federal government to control and direct Aboriginal governments for 150 years means that governments under contemporary treaties can experience similar impediments to achieving a principled basis for intergovernmental relations as those governments under the *Indian Act*. While contemporary treaties purport to use law to create certainty, it is inaccurate to presume bureaucrats on either side will rely on shared interpretations when determining their obligations. Instead, when there are interpretive differences, the parties are likely to develop interim arrangements for the purposes of governing that avoid developing a shared meaning.

40 *Tlicho Government v Canada (Attorney General)*, [2015] NWTJ 14. For discussion of co-management under contemporary treaties in the Mackenzie Valley, see Sari Graben, "Assessing Stakeholder Participation in Sub-Arctic Co-Management: Administrative Rulemaking and Private Agreements" (2011) 29:1 *Windsor Yearbook of Access to Justice* 195–221.

All of this means that the specificity of contemporary treaties as legal documents is not, in and of itself, able to rectify relations marked by colonialism. The role of courts in defining treaty terms and judging whether governmental practices conform to those terms instead remains essential to implementation. Yet, in order to avoid the pitfalls of treaty interpretation, which has turned historic treaties into instruments of management and control, courts must develop an understanding of treaties that reflects the parties' political goals and intentions. Without grounding contemporary treaties in their federalist aims, the redemptive power of law, even where painstakingly detailed, is likely to remain elusive.

PART II

The Role of Indigenous Legal Orders: Treaty Rights or Right Relationships?

7 Rights and Remedies within Common Law and Indigenous Legal Traditions: Can the Covenant Chain Be Judicially Enforced Today?

MARK D. WALTERS*

This chapter examines the Covenant Chain treaty relationship that was affirmed in the eighteenth century between the Crown and Indigenous peoples in Canada in light of ideas about rights and remedies today. It identifies reasons why judges may be reluctant to directly enforce the principles of self-determination embraced by this treaty in the present-day context. The chapter suggests, however, that if the treaty relationship is understood through the Indigenous legal traditions that first gave it life, creative judicial remedies might be articulated to establish a legal framework for the kind of political dialogue necessary for the treaty's principles to be vindicated. This framework would be informed by Indigenous legal ideas, but it would not introduce wholly new principles into Canadian law; indeed, it would resemble in many respects the principle of "cooperative federalism" that lies at the centre of Canadian constitutional law.

If the plaintiff has a right, he must of necessity have a means to vindicate and maintain it, and a remedy if he is injured in the exercise or enjoyment of it, and, indeed it is a vain thing to imagine a right without a remedy; for want of right and want of remedy are reciprocal …

– Sir John Holt, Lord Chief Justice of England, from *Ashby v White* (1703), 2 Ld. Raym. 938, 950, at 953

* The author wishes to acknowledge the funding assistance for research provided by the Social Sciences and Humanities Research Council of Canada.

Among the Indians there have been no written laws. Customs handed down from generation to generation have been the only laws to guide them. Everyone might act different from what was considered right did he choose to do so, but such acts would bring upon him the censure of the nation, which he dreaded more than any corporeal punishment ...

This fear of the nation's censure acted as a mighty band, binding all in one social, honorable compact. They would not as brutes be whipped into duty. They would as men be persuaded to the right.

– George Copway (*Kahgegagahbowh*), *The Traditional History and Characteristic Sketches of the Ojibway Nation* (London: Charles Gilpin, 1850), 144

1. Introduction

The idea that right and remedy are reciprocal is embedded deep within the common law tradition. Indeed, the insistence by Chief Justice Sir John Holt, quoted above, that where there is a right there is a remedy, is itself a variation upon an even more ancient common law idea that rights are simply the consequences of remedies.[1] So prominent were the forms of action at common law, such as writs of novel disseisin, debt, or detinue, that, it has been said, "substantive law" was for many centuries "secreted in the interstices of procedure."[2] However, the close relationship between the substance of right and the procedures associated with remedy is not unique to the common law tradition; indeed, it seems also to have been a feature of Indigenous legal tradition, at least among the Anishinaabe peoples of the Great Lakes region of North America. That people were to be "persuaded to the right," as Anishinaabe writer George Copway put it, reflected an understanding that what was right in any given situation could only really be appreciated through a particular procedure or form of discourse aimed at persuasion and agreement. And, in this respect, not any kind of persuasion would do. As another nineteenth-century Anishinaabe writer, William Warren, observed, it was at the council fire, the "symbol of their nationality," that the chiefs of clans and extended family lineages among the

1 F.W. Maitland, *The Forms of Action at Common Law*, A.H. Chaytor and W.J. Whittaker, eds. (Cambridge: Cambridge University Press, 1948) at 6.

2 Sir Henry Maine, *Dissertations on Early Law and Custom* (London: John Murray, 1883) at 389.

peoples of the Great Lakes met to resolve their problems through carefully structured forms of discourse.[3] The remedy for a wrong was, from this perspective, to *talk* according to the procedural customs of the council fire with a view to securing substantive right.

If there are similarities between common law and Indigenous legal traditions on the question of the substance of right and the procedure of remedy, there are, needless to say, differences too. It is easy to slip from the idea of *rights*, an idea which permeates the common law, to the idea of *right*, an idea which seems to inform Indigenous legal tradition. To claim *a* right is not always the same thing as seeking *right*. To ask what rights one has is to ask what one is owed by others, an inquiry that looks backward to an *a priori* conception of rights, whereas to ask what is right between people seems to involve asking what it is that they should do in relation to each other, an inquiry that looks forward towards establishing just relationships. The difference between approaches is not always clear, and indeed is best understood as a difference in emphasis rather than a conceptual difference. So it can be said, on the one hand, that rights are part of the Anishinaabe legal tradition, and, on the other hand, that this tradition focuses upon the relational aspects of law and right.[4] In the end, however, it is hard to deny that conceptions of right and rights are culturally entrenched and embodied in language. It may be helpful, then, to ask what word within the Anishinaabemowin language might capture the idea of right as it is used in the context of defining relationships around the council fire. One word that has been said to capture the Anishinaabe conception of right in this sense is *bimaadiziwin*, a word that connotes a special conception of the good life predicated upon securing harmony between individual, community, and the spiritual forces animating the natural world.[5] But if right should be vindicated by remedy, as the Lord Chief

3 William Warren, *History of the Ojibways Based upon Traditions and Oral Statements* [1853] (Minneapolis: Ross and Haines, 1957) at 99.

4 John Borrows, *Canada's Indigenous Constitution* (Toronto: University of Toronto Press, 2010) at 77–9; John Borrows (Kegedonce), *Drawing Out Law: A Spirit's Guide* (Toronto: University of Toronto Press, 2010) at 8.

5 See, for example, the work of Anishinaabe scholars Leanne Simpson, "Looking after *Gdoo-naaganinaa*: Precolonial Nishnaabeg Diplomatic and Treaty Relationships" (2008) 23:2 *Wicazo Sa Review* 29, and Aimeé Craft, *Breathing Life into the Stone Fort Treaty: An Anishinabe Understanding of Treaty One* (Saskatoon: Purich Publishing, 2013) at 69–71. For reflective criticism of the concept of *bimaadiziwin* by another

Justice of England said long ago, what remedy vindicates a people's aspiration for *bimaadiziwin*?

I will concede at the beginning of this essay that I do not have the answer to this question. My principal purpose in what follows is simply to argue that once the issue of right and remedy is framed in this way – that is, once we think about right and remedy as a cross-cultural legal question – then we may be in a better position to consider the question of what judicially enforceable legal remedies (if any) exist in Canadian law today for vindicating the rights of Anishinaabe peoples under the Covenant Chain treaty that was affirmed with the Crown at Niagara 250 years ago.

The Covenant Chain treaty was a type of constitution established at the council fires that were lit by Indigenous and Crown representatives in the seventeenth and eighteenth centuries – a constitution that drew far more from Indigenous than European notions of law and right.[6] It began as a treaty relationship between officials of the colony of New York and the Six Nations Iroquois, or Haudenosaunee, in the mid-seventeenth century, and by the end of the eighteenth century it had been extended to all of the nations surrounding the Great Lakes as well as to the Mi'kmaq and other nations of the east coast.[7] The Covenant Chain treaty relationship between the Crown and the Anishinaabe peoples who lived within the Great Lakes watershed was affirmed in a series of council meetings that culminated with the grand treaty council held at Niagara in the summer of 1764. At these meetings, the Crown's representative for Indian Affairs, Sir William Johnson, presented to the chiefs and Elders from the Anishinaabe Nation and other nations "the

---

Anishinaabe scholar, see Lawrence W. Gross, "Bimaadiziwin, or the 'Good Life,' as a Unifying Concept of Anishinaabe Religion" (2002) 26:1 *American Indian Culture and Research Journal* 15, and Lawrence W. Gross, "Cultural Sovereignty and Native American Hermeneutics in the Interpretation of the Sacred Stories of the Anishinaabe" (2003) 18:2 *Wicazo Sa Review* 127.

6 Mark D. Walters, "Brightening the Covenant Chain: Aboriginal Treaty Meanings in Law and History after *Marshall*" (2001) 24 *Dalhousie Law Journal* 75.

7 Francis Jennings, *The Ambiguous Iroquois Empire: The Covenant Chain Confederation of Indian Tribes with English Colonies* (New York: W.W. Norton and Co., 1984); Timothy D. Willig, *Restoring the Chain of Friendship: British Policy and the Indians of the Great Lakes, 1783–1815* (Lincoln: University of Nebraska Press, 2008); Donald Marshall Sr., Alexander Denny, and Simon Marshall, "The Covenant Chain" in Boyce Richardson, ed., *Drumbeat: Anger and Renewal in Indian Country* (Toronto: University of Toronto Press, 1989), 73–104.

great Covenant Chain," a belt of wampum shells "23 Rows broad, & the Year 1764 worked upon it."[8] The Covenant Chain treaty remains at the centre of the Anishinaabe idea of what Canada is today. Modern Canadian courts have enforced eighteenth-century treaties made between the Crown and Aboriginal peoples, but so far have only done so in relation to specific activities like hunting and fishing or engaging in trade or in a particular customary practice.[9] The Covenant Chain, however, contemplates not a right to do this or that practice or activity; it is, rather, a comprehensive constitutional relationship that seeks *right* in its broadest sense. It is a relationship, however, that gradually eroded as political circumstances changed in the nineteenth century. The Chain has, in the language of the council fire, rusted, perhaps even broken. Whether a judicial order today is capable of vindicating this kind of relationship, this kind of right, so many years after the rust set in, is, of course, a very good question. In this essay I will try to offer some preliminary thoughts about how this question might be answered.

2. Anishinaabe Conceptions of Rights and Remedies

The starting point for understanding legal remedies for vindicating the Covenant Chain treaty relationship must be located within the Indigenous legal traditions that shaped that relationship, including, in particular, Anishinaabe conceptions of legality. I am trained as a common lawyer and not in Indigenous law, and so my own comments on this topic will necessarily be those of an outsider and will thus be tentative and incomplete. Indeed, they are comments given in a spirit of humility and with no little amount of trepidation, and I hope that readers will take what I say about Anishinaabe conceptions of legality with caution. They may wish to consult Elders and experts in this field before coming to any firm conclusions about the arguments that I make.

---

8 James Sullivan, ed., "Treaty Council at Niagara, 9 July–14 August 1764" in *The Papers of Sir William Johnson*, vol. 11 (Albany: State University of New York, 1921–65) at 309–10. See in general John Borrows, "Wampum at Niagara: The Royal Proclamation, Canadian Legal History and Self-Government" in Michael Asch, ed., *Aboriginal and Treaty Rights in Canada: Essays on Law, Equality and Respect for Difference* (Vancouver: UBC Press, 1997) 155.

9 E.g., *R v Sioui*, [1990] 1 SCR 1025; *R v Marshall*, [1999] 3 SCR 456.

It may be helpful to begin by recalling the story of the Anishinaabeg from the Sault – the *Saulteaux* – who, after receiving their invitation to attend the council at Niagara, consulted *Mikinaak*, the Great Turtle, in a *jiisakiiwin*, or shaking-tent ceremony, about whether it was safe for them to attend the council.[10] The message they received was that if they attended the council, Sir William Johnson would fill their canoes with presents. Still the Saulteaux remained wary. Their journey to Niagara took them across the vast expanses of Lake Huron and Georgian Bay, and they felt a sense of unease within the waters around them. They encountered a snake *manitou* on one of the countless islands they passed, and, addressing the snake as grandfather, they gave it presents to ensure the safety of their canoes in the troubled waters that they encountered. In the end, they succeeded in reaching Niagara and they met Johnson at the treaty council.

I used to think that this was just an interesting story. Over time, however, I have come to think that the account of the journey that the Saulteaux made by canoe to Niagara reveals important insights into the *legal* context of the treaty relationship affirmed at Niagara. I have struggled through reading and talking to people to gain some understanding of Anishinaabe legal traditions. Canoes feature prominently in many stories that I have heard. I have learned that, from the Anishinaabe perspective, there was a time before there were Anishnaabeg in the world, when there were animals and there were *manitous* and there was the trickster figure known as Nanabush. In this time, Nanabush battled the *michebeshu*, the malevolent lynx and serpent *manitous* of the water, and after he killed one of their chiefs they flooded the world. Nanabush took refuge with the animals on a raft or canoe. He then asked the water animals to dive from the canoe into the waters to retrieve earth from the depths so that a new land might be created. The waters proved too deep for the beaver and even the otter, but finally the muskrat surfaced with some soil, and when Nanabush breathed upon the soil it grew into an island capable of providing a home for the animal-folk. The animals were soon joined by the Anishinaabeg who would come to rely upon their animal relations as well as benevolent *manitous*, especially the *animikeek* or thunderers of the sky, to help them to understand

10 Alexander Henry, *Travels and Adventures in Canada and the Indian Territories between the Years 1760 and 1776* (New York: I. Riley, 1809) at 165–81.

bimaadiziwin, the essence of right or good living, and its immanent *inaakonigewin* or laws.[11]

For the Anishinaabeg and other Indigenous peoples of the territories surrounding the five Great Lakes in North America, ideas about societal ordering were inseparable from ideas about the natural order of water, sky, and land within which they lived. The Great Lakes are the largest freshwater lakes in the world, drawing their waters from a complex system of muskegs, pools, ponds, creeks, streams, rivers, and smaller lakes, a labyrinth of water cutting between forests and meadows. In these territories of land and water, distinctive ideas about law emerged. Indeed, for the peoples indigenous to these territories, it was the very relationship between land and water, and their understanding of the place of people within that relationship, which grounded their ideas about legality.

The foundations for Indigenous legal traditions within the nations of the Great Lakes region may thus be located within the oral traditions about the very beginnings of the world. Although the region was divided culturally and linguistically between Algonquians and Iroquoians, nations within each group developed similar narratives on the world's origins. The tradition concerning the deluge and diving for earth of the Algonquian-speaking Anishinaabeg was similar to the narratives of their Iroquoian-speaking Wendat and Haudenosaunee neighbours.

---

11 For examples of the Anishinaabe narrative, in different forms, see Francis Assikinack, "Legends and Traditions of the Odahwah Indians" (1858) 3 *Canadian Journal of Industry, Science, and Art* 115 at 122–4; A.F. Chamberlain, "Nanibozhu amongst the Otchipwe, Mississagas, and Other Algonkian Tribes" (1891) 4:14 *Journal of American Folklore* 193; William Jones, *Ojibwa Texts, Part I*, Truman Michelson, ed. (Leyden, NY: Publications of the American Ethnological Society, 1917) at 89–101 and 145–59; Paul Radin and A.B. Reagan, "Ojibwa Myths and Tales: The Manabozho Cycle" (1928) 41:159 *Journal of American Folklore* 61; Basil Johnston, *Honour Earth Mother: Mino-audiaudauh Mizzu-kummik-quae* (Wiarton, ON: Kegedonce Press, 2003) at 1–9. In many accounts, Nanabush survives the deluge by making a raft from tree branches, but in some accounts he survives in a canoe. See Andrew J. Blackbird, *History of the Ottawa and Chippewa Indians of Michigan: A Grammar of their Language, and Personal and Family History of the Author* (Ypsilanti, MI: Ypsilanti Job Print House, 1887) at 75–6 (Nanabush had a "great canoe"); A.F. Chamberlain, "Tales of the Mississaguas. II" (1890) 3:9 *Journal of American Folklore* 149 at 150 (an account from the Scugog Island Mississaugas said Nanabush survived in his "ōtchīmāning" or canoe (boat)). On the relationship between *bimaadiziwin* and *inaakonigewin*, see Craft, *Breathing Life into the Stone Fort Treaty*, *supra* note 5 at 69–71.

These peoples told of how a spirit-woman fell from her home in the sky to the endless seas below, only to be saved by water animals who placed her upon a giant turtle and then dove to find soil from which a verdant land grew for the animals, and, in time, humans, on the island formed by the turtle's back.[12]

Different versions of the "Earth-Diver" story were told by other Indigenous peoples in North America, and all of these stories resonate with ancient narratives from other parts of the world – including, of course, the biblical story of the Flood and the ark.[13] There was something distinctive, however, about the Algonquian and Iroquoian narratives that the biblical story lacked. For the Indigenous peoples of the Great Lakes, the animals were not passive victims in need of rescuing from the deluge, but rather they were active participants in the formation of the world. The animals appear within Indigenous traditions as people themselves, as animal-folk, capable of holding their own councils in which collective decisions were made about how to respond to the perils they confronted.[14] Their world existed together with the worlds of the *manitous*, or spirit-beings, who had their own chiefs and councils in the skies above, in the watery depths below, and even within the rocks and trees of the new lands that had emerged. From the perspective offered by Indigenous Earth-Diver traditions, humans entered a place already peopled by animals and *manitous* capable of exerting

12 For examples of the Wendat (Huron) and Haudenosaunee (Five or Six Nations Iroquois) narratives, in different forms, see Elias Johnson [a Tuscorara chief], *Legends, Traditions and Laws, of the Iroquois, or Six Nations, and History of the Tuscorara Indians* (Lockport, NY: Union Printing and Publishing, 1881) at 40; William M. Beauchamp, *The Iroquois Trail, or, Footprints of the Six Nations in Customs, Traditions and History* (Fayetteville, NY: H.C. Beauchamp, 1892); C.M. Barbeau, "Supernatural Beings of the Huron and Wyandot" (1914) 16:2 *American Anthropologist* 288.

13 For comparisons of the Earth-Diver narratives within Algonquian, Iroquoian, and other societies, see Franz Boas, "Dissemination of Tales among the Natives of North America" (1891) 4:12 *Journal of American Folklore* 13; Gladys A. Reichard, "Literary Types and Dissemination of Myths" (1921) 34:133 *Journal of American Folklore* 269; Francis Lee Utley, "The Migration of Folktales: Four Channels to the Americas" (1974) 15:1 *Current Anthropology* 5; Frederic Baraga, *Abrégé de l'Histoire des Indiens de l'Amérique Septentrionale* (Paris: Société des Bons Livres, 1837) at 177–8: "La tradition du déluge s'est conservée généralement parmi les Indiens" (The tradition of the flood was generally maintained by the Indians).

14 William N. Fenton, "This Island, the World on the Turtle's Back" (1962) 75:298 *Journal of American Folklore* 283 at 292.

forms of jurisdictional influence.[15] The development of human laws would prove to be a very complex endeavour indeed within this world of related normative or jurisdictional spheres that emerged through the relationship between water, land, and sky.

For Indigenous peoples of the Great Lakes region, whether Iroquoian-speaking or Algonquian-speaking, legal order was thus a matter of seeking harmony between a complex series of shifting normative spheres or domains. Families, clans, villages, nations, and confederacies of nations represented overlapping and interconnecting jurisdictional spheres. Within and between these sphere, normative meaning evolved through constant discourse and the performance of duties of care through gift exchanges that ensured spiritual kinship. These shifting normative domains, however, were integrated within a dynamic physical environment infused with spiritual life that had its own shifting normative spheres, and the harmony needed for normative order among people involved seeking balanced relations with these spheres or domains too. In this sense, then, legal normativity was intensively grounded within the homeland of the people. Jurisdiction over homeland, however, was not territorial in the European sense, and so did not involve the assertion of dominion over the land by a single authority. Rather, territory was manifested through the constant negotiation of good relations with the shifting normative domains that bound people to each other and to the world around them. The canoe on the river is not, from this perspective, just a metaphor for a jurisdiction; it is literally a jurisdiction navigating through shifting currents of normative force within the river, along the shores, and in the sky above. Jurisdiction is not exercised *over* lands and waters, but *through* engaging with the multiple jurisdictions of a spiritually charged environment, and seeking to ensure, where possible, coherent and sound relationships between those different domains of order. There are, in this environment, lines of normative meaning that weave and interconnect in dynamic ways. These lines of normative meaning are, we could say, *like* the networks of countless rivers, lakes, and waterways that were canoed by the peoples of the Great Lakes. However, we could also say that these lines of normative meaning were actually *manifested*, in part at least, *by* the countless

15 Theresa S. Smith, *The Island of the Anishnaabeg: Thunderers and Water Monsters in the Traditional Ojibwe Life-World* (Moscow, ID: University of Idaho Press, 1995) at 21, 44, 49.

rivers, lakes, and waterways that were canoed. The canoe on the river is, at one level, a legal metaphor for a jurisdiction within a world of related jurisdictions. At a deeper level of meaning, however, it is not just a metaphor but a real jurisdictional space within a complex network of laws through which it must be navigated. One way of achieving legal order in its fullest sense, then, is through the experience of successfully navigating the river and completing a journey safely. From this perspective, the story of the Saulteaux' journey by canoe to the Covenant Chain council at Niagara takes on a very special meaning.

3. The British Canoe

If we want to understand the status of the British Crown from the Indigenous legal perspective under the Covenant Chain, we can do no better than to include within the legal landscape just painted the "great Canoe," as Indigenous people sometimes called it, of the English or British empire. The imagery of the Covenant Chain which was worked into wampum belts includes the image of this canoe. "[W]hen the Christians first arrived in this Country, we received them kindly," stated Sadakanahtie, an Onondaga chief, in 1694, "we tied the great Canoe which brought them, not with a Rope made of Bark to a Tree, but with a strong iron Chain fastened to a great Mountain."[16] In time, the iron Chain linked to the British canoe was exchanged for a silver Covenant Chain.

But as great as the British canoe might be, it enters the river as just *one* jurisdiction navigating a network of waterways and a series of shifting normative domains each of which requires respect through acknowledging reciprocal duties of care. In his oral tradition of the 1764 Niagara council, Anishinaabe chief Assiginack explained, in 1851, the wampum belt that Johnson gave at Niagara. Upon laying down the belt, Johnson said, according to Assiginack, "I speak the truth, the Great Spirit hears me also, you see the Waters present the appearance of white cloth being spread over their surface, the trees have no power to move, and in the sky not a particle of dust can be seen, all this confirm the truth

16 Treaty council with Five Nations, Albany, May 1694, in Cadwallader Colden, *The History of the Five Indian Nations of Canada, which are Dependent on the Province of New-York in America, and are the Barrier between the English and French in that Part of the World* (London: T. Osborne, 1747) at 167.

of my words."[17] In this belt, Johnson then explained, was depicted his "Canoe" which was "floating on the other side of the Great Waters" full of the "necessaries of life" for his children, and they needed only to "take hold of the Vessel" and pull this "Canoe" over to "this Land" on which they stood and their needs would be met, all of which was guaranteed by the "Great Spirit."[18] Yes, the Chain connected jurisdictions, but it was a connection defined by sacred duties of care and trust – and the British jurisdiction was moored at a distance until those living within Anishinaabe jurisdictions wanted to draw it closer.

I have read the written record of the Treaty of Niagara a number of times over the years. I think, though perhaps it is more of a vain hope than anything, that my understanding of the treaty council has become deeper and richer as my understanding of Indigenous legal traditions has slowly improved. The story of the canoe journey by the Anishinaabeg from the Sault to Niagara in 1764 is a story of navigating legal jurisdictions as much as the story of the council at Niagara is. Like Assiginack's oral tradition of the Niagara council, the written record abounds with references to canoes and the need to smooth the waterways.

This is not to say that the treaty negotiations were themselves altogether smooth. There is a tension between legal perspectives evident in the record. Johnson consistently adopts a hard line about rights and remedies. The Niagara treaty council was prompted by the so-called Pontiac uprising. Insofar as they had participated in that uprising, the Great Lakes nations had, in Johnson's view, violated the Covenant Chain and it was important for them to acknowledge their wrong and commit to specific remedial acts, such as the payment of compensation. However, Johnson was frustrated throughout by the fact that the chiefs and Elders assembled simply refused to see the issues in this way. They insisted on focusing the discussion on re-establishing, in a forward-looking manner, a relationship of trust and care, one in which the British Crown reassumed its proper role as *Father*. The lack of trade during the war had left the Great Lakes nations in need, and they looked to Johnson, as their Father's representative, to, in the words of an Ottawa

17 Untitled statement (no. 1), signed "J.B. Assekinawk, Indian Chief," Manitowawning (21 October 1851), Ottawa, National Archives of Canada (RG 10, vol. 613, file 440–2).

18 Untitled statement (no. 2), signed "J.B. Assikinawk, Indian Chief," Manitowawning (21 October 1851), Ottawa, National Archives of Canada (RG 10, vol. 613, file 440–3.

chief named Bildanwan, "supply our wants & fill our Canoes."[19] The Great Turtle, speaking in the shaking tent at Sault St. Marie, had used a similar expression. The expression may be taken literally as meaning that Johnson was to fill canoes with material goods of value. However, the canoe and the waters it travelled held a special spiritual and legal meaning for Indigenous peoples, and it is perhaps more accurate to say that filling the canoe with presents meant something like infusing nations with the spiritual and material benefits needed for their flourishing as free peoples at one with each other and the world around them.

The Niagara council was, in the end, all about re-establishing right – *right*, that is, in the special sense captured by the Anishinaabe ideal of *bimaadiziwin*. Johnson, the chiefs stated, had "cleared the Sky throughout this Country, and Smoothed the Waters of the Lakes, so that all was calm."[20] Johnson, for his part, stated in return that "he hoped before he left *Niagara* to render the Lakes, and Waters perfectly smooth ..."[21] We should not skip over these metaphors quickly. They contain the essence of a very complicated conception of legality. The metaphor of travelling by water appears in several parts of the written record. A Chippewa chief whose people lived "two days Journey from Toronto," stated: "That it gave them the most infinite pleasure to hear of Sir Wm's coming, that on his arrival the Lakes became placid, the Storms ceased & the Whole face of Nature was changed."[22]

We find also the mixing of pipe, road, and canoe images: "This Pipe is sent by all our Chiefs," one chief told Johnson, "We were obliged, several times along the Road, to Hoist up this Pipe in our Canoe to prevent our being Scratched on our way."[23] In the roughest sense, we may read this statement as meaning that to establish good relations – to establish right – with the British jurisdiction, the Anishinaabe jurisdiction struggled to overcome obstacles to peace and friendship. In the end, Johnson gave up on the idea of exacting specific remedies for what he perceived to be wrongs committed. Except for the Hurons of Detroit and the Senecas of Chenussio, no specific terms of peace were signed at Niagara; rather the unwritten Covenant Chain relationship was simply reaffirmed.

19 Treaty Council at Niagara, *supra* note 8 at 265.
20 *Ibid* at 273–4.
21 *Ibid* at 274.
22 *Ibid* at 271, 273.
23 *Ibid* at 300.

Stepping back and reflecting upon the treaty relationship in a general way, it is clear that the Covenant Chain was a mechanism through which the Great Lakes nations exercised sovereignty. This sovereignty was not asserted through an absolute political authority vested in a single entity. Rather, it was manifested by acknowledging the existence of multiple and interlocking centres or nodes of normativity. Family lineages, clans, villages, nations, confederacies, colonies, their "Father" the King and his representatives, and the spiritual forces within their lands and waters were all centres of interlocking normativity, each independent but also inseparable from the others. All of these centres are subject to the imperative of "right," the imperative of seeking coherent or harmonious relationships through honouring duties of care while at the same time respecting each group's field of equal freedom.[24] The Covenant Chain was a constitution, but not one in which rights and remedies were sharply divided concepts. As a system of interlocking centres of normativity that flourished through respecting reciprocal duties of care and domains of equal freedom through discourse and gift-giving, no such conceptual distinction could be made: the right it secured, which was a right or good relationship, was almost entirely subsumed by its remedial or procedural aspects captured by the customary laws of the council fire. It was a constant process of reinventing or brightening the Chain. It was about navigating within a system of dynamic normative forces. In this discursive legal order, the idea of a remedy that fixed a past wrong was as pointless as turning the canoe around and paddling up a raging river – it was an impossibility. Rust on the chain could only be removed by looking forward to a relationship once again based on integrity and coherence and the humility implicit within the duties of care and trust upon which it was based.

4. Recognizing Rights or Relationships

It should be apparent by now that I do not think that the Covenant Chain treaty relationship can be restored today through a simple judicial order. This conclusion, however, presents certain problems for the

---

24 Mark D. Walters, "'Your Sovereign and Our Father': The Imperial Crown and the Idea of Legal-Ethnohistory" in Shaunnagh Dorsett and Ian Hunter, eds., *Law and Politics in British Colonial Thought: Transpositions of Empire* (Houndmills: Palgrave Macmillan, 2010) at 91.

idea that treaties are sources of rights, at least in terms of the classical understanding of rights and remedies in the common law tradition. That understanding, as expressed by Chief Justice Sir John Holt in *Ashby v White*, is that if there is a right in law then the law must provide a remedy to vindicate that right. The idea that "where there is a right there is a remedy" was, and remains, a powerful one within the common law tradition – illustrated in Canada most famously, perhaps, by Justice Bertha Wilson's use of *Ashby v White* in crafting a common law tort of racial discrimination.[25] The difficulty, however, is that not all problems can be cured or remedied by orders issued by judges. Indeed, when Holt's dictum is pushed to its limit, it flips over onto its head. It is, in other words, a short step from saying that where there is a right there is remedy to saying that there can be *no* right *unless* there is a remedy. It follows, under this logic, that if there can be no judicial remedy today to fix the rusted or broken Covenant Chain, then there can be no treaty rights in law under the Covenant Chain.

Is there a judicial remedy that could fix the rusted or broken Covenant Chain? Much depends upon how the argument is framed. What is it about the Covenant Chain that Anishinaabe communities might wish to have judicially enforced today? The Covenant Chain certainly recognized a genuine sense of jurisdictional autonomy for Indigenous peoples. One option, then, is to invoke the Covenant Chain as the basis for a right to self-government in relation to a particular topic or subject matter and claim that this right is constitutionally protected as an existing treaty right under section 35(1) of the *Constitution Act, 1982*. This is what the Mississaugas of Scugog Island First Nation did: They claimed that pursuant to the Covenant Chain, as affirmed in 1764 at Niagara, they enjoyed a constitutional right to govern labour relations within the casino located within their reserve and that provincial labour laws were therefore inoperable within the casino. The remedy sought was therefore a traditional constitutional law remedy.

The argument was first put to the Ontario Labour Relations Board, which ruled against the First Nation, and this decision was then upheld

25 *Bhadauria v Board of Governors of Seneca College of Applied Arts and Technology* (1979), 27 OR (2d) 142 (CA). The Supreme Court of Canada rejected Justice Wilson's reasoning on the grounds that human rights legislation precluded common law developments in the area: *Seneca College of Applied Arts and Technology v Bhadauria*, [1981] 2 SCR 181.

by the courts on judicial review.[26] In writing the decision of the Ontario Court of Appeal in the case, Justice Robert Sharpe accurately summarized the essence of the Covenant Chain, noting that it was based on oral engagements and council fire ceremony, that it was informed by Aboriginal legal forms and customs, and that it came to embrace "an entire set of constitutional assumptions" about the relationship between the Crown and Aboriginal peoples, including the idea that Aboriginal peoples had a "right to self-determination."[27] But Sharpe then concluded that, in the absence of any evidence of a "specific term or promise" in this respect, the right to self-determination was simply too general and diffuse to be an enforceable constitutional right.[28]

It is worth pausing to consider the implications of the *Scugog Island* case. It can be said that, in one sense, the problem for the First Nation in this case was not the inability to identify an appropriate remedy for their claim, for once the decision was made to invoke the Covenant Chain in support of a standard section 35 treaty right argument the remedy followed as a matter of course. Had the treaty right been established, any unjustifiable legislative infringement of that right would have been unconstitutional and an order rendering such legislation inapplicable in relation to the First Nation would have been granted – a standard remedy in treaty rights cases. The real problem for the First Nation, then, was simply its failure to establish the treaty right. In another sense, however, perhaps the remedy was the problem. To put it bluntly, perhaps the Covenant Chain is simply too good to be true. The right to self-determination within the Covenant Chain relationship was so comprehensive, and the remedies that would attach to that right, if recognized today, so profound, that the judges were arguably overwhelmed by the implications of upholding the right. The result would have been, as Sharpe observed, "an aboriginal right of self-government on reserve lands of virtually unlimited breath and amplitude."[29]

---

26 *Mississaugas of Scugog Island First Nation v National Automobile, Aerospace, Transportation and General Workers Union of Canada (CAW-Canada), Local 444 et al.*, [2006] OJ No. 2159 (Div Ct); aff'd (2007), 88 OR (3d) 583 (CA); leave to appeal denied [2008] SCCA 35.

27 *Ibid* 88 OR (3d) at paras 49, 50. I should perhaps mention that Justice Sharpe's description of the Covenant Chain was drawn from the affidavit of the expert witness put forth by the First Nation, which happened to be me.

28 *Ibid* at paras 50, 52.

29 *Ibid* at para 52.

Of course, this conclusion is disputable. There are no doubt ways to reconceive the broad right of self-determination that was reflected in the eighteenth-century Covenant Chain so that it fits Canadian constitutional realities in the twenty-first century. Still, judges are understandably reluctant to engage in this reinterpretive process themselves. The *Scugog Island* case therefore suggests that traditional remedies may not be very helpful for Anishinaabe communities seeking to enforce the Covenant Chain treaty against provincial and federal governments in Canada today.

But what about non-traditional remedies? The law of remedies has evolved significantly since Chief Justice Holt pronounced upon the reciprocal nature of rights and remedies. It has been an accepted part of Canadian law for over twenty years that Aboriginal rights are best resolved through political negotiation and settlement and that judicial remedies should be crafted to encourage this political process.[30] Appropriate constitutional remedies in this respect include declarations, suspended declarations of invalidity, structured injunctions, and supervisory orders. Declaratory relief involves the issuance by the court of a mere declaration identifying the parties' legal rights without any additional order for consequential relief or action.[31] Declarations are particularly effective in cases in which designing a full remedy for the violation of a constitutional right involves policy decisions about sensitive political matters, legislative reform, and/or budgetary decisions that are best left to political actors.[32] In some cases, however, a mere declaration may not be enough to vindicate the right, and courts have developed more structured forms of remedy, such as suspended declarations of invalidity[33] and supervisory orders,[34] that tighten the parameters around political actors while still leaving them room to design the ultimate remedy themselves. In the area of Aboriginal and treaty rights, the Supreme Court of Canada has shown a marked preference over the

30 See in general Kent Roach, "Aboriginal Peoples and the Law: Remedies for Violations of Aboriginal Rights" (1992) 21 *Manitoba Law Journal* 498.

31 Lazar Sarna, *The Law of Declaratory Judgments*, 3rd ed. (Toronto: Thomson Canada, 2007) at 3.

32 *Mahe v Alberta*, [1990] 1 SCR 342; *Canada (Prime Minister) v Khadr*, 2010 SCC 3, [2010] 1 SCR 44.

33 *Eldridge v British Columbia (Attorney General)*, [1997] 3 SCR 624.

34 *Doucet-Boudreau v Nova Scotia (Minister of Education)*, [2003] 3 SCR 3.

course of the last decade or so for encouraging the "reconciliation" of Crown and Aboriginal peoples through treaty settlements and other forms of negotiation, and this remedial preference has been folded back into the concept of substantive rights producing a complex body of law on the duty of consultation and accommodation.[35] More recently the Court held in *Manitoba Metis Federation* that where official conduct in relation to Aboriginal peoples violated the "honour of the Crown" the remedy of a general declaration to that effect is appropriate "in order to assist them in extra-judicial negotiations with the Crown in pursuit of the overarching constitutional goal of reconciliation" so that the "ongoing rift in the national fabric" may be resolved. Furthermore, statutory law, common law, and/or equitable rules governing limitation periods and delays will not prevent such declaratory relief even where those wrongs were committed over a century ago.[36]

We are now in a position to rethink how the Covenant Chain might be enforced judicially today. Perhaps the most straight-forward approach is to argue: that through the Covenant Chain the Anishinaabe and other Indigenous peoples of the Great Lakes region were acknowledged as having certain rights to self-determination; that those rights were ignored by government officials beginning in the mid-nineteenth century to the dishonour of the Crown, causing a rift in the national fabric; and that a judicial declaration to that effect is appropriate in order to encourage negotiations designed at defining the scope of self-determination today. Until treaty relations are renovated pursuant to this declaration, governmental officials should be under a duty to consult with Aboriginal peoples and possibly accommodate their concerns before making decisions that affect them. Once stated in this bald form, however, the argument for declaratory relief in support of the Covenant Chain quickly runs up against the basic concern that Sharpe raised in *Scugog Island*: the wrong and remedy seem to be so general in nature that it is difficult to see what effect, if any, a judicial declaration of this kind would have. What did happen to the Covenant Chain

35 *Haida Nation v British Columbia (Minister of Forests)*, 2004 SCC 73, [2004] 3 SCR 511; *Taku River Tlingit First Nation v British Columbia (Project Assessment Director)*, 2004 SCC 74, [2004] 3 SCR 550; *Mikisew Cree First Nation v Canada (Minister of Canadian Heritage)*, 2005 SCC 69, [2005] 3 SCR 388; *Beckman v Little Salmon/Carmacks First Nation*, 2010 SCC 53, [2010] 3 SCR 103.

36 *Manitoba Métis Federation v Canada (Attorney General)*, 2013 SCC 14 at paras 137, 140.

after all? In his 1861 book, *History of the Ojebway Indians*, Peter Jones, who was an Anishinaabe chief among the Mississaugas of the Credit River, wrote that the "old chiefs" at that time still spoke of the treaties. He recalled how, after the British conquest of the French, "their great Father, the King of England, bound their hands together with a *silver chain*" – the Covenant Chain – which "placed them as allies with the British nation, and not subjects," and so they were considered, he continued, "until the influx of emigration completely outnumbered the aborigines" from which point "the Colonial Government assumed a parental authority over them, treating them in every respect as children ..."[37] In other words, the fate of the Covenant Chain, one might say, was sealed by the general phenomenon of *colonialism*. In light of the diffuse and general nature of the dishonour associated with colonialism in Canada, one wonders whether a court today could be persuaded to issue a general declaration concerning the wrong that led to the rusting of the Covenant Chain.

5. The Flow of Canadian Federalism

There is, I think, an alternative approach to conceptualizing the right, the wrong, and the remedy in relation to the Covenant Chain – and that is to return to the Anishinaabe legal traditions that informed the essence of the Covenant Chain relationship that was affirmed at Niagara 250 years ago. The solution may be to shift the focus of our analysis from the idea of *rights* that flow from the treaty back to the idea of *right* manifested through the activity of participating in the special form of discourse contemplated by the treaty. Sharpe was, in one sense, right when he stated in *Scugog Island* that the Covenant Chain was not a set of specific promises to do this or that. It was, first and foremost, a very particular mechanism for developing just relationships – the relationship of right associated with the Anishinaabe concept of *bimaadiziwin* – within a network of interlocking centres or nodes of normativity through ongoing discourse premised upon bonds that tightly linked independent groups through reciprocal duties of care and trust. What is missing in Canada today, one might say, is *that* kind of relationship. Perhaps a declaration could be issued by the courts stating so.

37 Peter Jones (*Kah-Ke-Wa-Quo-Na-By*), *History of the Ojebway Indians; with Especial Reference to their Conversion* (London: A.W. Bennett, 1861) at 216, 217.

It will no doubt be argued in response that such a declaration suffers from the same concerns about excessive generality noted above. Perhaps. However, I do think that there are differences between, on the one hand, declaring that a just treaty relationship was violated due to colonialism, a very open-ended statement that (even coming from a judge) would likely have little impact on the efforts already underway to redress the colonial legacy in Canada, and, on the other hand, declaring that a very particular form of intergovernmental discourse once served as the foundation for a just relationship, and that it should do so again, a statement that is targeted at specific processes for political engagement. Certainly, much more work would be needed on the question of how such a declaration might be framed – which is beyond the scope of this essay. It is worth recalling, however, that the Supreme Court of Canada has set forth a relatively detailed, though non-justiciable, "legal framework" for how a province might negotiate to secede from Canada.[38] If a framework for dismantling the constitutional order can be judicially articulated, it is perhaps conceivable that a framework for re-establishing a forum aimed at repairing the constitutional fabric of Canada might be articulated too.

A remaining concern, however, is simply that the vision of constitutionalism underlying the forms of political engagement implicit within the Covenant Chain may simply no longer fit modern realities in Canada. That vision is based largely on Indigenous conceptions of legality, including the general attitude that right relationships be established through discourse involving interlocking jurisdictional domains, an attitude captured by the image of the canoe and its navigation through a network of cascading laws. Can this vision of constitutionalism be accepted by non-Indigenous judges today? Is the common-law mind capable of grasping a constitutional order that exhibits this kind of jurisdictional interplay, flexibility, and, indeed, uncertainty?

The answer should be: yes. The legal narrative of federalism in Canada today is oddly close to the Indigenous conception of constitutional order – even down to the use of water and boat metaphors. The older view of federalism, expressed by Lord Atkin, was that the Canadian "ship of state" sails on international seas but retains the "watertight compartments" that define federal and provincial powers.[39]

---

38 *Reference re Secession of Quebec*, [1998] 2 SCR 217 at para 27.

39 *Reference re Weekly Rest in Industrial Undertakings Act*, [1937] AC 326 at para 15.

Despite this, the attempt to block the flow of jurisdictional waterways, of course, failed. As Chief Justice Brian Dickson famously stated, the doctrines of federalism associated with the watertight-compartment theory represent the "undertow" within Canadian constitutional thought, and the "dominant tide" of federalism is towards allowing "a fair amount of interplay and indeed overlap between federal and provincial powers."[40] Building upon this theme, the Supreme Court of Canada has stated more recently that Canadian federalism "is not simply a matter of legalisms" but rather that "[t]he Constitution, though a legal document, serves as a framework for life and for political action within a federal state." As a result, judges must leave room for "co-operation among government actors."[41] Doctrinally speaking, the result is that judges have only sparingly applied principles like interjurisdictional immunity, which are premised upon the exclusivity of power, and they have broadly applied principles like the double-aspect doctrine and the incidental-effect doctrine, which are premised upon overlapping power. One power may "overflow" into a constitutional space allocated to another power, but this reality is not necessarily a problem, for concurrent powers are generally favoured.[42] Although the "'dominate tide' of flexible federalism ... cannot sweep designated powers out to sea," interpreting federal and provincial powers to allow for overlap and overflow "encourages intergovernmental cooperation"; "complex governance problems that arise in federations" are not, in the end, solved by "either/or" solutions but rather are remedied "by seeking cooperative solutions" negotiated between levels of government.[43] We are, in other words, in "an era of cooperative, flexible federalism."[44]

Canada is a place of oceans, lakes, and rivers, and geographically appropriate metaphors have clearly shaped the non-Indigenous legal discourse on federalism just as much as they have shaped Indigenous

40 *OPSEU v Ontario (Attorney General)*, [1987] 2 SCR 2 at 17–18.

41 *Canadian Western Bank v The Queen in Right of Alberta*, [2007] 2 SCR 3, per Justices Binnie and LeBel at para 42.

42 *Reference re Assisted Human Reproduction Act*, [2010] 3 SCR 457, per Justices Deschamps and LeBel at para 188.

43 *Reference re Securities Act*, [2011] 3 SCR 837 at paras 57, 62, 132.

44 *Quebec (Attorney General) v Canadian Owners and Pilots Association*, [2010] 2 SCR 536, per Chief Justice McLachlin at para 42.

legal discourse on interlocking normativity. The similarities in metaphor may be coincidental, but the similarities between ideas about constitutionalism are not.[45] The point of significance to draw from recent federalism cases in Canada is that the Supreme Court has acknowledged that the interpretation of the constitutional provisions regarding federal and provincial legislative power is based upon the principle of cooperative federalism – which is, in essence, a judicial assumption that overlapping power produces the political conditions necessary for negotiated and cooperative arrangements between jurisdictions. In this respect, legal substance and legal procedure come together – right and remedy merge – for rather than ruling one way or the other about which level of legislature may do what, the remedial response from the courts tends to be, where possible, a non-remedy, a decision to let all levels of constitutional authority exercise their powers with a view to encouraging discussion, negotiation, and, in the end, cooperation.

The good life, the idea of right captured by the Anishinaabe conception of *bimaadiziwin*, may be incapable of vindication by judicial order as such. Even so, it does involve a process of cooperative discourse between domains of normativity not unlike the ideal of cooperative federalism that informs the Supreme Court of Canada's decisions on the federal-provincial division of powers. Perhaps, then, we will know when the Covenant Chain has been judicially vindicated when the courts extend the principle of cooperative federalism so that it embraces Aboriginal peoples too. Canada's constitutional system has already been acknowledged by the courts to be a complex, dynamic, and, yes, uncertain, network of interlocking centres of normativity. The explicit judicial acknowledgment that Aboriginal jurisdictions are as integrated within that system as federal and provincial governments is, we may say, simply a matter of right.

45 On applying the federalism principle to the question of Aboriginal rights, see James [Sákéj] Youngblood Henderson, "Empowering Treaty Federalism" (1994) 58 *Saskatchewan Law Review* 241; Jean Leclair, "Federal Constitutionalism and Aboriginal Difference" (2005–6) 31 *Queen's Law Journal* 521.

8 What Is a Treaty? On Contract and Mutual Aid

AARON MILLS / WAABISHKI MA'IINGAN

What role should Indigenous law play in how we think about treaties, and are courts equipped to perform it? This chapter argues that it is both an ethical and analytical error to interpret treaties as a unique species of contract. Rather, treaties are constitutional associations: they coordinate the relationship of distinct political communities, constituting a shared political community across them. A treaty is the relationship itself, not the (always contingent) exchange of goods and services it empowers at any given time. It follows that disputes arising are not to be managed by judges analysing a claimed breach of terms. They must be managed politically, as matters of citizenship. This chapter offers insight into one view of Anishinaabe constitutionalism, by way of inviting all now living on Turtle Island into this understanding.

1. From Interdependence

I sat transfixed the first time I heard Elder Fred Kelly speak. On that stifling August afternoon three years ago, Fred paced circles around the interior of the Wauzhushk Onigum (Rat Portage) roundhouse, sharing teachings about Anishinaabe law and about treaty.[1] Crown representatives from six provincial ministries were gathered to learn about the

---

* The author is grateful to John Borrows, Regan Burles, Keith Cherry, Molly Churchill, and James Tully for their helpful comments.

1 Fred Kelly, "History and Significance of Manito Aki Inakonigaawin (MAI)" (teaching presented at "Manito Aki Inakonigaawin Knowledge Forum," Grand Council Treaty #3, Wauzhushk Onigum Roundhouse, 20 August 2013).

Grand Council Treaty #3 Resource Law, *Manito Aki Inakonigaawin*,[2] and Fred spoke in a way that invited them in, in a way intended for their understanding. He made all of us laugh.

At one point towards the end of his address, Fred shared words that haven't let go of me. Given the context, it isn't for me to share his artful teaching. Fortunately, he shared a very similar teaching to a packed moot court audience at McGill Law two years later: "You can't sell what you belong to; you can only share it."[3] Fred was of course speaking about his traditional territory. It's more a statement of what is possible than it is of what is good: an ontological claim, not a normative one. I am not other than, but part of, creation. Importantly, as I understand Fred's teaching,[4] *part of* is not *reduced to*: within creation we're all unique. Ours is the gift and the struggle of standing side by side, different and together. Ours, to rise to live in right relation.

I met Fred two autumns past. I caught the ferry from Victoria earlier in the day just to sit with him that evening in Vancouver. I learned so much. At the end of the night, he invited a friend and me to meet for breakfast the next morning, where he continued to share teachings about Anishinaabe law and treaty almost until noon. He shared a dreamcatcher teaching and I understood from it that all of us on Earth are connected to and through spirit. I felt I was hearing the same message I heard him share at the Wauzhushk Onigum roundhouse: we're each unique *and* interdependent.

In a reflection contemplating the personal, interpersonal, and intersocietal aspects of reconciliation following the violence of Canada's legacy of colonialism, and especially of the Indian residential schools'

---

2 Readers can learn more about MAI here: Grand Council Treaty #3, "Laws and Policies" at http://www.gct3.ca/wp-content/uploads/2016/02/mai_unofficial_consolidated_copy1.pdf. This website contains links to MAI and to a regulation developed under it. I have written about MAI previously in Aaron Mills, "Aki, Anishinaabek, kaye tahsh Crown" (2011) 9:1 *Indigenous Law Journal* 107 at 142–8.

3 Fred Kelly, "Reconciling Sovereignties: Combining Traditional Law and Contemporary Western Law to see Truth and Reconciliation," public lecture presented at McGill Faculty of Law, Moot Court (NC DH 100), 21 September 2015.

4 When engaging with Elders' teachings, I try to be careful. First, I assess the extent, if any, to which I can speak on what was shared. Second, I insist that what I share is just my understanding of what was shared with me. This is important to assert, because I may have misunderstood the Elder's intended meaning and because even if I did understand, it isn't for me to speak on his or her intentions.

ethnocide program, Fred shared the following insight, which again emphasized this point about interdependence and uniqueness:

> While international conflicts are fought between enemies on a very clear and simple proposition of win or lose, the choice here in Canada is one that must be made among friends and neighbours. We must face the underlying tensions. We must understand them and we must resolve them. Neither side believes that the other is going anywhere. This is home. So, how do we live side-by-side and build a future of prosperity together? We share space in a common land. We constitute a society that is envied by other countries. We are economically interdependent. We have many social ties. Our children are married to one another through which we share generations of grandchildren. So inextricably tied are we that our options are also very clear and simple: we can all win or we can all lose.[5]

What are we – the Indigenous and settler[6] peoples of northern Turtle Island, Mikinaakominis, which many today call Canada – to make of a perspective so contrary to our inherited narratives of who the other is, and perhaps more importantly, of who we are to them? I want to suggest that the language of "friends and neighbours," "side-by-side," "interdependent," "married to one another" and most emphatically, the statement that "we share generations of grandchildren," suggests that the relationship – and a very tightly-connected one at that – is actually *the point*. So tightly are we bound that although we are *distinct*, *unique* peoples, we are not and have never been *autonomous* peoples: as interdependent persons and communities within creation, we're always-already in relationship. We need not contract into community; we just

5 Fred Kelly, "Confession of a Born Again Pagan," in Marlene Brant Castellano, Linda Archibald, and Mike Degagné, eds., *From Truth to Reconciliation: Transforming the Legacy of Residential Schools* [2008] (Ottawa: Aboriginal Healing Foundation, 2011) at 15, 29.

6 I don't intend my use of the descriptor "settler" to reduce the political identities of non-Indigenous Canadians to the fact of colonization. I doubt many of my Elders would support that move. But in an argument about treaty constitutionalism, where our respective political status on Turtle Island is the very thing at issue, centering settler and Indigenous locations is critical. Second, I take Fred's point that settler and Indigenous identities don't present themselves in a binary relation: many of us (me included) are both. However, the earth-centred Anishinaabe view of treaty constitutionalism I begin to articulate below locates settler legitimacy within Indigenous constitutional orders, shifting the emphasis from these descriptors.

need to learn how to live well together, across our difference, in a relationship that is always changing but which has always been.

In this chapter I argue that this teaching about our relation to one another is the driving force behind both (1) Anishinaabe constitutionalism[7] (how we constitute, sustain and change our political communities over time), and (2) an Anishinaabe conception of treaty. The second point follows from the first when treaty is understood as the intentional deepening of the intersocietal political community that always-already exists.[8] As I strive to disclose the logic of this relational view of treaty, you'll find that I'm not humbly tendering it into today's neoliberal marketplace of ideas. I'm hoping to speak within the discourse of invitation – like Fred Kelly, I want to speak across our difference – but I'm openly hostile to the reduction of treaty to contract.[9]

---

7 By "constitutionalism" in an Anishinaabe sense, I have in mind the ongoing act of constituting community, not an identifiable set of documents and/or unwritten conventions, preceded by a definite article, which purport to do the same but for all time and except for the never-finished business of interpretation, all up front.

8 I offer two qualifications here. First, I recognize that different Anishinaabeg will have different understandings to share. Like all communities, we're internally diverse in our individual perspectives. The view I offer here is my own. Second, I speak of this as an "Anishinaabe" conception of treaty because that's my identity and it references sources of knowledge available to me. However, I think that although the sources of knowledge vary widely across Indigenous constitutional frameworks, the view I present discloses a logic common to most of northern Turtle Island's Indigenous peoples, which elsewhere I've called "rooted constitutionalism." See for instance the perspectives of Anishinaabe, Nehetho, and Dakota Elders in Oshoshko Bineshiikwe-Blue Thunderbird Woman, Osawa Aki Ikwe (Florence Paynter); Zoongi Gabowi Ozawa Kinew lkwe, Strong Standing Golden Eagle Woman (Mary Maytwayashing); Nii Gaani Aki lnini, Leading Earth Man (Dave Courchene); Giizih-lnini (Dr. Harry Bone); Zhonga-giizhing, Strong Day (Wally Swain); Naawakomigowiinin (Dennis White Bird); Kamintowe Pemohtet, Spirit Walker (D'Arcy Linklater); and Mah Pe Ya Mini (Henry Skywater), *Ogichi Tibakonigaywin, Kihche Othasowewin, Tako Wakan: The Great Binding Law* (written at Turtle Lodge, 2015; delivered 28 November 2015 at Turtle Lodge) at http://www.turtlelodge.org/wp-content/uploads/2015/11/ScrollBanner_TheGreatBindingLaw_24x36-PROOFv03.pdf. Turtle Lodge: International Centre for Indigenous Education and Wellness, "Manitoba Elders Share a Message with National Energy Board and the Public at Turtle Lodge," 28 November 2015 at http://www.turtlelodge.org/2015/11/manitoba-elders-share-a-message-with-national-energy-board-and-the-public. See also Thomas J. Stillday, "Bawatig/Sault Ste. Marie" (2009) 7:1 *Oshkaabewis Native Journal* at 100, 119.

9 For a thoughtful survey of various conceptions of treaty, see Janna Promislow, "Treaties in History and Law" (2014) 47:3 *University of British Columbia Law Review* 1085.

Here's why. I think that contract (political and social theorists speak more particularly of the "social contract")[10] as a device for both imagining the genesis of political community and for justifying its continuity is a way of voicing a shared commitment to violence. This is of course a very different casting of social contract than what one might more ordinarily find in a university textbook or in contractarians' own works. I'll argue that contract as an account of Canada's constitutional order is uniquely violent to Indigenous persons, peoples, and lands. In the story it tells of itself, Canada is the better-behaved, non-rebellious child of the West's younger, progress-focused generation. What most of us, and certainly most settlers, understand as its constitution bears that genealogy.[11] Because of their common commitment to (1) contract as the source of our shared political community and (2) their reduction of treaties to minor contracts within the prior and unquestioned social contract, I'll argue that both the Crown and the Supreme Court of Canada are structurally committed to violence. Following this, I'll present a different way of thinking about the link between treaty and constitutionalism, one which derives from the logic of mutual aid. Given the availability of this alternative understanding, I'll argue that we ought not to accept violence as the ultimate authorization for citizenship[12] in our shared political community. Finally, I'll argue that through the 1764 Treaty of Niagara, this alternative account of the structure of Indigenous-settler relationships is actual, not ideal.

10 That is, as distinct from the Western legal tradition's sense of contract as voluntary obligation, an artefact of private law.

11 Recent years have seen counter-narratives, but their focus has been on remedying the ethnocentrism of Indigenous *exclusion* from Canada's constitutional story, not *setting aside* the contract. Although I reason differently than either of them, two of the best known counter-narratives are John Borrows, *Canada's Indigenous Constitution* (Toronto: University of Toronto Press, 2010) and John Ralston Saul, *A Fair Country: Telling Truths about Canada* (Toronto: Viking Canada, 2008).

12 Throughout this chapter I refer to "citizens" and "citizenship," even though I argue that the social contract and thus the state as a form of political community are inherently violent. The trouble with "membership" is that it sounds like the kind of belonging one has in a choral society, birding association, or points club. In my use of "citizenship" I mean belonging in political community generally, not in the form of the state specifically.

2. The Untargeted Violence of Contract

Before proceeding to this argument, I want to pause to share my view that Canada's origin in and ongoing commitment to contract means violence *for all,* settler citizens – the beneficiaries of the contract – included. I make the point now so you can attend to my use of it throughout the argument, because there is no separate section where I take it up as a standalone critique later.

A condensed version of my argument about the general violence of contract goes like this. Contract is offered as the solution to what is imagined as the problem of radical disconnection. We're told that but for the contract we share, we're disconnected individuals, each left to pursue our own self-interest. As such I have no reason to see you as anything more than a means to achieving my goals. Strange binary, that humanity should position itself on the precarious tip of a force/consent switch: we consent to live together under specified terms for mutual security because outside of the boundaries of the contract is a world of naked force freed from consequence.

Contractarian orthodoxy says that contract saves us from being used as a means to others' ends, most importantly from their violence. I say contract is the very means by which we commit citizenship to violence. Instead of cultivating the kind of genuine non-violent relationships that sustain our connections through periods of conflict, contract is a foundation for political community that commits citizens to non-relationships, on the understanding that the merely formal union of individuals through the device of the contract is sufficient to constrain harmful action. The sovereign, responsible for enforcing the formal union, replaces the need for actual relationships. Instead, only the lesser connection of direct transactional exchange (whether in law, politics, or economics) is necessary. Where individual autonomy is the most important political good, non-instrumental relationships are of secondary importance at best and necessarily so: otherwise the priority of individual autonomy is violated (that is, subject to what the formal union will allow, it's for me to choose with whom and how I relate with others, or I'm unfree).

The trouble with such a foundation for political community follows from the fact that social contract is a fiction. As such, the necessary presumptive citizenship commitment to disconnection, in the absence of lived relationships, allows for the possibility of only imagined and thus easily severable accountability. Citizens might strive to eschew accountability physically, for instance by believing that they can outrun the law, or that they can avoid detection in the performance of a harm. More frequently and more socially acceptable, they may also seek to eschew accountability discursively, by framing facts in a narrative that best suits their interests. This is a fundamental premise, for instance, of both the common law tradition and party politics in the party system.[13]

Beneath contract's fiction, therefore, is carefully contained violence, always threatening to irrupt the artificial peace and often doing so in ways that cause the settled majority to target minority parties whose needs and correlative demands surpass what the terms of the contract contemplate. While this violence can affect any kind of minority group, Indigenous peoples are uniquely affected by virtue of their prior constitution as political communities in the very territories that contractarian constitutional orders like Canada and the United States now imperially claim as their own.[14]

As such, contract is precisely the way of thinking about our relationship which, in Fred's language, necessitates that we all lose. And I do mean *all* – not just humans.[15] That today we live in the Anthropocene follows precisely from the reality that since the initial rumblings of the European Enlightenment through to today's global marketization of freedom, the West has been in the business of losing creation (in which we *are* all connected) for all of us. The Anishinaabe treaty vision I share below builds from this very different starting point, where the understanding is, rather, that we are and have always been interdependent.

Like Fred, therefore, I believe that we can all win, and I place my hope in folks like you. Not in a state institution or practice, but in living people who care enough about our relationship to pick up a book about treaties. I house my hope in all my relations, Indigenous and settler peoples, coming to realize that our difference is not the foundational

---

13 While an individual within any kind of political community is free to act unaccountably, I explain below why in political communities where relationships have primary significance, and hence where accountability is imminent, requiring no exercise of imagination through the role of a sovereign, such opportunities are severely constrained.

14 Robert Nichols has a terrific piece on this. See Robert Nichols, "Contract and Usurpation: Enfranchisement and Racial Governance in Settler-Colonial Contexts," in Audra Simpson and Andrea Smith, eds., *Theorizing Native Studies* (Durham, NC: Duke University Press, 2014) at 99.

15 The Reverend Dr. Stan McKay (Cree) explains this well in Stan McKay, "Calling Creation Into Our Family," in Diane Engelstad and John Bird, eds., *Nation to Nation: Aboriginal Sovereignty and the Future of Canada* (Concord: House of Anansi Press Limited, 1992) at 28, 29.

problem of political community, but rather the condition of its possibility. I'm hopeful I can show you that a shared political community need not have as its foundation the reduction of difference to sameness; that we can start instead with our need for one another's unique gifts and constitute ourselves in networks of mutual aid.

I'm hopeful also that if understandably you're nervous to accept this new foundation for our shared political community, you'll nonetheless stand atop it for a short while, even if only strategically, so as to have a vantage point beyond contract from which to gaze back at it. I believe that if you do so, you'll find two things. First, you'll see that our focus on linking our gifts with our needs points our community not towards justice, but harmony and that we get there not by policing autonomy, but by empowering mutual aid. Second, having begun to understand how mutual aid works as an organizing feature of political community, you'll see that fear – cold, nasty, and brutish – is the engine that drives contract onward. Fear is the driving force for the commitment to certainty of mutual security from one another's capacity for violence that the contract is said to have established. That is, contract, unlike the mutual aid of a Covenant Chain, doesn't link us together. It's a chain that binds us apart and anchors us in perpetuity and with certainty to division.

For most of us, that kind of fear is all it takes to inspire our consent. And we don't complain afterwards as contract becomes normalized and the fear that inspired our choosing it subsides. On the contrary, given enough time we cease noticing the binds of the contract against us. They become just another aspect of the world around us: water flowing, grass growing, sun shining, contract binding. Contract has slipped into the nothingness of the day; it is as if it always existed. And so a challenge to contract today has become a provocation of the sacred to be met with righteous condemnation, contract now mistaken as part of creation's order.

3. Autonomy Zombies

What a horrifying foundation for coming together. There's nothing natural about contract. Life under contract is a zombie horror.[16] Each

16 My chapter is concerned with the notion of social contract generally and political theorists will observe from my focus on violence that I often have Hobbes in mind, but here I'm intending an allusion to Rawlsian liberalism in particular because his account is so compelling and powerful today. Rawls wants us to think from

citizen is afforded his or her autonomy and has it respected by the others; none is at serious risk of violence (or lesser diminishments of liberty) from the others so long as they respect this. In large measure this is because all are now effectively the same. Stripped of their identities (memories, minds, habits, dispositions, abilities), there remains nothing over which significant conflict *could* arise. True enough, since each is an isolated unit pursuing interests of its own, intermittent conflicts still arise (for instance over access to valuable resources, like brains, which occasion the odd frenzy). And the particular incidents of what a day brings vary for each. But despite these small differences, each nonetheless ambles about with roughly the same gait (means), chasing different versions of the same thing (ends), being and knowing (or perhaps more accurately, not being and not knowing) just like all the others. Difference exists *within* but never *over* a single, hegemonic zombie MO. All are constrained to live and act under the conditions that bind.

Looking at zombies only ever through zombie eyes fails to disclose anything about the contract (including, for instance, that zombies are zombies) beyond the autonomy it affords them. They just feel free. But seen from another vantage point (*any* other vantage point given how non-discriminating the zombie diet is), what they've contracted begins to look like an affliction. Anything that isn't a zombie but which walks,

---

the location of an imaginary, pre-political "original position." To get there, he asks us to imagine passing behind a veil of ignorance, causing us to lose all sense of our unique identities (and thus of any possibility of reasoning according to policy preference) such that all judgment must issue from a common, public reason alone. In this way Rawls imagines citizens will agree on what should serve as the foundation for political community and he produces a sophisticated vision flowing from what he takes to be the necessary terms of agreement. Rawls developed this ideas in John Rawls, *A Theory of Justice* [1971] (Cambridge, MA: The Belknap Press of Harvard University Press, 1999) and revised his argument in *Political Liberalism* (New York: Columbia University Press, 1993). For a shorter introduction to Rawlsian thought, see John Rawls, "Justice as Fairness: Political not Metaphysical" (1985) 14:3 *Philosophy & Public Affairs* at 223.

It may thus seem that my zombie metaphor misunderstands Rawls, since his very point is that capacity for reason – which absent minds, zombies lack – is the only thing that survives behind the veil. For communities that don't accept that individual autonomy is the greatest political good, Rawls' concept of public reason is incoherent. For those who do give unrivalled priority to individual autonomy, I think Rawls makes zombies of citizens by reducing their difference to sameness; by transforming holders of *situated* reason into undifferentiated pursuers of as much self-interest as fully mutually recognized autonomy will bear.

wiggles, crawls, or blows in the wind is always at risk of being devoured. If you aren't one of the zombies, insofar as they're concerned you exist to feed their appetite. Zombies don't accept that their desire can't be sated; they believe they're progressing towards fullness. The thing with autonomy is that it only serves as a limit for action against those who, from one's own standpoint, are also understood to be autonomous. For many – like zombies – the set of autonomous beings is limited to the parties to the contract. Everyone else is an instrument. Or perhaps the better way to put the point is that everyone else is really just everything else.

From distance or from cover, the things – animals, plants, humans – watch the zombies stagger and drool profanely, haplessly lurching to and fro in pursuit of a burning desire limited only by the liberty of other zombies. For all their otherwise unbound autonomy, it's hard to see that any of them is free. For although the things often fight with each other – their communities are far from perfect – they never lose sight of the fact that despite all conflict, they need one another in order to be free. To them, the zombies aren't a community; They're just bodies roving in aggregate and swaying in the wind. None is capable of the insight that together they've become a plague on the Earth, each a wonderfully autonomous vector. And but for the fact that they lack brains, they might wonder where the violence they've contracted away has gone.

Contract was never alive and as the breeding ground for certainty and perpetuity – for *permanence*, in which change, the pulse of life, has been negotiated out – it yields only undeath in its participants. It has destroyed countless bodies, minds, and lands in violence sustained over centuries. Indigenous peoples, not having signed on but rather having had consent clubbed into them, experience the worst of it. Unsurprisingly, most have failed to contract the virus and remain painfully aware of the daily destruction contract causes. Most vicious of all, almost all of contract's violence has been performed in the name of freedom. But while freedom is the discourse invoked, liberty – freedom construed only in respect of the autonomy of individual persons – is the only meaning assigned. One vision of freedom is allowed to masquerade as the whole of it.[17]

17 The constitutional view from contract poses the question: Liberty or unfreedom? But of course the real question, the challenge that community poses, is always: Freedom or unfreedom? There are logics of freedom beyond liberty.

4. Fear and Treaty: Canadian Structural Violence Past and Present

It sometimes strikes me that many of us think that Indigenous peoples alone cling to origin stories. But no political community exists unstoried. Canada belongs to the family of nations that claims its origin in the mythology of social contract. So, that story goes (this is a highly sanitized version), a bunch of white folks got together and in 1867, through the exercise and upward delegation of their respective wills to a centralized, sovereign authority – the *Constitution Act, 1867* – established the political community, which today is internationally recognized as Canada. Notably absent from the negotiations but not the final agreement was Indigenous peoples. We're not party *to* the contract, yet strangely it nonetheless claims authority *over* us. As a consequence we're not subjects of popular sovereignty and the constitutional story most Canadians tell is thus premised on an insurmountable democratic deficit. The only way to dissolve it is to imagine Indigenous peoples as non-persons. Which is what happened under the law of nations (today, public international law).[18] Thus a fundamental commitment to the non-humanity of Indigenous peoples serves as a necessary condition of the Canadian contract.

This has never changed; Canadians never have given Indigenous peoples a voice *over* the contract. The most they've been willing to do is slowly and in pieces say that we too may live *under* it. As such, we now have most of the rights that other Canadians do,[19] but we remain in a state of subjugation because of one niggling but rather important detail: unlike all other peoples in Canada (including migrant communities), it can never be said of us that we choose this constitutional order for ourselves. Even if I exercise my right to vote, it still cannot be said that I'm a subject of popular sovereignty, for although Canada formally imprints me with the same level of freedom and constraint that it does other Canadians, my capacity to vote, or even to run for office myself – that is, to be one of the contract's contemporary legislators – exists only against the violence of Canada's total prohibition of my ability

18 Patrick Macklem, *Indigenous Difference and the Constitution of Canada* (Toronto: University of Toronto Press, 2001) at 113–15.

19 Quirks remain. For instance the *Indian Act* provides that upon my death, the Minister of Indian Affairs may direct the disposal of my property, even where I have a legal will. See the *Indian Act*, RSC 1985, c. I-5, ss.42–50.1, especially s. 46(1)(f).

to choose to live otherwise, under a political community constituted according to the ways of being, knowing, and conception of value that reflect who I am. It's only in the absence of my ability to have the world that controls me reflect me that I may vote or hold office.

Of course, we know well what the majority of Indigenous peoples do choose. As between settler and Indigenous peoples, the cry of Indigenous peoples has consistently been that treaty is the only legitimate justification for the constitution of shared political community on Turtle Island. Treaty, we are breathless from saying, constitutes political community without predication on violence. Why wouldn't settlers choose treaty over social contract as the foundation for our shared political community? On the contract story, citizenship is violent from the outset: instead of sharing, disagreeing, and slowly learning with and from one another – the treaty story – they strive to erase the existence of Indigenous peoples. Canadians have settled *on* Indigenous peoples' lands, *over* their existing constitutional orders, and hence *for* violence to Indigenous peoples. In excluding the peoples who were already here from the formation of our political community, they've accepted violence as a foundational constitutional principle. That's a hideous thing. Why would they do it? And perhaps more important, why sustain it now?

The answer is a hard one to accept but an easy one to apprehend. I think that to many settlers' minds it goes something like this. Fear. The kind of fear that if acknowledged in anything more than one's passing look of guilt at an Indigenous man clutching his blanket on the sidewalk, may never let go of us. Fear that if we acknowledge that Indigenous peoples are actual peoples, we'll have to acknowledge that they had politics and political communities long before settlers showed up. Fear that if all of this was already theirs, it clearly wasn't free for our taking and some kind of justification is required. Fear that because I have none, the home I live in and even my claim to call this country home are baseless and that a reckoning looms for all the years of Indigenous dispossession stacked so heavily upon each other. Fear that I'll lose everything because in the rare moments I contemplate this dispossession and taking over, I already feel the scream that none of this is mine and I know that only one thing allows me to keep it. A thing which can't be spoken publicly because it isn't justifiable at law, at church, at school, or even at the dinner table without recourse to violence: settler supremacy. For all my efforts, there's no principle, no historical moment I can turn to that avoids those two words. The only thing that allows me the life

I have is the bald exercise of power that keeps it from them. Though *I* displaced no one, I'm a direct beneficiary of settler supremacy, and supremacy cannot be justified. And I fear that looking at treaty as they do – this language of partners – risks unwinding the world I know and all I have in it. I have far to fall. So, Indigenous peoples, you are not my partner. And though I hate that you must suffer for it, I accept your suffering.

I think that internal monologues much like this one (although ordinarily less self-aware than this one suggests its holder is) is why Canada never changes when Indigenous peoples speak of treaty relationships and, in particular, why when we talk about being treaty *partners* it insists on hearing only treaty *rights*. What's at stake in the distinction? On the Crown's account, treaty consists of party-differentiated rights distributed through contract that attach to individual citizens of each party.[20] This means that treaties between British and Indigenous peoples don't have first-order constitutional significance; and wouldn't you know it, treaties are omitted from the contract-confederation story. No effort is made to tell a story that we constituted this community together. Instead, treaties magically arise as a second-order constitutional matter of distributive justice: they're how we strive to account for difference within the political community said to be already formed through contract.

5. Settler Supremacy: Three Forms of Canadian Domination of Indigenous Peoples

This foundational, structural inequality has conditioned the range of possibility for Indigenous-Canada relationships ever since. The existing relationship is one of domination exercised over Indigenous persons, peoples, and lands, and taken together, Indigenous constitutionalisms. First, consider Canada's domination over Indigenous persons. Through claimed sovereign authority, Canada purports to establish the framework of freedom and constraint which articulates how I may act and how others may act towards me. It bounds that framework with a monopoly on the legitimate exercise of violence to enforce my compliance. It doesn't care whether its imposed constitutional framework reflects my

---

20 *Constitution Act, 1982*, being Schedule B to the *Canada Act 1982* (UK), 1982, c 11, at s. 35(1).

ways of being, knowing, or conception of value. Nor does it care that in the absence of an identity between us it coerces and constructs me without my consent: a fact that should be noted with vicious irony, given that Canada's constitutional order is contractarian.

There are settlers who want to fight about this word, domination. They point to the quality of life that Canada has to offer compared to other places on Earth and say that domination (rendered in scare quotes) never looked so good. But this is a nonsense thing to say for it's an assertion that they've *solved the question of value* and therefore that we should want what they do. But no one can ever objectively claim which values are best for others. Such claims are inherently tautological: liberals will claim that illiberals ought to value liberty above all other values, *but only because they're already liberals*. This kind of claim presumes that Indigenous peoples' sense of value is broken. If we would just warmly accept what settlers have already figured out, we too would know what a good life looks like and we could stop this "we're still different" nonsense and accept that our cage is actually a home.

Domination also characterizes the relationship between Canada and Indigenous peoples. Canada claims total authority over how Indigenous communities may govern themselves. Any community which exercises a community code or traditional governance structure does so because Canada says it may; the only Indigenous communities Canada recognizes as Indigenous are those which bear the stamp of its constitutional imprint. Those seeking instead to act through their own, precolonial constitutional authority, which do not seek their legitimacy through Canada's recognition but rather through a direct appeal to the ways of being, knowing, and conceptions of value of their own citizens – that is, those which find their legitimacy generated from the citizens' bottom-up and not the imperial top-down – are treated as illegitimate by Canada.

Finally, the same holds true with respect to Indigenous lands. Consider the Crown's motivation for entering into "treaty" today. From its perspective, the primary impetus for doing so is to provide a secure property regime and a stable environment for economic development throughout Canada. The Crown openly calls treaties "comprehensive land claim settlements."[21] Under the Harper government,

---

21 Government of Canada, Aboriginal Affairs and Northern Development Canada, "Treaties with Aboriginal People in Canada," at "Modern Treaties – Comprehensive Claims," http://www.aadnc-aandc.gc.ca/eng/1100100032291/1100100032292.

comprehensive land claim settlements were intended to "establish certainty of ownership and control of lands and resources, and encourage economic activity."[22] Under the Trudeau government, the "Benefits of Settling Land Claims" include, amongst others, that doing so "gives certainty to ownership and use of lands and resources" and that it "propels economic growth by giving certainty and clear rules to investors and the public in general."[23]

In order to effect the level of absolute certainty so described, each and every modern treaty contains an extinguishment clause: a provision in which the Indigenous parties either acknowledge the formal extinguishment of all relevant claims not explicitly contemplated in the enumerated treaty provisions, or in which any such claims technically survive but are forevermore made non-justiciable. As if that weren't sufficiently oppressive, this provision isn't something the Crown bargains for within the treaty dialogue; instead in an exercise of bare power the Crown offers it as a precondition for the possibility of any treaty dialogue at all. Which, if you happen to believe that the interests of one side must be purchased at the cost of the other's, sounds great for settler peoples. It isn't clear how Indigenous peoples fit into modern treaties though, other than as means to empower the end of settler certainty.

Yet far more damning with respect to the land question is that, despite its participation in contemporary "treaty" processes, Canada nonetheless claims radical title to all of Turtle Island, knowing full well that Indigenous peoples were already living on it as persons, peoples, and confederacies of distinct constitutional orders before settlers arrived. As recently as the *Tsilhqot'in Nation* case, the Supreme Court of Canada asserted that Canada acquired radical title simply by willing it so.[24] The Court then enters into contortions. On the one hand it claims that the

22 Government of Canada, Aboriginal Affairs and Northern Development Canada, "Backgrounder – Canada Takes Action to Support Progress in the BC Treaty Process" at https://web.archive.org/web/20140822122335/https://www.aadnc-aandc.gc.ca/eng/1100100016314/1100100016315.

23 Government of Canada, Indigenous and Northern Affairs Canada, "Resolving Aboriginal Claims – A Practical Guide to Canadian Experiences," http://www.aadnc-aandc.gc.ca/eng/1100100014174/1100100014179.

24 *Tsilhqot'in Nation v British Columbia*, 2014 SCC 44, [2014] 2 SCR 256 at para 69.

doctrine of *terra nullius*[25] which existed under the law of nations "never applied in Canada." Yet it brazenly refuses to say how, in the absence of the belligerent racism of *terra nullius*, Canada *did* acquire a claim over Indigenous lands sufficiently powerful to dispossess Indigenous peoples of them.[26] The Court explicitly denies the application of *terra nullius* in Canada and thereby attempts to disclaim a legacy of domination at law, yet amazingly accepts no obligation to articulate how Canada's mere assertion of sovereignty translated to a legitimate claim of radical title. Only under conditions of domination is governance in the face of so flagrant an omission, and even of the need to offer a pretense of its justification, imaginable.

This domination is organized along clear lines: it organizes a power relation that distributes privilege to settlers and oppression to Indigenous peoples. We can more accurately call this domination settler supremacy. It lacks only the open physical state violence to make supremacy obvious. Yet through systematic police racism, sustained policies of economic underdevelopment, the status quo of mass First Nations poverty, the deployment of the state's anti-terror and mass-surveillance apparatuses in contexts of non-violent Indigenous assembly, urban Indigenous homelessness, intermittent military confrontation, and the scourge of missing and murdered Indigenous women, many of us are willing to say that it has that too.

6. Treaty Interpretation Is Properly Framed as a Question of Citizenship, Not Remedy

The structural relation of settler supremacy that characterizes Canada-Indigenous relationships means that even if somehow the Supreme Court of Canada could get the doctrine right, inequality between Indigenous and settler peoples would persist. Yet the overarching theme of this book is treaty *remedies*. It will be clear by now that I think that's the wrong frame for thinking about changing treaty relationships today because it assumes too much, namely that the courts have a leading role to play in reorganizing treaty relationships. The courts are an institution

25 If land was vacant – or "vacant" in the sense that is was populated by non-persons – the settlement of a European population upon it was said to justify its acquisition by the European sovereign.

26 *Tsilhqot'in Nation v British Columbia*, 2014 SCC 44, [2014] 2 SCR 256 at para 69.

internal to Canada's constitutional order and, as creations by and under its authority, are by definition incapable of taking up the very issue at stake in treaty: the coordination of distinct constitutional orders.[27] But the situation with courts is worse still: they lack also the power in practice to account for Indigenous understandings of treaty as honourably as they might *even under* the boot of imposed Canadian constitutionalism.

This is deeply regrettable for although the courts can't play a leading role in changing treaty relationships, they could still play a meaningful role by opening up whatever small space they feel capable of to reflect on their own exercise of power and its implications for the Indigenous and settler parties before them. But the low level (in many jurisdictions, nearly wholesale absence) of the judiciary's cultural competence, the centralization of interpretive authority, and the European epistemological commitments and cultural embeddedness of the courts all necessitate that the vast majority of them are incapable of building a doctrine around treaties that would reflect even a common law translation of Indigenous understandings, which working exclusively within their own framework the courts would see as doing justice by Indigenous peoples. Again, I'm not promoting this. To be very clear, I'm strongly against the translation of Indigenous understandings out of their own ontological and epistemological (and generally, constitutional) frameworks and into the liberal language of Canadian constitutionalism. My point is rather that the courts aren't set up to do even what one would imagine is the honourable thing from their own internal perspective.

Given all of this, just as one should expect, the Supreme Court of Canada consistently chooses to account for the unique political status of Indigenous peoples *within* the contract-confederation story. Instead of situating treaties as the very things which empower settler legitimacy, settler legitimacy requires no justification and is simply presumed (i.e., settler supremacy), and treaties are imagined as contracts executed under the logic of distributive justice,[28] albeit subject to unique

27 Peter Russell has thoughtfully addressed this issue specifically in the context of the legal claims of Indigenous peoples. See Peter H. Russell, "High Courts and the Rights of Aboriginal Peoples: The Limits of Judicial Independence" (1998) 61 *Saskatchewan Law Review* 247.

28 In fairness to the courts, it should be acknowledged that the path for this choice has been cleared by the section 35 framework, which explicitly presents treaties within rights discourse. However, this doesn't in any way mean that the Supreme Court of Canada was required to construct treaties in a narrow, provision-by-provision way, under the logic of distributive justice.

interpretive principles that don't apply to other kinds of contracts.[29] Specifically, they distribute unique rights thought within this framework to account for Indigenous difference.

From an Anishinaabe constitutional standpoint, this is outrageous. Not only is treaty not a form of contract, treaty isn't even the sort of thing capable of giving rise to a legal remedy. Treaties aren't legal instruments; they're frameworks for right relationships: the total relational means by which we orient and reorient ourselves to each other through time, to live well together and with all our relations within creation. They have a legal quality in the sense that they constrain behaviour and they are at once political, social, economic, spiritual, and ecological.[30] They're how we constitute ourselves as communities of communities, across our difference.[31]

As such treaties are at the heart of citizenship on Mikinaakominis, Turtle Island. Instead of framing the crisis of treaty relationships in terms of legal remedies, we should be situating it within a much larger question about what we want citizenship in Canada to mean. That kind of inquiry holds the potential to get us out from under the violence of the contract story, but it can only be achieved with a *structural* program of change: our constitutional dialogue must be open to change over, not merely under the contract. This means that our shared political community will be constituted in respect of the ways of being, knowing, and conceptions of value of the peoples who were already here, already constituted as political communities, already relating to one another across considerable difference. Settlers *should* feel unsettled by this proposal. For most of us, against a constitutional context of normalized, even invisible settler supremacy, feeling unsettled is necessary. After

---

29 *R v Badger*, [1996] 1 SCR 771 at 41, 52, 76; *Marshall v Canada*, [1999] 3 SCR 456 at 78(3); *Tsilhqot'in Nation v British Columbia*, 2014 SCC 44 at para 4.

30 Sociologists and anthropologists may recognize in this description a similarity to Marcel Mauss' "total social phenomenon." While Mauss misunderstood much about the internal organization of Indigenous societies and what this means for both intra- and intersocietal exchange, he had a remarkable grasp on the intrinsic interconnection of all spheres of being that characterize Indigenous lifeways, and this should be acknowledged. See Marcel Mauss, *The Gift: The Form and Reason for Exchange in Archaic Societies*, trans. W.D. Halls (New York: W.W. Norton, 2000).

31 For Anishinaabe, Nehetho, Ininiw, Denesuline, and Dakota Elder perspectives on treaty, see the remarkable text by Joe Hyslop et al., *Dtantu Balai Betl Nahidei, Our Relations to the Newcomers: Treaty Elders' Teachings*, vol. 3 (Winnipeg: Treaty Relations Commission of Manitoba and Assembly of Manitoba Chiefs Secretariat, 2015).

that, we can work together. After that, I can tell them why they're legitimate citizens here and that I'll be among those defending their presence against those who would deny their legitimacy. But they're required to know that their legitimacy isn't simply to be presumed – which is exactly what settler supremacy promotes – and they must be able to teach their children how it is that they came to fit into the existing Indigenous constitutional framework.

7. Seeds Planted for a Total Reroot?

Although there continue to be many Indigenous communities appealing to Canadian constitutional authority for change through Aboriginal and treaty rights litigation or through comprehensive claims processes, there are also many who see that the change in our relationship must be *structural*. The Indigenous resurgence movement, for instance, takes this commitment as its starting point.[32] Much of the contention practised and given voice through Idle No More also expressed this understanding. As more settlers come to understand that they always stand in relation to Indigenous persons, peoples, and places and begin to accept responsibility for and in those relationships, many of them are holding it too. In his extraordinary speech, "The Duty to Learn," then Chief Justice of British Columbia Lance Finch argues that both the honour of the Crown and the rule of law impose upon legal actors a duty to learn about Indigenous legal traditions.[33] There are many important statements in Finch's essay, but perhaps most salient with respect to the responsibility of settler peoples vis-à-vis the prior existence of Indigenous constitutionalisms is the following:

> I suggest the current Canadian legal system must reconcile itself to coexistence with pre-existing Indigenous legal orders. This conference poses the question: How can we make space within the legal landscape for Indigenous legal orders? The answer depends, at least in part, on an inversion of the question: a crucial part of this process must be to find space for

32 As a thoughtful example of this robust literature, see Jeff Corntassel, "Re-envisioning Resurgence: Indigenous Pathways to Decolonization and Sustainable Self-determination," (2012) 1:1 *Decolonization: Indigeneity, Education and Society*, 86.

33 Hon. Lance S.G. Finch, "The Duty to Learn: Taking Account of Indigenous Legal Orders in Practice" (paper delivered at "Indigenous Legal Orders and the Common Law," Vancouver, BC, 15–16 November 2012) at 2.1.1.

> ourselves, as strangers and newcomers, within the Indigenous legal orders themselves.[34]

If Canadians generally took this view, the question of treaty "remedies" would be moot; they'd have recognized that the challenge they face in organizing their relationship with Indigenous peoples is one of citizenship. Especially significant for me is that in Finch's formulation, responsibility for addressing the fact of contemporary state domination isn't left to the institutions of representative government, but is rather to be claimed and picked up individually. I have more to say about this below.

The other statement I wish to draw your attention to is a passage in a book review authored by the Honourable John Reilly (of the Provincial Court of Alberta, retired) in 2012.[35] After having acknowledged that his well-meaning efforts with Indigenous persons involved in Canada's criminal justice system were paternalistic ("I tried to ameliorate the law by imposing treatment-oriented sentences that did not comply with precedents that mandated imprisonment"),[36] Reilly wrote,

> [I]f I had it to do over, I would continue my efforts to ameliorate the criminal law in relation to Aboriginal offenders, but rather than do this on a basis of attempting to right wrongs, past and present, I would advance the following reasoning:
>
> 1. The Aboriginal offender is a member of a separate nation and is entitled to have his traditional laws recognized.
> 2. My jurisdiction over this offender is an anomaly. He should be answering to his own judicial system. The process of attrition by which Canada has assumed jurisdiction over him is contrary to the legality of the historic relationship between Euro-centric Canada and Aboriginal Canada. I only assume jurisdiction by reason of necessity. I find that in doing so I must give recognition to his traditional laws.
> 3. His traditional laws emphasized healing and teaching as the accepted methods of behaviour modification and only resorted to banishment

34 *Ibid* at 44.

35 Hon. John Reilly, review of *Ghost Dancing with Colonialism: Decolonization and Indigenous Rights at the Supreme Court of Canada*, by Grace Li Xiu Woo (2012) 50:1 *Alberta Law Review* at 219.

36 *Ibid* at 221.

> as a last resort. Therefore, in order to give recognition to his traditional laws, I will emphasize healing and teaching in passing sentence and only resort to imprisonment (the equivalent of banishment) as a last resort.[37]

Of course I find things to challenge in these passages too, but these judges' insistence on the ongoing relevance of Indigenous peoples' own legal systems is remarkable given that they worked within a legal system premised on settler supremacy. I felt joy when I read these essays! Public actions like these ones, although not taken while on the bench, promote engagement with Indigenous legal traditions today within *their own* constitutional frameworks. That's the critical awakening all Canadians need to experience.

In its absence, our judiciary absorbs Indigenous experiences and legal traditions into Canada's hegemonic constitutional framework. Canada's theory of constitutional change was first articulated in *Edwards v Attorney General for Canada*[38] in 1929 by the Judicial Committee of the Privy Council (Canada's then-final legal arbiter). Speaking for the council, Lord Sankey stated that "The British North America Act planted in Canada a living tree capable of growth and expansion within its natural limits."[39] Every law student learns this passage as a powerful constitutional commitment *against* originalism. However not many of us are taught that it's just as strongly a constitutional commitment *to* imperialism. The living tree stands alone, self-contained, oblivious to the surrounding creation with which it depends. Instead of relating with and through the myriad others that live in, under, over, and alongside it, the living tree "grows and expands" by absorbing creation into itself and then reconfiguring and re-expressing it within the tree's own forms of trunk, branches, and leaves. Within the given structure – that is, provided that no leaf damages or tries to transform the trunk and branches that sustain them together – each is at liberty to flutter or express itself

37 *Ibid* at 221–2.

38 *Edwards v Canada (Attorney General)*, [1929] J.C.J. No. 2, [1930] A.C. 124. (J.C.P.C.). *Edwards* is better known as the *Person's Case*. Within it, five women sought to prove that they were "persons" within the meaning of section 24 of the *British North America Act, 1867*, which regards senate appointments.

39 *Ibid* at 136.

as it wishes. Although the tree will expand and its shape will change, all change occurs within the sole, given structure.[40]

The "living" tree isn't really living at all. Let me suggest that Lord Sankey was right to describe its movement as expansion but mistaken to also call it growth because it has no intention of ever dying. It's unliving, in need of neither care nor renewal for its continuation. It needs only resources, which is how it regards the earth – all others with whom it shares creation. There's nothing in the metaphor about the tree's relationship to the world beyond itself that would impose an external limit[41] on its expansion: other trees, plants, or animals whose needs are impacted, or even transpiration and photosynthesis – its relations with sun, water, and Earth which connect it to the world above and below it. It presumes entitlement to expand forever precisely because it *isn't* growing: growth presupposes interdependent relationships with others, whose needs present limits on one's field of possible action.

But there *are* others. Indigenous peoples and their constitutional orders were already rooted on Turtle Island before Canada's living tree was imported from Britain. I've thus argued that we don't escape settler supremacy if all we're prepared to do is *tolerate* Indigenous legal traditions as a sort of quirky addition to Canada's otherwise uninterrupted constitutional order. We have to transform that very structure to allow Indigenous legal traditions to stand within their own constitutional worlds, not contain and re-express them post-fact within the existing terms of the settler contract.

That's the work of treaty and it places a much larger demand on Canadians than toleration-absorption. And so I'd like to take advantage of the movement supported by folks who think like Chief Justice of British Columbia Finch (as he then was) to urge Indigenous practitioners of Canadian law and Indigenous academics embedded in their

40 For an unpacking of the imperial form of citizenship I'm identifying here, see James Tully, *Public Philosophy in a New Key: Imperialism and Civic Freedom*, vol. 2 (Cambridge: Cambridge University Press, 2008) at 116–17.

41 In *Reference re Same-Sex Marriage*, the Supreme Court of Canada further develops the living tree doctrine. In so doing, the Court takes up Lord Sankey's caveat that Canada's constitution is capable of adaptation "within its natural limit." The Court clearly reads this as only an internal limit, linking it with "an objective core of meaning which defines what is 'natural' in relation to," in this case, marriage. See *Reference re Same-Sex Marriage*, [2004] 3 S.C.R. 698, 2004 SCC 79 at paras 27–8.

own constitutional orders to plant wherever relevant within their work a vision of treaty originating within their own constitutional order.[42] And that's what I'm about to do.

8. Anishinaabe Constitutionalism

Of course while easy to *say*, the prospect of reaching into our own Indigenous constitutional orders may pose an enormous challenge. As colonized peoples, many of us, myself certainly included, face serious obstacles not only in using but also simply in knowing our own legal traditions, much less the constitutional orders which allow us to make sense of them. My process for coming to understand Anishinaabe constitutionalism is always growing. So far it has involved *kakinamatiwinan* and *izhitwaawinan* (diverse teachings about Anishinaabe *inaadiziwin*: lifeways) with Anishinaabe Elders, knowledge-keepers, and others seeking this knowledge; experiences on the land (*akinoomaagewin/ manido aki inaajimowin*); ceremony (*manido ichigewinan*) and material culture; *dibaajimowinan* (family and community narratives); *aadizookaanan* (sacred stories, from time immemorial); archival records; Anishinaabe-authored texts (contemporary and historic); and perhaps for some controversially, ethnography. Although many ethnographic accounts of Indigenous lifeways and world views are deeply problematic and have proven harmful, if we learn to read them carefully many are also powerful resources for us. I've learned much from them.

I'd like to share a simple sketch of my[43] understanding of Anishinaabe constitutionalism so far. My entire dissertation is an articulation of this framework; to offer more than a sketch here would allow it to take over this chapter.

Garry Potts, formerly chief of the Teme-Augama Anishnabai – an Anishinaabe community which has known its share of conflict with

---

42 For a brilliant (and much more developed) Cree example, see Harold Johnson, *Two Families: Treaties and Government* (Saskatoon: Purich Publishing Ltd, 2007).

43 This is important; others will see differently and each must allow for others' truth. One published version of this teaching is available from Anishinaabekwe Elder Nancy Jones in Ogimaawigwanebiik [Nancy Jones], "All Teachings are Correct," in H. James St. Arnold and Wesley Ballinger, eds., *Dibaajimowinan: Anishinaabe Stories of Culture and Respect* (Odanah, WI: Great Lakes Indian Fish & Wildlife Commission, 2013). My understanding is based on what has been shared with me, what I've experienced, and my engagement with diverse Anishinaabe sources.

settler peoples – said the following, which I find such a compelling way into Anishinaabe constitutionalism:

> I remember once coming across an old white pine that had fallen in the forest. In its decayed roots a young birch and a young black spruce were growing, healthy and strong. The pine was returning to the earth, and two totally different species were growing out of the common earth that was forming. And none was offended in the least by the presence of the others because their own identities were intact.[44]

What an amazing image of Fred Kelly's message of interdependence *and* uniqueness! Here each society is its own unique tree, but sharing a common ground and growing together. As such, neither tree is *autonomous*. We're *unique* to be sure, but we're interdependent. As Chief Potts' constitutional observation reveals, both the birch and the black spruce depend on the fallen white pine for their being and for its part, the white pine is returning to the Earth, part of a cycle of growth, decay, and renewal. None stands alone. Each of us, individually and in kind, is small and finite. Even the most towering oak has only a humble slice of life and collapses without its relations to root and sustain it. Unlike Canada's constitutional living tree, Potts' image of trees constituting themselves interdependently recognizes that we're each conscious of our humble smallness within and our dependence upon other orders of creation and those who've come before – all our relations – for our freedom. Freedom isn't experienced when most fully severed from the needs and demands of others; it's experienced only ever with and through them.

Within creation, each being serves as a condition of the freedom of all others. Each of us needs the gifts we don't have in order to be free and, in many instances, simply to survive. As deeply incomplete beings, the ubiquitous need for the gifts we lack means that each of us is inherently connected to all others – and not just human others. Our ontological foundation is one of interdependence; our normative foundation for political community had better be too, lest we allow the conditions

44 Gary Potts, "Growing Together From the Earth" in Diane Engelstad and John Bird, eds., *Nation to Nation: Aboriginal Sovereignty and the Future of Canada* (Concord: House of Anansi Press Limited, 1992) at 199.

which make our unique community possible to overrun the conditions which sustain Earth community.[45] That might result in a climate crisis.

Contractarians who don't outright reject this account of persons, community, and freedom as incoherent are likely to reject it as unethical. They may worry that it surrenders community to the unbound violence of individual caprice. To this anxiety I acknowledge that yes, an interdependent self and an autonomous self are indeed incommensurable understandings. But non-autonomy need not mean unfreedom for interdependent citizens. A self whose mode of being in the world is relational *is not a collective self*. An interdependent self neither stands independent of (autonomy) nor is subsumed within (heteronomy) the groups of his or her life's experience, but is rather constituted *through* his or her membership in groups, including with non-humans.

Far from erasing the moral significance of individuals, the constitutional view from interdependence privileges it: without identifiable, secure, unique selves, the creative order collapses. We need the other's gifts and this simple fact presupposes our recognition of and interest in protecting their unique, respective identities. Without those identities, their gifts disappear. Thus within this constitutional framework, it turns out that most of the time my interests aren't actually served if yours are the cost of my benefit. It's rather like Elder Fred Kelly says: we win and lose together. Since I need your gift, when you're empowered, so too am I. In this way we see that difference between citizens isn't the foundational problem of political community, but rather the condition of its possibility; difference is therefore to be embraced, not overcome. If each bore the same gift, none would have its needs met and the world would wind to a close. Deep diversity isn't an unfortunate consequence of the fact of life; it's what allows for life. Elder Basil Johnston, writing as Epingishmook, put the earthly point like this:

> There are four orders in creation. First is the physical world; second, the plant world; third, the animal; last, the human world. All four parts are

45 James Tully, "Reconciliation Here on Earth" (paper presented at "Environment, Sustainability and Society" lecture series, College of Sustainability and King's College, Ondaatje Auditorium, Dalhousie University, Halifax, NS, 20 March 2014) [unpublished; copy with author] at 6, 14 (available also at http://www.youtube.com/watch?v=QGzGvxvHz2o).

> so intertwined that they make up life and one whole existence. With less than the four orders, life and being are incomplete and unintelligible. No one portion is self-sufficient or complete, rather each derives its meaning from and fulfils its function and purpose within the context of the whole creation.[46]

In terms of human intrasocietal relations, he offers the same message:

> The community had a duty to train its members as individuals not so much for its own benefit though there was that end, to be sure, but for the good of the person. The man or woman so trained had received a gift from the community which he was to acknowledge in some form; and that form consisted simply of enlarging one's own scope to the fullest of his capacity. The stronger the man, the stronger the community; and it was equally true that the stronger the community, the firmer its members.[47]

If we understand persons as inherently interdependent, the central challenge of community isn't how to constrain transgressions of individual autonomy (a just society), but rather how to meet the condition of ubiquitous need for all (a harmonious society, but one wherein harmony requires conflict). Instead of mutual security, constitutionalism coordinates mutual aid. We don't need to contract into community for that. But if there's no contract and thus no sovereign to legislate for citizens and to enforce order over them, in what does a constitutional order premised on mutual aid inhere?

The answer is each of us. Law doesn't live in a set of abstract rules external to our lives or in the small set of duly-elected or carefully trained arbiters of them. It lives inside every citizen. In our bodies, minds, hearts, and spirits. Mutual aid – the sharing of our gifts to meet each other's needs – is embodied in our practices of self.[48] Instead of obedience to formal rules knowable by all, our behaviour is conditioned through a carefully-developed orientation towards the other. Thus the

---

46 Basil Johnston, *Ojibway Heritage* [1976] (Toronto: McClelland and Stewart, 1990) at 21.

47 *Ibid* at 70.

48 For an accessible introduction to this idea, see Robin Kimmerer, "Returning the Gift" (2014) 7:2 *Minding Nature*, 18.

image of "the gift" is not any particular good held within or service offered through an outstretched hand, but the act of reaching.

Critics may worry that this is nothing more than a romantic idea if it isn't enforceable. In the absence of a contract-constituted sovereign with a monopoly on the legitimate exercise of violence, how is the community to enforce compliance from individuals?

The answer comes in two parts, only one of which I can share here. The other, *onjine'itizowin*, requires an immersion in Anishinaabe world view beyond the bounds of what this paper can provide.[49] It regards the fact that within Anishinaabe constitutionalism, persons are interdependent not only in a political-ecological sense, but also spiritually. As such, it isn't always the case that humans need to take action to address harms done.

The part of the answer I can take up here concerns relational force, which is informal, decentralized, and persuasive. To a contractarian sold on the supposed guarantee of enforcement that the social contract is said to provide, this may seem frightful. But where each citizen understands that he or she needs the others to be free and, in some instances, simply to survive, the cost of failing to meet one's responsibilities of mutual aid is prohibitive. First, no interdependent self can run the risk of falling outside of right relation with the community for fear of its refusal to meet his or her needs.[50] Citizens are thus raised to exercise enormous self-control for the very reason that diffuse, persuasive authority *is* enormously powerful and they wish to avoid having it brought to bear on them. Within the logic of mutual aid, a society doesn't have a sovereign *because the role of the sovereign would be redundant*. Our leaders, *ogimaag*,[51] are rather spokespersons and facilitators.

Second, part of Anishinaabe constitutionalism includes the citizenization processes we've developed to ensure that our community members are taught how to create and sustain diverse but always respectful

49 I've learned about *onjine'itizowin* from different sources, but most directly from *nokomis* (my grandmother), Bessie Mainville of Couchiching First Nation.

50 It's important not to conflate harm and dissent here. As I said above, mutual aid requires vibrant, empowered individuals. We have strong, long-established practices of dissent.

51 "Leaders." "Chiefs" is and has always been an awful translation because it suggests leadership vested with coercive authority, which is precisely to misunderstand leadership outside of social contract, within mutual aid.

relationships. Citizens are motivated to behave accordingly by the social affirmation they receive for doing so. The winter telling of the *aadizookaanan*, our sacred stories, is a critical Anishinaabe citizenship institution that identifies different kinds of relationships and how to orient our behaviour to the diverse kinds of others within them. They not only disclose normative content, but owing both to their intentional ambiguity and their demand for listener agency in individual meaning-making, also instil skills for normative reasoning and discernment. They not only teach us about law, but also empower us to reason with it in new situations.

But even if as a general matter this relational logic of force is understood, what about when responsibilities aren't met? Even in a good system, even the most respectful and well-intentioned of us sometimes behaves badly. For such occasions, does the diffusion of power in a society organized around mutual aid really have teeth or are the boundaries around mutual aid too fuzzy to give rise to anything actionable? How could one citizen try to hold another to account, saying he or she has, in some specific way, failed in his or her practices of self towards another? This is an important question. After all, without the supposed certainty of contract, how are citizens to identify the boundaries of appropriate behaviour?

My answer proceeds by identifying a deep flaw in the objection. From the internal view of Anishinaabe constitutionalism, the absence of certainty isn't a structural failing in dire need of justification, but rather the only coherent position. For dynamic, living relationships, the *a priori* imposition of certainty is both incoherent and strangling. It requires an orientation to nonsense and death. Instead of the universality, abstraction, formality, and certainty of rights distributed through contract and policed by a sovereign, citizen behaviour is conditioned by substantive, living bundles of responsibility that empower and constrain the sharing of gifts. And here's the critical bit: being *substantive*, these bundles can't be articulated *formally*, across widely differing contexts. Each kind of relationship calls for a shift in responsibility. The practices of self that a father engages towards his daughter vary markedly from those which a trapper engages towards her kill, or an educator to his community. More complicated still, every particular relationship calls into being its own unique set of responsibilities. The gifts that one father is called to provide for his daughter may vary from those of another father: the specific nature of the gifts will be a function of their respective daughters' needs, and as unique persons, the needs of the daughters, despite substantial overlap, will vary.

When our own constitutional orders governed our lives, beginning when we were children, Anishinaabeg internalized how to think about mutual aid and thus how to identify the complex, shifting responsibilities we carry as we move through each of the four hills of life. This isn't magic; no one's born knowing. It requires a discipline and follows a logic very different from that of Canadian law. On the understanding that people exist interdependently instead of autonomously in the world, the work of normative ordering is to coordinate right relationships through mutual aid, not to resolve rights-claims through contract. It's about a particular way of being-with, not claiming-over. The logic of mutual aid replaces the need for a theory of obligation.

A. The Logic of Mutual Aid Replaces the Need for a Theory of Obligation

That speaks of the means of normative ordering under Anishinaabe constitutionalism; now, the ends. Having no concept of autonomy to be violated and thus no rights to be vindicated, the goal towards which Anishinaabe constitutional order strives isn't justice, it's harmony. Importantly however, this isn't harmony in the romantic sense of non-conflict. This is harmony understood as the ceaselessly changing but grounded state of interdependent selves engaged with each other in personal practices of mutual aid, which we may call *living in right relation*. And that necessitates conflict. Wolves eat deer; neighbouring communities disagree over land use; fathers and daughters fight. Each needs healthy conflict if it is to grow strong and be fully empowered to share its gifts with all others.

I think this clarified understanding of what harmony means speaks to Borrows' concern that "the rejection of Canada's discriminatory constitutional principles should not be replaced with another false narrative. We should not construct an unremittingly positive, glorious past."[52] I agree: false, ideal stories about Indigenous constitutionalism are unhelpful. I'd go further and say that to the extent that they create nervousness around the possibility of leaving the existing violence of Canadian constitutionalism behind, they're harmful. If we're going to consider constitutional alternatives, we ought not to bother unless we're prepared for the hard work of understanding them on their own terms.

52 John Borrows, "Canada's Colonial Constitution," chapter 1 in this volume.

However, we should also be clear that an obstacle to doing that can be having too romantic a vision of *Canadian* constitutionalism. That is, we must also identify the other side of the tension Borrows raises: we have to exercise equal care to guard against allowing conservative, pro-Canada deference to predispose us to the view that anything that deviates from the statist constitutional status quo is automatically taken as dreamy and romantic,[53] and thus dismissible without even stopping to inquire whether it might operate according to a rigorous but distinct and thus not immediately discernible logic. Difference itself isn't dangerous. Cynicism sure is though. If we give too much oxygen to it and unreflectively mistake the given constitutional order as the one we *ought* to have as opposed to the one that has proven most effective in exercising power over us, we run the risk of eliminating genuine alternative constitutional pathways before walking them. It seems to me that essentialism road runs in both directions, and that the right constitutional path will steer clear of it no matter which way its arrows point.

9. The Treaty of Niagara, 1764

Above I've shared my understanding that Anishinaabe constitutionalism responds to the problem of ubiquitous individual need, functions through the logic of mutual aid, and is pointed towards harmony (as right relations, not as non-conflict). This differs profoundly from liberal constitutionalism which centres instead on the risk of one person being used as a means to another's end (and in particular, of violence) that follows from the problem of radical individual disconnection, functions through the logic of contract, and is pointed towards justice – the contract's enforcement. I then observed that the account a society offers of treaty follows from its constitutional self-understanding: treaties are a constitutional form insofar as they constitute shared political community. As such, settler society's contract treaty narrative perpetuated formally through the executive and judicial orders of Canadian government merely reinscribes the original colonial violence of liberal constitutional imposition over Indigenous persons, peoples, and lands in the face of existing Indigenous constitutionalisms.

53 Jeffrey Simpson, "Too Many First Nations People Live in a Dream Palace," *Globe and Mail*, 5 January 2013.

With both pictures in view, I suggested that treaty vested in Anishinaabe constitutional forms is a better option because it empowers us to build a shared political community across our deep diversity without recourse to the violence of settler supremacy. I suggested that the fear that stops settlers from choosing this other path is deeply regrettable, because it offers a constitutional vision in which settler lives can be accounted for and legitimized.

Now I want to develop the argument further still: this alternative vision of treaty is actual, not ideal. It isn't a dream to be realized one day, forever in the future. The Treaty of Niagara, 1764 represents the intercultural achievement of this understanding on Mikinaakominis, and Indigenous peoples have never legitimated a new constitutional relationship, although we have struggled to participate as best we can within Canada's imposed, displacing constitutional order. I can't make the case for this claim convincingly here; to do so would require this argument to be its own paper. I aim rather just to offer an initial sketch.

The Treaty of Niagara, 1764 is our (i.e., Indigenous and British-become-Canadian)[54] commitment to a relationship based in practices of mutual aid, oriented towards harmony. This treaty understanding is visually represented in the bead patterning of the two wampum belts which together physically embody the relationship (many other wampum belts contributed to the dialogue that led to this ultimate characterization).[55]

Our orientation towards one another is represented in the 1764 Covenant Chain belt. At its centre it depicts two human figures holding hands. The creator(s) of the belt beaded hearts for each of these figures and importantly they were beaded differently, identifying them as representatives of peoples who remain distinct.[56] Thus more than 250 years ago we had the same teaching that Elder Fred Kelly offers today: we

---

54 By 1764 New France had fallen and thus residents of what had been New France were also represented by Britain.

55 Some of these other belts are described or simply mentioned in Sir William Johnson and various *ogimaag*, "An Indian Congress, Contemporary Copy [Niagara July 17-August 4, 1764]," in Milton W. Hamilton and Albert B. Corey, eds., *The Papers of Sir William Johnson*, vol. 11 (Albany: The University of the State of New York, 1953) at 278.

56 A. F. Hunter, "Wampum Records of the Ottawas," in *Annual Archaeological Report 1901: Being Part of Appendix to the Report of the Minister of Education Ontario* (Toronto: L. K. Cameron, 1902) at 52. This amazing document provides the exact bead count (10,076) and positioning of beads in the belt, and it offers an image made from a facsimile copy of the belt.

are interdependent *and* unique. Neither community absorbs the other but neither community stands alone. This belt exists as testimony to the simple fact that the heart of the Treaty of Niagara, 1764 isn't any particular exchange, but rather our choice to stand together in a relationship strengthened beyond what the given relationship through which we're always already connected provides for. Once this connection is affirmed, then exchange, as a second-order consideration, follows.

The next step – mutual aid, in which each shares its gifts to help meet the needs of the other – is embodied in the Twenty-Four Nations Belt. On the far left of the belt is an image of Mikinaakominis. To the right of it are twenty-four figures holding hands. On the other end of the belt the figures connect to a British vessel. Reminding the British of the Treaty of Niagara, 1764 almost ninety years earlier, *ogimaa* Assikinawk, keeper of the Niagara wampum belts, explained this belt's meaning precisely in the language of British aid. Deploying the belt's metonymic function, he orated the following British commitment, spoken as if from their representative's mouth:

> My children, see, this is my Canoe floating on the other side of the Great Waters, it shall never be exhausted but always full of the necessaries of life for you my Children as long as the world shall last.
>
> Should it happen anytime after this that you find the strength of your life reduced, you Indian Tribes must take hold of the Vessel and pull, it shall be in your power to pull towards you this my Canoe, and when you have brought it over to this Land on which you stand, I will open my hand as it were, and you will find yourselves supplied with plenty.[57]

This is to say that at the Treaty of Niagara, 1764, Sir William Johnson, Superintendent of Indian Affairs of the Northern Colonies and the highest ranking representative of the British Crown, made a point of engaging us in our own constitutional forms, making the British

57 National Archives of Canada, Record Group 10, vol. 613 at 443, as cited in Darlene Johnston, "Aboriginal Traditions of Tolerance and Reparation: Introducing Canadian Colonialism" in Micheline LaBelle, Rachad Antonius, and Georges LeRoux, eds., *Le devoir de mémoire et les politiques du pardon* (Québec: Presses de l'Université de Québec, 2005) at 153n32 and in Darlene Johnston, *Respecting and Protecting the Sacred, A Report Commissioned for the Ipperwash Inquiry*, 24n67 (2006), Attorney General at http://www.attorneygeneral.jus.gov.on.ca/inquiries/ipperwash/policy_part/research/pdf/Johnston_Respecting-and-Protecting-the-Sacred.pdf.

people participants within Indigenous constitutionalism.[58] Thus wonderful as it is, Chief Justice of British Columbia Finch's injunction for Canadians to find their place within existing Indigenous legal traditions isn't trailblazing, but rather a call for a return to an understanding already achieved.

As an important aside, achieved *between whom* exactly is a critical question. By 1764, the Haudenosaunee had already enjoyed a mutual aid relationship with the British peoples, also represented by the Covenant Chain, for 100 years. They attended Niagara at Johnston's request but the purpose of the treaty was to extend the Covenant Chain to the Western (or Ottawa) Confederacy, which consisted of the Great Lakes Anishinaabeg and their allies.[59] Anishinaabeg travelled from at least as far away as "the North West Side of Lake Superiour [sic]" and Cree came from "the Neighbourhood of Hudsons Bay."[60] There remains a question about those peoples who lived east of Niagara, such as the Algonquian peoples of the eastern seaboard. I have yet to do this research, but existing work by Sákéj Henderson, while of course recognizing important differences, suggests direct continuity with the Anishinaabe treaty understanding I've shared above.[61] Then there are the Indigenous peoples who, for various reasons, chose not to attend. These included the Dakota[62] to the far west, the Pottawatomi,[63] and

58 For example, see William Johnson, [Untitled Document] dated 31 July 1764, in Milton W. Hamilton and Albert B. Corey, eds., *The Papers of Sir William Johnson*, vol. 11 (Albany: University of the State of New York, 1953) at 309–10, in which Johnson deploys both the material and oratorical forms of wampum belts in treaty-making.

59 William Johnson, "Nations at the General Meeting," in Alexander C. Flick, ed., *The Papers of Sir William Johnson*, vol. 4 (Albany: University of the State of New York, 1925) at 481; "Memorandum on Six Nations and Other Confederacies," in Alexander C. Flick, ed., *The Papers of Sir William Johnson*, vol. 4 (Albany: University of the State of New York, 1925) at 240, 243–4.

60 "William Johnson to Thomas Gage, Johnson Hall August 22^{d}. 1764," in Milton W. Hamilton and Albert B Corey, eds., *The Papers of Sir William Johnson*, vol. 11 (Albany: University of the State of New York, 1953) at 336, 337.

61 James (Sákéj) Youngblood Henderson, Marjorie L. Benson, and Isobel M. Findlay, eds., "Aboriginal Treaty Order of North America," in *Aboriginal Tenure in the Constitution of Canada* (Scarborough: Carswell Thomson, 2000) at 94–9, especially at 98.

62 William Johnson to Thomas Gage, "To Thomas Gage," in Milton W. Hamilton and Albert B. Corey, eds., *The Papers of Sir William Johnson*, vol. 11 (Albany: University of the State of New York, 1953) at 336.

63 William Johnson to Cadwallader Colden, "To Cadwallader Colden, Johnson Hall, August 23^{d}. 1764," in Alexander C. Flick, ed., *The Papers of Sir William Johnson*, vol. 4 (Albany: University of the State of New York, 1925) at 511.

groups of Shawnee, Delaware, Seneca, Anishinaabeg, and Wyandot who opted instead for war with *ogimaa* Pondiac,[64] although many of these later joined the treaty. Although it isn't determinative, we should note that Johnson's intent was that "all Nations of Ind[ians]" in what Britain identified as the northern territory – which covers much of what is today called Canada – were to be included in the treaty.[65] Of course whether a community that didn't attend understands itself as part of the Niagara treaty relationship is for it and not for Johnston, me, or anybody else to decide.

10. Treaty Citizenship: Beyond the Binary of Settler Supremacy/Illegitimacy

If treaty is a constitutional form and the Treaty of Niagara, 1764 in particular is how settler and Indigenous peoples constituted a shared political community respectful of existing Indigenous constitutional orders, then it's this living relationship and not a state called Canada that serves as the foundation for settler citizenship. I don't mean that treaty is the substantive keystone of citizenship; rather it's the condition of the possibility of any settler citizenship at all. This is the thickest sense of "we're all treaty people."[66]

In making so strong a claim, I'm careful to note Borrows' worry that "The strength of the treaty narrative makes it difficult to develop policy with some First Nations. Any step which does not accord with the original treaty relationship is deeply suspect."[67] To the extent that Indigenous persons and peoples hold this view, I too am concerned. Having Indigenous peoples be the ones to call for contract doesn't make any of its problems disappear. But I don't share Borrows' worry in a strong way because as I've been explaining, I don't think this is what most of us are calling for. For the most part I don't understand

64 Thomas Gage to William Johnson, "From Thomas Gage, New York August 15th: 1764," in Alexander C. Flick, ed., *The Papers of Sir William Johnson*, vol. 4 (Albany: University of the State of New York, 1953) at 508, 509.

65 "William Johnson to Thomas Gage, Johnson Hall August 22nd, 1764" in Milton W. Hamilton and Albert B. Corey, eds., *The Papers of Sir William Johnson*, vol. 11 (Albany: University of the State of New York, 1953) at 336–7.

66 This is illustrated in a wonderful graphic publication of the Anishinabek Nation in Maurice Switzer and Charley Hebert, *We Are All ... Treaty People* (North Bay, ON: Union of Ontario Indians, 2011).

67 John Borrows, "Canada's Colonial Constitution," chapter 1 in this volume.

Indigenous claims for a return to our treaty relationship as originalist calls for a return to a timeless contract. In fact I hear a yearning to get out from under contract and into partnership. The "return" I hear far more often isn't directed at times past, but towards our formerly shared understanding that we're interdependent, that we need each other, and that if we would think of ourselves as partners in open-ended creation rather than as adversaries in zero-sum negotiation, we could all win. It isn't originalist because our needs and hence our responsibilities to one another are always changing. The core temporal value that the call for "return" invokes isn't stasis, but renewal.

Living in right relation would mean that Indigenous peoples are free to live on Mikinaakominis within treaty confederacies composed of their own unique constitutional orders. It would mean that any settler constitutional order will have to reconcile itself to the confederal treaty superstructure that holds distinct Indigenous constitutionalisms together: interdependent but unique; aiding one another through their differences. Importantly, because Indigenous constitutional orders are designed to orient Indigenous societies in right relationship with the rest of the creative order (i.e., the earthway), the confederal constitutional structure shares their creative-ecological orientation and requires that as existing treaty partners grow and change and as new constitutionalisms join the treaty relationship, each unique constitutional order within it sustains that foundational understanding for itself.[68] As a participant in the treaty order, this means that settler peoples have to reconcile their liberal foundation with the Earth-first relationalism of the treaty superstructure.[69] That won't be an easy task. For one thing, an Earth-first orientation is incommensurable with Earth-alienation, a foundational postulate of liberalism (i.e., how was Earth represented in the contract?). Stated bluntly, any contractarian account of political community on Mikinaakominis will have to give way.

---

68 By way of pre-empting Rawlsian critics, this is nothing like an overlapping consensus: it's only the starting point of an ontological claim of an interdependent self and the concomitant relational mode of being which are common throughout the confederal treaty order, not determinate norms or even processes of norm-generation. Further, the treaty order derives from the participation of its members in their unique situatedness, not stripped of their identities.

69 I take this up in Aaron Mills, "Rooted Constitutionalism: Growing Political Community" in Michael Asch, John Borrows, and James Tully, eds., *Resurgence and Reconciliation* (Toronto: University of Toronto Press, forthcoming).

That's what reconciliation in the Canadian context means. Once it's accomplished settler people will[70] be able to claim that they truly belong here – that's a gift that Anishinaabe (and I suspect many other indigenous) constitutionalism offers to all. Settlers are part of creation and they aren't to be left out. More important, their political status won't be predicated on violence. That should be a foundation for citizenship that everyone demands. And as for Indigenous peoples, if our constitutional orders were again vibrant and empowered to govern our lives (and the violence that does so now was ended), presumably many more of us would find good reason to *want* to identify as citizens of a shared political community.[71]

All my relations, the arrangement our ancestors made in 1764 is so very different from our reality now. There was a time when we agreed to live in right relation together, when Indigenous peoples were understood as partners, not as minorities seeking toleration.[72] It isn't a vision of treaty that can ever be achieved so long as we're content to think of treaty as a contract, in the way that the Crown and the courts do and which section 35 has been interpreted to demand. I have a stark view of

---

70 I mean that the claim becomes possible, not that it is accomplished. This shift would of course be the beginning, not the end, of a constitutional dialogue.

71 See the remarkable dialogue between Mary Ellen Turpel-Lafond and Trish Monture on this tension in M.E. Turpel and P.A. (Trisha) Monture, "Ode to Elijah: Reflections of Two First Nations Women on the Rekindling of Spirit at the Wake for the Meech Lake Accord" (1990) 15:2 *Queen's Law Journal* 345, 347.

72 Sir William Johnson's papers clearly indicate his knowledge that Anishinaabeg understood themselves as free peoples standing in partnership with, not subjection under, British constitutional authority and that any effort by the British to exercise sovereignty over them would destroy the existing relationship: "Sir William Johnson to the Lords of Trade, Johnson Hall Novr 13. 1763," in E.B. O'Callaghan, ed., *Documents Relative to the Colonial History of the State of New York,* vol. 7 (Albany: Weed, Parsons and Company, 1856) at 572, 575; "Sir William Johnson to the Lords of Trade," in E.B. O'Callaghan, ed., *Documents Relative to the Colonial History of the State of New York,* vol. 7 (Albany: Weed, Parsons and Company, 1856) at 661, 665; "Sir William Johnson to the Lords of Trade, Johnson Hall, October 30, 1764," in E.B. O'Callaghan, ed., *Documents Relative to the Colonial History of the State of New York,* vol. 7 (Albany: Weed, Parsons and Company, 1856) at 670, 674; "William Johnson to Thomas Gage, Johnson Hall Octbr. 31st. 1764," in Milton W. Hamilton and Albert B. Corey, eds., *The Papers of Sir William Johnson,* vol. 11 (Albany: University of the State of New York, 1953) at 394, 395. See also "Journal of Colonel Croghan's Transactions with the Western Indians" in E.B. O'Callaghan, ed., *Documents Relative to the Colonial History of the State of New York,* vol. 7 (Albany: Weed, Parsons and Company, 1856) at 779, 788.

that vision: thus far, the concept of treaty rights – and section 35 more generally – has been one more tool to effectively neutralize the unique political status of Indigenous peoples by transmuting claims for partnership *with* a reformed, non-contractarian settler society into claims for recognition *under* Canada's imposed constitutional order.

If ever we're to live in right relationship again we'll have to inspire Canada to decolonize itself.[73] There are many things that could mean but one thing it *must* mean is education. We have to make clear the relationship between colonialism and Canadian citizenship *today*. Insofar as Canadians can thoughtlessly relegate colonialism to the past, the cognitive barrier to empowering Indigenous freedom will remain unbreakable. Canadians pride themselves on a (carefully-tailored) narrative of what their nation stands for and of what they think their membership in it says about them. At the same time, the vast majority of Canadians don't identify as agents of colonialism, thinking they have no personal connection to that word. Colonization is taken as an historical fact – one completed long before any of us living today were born. Since they're not causal agents of colonial harm, they bear no contemporary responsibility for its violence.

---

73 There's a contemporary indigenist line of thought that disagrees with the attribution of onus in this statement, thinking instead that it isn't up to us to do anything with respect to Canada's process of decolonization. I understand that feeling. Yet I can't help but hear a discourse quietly invoked that I find worrisome. It seems to me that what we're really saying in forwarding that view is that we *ought* (obligation) not to have to do it because at no time did we undertake to do so – which is to deploy the logic of contract. This follows, we say, from the fact that it's about them, not us. But if instead of turning to contract we think that we're always already in relationship with settler Canadians, that we all win or we all lose because it's always about both of us, and that the goal of intervening is harmony as right relations, not justice – then as plainly unfair as it is (and it is plainly unfair, infuriating, and worse), the only thing that makes sense is to address what's wrong in the relationship. Both the normative and the strategic questions are thus all about *how*, not *whether* to engage. I fully support the commitment to prioritize the thickening of our own cultural vitality that sits at the heart of the Indigenous resurgence movement. While this means a turn away from settler constitutional forms, it doesn't mean that we reject settler people. There are practices of Anishinaabe constitutionalism which derive from our connections with other societies (for instance the jingle dress and the traditional drum) and hence which go directly to the very sense of self we want to thicken. I reject the possibility of a turn-away from settler *people* because of its anti-relationalism which I cannot square with Anishinaabe constitutionalism.

Colonization *isn't* completed. It isn't reducible to an imagined initial act of settler arrival and Indigenous displacement. It's a relationship Indigenous peoples and settlers live out today through the three forms of domination that constitute settler supremacy and which culminate in the imposition of settler constitutionalism over existing Indigenous constitutionalisms. Canadians enjoy the incredible level of privilege they do *because* Indigenous peoples remain colonized. Indigenous suffering is the cost of the settler benefit that Canadian citizenship allows to be taken for granted. Contemporary settlers are responsible not only because indirectly they *are* causal agents, but also because they benefit, and the ongoing desire to sustain this benefit for settler citizens is among the most important factors in Canada's daily decision to continue its colonial relationship with Indigenous peoples today.

We'd all be much further ahead if settler children and youth were educated about this. But beyond including these truths as mandatory components of elementary and secondary school curricula, there's much more we can do. When I look to my *nokomis*, Bessie Mainville, I see how it's possible to live the practices that generate right relationship within my own life, even under conditions of contemporary colonialism. Our Elders aren't waiting for Canadian institutions to internalize a commitment to right relations. No, they start with themselves. They endeavour to carry their responsibilities through practices of self that are intended to draw them into right relation with the world around them. My sense is that from their perspective this is simply what engaged citizenship means. Our Elders lead, as they always have, through example. Albeit clumsy, unskilled, and with a colonized mind, I'm learning how to follow. As I understand it, you're welcome to follow, too. One need not be an ethnic Anishinaabe to follow Anishinaabe constitutionalism (or more generally, the rooted mode of constitutionalism of which Anishinaabe constitutionalism is but one kind). Though your stories may be different and you and I may not read the Earth in just the same way, this is a constitutional framework available to all. I hope you understand that I've chosen to share my deep criticism of liberal constitutionalism and to call settler supremacy exactly what it is in order to make this invitation possible.

And as I grow my understanding of what it means to exist interdependently, to be a fully relational self, and to discover the extraordinary strength that comes from seeing the world and myself in it that way, I'm also learning this: on my own I have no power over anything but myself. But, all my relations, when we accept our interdependence and aid one another, I believe no form of state violence can stop us from calling a community beyond settler supremacy into being. We have only to learn and to live these practices for them to manifest as mass resistance to the violence of contract. We don't need to tear the state down (or the contract up). We can simply make it redundant. If that seems an overwhelming prospect to you, fortunately there's experience and leadership in the Indigenous communities of Mikinaakominis, and I bet that if you dedicate yourself, those are gifts most of them are willing to share.

The Anishinaabe conception of constitutionalism and thus also of treaty that I've presented in this chapter is captured in this quotation taken from a talk by Anishinaabe Elder Ed Onabigon:

> This is the way it has to be. Just like those trees, look at them, there's maybe fifty, sixty plants right in front of us. But they're all connected, they're all reaching out, and they never have to worry, they're each doing their job. So is each and every one of those blades of grass – they're unique, they're all unique. If you take any two, they're not exactly the same, just as with people. That shows us the harmony and balance, and that they adapt to their environment. Man and woman have to do the same thing, adapt and see our connection to everything around us.[74]

By offering contract as the sole framework within which we can imagine treaty, Canada succeeds in silencing my Anishinaabe understanding. The problem I have isn't that my view isn't sufficiently persuasive to carry the day. It's that I may not speak it.[75] A judiciary vested in colonial supremacy and concerned with a citizenry that benefits from it isn't willing to hear. It has explicitly said so.[76] It's as if the Treaty of Niagara, 1764 never happened.

---

74 Ed Onabigon, "Elder's Comments," in Roger Neil, ed., *Voice of the Drum: Indigenous Education and Culture* (Brandon: Kingfisher Publications, 2000) at 282–3.

75 Johnny Mack makes a similar point in Johnny Mack, "Hoquotist: Reorienting through Storied Practice," in Hester Lessard, Rebecca Johnson, and Jeremy Webber, eds., *Storied Communities: Narratives of Contact and Arrival in Constituting Political Community* (Vancouver: UBC Press, 2011) at 287, 298.

76 *R v Van der Peet*, [1996] 2 SCR 507 at para 49; *R v Marshall; R v Bernard*, [2005] 2 SCR 220 at para 51; *Tsilhqot'in*, at para 50.

To my mind this leads to two simple questions about responsibility. For settler Canadians: As beneficiaries of settler supremacy, is citizenship premised on domination good enough for you? And as for Indigenous peoples: *Can* citizenship in a state imagined through a social contract allow us to meet our responsibilities to the land, to those who came before us, to those yet to come, and to all of creation? Can policy development within a state framework ever afford us the freedom these responsibilities call us to exercise? I've given my answer. But however one might reply to these questions, it's at least clear that they aren't challenges we can litigate to a meaningful close.

I'm certain the relationship with Canada that I've inherited isn't what my ancestors agreed to at Niagara, or what my *ogimaag* Manidobines, Powassin, or Blackstone intended in 1873 at the congress that finally resulted in the Treaty 3 relationship. I don't intend to disappoint them.

9 Changing the Treaty Question: Remedying the Right(s) Relationship

HEIDI KIIWETINEPINESIIK STARK[1]

How do we understand treaty relationships and the responsibilities and obligations that flow from these diplomatic accords? What would happen if we approached these questions from a different starting point? This chapter explores how Anishinaabe law produces a different set of questions, focusing not on the rights retained/attained via treaties, as a Western orientation often centres on, but instead explores the responsibilities and obligations we have to one another. The narrow construction of rights that has been the focus of treaty litigation has contained and constrained alternate visions for mutual coexistence.

1 Boozhoo indinawemaaganidog minaawa niijiiywag. Kiiwetinepinesiik indigo idash Heidi nindizhinaakaaz zhaaganaashiimong. Mikinaak wajiwiing izhinikaate ishkonigan wenjibaayaan. Bizhiw indoodem. Apegish miigwechiwenimaag Michael Coyle and John Borrows. I am grateful for this opportunity to reflect on treaties and think through potential remedies when the relationship is impaired or damaged by failure to carry out responsibilities and duties. I appreciate and want to acknowledge Michael Coyle's and John Borrows' efforts to facilitate engagement between and among the contributors through conferences and forums. This chapter is richer due to this engagement. In addition to the contributors in this collection, this chapter is significantly improved by comments from and conversations with Rita Dhamoon, Kekek Jason Stark, Jason Manidoonoodin Schlender, and Maajigwaneyash Gordon Jourdain. All errors and mistakes are nonetheless my own.

And some earth he took, using it to create the human being. Truly did he accomplish the work of creating a man. Speaking to him, he said: "In this place do you remain." – Bois Fort Anishinaabe recounting when Nenabozho and his younger brother created man

****

The Earth is said to be a woman … She is called Mother Earth because from her come all living things. Water is her life blood. It flows through her, nourishes her, and purifies her.

On the surface of the Earth, all is given Four Sacred Directions – North, South, East, and West. Each of these directions contributes a vital part to the wholeness of the Earth …

The Creator sent his singers in the form of birds to the Earth to carry the seeds of life to all of the Four Directions … On the Earth the Creator placed the swimming creatures of the water. He gave life to all the plant and insect world. He placed crawling things and the four-leggeds on the land. All of these parts of life lived in harmony with each other.

Gitchie Manito then took four parts of Mother Earth and blew into them using a Sacred Shell. From the union of the Four Sacred Elements and his breath, man was created.

It is said the Gitchie Manito then lowered man to the Earth. Thus, man was the last form of life to be placed on the Earth. From this Original Man came the A-nish-i-na'-be people. – Edward Benton-Banai

Although an interpretation of a treaty should be made in the light of conditions existing when the treaty was executed, as often indicated by its history before and after its making, the exact situation which caused the inclusion of a provision is often difficult to ascertain. – Felix Cohen

****

In construing any treaty between the United States and an Indian tribe, it must always (as was pointed out by the counsel for the appellees) be borne in mind that the negotiations for the treaty are conducted, on the part of the United States, an enlightened and powerful nation, by representatives skilled in diplomacy, masters of a written language, understanding the modes and forms of creating the various technical estates known to their law, and assisted by an interpreter employed by themselves; that the treaty is drawn up by them and in their own language; that the Indians, on the other hand, are weak and dependent people, who have no written language and are wholly unfamiliar with all the forms of legal expression, and whose only knowledge of the terms in which the treaty is framed is that imparted to them by the interpreter employed by the United States; and that the treaty must therefore be construed, not according to the technical meaning of its words to learned lawyers, but in the sense in which they would naturally be understood by the Indians. – 1899 *Jones v Meehan*

****

Out of nothing he made rock, water, fire, and wind. Into each one he breathed the breath of life. On each he bestowed with his breath a different essence and nature. Each substance had its own power which became its soul-spirit.

From these four substances Kitche Manitou created the physical world of sun, stars, moon, and earth.

To the sun Kitche Manitou gave the powers of light and heat. To the earth he gave growth and healing; to waters purity and renewal; to the wind music and the breath of life itself …

Last of all he made man. Though last in the order of creation, least in the order of dependence, and the weakest in bodily powers, man had the greatest gift – the power to dream. – Basil Johnston

****

The treaty was entered into for the benefit of both the British Crown and the Micmac people, to maintain peace and order as well as to recognize and confirm existing hunting and fishing rights of the Micmac. In my opinion, both the Governor and the Micmac entered into the treaty with the intention of creating mutually binding obligations which would be solemnly respected. It also provided a mechanism for dispute resolution. – Chief Justice Dickson in *Simon v R*[2]

2 Truman Michelson, ed., and William Jones, comp., *Publications of the American Ethnological Society*, vol. 7, bk. 1, *Ojibwa Texts* (Leyden, NL: E.J. Brill, Ltd., 1917) at 549; Basil Johnston, *Ojibway Ceremonies* (Lincoln: University of Nebraska Press, 1990) at 2–3; Edward Benton-Banai, *The Mishomis Book: The Voice of the Ojibway* (Saint Paul, MN: Red School House, 1988) at 5; Felix S. Cohen, *Handbook of Federal Indian Law: With Reference Tables and Index* (Washington, DC: U.S. Government Printing Office, 1942) at 38; *Jones v Meehan* (1899) 175 U.S. 1; *Simon v R.*, [1985] 2 SCR 387.

The narratives that open this chapter bring to light the different starting points that often ignite discussions of treaties. While it may seem odd to set Anishinaabe creation stories alongside Canadian and American legal opinions and Cohen's commentary on federal Indian law, I think this is fitting for two reasons. First, Canadian and American legal opinions are critical components to Canadian and American stories of nation-building. Indeed, federal Indian law and Aboriginal law say more about the two settler states than they do about the Indigenous nations of which they speak. Take, for example, that Indigenous nations were not party to the original title cases foundational for both states.[3] While seemingly obvious, but frequently obscured, federal Indian law and Aboriginal law are Western laws that detail the *obligations* and *responsibilities* these nation states have to the Indigenous nations on whose lands they have erected themselves. This is despite the fact that, too often, the courts have utilized legal rulings to instead reflect upon a question of the *rights* Indigenous nations and their citizens have retained. Second, much in the same way that American and Canadian law produces the creation stories of the settler states, Anishinaabe creation stories give shape and meaning to Anishinaabe law. The philosophical underpinnings of Anishinaabe law are found in these rich narratives and were drawn on by Anishinaabe leaders as they negotiated treaties with Canada and the United States.

I argue that by taking a different starting point – Anishinaabe law rather than Western law – a different set of questions about treaty relationships arise than that produced by Western legal narratives. Instead of questioning the rights retained or attained via treaty, Anishinaabe law shifts our orientation towards a possibly more fruitful exploration of the responsibilities and obligations we have to one another. This is not to say that Canadian and American law fails to take up questions of responsibility. Indeed, as the opening epigraphs seek to illuminate, Western law has, at times, recognized that treaties created "mutually binding obligations which [should] be solemnly respected." However, as I aim to show in section 3, these obligations are consistently contained and constrained through a narrow construction of rights.

3 *Johnson v M'Intosh*, 21 U.S. (8 Wheat) 543 (1823) and *St. Catharine's Milling and Lumber Company v The Queen*, [1887] 13 SCR 577.

To illuminate this point, I first consider Anishinaabe law. I argue that taking Anishinaabe law as a starting point provides an alternate vision for coexistence that has routinely been eclipsed by a narrow court-driven focus on rights. I focus on Anishinaabe invocations of the Creator throughout treaty negotiations, positing that a focus on Anishinaabe law encourages us to ask, How are we to honour treaties and our obligations to creation? I conclude by reflecting on what does not constitute a remedy in order to illustrate how court-driven interpretations of treaties have limited our abilities to envision a better way forward.

Anishinaabe understandings of their creation, recorded in stories, songs, birch bark scrolls, rock paintings, and teachings, were and remain foundational to Anishinaabe legal and political thought and practice. Creation was a critical component of the rich discourses that embodied and sustained Anishinaabe political and legal thought and shaped their engagement with others. As Creek scholar Craig Womack notes, "… there is always an interrelationship between the political and the spiritual."[4] But what is this interrelationship? And how does this interrelationship shape and inform treaty relationships?

John Borrows notes, in his contribution to this collection, that a prominent narrative of treaties maintained by Indigenous peoples, one which is especially prevalent among the Prairie First Nations and Numbered Treaties signatories, is that treaties are sacred covenants. Laying out the principles driving treaty federalism, he cautions us to be wary of treaty fundamentalism. With these concerns in mind, I want to consider this understanding of treaties as sacred agreements. I came to think about these assertions in a new way when considering the treaty speeches of Anishinaabe chiefs in their negotiations with Canada and the United States. Throughout these negotiations, the chiefs spoke of their relationships to their homelands through a delineation of their placement on these lands by the Creator. But what does this mean? Why were Anishinaabe leaders invoking the Creator throughout treaty negotiations? Why do our Elders and leaders continually reference these treaties as sacred agreements today? How did Anishinaabe laws of creation, *inaakonigoowin*, shape and inform these engagements? How can a richer understanding of Anishinaabe law inform possibilities and pathways for remedies today?

---

4 Craig S. Womack, *Red on Red: Native American Literary Separatism* (Minneapolis: University of Minnesota Press, 1999) at 53.

1. Anishinaabe Laws of Creation

As legal scholar Aharon Barak notes, "The world is filled with law. Every human behavior is subject to a legal norm ... Wherever there are living human beings, law is there. There are no areas in life which are outside of law."[5] Anishinaabe law predates the arrival of Europeans, ordered historical diplomatic practices, and has continued meaning and application in Anishinaabe political, legal, and cultural practices. As Anishinaabe legal scholar John Borrows notes,

> Many Indigenous people believe their laws provide significant context and detail for judging our relationships with the land, and with one another. Yet, Indigenous laws are often ignored, diminished, or denied as being relevant or authoritative in answering these questions.

As Borrows details in his extensive study of Indigenous legal traditions, law is an important organizing force and "pivots around deeply complex explicit and implicit ideas and practices related to respect, order, and authority."[6]

Indeed, the Anishinaabe live across a legally pluralistic landscape that is ordered by federal, provincial/state, and Indigenous/tribal law. Anishinaabe laws flow from many sources, which influence and give shape to Anishinaabe jurisprudence.[7] In analysing the sources and scope of Indigenous legal traditions, Borrows finds that

5 Aharon Barak, "Judicial Philosophy and Judicial Activism" (1992) 17 *Tel Aviv University Law Review* 483.

6 See John Borrows, *Recovering Canada: The Resurgence of Indigenous Law* (Toronto: University of Toronto Press, 2002); John Borrows, *Drawing Out Law: A Spirit's Guide* (Toronto: University of Toronto Press, 2010) [Borrows, *Drawing Out Law*]; John Borrows, *Canada's Indigenous Constitution* (Toronto: University of Toronto Press, 2010). John Borrows, the Robina Chair in Law, Public Policy and Society, is a leading scholar in Indigenous, constitutional, and environmental law. He is a member of the Chippewas of Nawash First Nation. Canadian Supreme Court justices have cited his articles and legal texts when ruling on Aboriginal rights.

7 See for example Larry Nesper, "Negotiating Jurisprudence in Tribal Court and the Emergence of a Tribal State: The Lac Du Flambeau Ojibwe" (2007) 48:5 *Current Anthropology* 675; Matthew L.M. Fletcher, *American Indian Tribal Law* (Austin, TX: Wolters Kluwer Law and Business, 2011); Nicholas J. Reo, "The Importance of Belief Systems in Traditional Ecological Knowledge Initiatives" (2011) 2:4 *International Indigenous Policy Journal* 1–4.

> [u]nderstanding their communities' legal foundations can lead to a better appreciation of their contemporary potential, including how they might be recognized, interpreted, enforced, and implemented. The underpinnings of Indigenous law are entwined with the social, historical, political, biological, economic, and spiritual circumstances of each group.[8]

Similar to other legal traditions, one component of Anishinaabe law is sacred law. Anishinaabe laws are often referred to as sacred if, for example, they stem from the Creator, creation stories, ancient teachings, and spiritual principles. Much of Anishinaabe law is informed by sacred teachings that illustrate the interconnectivity of creation; encouraging particular ways of relating to creation. Borrows finds, "Within Indigenous legal traditions, creation stories are often one source of sacred law. These accounts contain rules and norms that give guidance about how to live with the world and overcome conflict. Their reach can be quite expansive because they contain instructions about how all beings should relate to specific territories."[9]

These laws, because of their expansive application to creation, are often less flexible than laws flowing from other sources. This is partially because, as will be laid out below, these laws pertain to obligations and responsibilities that Anishinaabe maintain to those that came before the placement of human beings on the Earth. Treaties are understood as flowing from this source of law. They are revered by the Anishinaabe as sacred agreements because they not only brought the Creator and their pre-existing responsibilities and obligations to creation into their relationships with the United States and the Crown, but also brought the United States and the Crown into these relationships with creation.

The historical record pertaining to Anishinaabe treaties with the United States and Canada captures some of these sacred elements. The journal of the proceedings to an 1837 treaty with the United States notes, "The usual ceremonies for opening a council with the Indians, having been duly observed, Governor Dodge addressed them ..."[10] The usual ceremonies involved the exchange of gifts such as tobacco and the

---

8 Borrows, *Drawing Out Law*, *supra* note 6; Borrows, *Canada's Indigenous Constitution*, *supra* note 6.

9 *Ibid.*

10 *Ratified Treaty No. 223 Documents Relating to the Negotiations of the Treaty of July 29, 1837, with the Chippewa Indians*, NAMP RG 75, M T-494 Roll 3:F559 at http://digicoll.library.wisc.edu/cgi-bin/History/History-idx?id=History.IT1837no223. Also see president's message, 19 December 1837, "Treaty of July 29, 1837 with the

smoking of the pipe. The use of the pipe, exchange of wampum, and practice of gift giving are well-documented Indigenous political practices that continued in their relations with European nations and, later, the United States and Canada.[11] Nell Jessup Newton et al. argue,

> [T]he initial "treaties" between the Americans and the Indian tribes were not written documents, but instead were formal diplomatic ceremonies lasting several days and marked by the exchange of presents, ceremonial objects, and solemn promises of friendship.[12]

Even for treaties created during the early formation of the United States and for those made with the British Crown, little attention was paid to the written agreement.[13] Many of these important Indigenous legal and diplomatic traditions continued into the nineteenth century. By using the pipe and opening the treaty proceedings with ceremony, the Anishinaabe not only brought Gichi-Manidoo (the Creator) into the proceedings, but also brought in all of Creation. Throughout the proceedings the Anishinaabe chiefs spoke of the Creator and the Earth. For example, Sha-wa-nig-wa-nabe noted,

> My Father, What I have to say to you, place it strongly in your heart. The Master of life and the Spirit of the Earth listen to us. The Master of life made the Earth, the grass and the trees that grow upon it, and the animals

---

Chippewas," Indian Treaty Files, SEN 25B-C4, RG 46. For additional information on the 1837 treaty, see James M. McClurken, comp., *Fish in the Lakes, Wild Rice, and Game in Abundance: Testimony on Behalf of Mille Lacs Ojibwe Hunting and Fishing Rights*, with Charles E. Cleland, Thomas Lund, John D. Nichols, Helen Tanner, and Bruce White (East Lansing: Michigan State University Press, 2000); Ronald N. Satz, *Chippewa Treaty Rights: The Reserved Rights of Wisconsin's Chippewa Indians in Historical Perspective* (Madison: Wisconsin Academy of Sciences, Arts and Letters, 1991).

11 Robert A. Williams, Jr., *Linking Arms Together: American Indian Treaty Visions of Law and Peace, 1600–1800* (New York: Routledge, 1999) [Williams, *Linking Arms Together*]; Colin G. Calloway, *New Worlds for All: Indians, Europeans, and the Remaking of Early America* (Baltimore: Johns Hopkins University Press, 1998).

12 Nell Jessup Newton et al., eds., *Cohen's Handbook of Federal Indian Law* (Newark, NJ: LexisNexis, 2005) at 20.

13 Francis Paul Prucha, *American Indian Treaties: The History of Political Anomaly* (Berkeley: University of California Press, 1994) at 26; Alden T. Vaughan, *Early American Indian Documents: Treaties and Laws, 1607–1789*, vol. 1–4 (Washington, DC: University Publications of America, 1979).

> that roam over it. When the Great Spirit made the Earth, he placed the Red Men upon it, and when the chiefs were put upon it, it became very strong.[14]

The use of pipe and other diplomatic traditions incorporated the Creator into the treaty negotiations. Therefore, treaty rights are not restricted to those mentioned expressly in the written agreements, but must also account for pre-existing relationships and responsibilities across Anishinaabe *aki* (the Earth) that were impacted by these agreements. The use of the pipe in treaty-making incorporated the Creator into the treaties and established a commitment between the various parties to the treaty.

When Commissioner Alexander Morris arrived at the Northwest Angle to establish a treaty with the Lake of the Woods Anishinaabe in 1873, they immediately approached him. In his reports for Treaty 3, Morris recorded that "they asked leave to perform a dance in [his] honor, after which they presented to [him] the pipe of peace."[15] By offering the sacred pipe to the commissioner, the Anishinaabe of Lake of the Woods were carrying out a treaty practice that recognized both the political and spiritual relationship the treaty agreement would create in the lives of the Anishinaabe. Anishinaabe Elder Melvin Huntinghawk further addressed this relationship. He stated,

> Our treaties were entered into by using the sacred ways of our First Nations people, that is, the sacred pipe, sacred tobacco, sacred sweetgrass, and sacred power of our Mother Earth. Our treaties were made to last forever: As long as the sun shines, the river flows, and the grass grows … The importance of these negotiations by the First Nations was marked by the pipe ceremonies.[16]

---

14 *Ratified Treaty No. 223 Documents Relating to the Negotiations of the Treaty of July 29, 1837, with the Chippewa Indians*, NAMP RG 75, M T-494 Roll 3 at http://digicoll.library.wisc.edu/cgi-bin/History/History-idx?id=History.IT1837no223 at 20.

15 Alexander Morris, *The Treaties of Canada with the Indians of Manitoba and the North-West Territories: Including the Negotiations on Which They Were Based, and Other Information Relating Thereto* (Toronto: Belfords, Clarke, 1880) at 47.

16 Mervin Huntinghawk, "Since Time Immemorial: Treaty Land Entitlement in Manitoba," in Jill Oakes, Rick Riewe, Kathi Kinew, and Elaine Maioney, eds., *Sacred Lands: Aboriginal Worldviews, Claims, and Conflicts* (Edmonton: University of Alberta Press, 1998) at 40–1.

By using their sacred laws, the Anishinaabe were engaging in a process that incorporated the Creator and all of creation in their political practices. In doing so, the Anishinaabe were simultaneously recognizing their sovereignty (and thus responsibilities to their lands) as being derived from the Creator and the Anishinaabe were bringing the newcomers into these pre-existing relationships by including the Creator in any dealings or transactions that pertained to this "inheritance." This was critical because of the responsibility Anishinaabe people had both to the Creator and to their lands.

Lumbee scholar Robert Williams, in his analysis of American Indian treaty visions of law and peace in the encounter era, finds that "[w]hen smoked in the context of treaty negotiations, the pipe evoked a vision of a universally conceived society in which different peoples were connected to each other as relatives."[17] Intersecting spiritual practices with political acts enabled the Anishinaabe to develop political relationships that carried the additional obligations and commitments of kin relations. This language of diplomacy was carried into the nineteenth-century treaty practices of the Anishinaabe, as the treaty journals reflect. Thus, colonial nations that sought to establish and maintain political and economic alliances with Anishinaabe nations often found themselves engaging with and employing Anishinaabe cultural practices and discourses that were driven by Anishinaabe laws of creation.

Williams finds that Indigenous visions of law and peace were articulated throughout the treaty process as a means to create a shared understanding between the various participants. He argues,

> [T]he parties to a treaty had to agree to create and sustain a *nomos*, a normative universe of shared meanings – "a present world constituted by a system of tension between reality and vision." The smoking of the calumet of peace sought to resolve this tension by invoking the larger forces at work in the affairs of human beings.[18]

This shared vision placed responsibilities on all the parties involved.

Indeed, Anishinaabe chiefs recognized the importance of accounting for pre-existing relationships in the 1837 negotiations. This was done in a number of ways. For example, Aish-ke-bah-ge-ko-zhay (Flat Mouth) stated,

---

17 Williams, *supra* note 11 at 50.

18 *Ibid*, 47.

> They [chiefs from the Chippewa River] have granted a privilege to some men of cutting timber on some of their lands; for which they are paid in tobacco, & ammunition for hunting. They wish you not to break their word with these people – but to allow them to continue to cut timber.[19]

But pre-existing relationships were also recognized in more nuanced ways. For example, Aish-ke-bah-ge-ko-zhay stated,

> My Father, Your children are willing to let you have their lands, but they wish to reserve the privilege of making sugar from the trees and getting their living from the Lakes and Rivers, as they have done heretofore, and of remaining in their country. It is hard to give up the lands. They will remain and cannot be destroyed – but you may cut down the trees, and others will grow up. You know we cannot live deprived of our Lakes and Rivers. There is some game on the lands yet; and that that reason also, we wish to remain upon them, to get a living. Sometimes we scrape the trees and eat the bark. The Great Spirit above, made the Earth and causes it to produce, which enables us to live.[20]

Later in the negotiations, Aish-ke-bah-ge-ko-zhay repeated this important point, stating, "You know that without the lands and the rivers and the lakes, we could not live. We hunt and make sugar, and dig roots upon the former, while we fish and obtain rice and drink from the latter."[21] Aish-ke-bah-ge-ko-zhay's speeches not only speak to Anishinaabe recognition of our dependence on the Creator and creation for our ability to live, but also recognizes that the Earth was a gift from the Creator. By acknowledging Gichi-Manidoo, both through diplomatic practices such as smoking the pipe and in speeches delineating Gichi-Manidoo's role in producing resources upon the Earth, the Anishinaabe brought their pre-existing relationships with the land, animals, and flora into the treaty. In doing so, Anishinaabe not only reserved the rights to hunt, fish, and gather in shared territories, but also, importantly, reserved the ability to regulate these rights according to Anishinaabe legal traditions.

---

19 *Ratified Treaty No. 223 Documents Relating to the Negotiations of the Treaty of July 29, 1837, with the Chippewa Indians*, NAMP RG 75, M T-494 Roll 3, http://digicoll.library.wisc.edu/cgi-bin/History/History-idx?id=History.IT1837no223 at 26.

20 *Ibid*, 25.

21 *Ibid*, 27.

2. Honouring Our Relationship with Creation

Borrows, in analysing Anishinaabe legal traditions notes,

> In an Anishinabek legal context, *rights and responsibilities are intertwined* ... W.N. Hohfeld observed: "[A] duty is the invariable correlative of that legal relation which is most properly called a right or claim." An 1894 legal citation reads: "A duty or a legal obligation is that which one ought or ought not to do. 'Duty' and 'right' are correlative terms. When a right is invaded, a duty is violated." This is the case with Anishinaabek law. Wherever a potential right exists, a correlative obligation can usually be found, based on individual's relationship with the other orders of the world.[22]

He further notes,

> The Anishinaabek have strong legal traditions that convey their duties relative to the world. These are steward-like concepts (*bimeekumaugaewin*) and apply to their use of land, plants, and others. Principles of acknowledgement, accomplishment, accountability, and approbation are embedded in the Anishinaabek creation epic and associated stories.[23]

There are a multitude of stories among the Anishinaabeg, contained in various forms, that all work towards the same end: providing meaning to the world we live in, teaching us how to relate to one another, and helping us understand our place in creation. As Hester Lessard, Rebecca Johnson, and Jeremy Webber remind us,

> We come into existence ... as embodied beings, processing the partial fragments of sensory experience (sounds, images, smells, touches), sorting them into patterns of consequence, patterns of meaning. Narrative – or "story" – is one of the primary vehicles through which we sort, arrange, and produce those patterns.[24]

---

22 Borrows, *Canada's Indigenous Constitution*, *supra* note 6 at 79.

23 *Ibid.*

24 Hester Lessard, Rebecca Johnson, and Jeremy Webber, "Stories, Communities, and Their Contested Meanings," in Hester Lessard, Rebecca Johnson, and Jeremy Webber, eds., *Storied Communities: Narratives of Contact and Arrival in Constituting Political Community* (Vancouver: UBC Press, 2011) at 7.

It is through lived experiences, through interaction with all of creation, that we come to produce the stories that help us make sense of the world. By using these stories, and the important philosophies contained within them, we are able to draw out and develop laws that ensure we are relating to the land, animals, flora, *manidoog* (spirits), and one another as human beings in ways that are respectful and that account for our responsibilities to one another.

As many Indigenous peoples look to their stories to draw out law, they are careful in determining whether to codify these stories, instead often using the philosophies contained within the stories to serve as guiding posts in developing codes and regulations. For example, the stories that open the Great Lakes Indian Fish and Wildlife Commission's "Waawaashkeshi Waaswaa Ayaangwaami-Doodamowin: Tribal Manual on the Safe Conditions of Tribal Deer Hunting At Night While Shining Within an Established Safe Zone of Fire from a Stationary Position" outline the reciprocal relationship that exists between Anishinaabe and deer. As Ogimaagwanebiik's story "Mashkiki-Awesiiyag" denotes, the animals are gifts from the Creator and they offer themselves to the Anishinaabe as food. In doing so, the Anishinaabe have a responsibility to first offer tobacco, to additionally maintain respect for the animals, and, as cultural practices outline, to return particular parts of the animal to the woods to ensure their regeneration. Offering tobacco and treating the deer with respect is also outlined by Andy Favorite in "Waawaashkeshi and Asemaa." In this story, the old man, after living among the deer and learning the proper ways in which the Anishinaabe should relate to the deer, detailed these responsibilities to the hunter that shot him. This story delineates how the Anishinaabe came to engage in the practice of offering *asemaa* (tobacco) when petitioning an animal and is also told as a continuous reminder of why this act is so important.

Stories detail relationships. They teach us how to conduct ourselves and how to make sense of our actions vis-à-vis one another.[25] Julie Cruikshank found that "such narratives depict humans, animals, and other nonhuman beings engaged in an astonishing variety of activities and committed to mutually sustaining relationships that ensure the

25 See, for example, Heidi Kiiwetinepinesiik Stark, "Respect, Responsibility, and Renewal: The Foundations of Anishinaabe Treaty Making with the United States and Canada" (2010) 34:2 *American Indian Culture and Research Journal* 145–64.

continuing well-being of the world."[26] Stories are clearly a source of law as they lay out critical principles for how Anishinaabe order their world. The creation story did not cease at a particular moment for Anishinaabe. Our continued interaction with creation – in all her forms – continues to generate stories that teach us how to be in the world. In the same way, Anishinaabe legal traditions continue to adapt to an ever-changing world while remaining rooted in underlying principles that inform how we are to relate to the land and animals.

For example, on 9 September 1998, the Anishinaabeg of Kabapikotawangag Resource Council, which services six Anishinaabe First Nations surrounding Lake of the Woods, signed a formal protocol regarding the Earth with the Great Lakes Indian Fish and Wildlife Commission, which represents eleven Anishinaabe nations within the borders of Minnesota, Wisconsin, and Michigan.[27] This agreement, known as the Anishinaabe Akii Protocol, "recognized the bond between Ojibwe people from the United States and Canada due to common origins, traditions and clan and considers them 'brothers and sisters of the Sovereign Anishinaabe Nation,' in essence cutting through national, state and provincial boundaries that seem to separate the Anishinaabe Nation."[28]

The Anishinaabe Akii Protocol reaffirms "our sacred trust to protect the natural environment and resources for all peoples and generations yet unborn," stating, among other things, that "we hereby covenant and agree to work jointly and actively in: the conservation, control, and prudent use of the land, air, water, and all resources including the rock, soil, minerals, fish, flora, fauna, and all other life within our traditional territory."[29]

---

26 Julie Cruikshank, *The Social Life of Stories: Narrative and Knowledge in the Yukon Territory* (Lincoln: University of Nebraska Press, 1998) at xii.

27 See Sue Erickson, "GLIFWC Hosts Northern Anishinaabe Relatives," *Mazina'igan: A Chronicle of the Lake Superior Ojibwe* (Summer 2008) at 1, 17, available at http://glifwc.org/publications/mazinaigan/Summer2008.pdf. Also see Sue Erickson, "GLIFWC Brings Home Gifts for the Spirit: Protocol between Kabapikotawangag Resource Council and GLIFWC Bands Proposed," *Masinaigan* (Fall 1997) at 2; Sue Erickson, "Anishinaabe Akii Protocol Signed at Madeline Island Treaty Conference: Solidarity between U.S. and Canadian Ojibwe Confirmed," *Masinaiganm* (Fall 1998/Winter 1999) at 5–6; Dylan Jennings, "No Borders for Anishinaabeg: Manoomin, Education Highlight Treaty 3 Visit," *Mazina'igan: A Chronicle of the Lake Superior Ojibwe* (Spring 2016) at 1, 3. For additional information about the Great Lakes Indian Fish and Wildlife Commission, see glifwc.org.

28 Sue Erickson, "GLIFWC Hosts Northern Anishinaabe Relatives," *Mazina'igan*, summer 2008 at http://www.glifwc.org/publications/mazinaigan/Summer2008.pdf.

For Anishinaabe, *aki* (also referred to as *akii*) is an all-encompassing term for the Earth which recognizes the interconnectivity of all of creation. This term is also relational. Indeed, the protocol begins by stating "knowing that our sacred grandfather, Saagima Manitou, placed us here upon grandmother earth under the sky; in the forest hills and valleys, in the lakes, rivers, and islands of our ancestors." We have a relationship to *aki*, delineated in our creation stories through our placement on the land by Gichi-Manidoo or Saagima Manitou, the Creator.[30]

The rich stories among the Anishinaabe demonstrate our awareness of, and indeed seek to teach us about, the interconnectivity and interdependence within and across *aki*, the Earth. Stories about Nenabozho (also known as Nanaboozhoo or Nanabush), a central trickster figure among Anishinaabe, outline our interactions with creation and detail how these interactions transform all those involved: land, animals, Anishinaabe, and so on. These stories also describe how our relationships to one another are generated through our actions.[31] As we engage with one another, we transform and are transformed. The names we maintain for much of the landscape we traverse outline these interactions and contain vibrant stories about how we relate to *aki*.[32] Thus, this Anishinaabe Akii Protocol not only reflects our responsibilities to the land, but also to the plants, animals, spirits, and humans. We have relationships, often established through treaty and diplomacy, with the land and animals. These early treaties between Indigenous peoples and the animal and star nations are perhaps the oldest recorded treaties;

---

29 "Sky, Land, and Water of the Anisinaabe: The Anishinaabe Akii Protocol," signed 9 September 1998 at Madeline Island by Tom Maulson, chairman, on behalf of the Great Lakes Indian Fish and Wildlife Commission and by Chief Wesley Big George, chairman, on behalf of the Kabapikotawangag Resource Council.

30 For additional information on Anishinaabe creation see Benton-Banai, *supra* note 2; Basil Johnston, *Ojibway Ceremonies*, *supra* note 2; Basil Johnston, *Ojibway Heritage* (Lincoln: University of Nebraska Press, 1976); Basil Johnston, *The Manitous: The Spiritual World of the Ojibway* (St. Paul: Minnesota Historical Society Press, 2001).

31 Benton-Banai, *supra* note 2; Truman Michelson, ed., and William Jones, comp., *Publications of the American Ethnological Society*, vol. 7, bk. 1, *Ojibwa Texts* (Leyden, NL: E.J. Brill, Ltd., 1917); Truman Michelson, ed., and William Jones, comp., *Publications of the American Ethnological Society*, vol. 7, bk. 2, *Ojibwa Texts* (New York: E.J. Brill, Ltd., 1919).

32 Keith H. Basso, *Wisdom Sits in Places: Landscape and Language among the Western Apache* (Albuquerque: University of New Mexico Press, 1996); Benton-Banai, *supra* note 2.

they are contained in stories that lay out many of the foundational principles of treaty-making, and that teach us about how we are supposed to relate to *aki*, the Earth.[33]

How do we honour these treaties today? One way is to honour our relationships with *aki*, with the animals, plants, spirits, and so on, regardless of the state's recognition of our responsibilities to do so. And indeed, Anishinaabe, and for that matter Indigenous peoples across Turtle Island, have continued to carry out these relationships even though the ways in which they have done so have been impacted by a lack of recognition by the state of their responsibilities to creation. The United States and Canada have instead narrowly defined these relationships through the language of rights guaranteed by treaties. For example, Anishinaabe, who were party to the 1837 treaty with the United States have found their relationships to *aki* has been construction through a rights discourse that narrowly defines their obligations to creation as rights to hunt, fish, and gather in their "ceded" Anishinaabe homeland. Despite explicitly reserving the rights to carry out these relationships across what Anishinaabe consider to be shared, not ceded, territories, Wisconsin, Minnesota, and Michigan laws previously failed to account for these treaty rights. Nonetheless, the Anishinaabe continued to carry out these relationships, knowing they would likely be constructed as criminal activities by the state.[34] Furthermore, the Anishinaabe resisted the curtailment of their responsibilities to carry out their long-standing relationships through hunting and fishing, securing judicial recognition of their rights to hunt, fish, and gather in these shared territories.

Another way we honour these traditions is to continue to carry out long-standing Anishinaabe legal traditions that teach us how we are supposed to relate to Anishinaabe *aki*. This is done each time Anishinaabe offer *asemaa*, tobacco, and return particular parts of the animal to the land and water that enables their regeneration.[35] These traditions are all good and necessary.

---

33 Stark, *supra* note 25; Heidi Kiiwetinepinesiik Stark, "Marked by Fire: Anishinaabe Articulations of Nationhood in Treaty-Making with the United States and Canada" (2012) 36:2 *American Indian Quarterly* 119–49.

34 See Larry Nesper, *The Walleye War: The Struggle for Ojibwe Spearfishing and Treaty Rights* (Lincoln: University of Nebraska Press, 2002).

35 See Stark, *supra* note 25; Reo, *supra* note 7; Andy Favorite, "Waawaashkeshi & Asemaa: A Story for Hunters, Gatherers and Fishermen," *Anishinaabeg Today*, 25 April 2011; Val Napoleon, "Living Together: Gitksan Legal Reasoning as a

Yet a question remains: What obligations and responsibilities do we have to Anishinaabe *aki* – to the animals, the plants, the water, the *aadizookaanag* and *manidoog* (spirits) – that are being impacted by external forces such as the United States and Canada? Put another way, How are our relationships to land, animals, all of creation, being impacted and transformed by non-Anishinaabe humans' engagement with creation? As Aimée Craft reminds us in her recently published study of the Stone Fort Treaty, citing the speeches of Anishinaabe chiefs negotiating Treaty 1, "the land cannot speak for itself. We have to speak for it."[36]

While the land, animals, and *manidoog*, constantly speak to us if we are willing and able to listen, as this chief's words connote, we have a responsibility to give voice to the land; we must acknowledge we have heard the land by acting accordingly. Through treaty we did so in a number of important ways, two of which I want to briefly reflect upon. The first is creation. Anishinaabe asserted their sovereignty through an expression of creation. They spoke of the land as an inheritance from the Creator. For example, Anishinaabe Chief Mash-i-pi-nash-i-wish, at the 1795 Treaty of Greenville, stated,

> Listen! The Great Spirit above hears us, and I trust we shall not endeavor to deceive each other. I expect what we are about to do shall never be forgotten as long as we exist ... Remember, we have taken the Great Spirit to witness our present actions; we will make a new world, and leave nothing on it to incommode our children.[37]

Chief Hole-in-the-Day also spoke of the Creator in treaty negotiations, reminding U.S. Treaty Commissioner Henry Dodge, "The Great Spirit who placed us on this Earth hears both you and me. He put us upon it to live." He further stated, "And I call the Great Being to witness what I say. We agree to what has just been done, & are satisfied with it."[38]

Foundation for Consent," in Jeremy Webber and Colin M. Macleod, eds., *Between Consenting Peoples: Political Community and the Meaning of Consent* (Vancouver: UBC Press, 2010).

36 Aimée Craft, *Breathing Life into the Stone Fort Treaty: An Anishinabe Understanding of Treaty One* (Saskatoon: Purich Publishing, 2013) at 94.

37 Quoted in Williams, *supra* note 11 at 99.

38 *Ratified Treaty No. 223 Documents Relating to the Negotiations of the Treaty of July, 29, 1837, with the Chippewa Indians,* NAMP RG 75, M T-494 Roll 3:F564.

Perhaps one reason they shaped their speeches in this way was to mitigate American and Canadian claims of sovereignty, demarcating their relationships to *aki* through a declaration of their relationships as rights to the land, water, and resources that were distinct from the claims of the state. Indeed, Anishinaabe noted in these speeches that these newcomers had been placed on lands across the great sea.[39]

I think, however, that this invocation of the Creator is essential to understanding how Anishinaabe comprehend their relationship to *aki*, a relationship that is often narrowly constructed through the Western language of sovereignty. The Anishinaabe term often used to express sovereignty is *ezhi-ogimaawaadizid*. This word has at its root the term *ogimaa*, which roughly translates as a leader. Anishinaabe legal scholar John Borrows, drawing on the definition provided by Mary Black, has defined the word *ogimaa*, as "those who I am responsible for."[40] Using Borrows' definition of *ogimaa*, the Anishinaabe term often used to express sovereignty, *ezhi-ogimaawaadizid* would translate roughly as "to act in a way that recognizes those who I am responsible for." This is a nice way to think about Anishinaabe sovereignty that recognizes that our relationships to one another and to Anishinaabe *aki* entail responsibilities. While this is a useful term and concept for understanding how we think about sovereignty, I would like to offer another, one that is directly connected to our creation.

I think at its very essence the Anishinaabe word for sovereignty is *Anishinaabe*. Who we are as a people, how we see ourselves is the very essence of our sovereignty. The term Anishinaabe references the creation of the people. It alludes to how the Creator lowered our people to the Earth. This act of creation was invoked again and again by Anishinaabe leaders to assert their sovereignty and relationships to *aki* in treaty negotiations – relationships carrying responsibilities that were inherited from the Creator.

Perhaps another reason Anishinaabe leaders across Anishinaabe *aki* repeatedly spoke about their relationships to the land through a

39 Heidi Kiiwetinepinesiik Stark, "Nenabozho's Smartberries: Rethinking Tribal Sovereignty and Accountability" (2013) 2 *Michigan State Law Review* 339.

40 Personal correspondence with John Borrows. Mary Black, "Ojibwa Power Belief System," in Raymond Fogelson and Richard Adams, eds., *The Anthropology of Power: Ethnographic Studies from Asia, Oceania, and the New World* (New York: Academic Press, 1977) at 147.

discussion of their placement on these lands by Gichi-Manidoo was to recognize and account for pre-existing responsibilities to the land. These responsibilities are created out of our relationships; our relationships to the land, to the animals, to the plants, and so on. While Anishinaabe are encouraged to pursue our individual gifts (*andobawaajigen*, seek your dream or purpose) and exercise a high degree of personal autonomy while simultaneously recognizing our connection and relationship to the Anishinaabe collective by acting in ways that allow personal growth while remaining rooted in collective well-being, Anishinaabe also understand ourselves as merely one part of creation. While we should be working towards our collective maturation, we are also deeply connected to and interconnected with the larger collectivity known as creation.

Indeed some people translate the word Anishinaabe to mean the humble people or the pitiful people. *Anishinaa*, which means "just for nothing" or "without purpose,"[41] connotes that we were the last of creation to be made and implies that, because we are not born knowing our purpose in life, we must seek out a vision.[42] Thus, treaties were not just made between nations but also necessarily incorporated all of creation, as this collective creation would be impacted and transformed by the actions of Anishinaabe. The web of relationships in existence across Anishinaabe *aki* brought all these entities into the treaty relationship.

This brings me to the second point of reflection: relationships. Treaties created relationships.[43] When Anishinaabe entered into treaties with the United States and Canada, Americans and Canadians became relatives of the Anishinaabe. It could be said that these relationships were bound not by blood, but instead by ink. But neither blood nor ink carry much weight among Anishinaabe. It is words that have force. Words can possibly be seen and understood as a law of creation as it was the breath of Gichi-Manidoo, the Creator, when combined with the Earth that made the Anishinaabe. Thus, any word we utter is intimately connected not only to the act of our creation, but also to the one we call the kind-hearted spirit, Gizhe-Manidoo. Our breath is an extension of the Creator's.

---

41 John Nichols and Earl Nyholm, *A Concise Dictionary of Minnesota Ojibwe* (Minneapolis: University of Minnesota Press, 1995).

42 Dennis Jones, "The Etymology of Anishinaabe" (1995) 2:1 *Oshkaabewis Native Journal* 43–8.

43 Stark, "Marked by Fire," *supra* note 33.

Throughout the treaties, Anishinaabe acknowledged they were speaking clearly and freely so all of creation could hear them, recognizing our relationship to and interconnectedness with creation. Chief Little Rock, in the 1863 "Old Crossing Treaty" between the United States and the Red Lake and Pembina Anishinaabe, perhaps most eloquently illustrated this point. He stated, "Now, my friend, I am going to show you how we came to occupy this land. The Master of Life placed us here, and gave it to us for an inheritance."[44] He continued,

> I want the earth to listen to me, and I hope also that my grandfather may be present to hear what I have to say, and I invoke the Master of Life to listen to the words I have to speak. I hope there is not a single hole in the atmosphere in which my voice shall not be heard. My friend, the question you have laid before us is of great importance.[45]

Anishinaabe conceptions of sovereignty were intimately connected to Anishinaabe identity and land. These intersections are eloquently articulated by Red Lake Chief Little Rock in the 1863 Old Crossing treaty negotiations with the United States. He asserted, "My grandfather made my heart, and he also made my mouth, that all the land and the inheritance may listen to my voice when I speak his words." He returned to this point later in his speech, stating, "We have made reference to the Master of Life; we speak of him again. He is present now, and hears what we have to say."[46]

Little Rock's words reflect the intersections among Anishinaabe conceptions of creation, sovereignty, and land tenure. The Anishinaabe, made from the Earth and the Creator's breath, are connected to the land through our bodies. As Little Rock spoke from his heart and breath, placed in him by the Creator, the Creator and the Earth could hear his words. Anishinaabe creation delineated a relationship between all beings, the Anishinaabe just one of many. Little Rock recognized that Anishinaabe actions, such as negotiating treaties, involved and affected all of creation. In uttering these agreements, which simultaneously

44 President's message, 7 and 8 January 1864; *Treaty of October 2, 1863 with the Red Lake & Pembina Bands of Chippewas*; Indian Treaty Files (SEN 38B-C9): p. 18, RG 46.

45 *Ibid.*

46 *Ibid* at 28.

established and renewed relationships, we not only brought Anishinaabe *aki* into our relationships with the United States and Canada, but also brought the United States and Canada into our relationship with *aki*. We spoke not only for the land, but also for the newcomers to this land. We vouched for these newcomers. In doing so we became responsible for Americans and Canadians, for how they would relate to *aki*. We brought them into our long-standing relationships with *aki* and thus took on a responsibility for how they would relate with all of creation.

This may be another way for us to reflect on the term Anishinaabe. In invoking creation, in defining ourselves as those last to be placed within creation, we recognize that we were brought into a complex web of relationships operating across *aki*. How we relate to *aki* must reflect this. While our relationships to *aki* enable us to engage the land, animals, plants, and *manidoog* in meaningful ways that nourish us physically and spiritually, these relationships carry responsibilities. As the last placed within creation, we cannot act in ways that would violate those relationships that came before us, that were already in existence across creation. Indeed some say that the term Anishinaabe means the second people, as it is connected to the word *niizh*, which means two. Anishinaabe at one time were not relating to *aki* in a way that accounted for these pre-existing relationships. We had created great imbalance and the Earth was flooded. When the Earth was created anew, the animals stood up for us, they vouched for the Anishinaabe and said they would teach us how to relate to creation. This is one of the origin stories of our clan system.[47] The animals created a relationship with Anishinaabe and took responsibility for our actions. We did the same for the newcomers when we negotiated treaties with the United States and the Crown.

This brings me to my present question: How do we honour our treaties with *aki*? How do we implement these agreements and protocols in meaningful ways that take seriously our responsibilities for the newcomers we brought into the fold? As we call on the United States and Canada to fulfill the commitments outlined in our treaty relationships in accordance with the spirit and intent of these relationships, how can we make sure we are not replicating these shortcomings in our commitments and relationships with *aki*? This is a question facing the Lake Superior Anishinaabe.

---

47 See Benton-Banai, *supra* note 2; Johnston, *Ojibway Heritage, supra* note 30; Johnston, *The Manitous, supra* note 30.

Represented by the Great Lakes Indian Fish and Wildlife Commission, Anishinaabe are seeking to ensure that Anishinaabe legal traditions which are rooted in rich understandings of our interconnectivity and interdependence with all of creation are not only given space to flourish but also inform how we relate to one another. For example, current wild rice management plans attempt to account for the ways our actions impact *aki* by requiring tribal members to move through the rice beds following particular patterns and to use wild rice knockers made out of cedar as this lightweight wood enables Anishinaabe to minimize their impact on this vital resource. Anishinaabe also have tribal ordinances that recognize the centrality of respect for animals who gave their lives to ensure our survival, fining hunters who are found guilty of wasting the animal.[48] Anishinaabe continue to offer *asemaa*, tobacco, to the water, land, plants, and animals prior to harvest, acknowledging their gratitude and ensuring the regeneration of these essential parts of creation.[49]

While Anishinaabe continue to strive towards the adherence of the protocols outlining how we relate to *aki*, Anishinaabe also continue to be confronted with the challenges of not only holding Americans to their treaty commitments but also accounting for what it means that these Americans were brought into our long-standing relationships with *aki*.

This question was made starkly present for Anishinaabe when the state of Wisconsin began considering, and subsequently implemented, a wolf hunt following the removal of the grey wolf from the endangered species list in January 2012. The Anishinaabe vehemently opposed this hunt, as it is antithetical to the particular relationship Anishinaabe have to wolves, whom we see as our brothers. As Anishinaabe treaty rights were recognized in the *Voigt* decision (1983), the Anishinaabe have a recognized right to a portion of the "resources" in "ceded" territories and must work in conjunction with the state in the management of these resources. While many have seen this affirmation of treaty rights as a victory for Anishinaabe in our pursuits to exercise our sovereignty, the contentions surrounding the 2012 wolf hunt, ever so briefly outlined

48 Nesper, *supra* note 7.

49 Reo, *supra* note 35; Favorite, *supra* note 35.

here, demonstrate the limitations of a rights-based system in which the state is willing to recognize that Anishinaabe have "rights" to a particular quantity of the entities that comprise *aki*. The rights framework was deployed by the state to foreclose conversations about our responsibilities to wolves, positioning wolves as "resources" that could be portioned out between the tribes and the state in their management. This left little recourse for the tribes in voicing their concerns regarding state action toward their "portion" of this "resource."

As Anishinaabe pursue a number of approaches to address the contentions that arise from this rights framework, it is unclear whether the United States and Canada will be willing to reframe their focus on rights to a more fruitfully examination of our relationships and responsibilities to one another and ask not what our rights to land and resources are, but instead question how we are supposed to relate to *aki*. As Anishinaabe that stood up for the newcomers brought into the fold through treaty, what responsibilities do we have to ensure Americans and Canadians are acting in accordance with pre-existing agreements operating across *aki*? How do we ensure that we do not let the narrow rights-based framework of these nation-states blind us to our larger relationships and responsibilities to Anishinaabe *aki*?

These reflections raise more questions than answers. Reflecting on the Anishinaabe Akii Protocol, we must consider what it means as Anishinaabe to reaffirm "our sacred trust to protect the natural environment and resources for all peoples and generations yet unborn." What responsibilities do these relationships entail for Anishinaabe? What is our duty to consult with creation? How do we ensure we are relating to *aki* in meaningful ways that account for the pre-existing relationships across creation? And what responsibilities do we have to teach the newcomers whom we vouched for how to relate to *aki*?

3. More Questions than Answers: Reframing the Right(s) Relationship

When I was invited to consider treaty remedies, the aim of this collection, I instinctually found myself giving deep consideration to treaty interpretation. I believe that any discussion regarding a framework for addressing treaty remedies, for treaty signatories to hold each other accountable for breaches of treaty promises, brings us back around to the central question that continues to plague treaty relationships today: How are we to interpret treaties? What were the treaty signatories agreeing to? What was the spirit and intent of the treaty? Before we can consider what a particular treaty entailed, in terms of the relationships created or renewed and the correlating responsibilities that gave meaning to these relationships, we should consider the normative world views that informed and conditioned these relationships. This is the question I have sought to explore here, with a focus on Anishinaabe political and legal thought. Specifically, my aim is to unearth the political and legal philosophies that informed and continue to inform Anishinaabe engagement with others, namely, with Canada and the United States, in order to bring forth a different set of questions and concerns that, though offering little in the way of answers, I hope may provide new or alternate paths for consideration in thinking through remedies.

The courts have sought to address some of these quandaries through the development of canons of treaty interpretation, calling for treaties to be interpreted as they were understood by the signatories. Treaties are to be given large, liberal, and generous interpretations in favour of Indigenous peoples, ambiguities in treaties are to be resolved in favour of Indigenous peoples, treaties are to be interpreted in a flexible manner, and extrinsic evidence should be used to determine the meaning and intent of treaties.[50] The courts in the United States have even applied and upheld the "reserved rights" doctrine, which notes that any Indigenous nations' rights, not expressly ceded or extinguished, remain intact.[51]

While these canons, when they are adhered to, can be favourable for unearthing Indigenous interpretations of their treaties, they nonetheless compete with legal principles that enable an infringement of treaty

---

50 For discussion of Canadian canons of treaty interpretation, see: Leonard I. Rotman, "Taking Aim at the Canons of Treaty Interpretation in Canadian Aboriginal Rights Jurisprudence" (1997) 46 *University of New Brunswick Law Journal* at 11; John Borrows and Leonard I. Rotman, *Aboriginal Legal Issues: Cases, Materials & Commentary*, 4th ed. (Markham, ON: LexisNexis Canada, 2012); Gordon Christie, "Justifying Principles of Treaty Interpretation" (2000) 26 *Queen's Law Journal* 143.

51 For discussion of U.S. canons of treaty interpretation, see David E. Wilkins and K. Tsianina Lomawaima, *Uneven Ground: American Indian Sovereignty and Federal Law* (Norman: University of Oklahoma Press, 2001); Charles F. Wilkinson and John M. Volkman, "Judicial Review of Indian Treaty Abrogation: 'As Long as Water Flows, or Grass Grows Upon the Earth' – How Long Is That?" (1975) 63:3 *California Law Review* 601–61; Cohen, *Handbook, supra* note 12.

rights when such an infringement is deemed justifiable.[52] In addition, though calling for flexible interpretation the canons still rely heavily on historical evidence to shed light on the spirit and intent of treaties. This reliance on historical evidence has, at times, been favourable for Indigenous nations. Indeed, the field of ethnohistory arose out of the study of Indigenous treaties and Aboriginal occupancy, lines of inquiry that were necessitated by the Indian Claims Commission.[53] The commission created a process for tribes to address their grievances against the United States, and offered monetary compensation for territory lost as a result of broken federal treaties.

Ethnohistorical methodologies have enabled the production of in-depth analyses of treaties, as ethnohistorians seek to understand culture on its own terms and according to its own cultural codes. It is especially important because of its ability to bridge differing frameworks and access a more informed context for interpreting the past. Nonetheless, much of this work has paid little attention to how these interpretations get carried into the present. This is partially due to the fact that the courts have primarily focused their attention on historical interpretations of treaties, notwithstanding their willingness to recognize that Indigenous peoples should be able to carry out treaty rights in modern forms.[54] This attention to interpreting and understanding the past, while important, has nonetheless constrained our understanding of treaties, putting us at risk for thinking narrowly about treaty remedies.

This raises the question of how historical interpretation of treaties may be creating an incomplete picture of how we understand these binding agreements. This occurs in two forms. The first is the court-driven agenda that has shaped and contained how we understand treaties. Indeed, we recognize that much was left out of the written documents and

52 N. Bruce Duthu, "Implicit Divestiture of Tribal Powers: Locating Legitimate Sources of Authority in Indian Country" (1994) 19:2 *American Indian Law Review* 353–402; Samuel E. Ennis, "Implicit Divestiture and the Supreme Court's (Re)Construction of the Indian Canons" (2011) 35:3 *Vermont Law Review* 563; Gordon Christie, "A Colonial Reading of Recent Jurisprudence: *Sparrow, Delgamuukw* and *Haida Nation*" (2005) 23:1 *Windsor Yearbook of Access to Justice* 17–53.

53 See "About ASE," *The American Society for Ethnohistory* at http://www.ethnohistory.org/about-ase/; Christian W. McMillen, *Making Indian Law: The Hualapai Land Case and the Birth of Ethnohistory* (New Haven: Yale University Press, 2007).

54 For example, see *R v Sundown* [1999] 1 SCR 393.

yet, we continue to focus our attention on the interpretation of particular clauses. We spend a great deal of time focused on rights to hunt, fish, and gather – which, indeed, are important and worthy of this attention – but I cannot help but wonder if this has locked us into framing our treaty rights in language that is comfortable and recognizable to the state. Courts are culturally subjective institutions, and judges are indeed influenced by their archaic notions about Indigenous peoples. For example, judges are often able to recognize Indigenous rights to hunt and fish for subsistence but they struggle in extending these rights to commercial activities. Similarly, judges in Canada struggle to envision treaty signatories as having reserved their sovereignty in their treaty relationships with the Crown while putting forward a vision for coexistence across a multinational terrain in which Indigenous nations and Canada are bound by their obligations and treaty commitments.

We look to section 35 of the Canadian constitution as an affirmation and recognition of treaty and Aboriginal rights that have constitutional standing, and it is indeed the case that these rights are constitutionally guaranteed. In celebrating this affirmation and recognition, however, I continue to wonder whether we must also be aware of the dangers posed by the constitutional inclusion of Aboriginal and treaty rights. Has the attention to section 35 enabled people to slip from understanding pre-existing treaty-protected rights as inherent rights that were merely recognized and affirmed by the constitution to instead understanding these rights as derived from the constitutional framework. While legal scholars have, of course, been careful to position these rights as pre-existing, the attention to section 35 has nonetheless locked these discussions, in some ways, within a state framework instead of situating them as part of a dialogue about nation-to-nation relationships.

Indeed the Canadian courts often close off and contain discussion of self-government and fail to affirm and recognize Indigenous sovereignty. They have failed to consider even more narrow questions about treaty rights that focus, for example, on taxation, small business enterprises, or Indigenous economic development efforts that fall outside of capitalist market-driven, extraction-oriented agendas. If we are going to take Indigenous assertions of sovereignty and nationhood seriously, as well as the laws and political traditions that give shape and meaning to Indigenous sovereignty and nationhood, we must also ask what treaty rights exist beyond the scope of hunting and fishing. If Indigenous peoples were not ceding lands, but instead creating a shared territory that would enable peaceful and mutually beneficial coexistence of separate nations, how must our understandings of treaty rights expand to account for these interpretations?

This brings me to my second point for consideration. In focusing on the historical interpretation of treaties, we continue to put forward an agenda shaped by our belief that the answers lie in understanding the original spirit and intent of treaties. While Indigenous leaders invoke this language to call for more expansive engagement with the Indigenous philosophies and laws that undergird treaties, the courts have too often restricted this language of spirit and intent to questions of what Indigenous signatories understood about particular clauses within written treaties or to the historical context of a particular treaty. While these questions are important, I believe that this has also limited our understanding of treaty relationships. I instead argue that the answers lie in understanding the larger framework of Indigenous governance and legal traditions that gave meaning to our historical treaties.

Let's take, for example, Anishinaabe teachings about the Earth and our relationships to creation. How might our understandings of Anishinaabe governance and legal principles regarding creation impact our interpretations of treaties?

In order to understand our treaties, and the rights we reserved, it is imperative that we account for the pre-existing relationships and legal frameworks that informed and gave meaning to these treaties. In order to do so, we must pay attention to Anishinaabe governance and legal traditions that gave shape and meaning to our treaty relationships. By looking to the broader philosophies and legal traditions that informed our treaty relationships with the Crown, we bring forth a new set of questions regarding treaty rights. If we take the ways in which Anishinaabe relationships with creation shaped treaties into consideration, for example, in thinking about a legal framework for breaches of treaty relationships, then we must make space for Indigenous peoples to hold the state accountable to the pre-existing relationships with creation. Better yet, we would need to make space for Indigenous peoples to teach the state how to properly engage in relationships with creation.

4. Bringing Indigenous Law to the Surface

When the Earth was out of balance, before the animals stood up for the Anishinaabe, the Earth was flooded. Nenabozho was floating on a log and was joined by a number of animals who took turns diving into the depths of the ever-rising water in order to fetch some earth. Many attempted and failed until finally the tiny muskrat volunteered to dive for earth. He was gone for a long time but eventually floated up to the surface, having drowned for his efforts. Clenched in his little paw, however, was a small amount of earth. Nenabozho was able to use this earth to make the land anew. In doing so, he was careful to consider those to come, the many who have yet to be born. He sent out runners to measure the earth and continued to expand it until they were unable to return, thus ensuring he had considered the future generations.

Anishinaabe stories about restoring balance may generate insight about how we can envision new remedies, not just for treaty-specific violations, but for what it means to coexist. As Anishinaabe, we must remain rooted in our foundations, just as the new Earth was rooted in the earth of the lands that came before. We cannot, however, bring up all the land as it was. This land is submerged under the water. We cannot ignore the fact that treaty relationships have not been upheld. Actions cannot be undone, but balance can again be restored. We must draw on our historical treaties, but we must also account for the need for a renewed relationship. In remoulding the Earth, we must have the foresight to think of those yet to come, making sure we have made room for them. We must create space for growth. With treaties, we must not only draw on the responsibilities impacted, created, and protected by these agreements, but also enable space for growth by moving away from a rights discourse that precludes us from focusing on treaties as relationships, relationships that must be nurtured and renewed.

Indeed, our historical treaties faced similar challenges. The relationships established through the Covenant Chain were thoroughly tarnished by the time our ancestors negotiated the Numbered Treaties. In their desire to renew relationships, however, our ancestors delved deep into our philosophical waters to unearth and bring to the surface Anishinaabe conceptions of sovereignty and nationhood. Our ancestors spoke at length about our relationships to land, rooted in our creation stories, and outlined these relationships through a legal and political discourse that provides insight into how we saw ourselves as nations. Our obligations and responsibilities to our lands and our kin responsibilities, not only to our people, but also to the animals and plants that reciprocated in providing us nourishment and health, necessitated our engagement with newcomers to our lands. Our obligations and responsibilities to speak for the land and to account for our pre-existing relationships with creation would motivate us to engage in treaties that had complicated and unforeseen consequences. Indeed, throughout and following our treaty negotiations, we faced the rising waters of colonialism that threatened to submerge us. Yet, like Nenabozho, our people were able to remain afloat.

Our treaties are our vessels, the logs that have kept us afloat. We risk being lost at sea, however, if we do not navigate these agreements by diving down and unearthing the deeper political philosophies that inform our understandings of who we are as nations. We must take turns diving deep into the waters in order to bring our rich philosophies to the surface and to remould our legal traditions that give shape and meaning to treaty relationships. We must not be constrained by the narrow articles and interpretations that too often distract us from the deeper meanings that gave shape to our treaties. We must understand that, while our treaties are critical, they are still merely the vessels that keep us afloat. We must still envision creating the Earth anew.

10 (Re)Defining "Good Faith" through *Snuw'uyulh*

SARAH MORALES

The chapter speaks to the role that Indigenous legal traditions should play in creating and defining the processes of modern-day treaty negotiations. It uses the Hul'qumi'num treaty table as a case study to illustrate how current negotiations are not being conducted in "good faith" (neither in relation to domestic or international standards) and how that is leading to insurmountable stalemates within the BC treaty process. The author argues that Indigenous peoples, like the Hul'qumi'num people, have well-established principles of dispute resolution and teachings about proper negotiations, or "good faith," and that these principles and practices should also be reflected within the treaty negotiation process if true reconciliation is the goal.

"I'm tired of talking about those damn bones!" As soon as the words crossed the lips of the government negotiator the room fell silent. The Elders sat stunned and tears started to well up in some of their eyes. Immediately many of them got up and left the room – it had become apparent that consensus would never be reached.

They had come to the negotiating table hoping to find a resolution to the issue of the destruction of their sacred sites within their territory. They had spent the morning trying to explain the significance of these sites to the provincial and federal negotiators; however, as they recounted the teachings that they had been given by the Old People concerning these sites, their *snuw'uyulh*, the government negotiators occupied themselves with emails and by passing notes to one another. They weren't listening to their words. They weren't hearing their concerns.

Now, just as they were about to break for lunch and share a meal together, they heard it ... the words that they had feared all along. What was it going to take to make them understand? Why were the resting places of their ancestors so much more important than the resting places of ours? Were they really here to resolve these issues? Was this just another process aimed to strip them of their rights and dignity? Why should they continue in this process? They had been "negotiating" for over twenty years, and they were no closer to a resolution than they had been at the beginning of this process?

But they had to continue with their fight. Not just for the Old People who had gone before them, but for their future generations. So that they could one day visit those places and feel the strength of their ancestors, reflect on their laws and teachings and navigate their place within the world.

1. Introduction

The story told above is a recounting of true events that happened during the negotiations at the Hul'qumi'num treaty table. I have had the opportunity to work with this treaty table off and on for almost fifteen years. My participation in this process has greatly influenced my research agenda over the past decade, inspiring me to examine further the nature of the Hul'qumi'num legal tradition and their own processes of dispute resolution. Although the frustrations and stalemates I witnessed at the tripartite negotiating table influenced me to research and study the Hul'qumi'num legal tradition, it was not until I began to explore the intricacies of this legal tradition that I began to realize that it was not just substantive differences causing issues at the negotiating table; the process itself was flawed due to its inability to reflect the dispute resolution principles and practices of all parties involved. By failing to consider Indigenous legal traditions within the dispute resolution process itself, Canada is choosing to overlook the colonial history of its past land policy practices and is embedding the racism and structural inequalities mentioned by John Borrows in his chapter, "Canada's Colonial Constitution," into this process of reconciliation.[1]

The Hul'qumi'num Treaty Group (HTG) was founded in 1993 to jointly negotiate a comprehensive treaty on Aboriginal title, property, self-government, and other rights with Canada and British Columbia in the British Columbia treaty process. HTG's member First Nations are socially, culturally, and economically interconnected by marriage, travel, trade, ceremony, and sacred beliefs. There are also vitally important,

1 See John Borrows, "Canada's Colonial Constitution," chapter 1 in this volume.

life-giving and ongoing ties to the land that have sustained these Indigenous peoples, their unique culture, and their way of life since time immemorial.[2] The current member First Nations[3] are (1) Cowichan Tribes, (2) Penelakut Tribe, (3) Halalt First Nation, (4) Lyackson First Nation, and (5) Lake Cowichan First Nation.

Like so many other First Nations in British Columbia, the Hul'qumi'num people have been involved in this modern-day treaty-making process, established under Canada's comprehensive claims policy, because their rights to and governance of their territories has yet to be formalized with the state. No treaty or any other formal arrangement has resolved the issues surrounding the competing interests of the Hul'qumi'num First Nations and the Canadian state. After over sixteen years of negotiation talks within the British Columbia treaty process, the Hul'qumi'num Treaty Group and other British Columbia First Nations have begun to question whether the governments of Canada and British Columbia are negotiating in "good faith."[4]

In this chapter, I want to critically assess the notion of "good faith" and examine the critique that the governments have not been upholding their domestic, international and Indigenous legal obligations to negotiate in good faith. In the first section of this chapter, I will explain in more detail some of the main issues hampering progress at the Hul'qumi'num treaty table. I will then discuss how government mandates and negotiating practices within this context illustrate bad faith negotiation on their part. Second, I will rely on international law to demonstrate that the positions of the Hul'qumi'num leadership are not evidence of bad faith on their part; rather, they are acknowledged as expressions of fundamental rights under international law. Finally, I will attempt to illustrate how engaging a process that draws from both the Hul'qumi'num legal tradition and the common law tradition

2 See generally Sarah Morales, "Snuw'uyulh: Fostering an Understanding of the Hul'qumi'num Legal Tradition" (PhD diss., University of Victoria, Faculty of Law, 2015).

3 Indicative of the issues explored in this chapter, in early 2014 the Stz'uminus First Nation decided to withdraw from the British Columbia treaty process, and subsequently from the Hul'qumi'num Treaty Group, to focus their resources and attention on asserting their rights on the ground.

4 Brian Thom, "Reframing Indigenous Territories: Private Property, Human Rights and Overlapping Claims" (2014) 38:4 *American Indian Culture and Research Journal* 3 at 6 [Thom, "Private Property"].

is needed in order to resolve the current issues within the modern-day treaty-making process in British Columbia.

2. Evidence of Bad Faith in the British Columbia Treaty Process: The Hul'qumi'num Case Study

As previously mentioned, the Hul'qumi'num Treaty Group (HTG) has been participating in the modern-day treaty-making process since 1993. However, despite concerted efforts, a treaty has yet to be signed or ratified between the five member First Nations and the governments of British Columbia and Canada. The leadership of the Hul'qumi'num Treaty Group has made the argument, domestically and internationally, that this failure is due to the governments' bad faith negotiation practices throughout the process.[5]

At the heart of the tension at the Hul'qumi'num negotiating table is the fact that the state disregards Hul'qumi'num property, cultural, and other fundamental human rights, and remains unwilling to reconcile the near-complete privatization of Indigenous territories on Vancouver Island by the 1884 Esquimalt and Nanaimo (E&N) Railway land grant, which resulted in the loss of approximately 85 per cent of the lands traditionally used and occupied by the Hul'qumi'num communities to private landowners.[6] In particular, a huge tract of land, approximately 237,000 hectares (or 70 per cent of the Hul'qumi'num ancestral territories) was granted to a private railroad corporation.[7] That corporation in turn has re-granted many of these same Hul'qumi'num communal lands to private third parties under Canadian domestic law. The state has claimed the unilateral right to confiscate these Hul'qumi'num traditional lands without ever offering any form of restitution, either through return, replacement, or payment of just compensation to the Indigenous communities affected (both within and outside of the modern-day treaty process).

The Hul'qumi'num First Nations view the modern-day treaty process as a way to re-establish a territorial land base, and as such, are seeking

5 *Hul'qumi'num Treaty Group v Canada* (2009), Inter-American Commission on Human Rights, No 105/92, *Annual Report of the Inter-American Commission on Human Rights: 2009*, OEA/Ser.L/V/II.

6 Thom, "Private Property," *supra* note 4 at 7.

7 *Ibid.*

a combination of land transfer or purchase and jurisdictional recognition through negotiations. In addition, they are seeking recognition of shared decision-making authority on lands where they have rights, but no jurisdictional recognition. The Crown has remained largely opposed to pursuing these solutions.[8] Instead, the state, through these negotiations, is working towards the complete extinguishment of Indigenous title over all but a few thousand hectares of their ancestral territories, where Hul'qumi'num people would have municipal-style Indigenous governance and limited authorities to administer some social services.[9] Small commercial forestry and fisheries opportunities are on the table for negotiation, but they are narrowly defined and only non-exclusive subsistence, cultural, and consultative rights could be recognized under this model of self-governance.[10]

Although the limited availability of Crown land, and vast amount of private land, is a defining feature of the Hul'qumi'num Treaty Group's negotiations, the state has allowed little space for its discussion at the treaty table. Governments have proposed that some of the anticipated settlement funds would be used to purchase small areas of land from willing sellers. On private land, however, the state has refused to consider co-management, revenue sharing, shared decision-making, or recognition of Indigenous jurisdictions.[11] Federal and provincial governments have said "no" to the proposals of the Hul'qumi'num negotiators to constitutionally protected interjurisdictional arrangements on private land, as well as arrangements for the exercise of cultural rights that are not subject to landowner veto.[12] Remarkably, at the negotiating table governments have refused to even recognize or discuss the Hul'qumi'num peoples' claims to restitution, or at the very least compensation, for these lost ancestral lands.

It is hard to classify this refusal as "good faith" negotiations. Despite repeated requests by the HTG to responsible government officials involved in the BC treaty process, the state has adamantly refused to recognize the specific existence of any property rights or other interests based on customary tenure belonging to the Hul'qumi'num Indigenous

8 *Ibid* at 8.
9 *Ibid.*
10 *Ibid.*
11 *Ibid.*
12 *Ibid.*

communities in their traditional lands that were confiscated by Canada for the benefit of the railroad company and other private development interests. Instead, government steadfastly refuses to provide a fair process by which to address the ongoing claims of the Hul'qumi'num people to these ancestral communal lands.

Furthermore, Canada's continuing practice of allowing the granting and re-granting of Hul'qumi'num traditional territory and property rights without offering any form of restitution and without engaging in any form of meaningful consultation with the Hul'qumi'num communities has led to the wholesale destruction of the environment within this territory. As a result of logging and mining operations, the Hul'qumi'num peoples have lost the ability to utilize their lands for subsistence fishing, hunting and gathering, important ceremonies, and other customary practices. It is difficult to overstate the impact of this privatization on Hul'qumi'num communities. The E&N land grant removed vast areas of land from Hul'qumi'num jurisdiction. In the words of one of our Elders, August Sylvester, "That's our private land ... They need to hear that the land they are sitting on, the land where my ancestors lived and are buried is our private land."[13] As these private lands were "developed," fences and locked gates went up to block the entry to places where the Hul'qumi'num people have always hunted, harvested plant foods, and gathered other resources to meet our material needs. Excerpts from the affidavit of Ts'ules (William Seymour), a Cowichan Tribes member, describes how private lands restrict his hunting practices:

> There are places where I've been shown to hunt, up in the Shawnigan division, where you have to pay a fee. The gatekeeper for the logging companies charges a fee for cars to get through the gates. Other areas I've done hunting, some of them are gated completely and the gates are open at certain times and closed at certain times. As a result, I don't go out hunting anymore.[14]

---

13 *Hul'qumi'num Treaty Group v Canada* (2009), Inter-American Commission on Human Rights, No 105/92, *Annual Report of the Inter-American Commission on Human Rights: 2009*, OEA/Ser.L/V/II (Affidavit August Sylvester).

14 *Hul'qumi'num Treaty Group v Canada* (2009), Inter-American Commission on Human Rights, No 105/92, *Annual Report of the Inter-American Commission on Human Rights: 2009*, OEA/Ser.L/V/II (Affidavit of William Seymour).

The government, despite repeated requests and appeals by the HTG, has adamantly refused to discuss the recognition or protection of Hul'qumi'num property and user rights in these so-called private lands granted to the railroad company and other third parties. Government officials have repeatedly made it clear that the traditional lands belonging to the Hul'qumi'num peoples in British Columbia unlawfully seized and parcelled out to third parties by the state are not part of the British Columbia treaty negotiation process. For example, in a letter to the Hul'qumi'num Treaty Group dated 19 January 2007, the provincial government stated that the issue of compensation for the E&N land grant was technically "on the table," but only because it had been raised by the HTG. However, the province reiterated that it "does not approach land negotiations as a matter of compensating First Nations for past dispositions of Crown land."[15] The state's refusal to address past grants of these "private lands" in negotiations means that the issue remains effectively "off the table." Thus, the lands regarded as having been privatized by the government, comprising the bulk of all Hul'qumi'num traditional territory, are unavailable for treaty settlement purposes, both through restitution and compensation, as far as Canada is concerned. Again, one has to question – is this negotiating in good faith? Is it in good faith to unilaterally take 85 per cent of the traditional territory off the table for negotiation? Is it good faith to speak of reconciliation, when one party is knowingly left without an effective remedy for the majority of its interests?

3. Recourse to International Law: Evidence of Bad Faith, Violations of Fundamental International Human Rights, or Both?

Frustrated with the lack of progress on these issues at the negotiating table, the Hul'qumi'num First Nations have appealed to the international community for help in resolving the private land question in their traditional territory. In doing so, they have strengthened their argument that they are not being unreasonable in their negotiating positions, or themselves acting in bad faith by seeking to put these issues on the table for negotiation. Their international efforts illustrate

15 Letter from the Province of British Columbia, Ministry of Aboriginal Relations and Reconciliation, to the Hul'qumi'num Treaty Group (19 January 2007) held in the HTG archives.

that the concerns they are bringing forward to the government through negotiations are, in fact, expressions of fundamental human rights, and therefore the positions of government negotiators are even less defensible in terms of believing that they are attempting to reach a just resolution through good faith negotiations.

This type of legal recourse is not unchartered territory for the Hul'qumi'num people. These First Nations have a long history of using international law to resolve their domestic disputes. As early as 1901, Hul'qumi'num leaders began to operationalize a plan to bypass the provincial and federal governments to resolve the land question within their territories. The resulting 1906 Cowichan Petition to King Edward of Great Britain represents one the most notable and well-documented instances of the Hul'qumi'num peoples' resistance and efforts at negotiation and demands for restitution. Almost 100 years later, chiefs, Elders, and lawyers representing the Hul'qumi'num communities travelled to Washington, DC, in an effort to petition the Inter-American Commission on Human Rights (IACHR) to hear their grievances about the modern-day treaty-making process and send a third-party observer to comment on the situation of the Hul'qumi'num people in British Columbia.

Drawing on international human rights law and the development of its application to Indigenous peoples, the Hul'qumi'num communities have alleged that the British Columbia treaty process is violating their right to property. The right to property affirmed in Article 23 of *the American Declaration on the Rights and Duties of Man* affirms the "right to own such property as meets the essential needs of decent living and helps to maintain the dignity of the individual of the home."[16] This right includes the right to be free from unreasonable state interference with the enjoyment of property and from uncompensated takings thereof.[17]

---

16 *American Declaration of the Rights and Duties of Man*, Organization of American States, Resolution 30, reprinted in Basic Documents Pertaining to Human Rights in the Inter-American System, OAS/Ser.L/V/I.4 Rev 9 (2003) at Article 23.

17 The relevant general principle of law is reflected in Article 21.1 of the *American Convention on Human Rights*, which states: "No one shall be deprived of his property except upon payment of just compensation for reasons of public utility or social interest, and in the cases and according to the forms established by law." Additionally, the commission has understood property to refer to "the right to dispose of a thing in any legal way, to possess it, to use it and to exclude everyone else from interfering with it." Report No. 47/97, Tabacalera Boquerón Petition (Paraguay), Inter-American Commission on Human Rights, OEA/Ser.L/II.98, doc. 7 rev. (1998) at 230.

The right to property affirmed in Article 23, especially when considered in light of the fundamental principle of non-discrimination, embraces those forms of individual and collective land tenure and resource use that derive from the customary laws of the Hul'qumi'num people.[18] As such, Canada's confiscation of their traditional lands for the benefit of private third parties, and its subsequent position that Hul'qumi'num title and property rights of "private lands" have been extinguished by the nature of fee simple grants from the state to third parties, is not only evidence of bad faith negotiations but also violations of international human rights law.

At a minimum, to make extinguishment lawful under international law, Canada must provide restitution for the expropriation of those lands belonging to the Hul'qumi'num communities. However, the Hul'qumi'num people are also arguing that their right to restitution[19] has been violated by the refusal of the state to settle their land claims through the modern-day treaty process. As the Inter-American Court has explained, the state is obligated to recognize the property rights of Indigenous peoples, even when their ancestral Indigenous lands have been granted by the state to private individual owners. The jurisprudence of the inter-American system has clearly established and affirmed that the right to property belonging to Indigenous peoples in their traditional lands includes the right to restitution, even when those lands have been confiscated and granted by the state to good faith third party purchasers.[20] Otherwise, the cultural survival of an Indigenous community would be at risk until the state took effective measures to provide redress for its taking of the lands and resources belonging to those peoples. To date, no Canadian court has ever awarded any form of restitution or payment of just compensation to the Hul'qumi'num or any other First Nation in British Columbia for such extinguishments.

---

18 See generally Organization of American States, Inter-American Commission on Human Rights, *Indigenous and Tribal Peoples' Rights over Their Ancestral Lands and Natural Resources*, OEA/Ser.L/V/II.Doc.56/09 (2009).

19 The right to restitution refers to the right to lawful recovery of one's property interest.

20 *Case of Mary and Carrie Dann v United States ("Dann")*, Inter-American Commission on Human Rights, Case No. 11.140, Report No. 75/02 (27 December 2002) at para 30; *Case of Sawhoyamaxa v Paraguay ("Sawhoamaxa")*, Judgment of 29 March 2006, Inter-American Court of Human Rights Series C. no. 146 (2006) at paras 131–4; *Yakye Axa* at para 151.

Despite repeated requests, Canada and British Columbia have refused to even consider discussing the issue of fair compensation for confiscating the Hul'qumi'num property rights of "private lands" in treaty negotiations with the Hul'qumi'num Treaty Group. This effectively means that the Hul'qumi'num peoples are left without any effective remedy for the state's taking of their traditional territory, a process outlined in the previous section.[21]

Faced with this unsatisfactory result, the Hul'qumi'num communities have put their efforts into petitioning the international community to support them in their endeavour to re-establish their legal footprint within their traditional territory. An early victory came with the decision on admissibility by the Inter-American Commission on Human Rights (IACHR) in the fall of 2009. In ruling that the HTG's petition against Canada on the cumulative impacts of the privatization of Hul'qumi'num traditional territory was admissible for further investigation on the merits of the case, the IACHR made several highly critical observations of the remedies available to Aboriginal people in Canada. In particular, they referred to the fact that the British Columbia treaty process has not permitted negotiations on the subject of restitution or compensation for the Hul'qumi'num people's ancestral lands in private possession, despite the fact that the Hul'qumi'num leadership has brought this issue to the attention of official authorities since 1994, and determined that "by failing to resolve the HTG claims with regard to their ancestral lands, the BCTC process has demonstrated that it is not an effective mechanisms to protect the right [to property] alleged by the alleged victims."[22] Although it still remains to be decided if the

---

21 On 26 June 2014, the Supreme Court of Canada rendered its decision in *Tsilhqot'in Nation v British Columbia*, 2014 SCC 44 and made a declaration of Aboriginal title for the Tsilhqot'in Nation. While Aboriginal title theoretically existed in Canada prior to this decision, this is the first time an Indigenous group can actually claim the full protection for their lands rights in Canadian courts. This decision has huge implications for the Hul'qumi'num Nations who, like the Tsilhqot'in, never ceded their lands through surrender or treaty. Although the Hul'qumi'num First Nations are still pursuing a negotiated agreement, this decision will be of immense importance if they choose to litigate.

22 *Hul'qumi'num Treaty Group v Canada* (2009), Inter-American Commission on Human Rights, No 105/92, *Annual Report of the Inter-American Commission on Human Rights: 2009*, OEA/Ser.L/V/II.

Hul'qumi'num people will have more success in international law than their ancestors did in 1906, it is significant to note that the admissibility decision from the IACHR further supports the argument made by the Hul'qumi'num Treaty Group that the state is negotiating in bad faith.[23]

4. (Re)Defining Good Faith through *Snuw'uyulh*

As the previous sections have demonstrated, the treaty-making process in British Columbia is highly unsatisfactory for many of the parties, Indigenous and non-Indigenous, currently engaged in the process. Indigenous groups, like the Hul'qumi'num Treaty Group, believe that the positions taken by government at the treaty table reflect not only bad faith negotiation tactics, but also violations of their fundamental human rights. The state has taken the position that the treaty process is not the correct forum for discussing issues related to private property, compensation, or restitution. Arguably, these positions will be difficult to resolve through this domestic process if things continue as they are. However, a possible remedy would be to come to a mutual understanding of what it means to negotiate, or dialogue, in "good faith." Indigenous peoples, like the Hul'qumi'num people, have established dispute resolution processes, grounded in their legal traditions, which could help inform and define modern-day processes such as the British Columbia treaty negotiations. This mutual understanding, informed by Indigenous legal traditions, but not to the exclusion of common law understandings, can help to establish a new framework of what it means to engage one another in good faith. To this end, the following section will discuss the concept of "good faith" in the Canadian common law, in international law, and in Indigenous law, specifically the Hul'qumi'num legal tradition. Through this discussion, we can come to a better understanding of mutually acceptable dispute resolution practices and consider different approaches to the treaty-making process itself, both of which may help the parties make progress on some of their substantive differences.

23 In 2011 the Hul'qumi'num leadership and representative lawyers presented their arguments on the merits of this complaint before the Inter-American Commission on Human Rights. They are still awaiting the results from the Organization of American States.

A. "Good Faith" at Canadian Common Law

What does Canadian common law currently tell us about the principle of "good faith" negotiation? The Supreme Court of Canada's judgment in *Delgamuukw* concluded with the words, "Let us face it, we are all here to stay."[24] As such, it encouraged the parties to forego litigation and engage in meaningful negotiations to resolve Indigenous constitutional rights to land and self-government within Canada and to ultimately achieve reconciliation. In doing so, the Court expressed that these negotiations must be guided by the principle of "good faith and give and take on all sides" if reconciliation is to be achieved.[25]

This standard of good faith and its application to the governments' processes of negotiation with Indigenous peoples was taken up again in the Court's decision in *Haida Nation v British Columbia (Minister of Forests)*. In this case, we begin to see the Court articulate some of the practices associated with this standard of good faith founded on the related concepts of the honour of the Crown and reconciliation. In making and applying treaties, governments must act with honour and integrity and avoid any appearance of "sharp dealings."[26] Negotiations must work towards a just settlement of Aboriginal claims.[27] Reconciliation will only be realized through "the process of honourable negotiation."[28] Despite the articulations of these standards, the question still remains: What does it mean to negotiate in "good faith"? How do we measure the integrity of a government negotiator? What distinguishes "sharp dealings" from skilled and pragmatic negotiation practices? Can one classify a negotiation process as honourable if consensus is never achieved?

Arguably, there is no "doctrine" of good faith in the common law that might describe a process for a good faith negotiation, and currently no policy direction exists with respect to the implementation of good faith negotiations. As described above, there is common law direction from the Supreme Court that governments are under a legal duty to negotiate in good faith to resolve the land claims of Indigenous peoples in Canada; however, there is no indication of what practices good faith

24 *Delgamuukw v British Columbia* [1997] 3 SCR 1010 at para 186.
25 *Ibid*.
26 *Haida Nation v British Columbia (Minister of Forests)*, 2004 SCC 73 at para 19 [*Haida*].
27 *R v Sparrow*, [1990] 1 SCR 1075 at pp. 1105–6 cited in *ibid* at 20.
28 *Haida, supra* note 26 at para 20.

negotiations should include. There is very little direction in terms of the conduct of the parties at the negotiating table; as one government negotiator expressed, "as long as I am telling the truth than I am here in good faith." Many First Nations in British Columbia currently engaged in the modern-day treaty process, including the Hul'qumi'num First Nations, argue that the principle of good faith negotiations as encouraged by the courts must require more than this.

A negative definition of good faith is probably the easiest to describe. One simply eliminates what would be clear instances of bad faith to arrive at a definition of good faith. The difficulty is that this still provides little guidance. Positive definitions of good faith include notions of "fairness," "reasonableness," "fair dealings," and so on, but these are confusing because they are not easily distinguishable from one another and seem to connote moral and ethical principles and not strict legal standards. Arguably, the meaning of "good faith" in law seems to be predicated on one's intuitive sense of justice. Given the colonial nature of the concept of "reconciliation," as described in John Borrows' chapter in this book, one can understand why diverging viewpoints about what constitutes good faith negotiations exist at some of the tables in the British Columbia treaty process.[29]

Case law in Canada has begun to articulate the standards associated with good faith negotiations in the commercial contract context.[30] The Canada Labour Code sets out the duty to bargain in good faith and states that parties must "meet and commence … to bargain collectively and in good faith" and "make every reasonable effort to enter into a collective agreement."[31] The duty, as one can see, is similar to the duty articulated in *Delgamuukw*. First, there is a requirement to negotiate in good faith; second, the parties must make every reasonable effort to enter into a collective agreement; and third, the purpose is to conclude an agreement. It has been argued that the "give and take on all sides" required in *Delgamuukw* is the same standards as "a reasonable effort."[32] Furthermore, the Supreme Court has broadened the duty to bargain in

29 See generally Borrows, *supra* note 1.
30 *Bhasin v Hrynew* 2014 SCC 71 at 33.
31 *Canada Labour Code*, RSC 1985, c L-2, s 50(a)(i)(ii).
32 Stuart Rush, "The Duty to Bargain in Good Faith Arising Out of Delgamuukw" (paper presented at "The Supreme Court of Canada Decision in *Delgamuukw*" conference sponsored by the Pacific Business & Law Institute, Vancouver, 12–13 January 1998) [unpublished].

good faith in order to assess the reasonableness of the party's substantive positions in bargaining. In its *Royal Oak Mines* decision, the Court found that not only must the parties negotiate in good faith, but they must also make every reasonable effort to enter into a collective agreement. Both requirements were found to be equally important and the Court stated that

> ... the duty to enter into bargaining in good faith must be measured on a subjective standard, while the making of a reasonable effort to bargain should be measured on an objective standard ... It is this latter part of the duty which prevents a party from hiding behind an assertion that it is sincerely trying to reach an agreement when, viewed objectively, it can be seen that its proposals are so far from the accepted norms of the industry that they must be unreasonable.[33]

The Court found that the employer was engaging in "surface bargaining" and stated that this approach was "unlawful, unjustifiable and contrary to what is permitted in good faith bargaining."[34] Arguably, this is the very practice illustrated in the Hul'qumi'num example. Therefore, Canadian common law itself supports the arguments of Indigenous people that the state is not making every reasonable effort to enter into a final agreement or treaty.

B. "Good Faith" at International Law

While the case law relating to the Canadian commercial context can certainly inform our understanding on whether or not the state is negotiating in good faith with the Hul'qumi'num people, I would argue that it represents a minimum standard and that good faith standards and practices should be higher when considered in the context of reconciling competing constitutional interests between nations. Accordingly, I believe that the standards and practices associated with the concept of good faith in international law are of use to this discussion, especially when one considers that a *treaty* is, according to standard academic and political usage, a formal agreement between two or more recognized,

---

33 *Royal Oak Mines Inc v Canada (Labour Relations Board)* (1996) 133 DLR (4th) 129 (SCC) at para 42.

34 *Ibid* at para 43.

sovereign nations operating in an international forum, negotiated by designated representatives, and ratified by the governments of the signatories.[35] International standards include these requirements for parties:

- to deal honestly and fairly with each other;
- to represent their motives and purposes truthfully;
- to refrain from taking unfair advantage;
- to sustain the upkeep of the negotiation, awareness of the interests of the other party and a persevering quest for an acceptable compromise, with a willingness to contemplate modification of one's own position;
- to refrain from acts incompatible with the object and purpose of the negotiations;
- to respect the integrity of the process;
- to prohibit abuse of process, such as fraud and deceit;
- to prohibit unjustified termination of negotiations; and
- a general obligation of information and communication.[36]

Just as the previous section has demonstrated how international law can inform the substantive legal issues at the HTG negotiating table, at a very minimum, given the history, object, and purpose of this modern-day process, international standards should also be used to help define the practice of good faith negotiations in the modern-day British Columbia treaty-making.

C. "Good Faith" at Hul'qumi'num Law

Given that the obligation of good faith seems to stem from the honour of the Crown and the need for true reconciliation, standards based

---

35 UN Commission on Human Rights, *Study on Treaties, Agreements and Other Constructive Arrangements between States and Indigenous Populations*, final report by Miguel Alfonso Martinez, Special Rapporteur, Sub-Commission on the Prevention of Discrimination and Protection of Minorities, 51st Session, 22 June 1999.

36 See generally Anthony D'Amato, "Good Faith" in Rudolf Bernhardt, ed., *Encyclopedia of Public International Law*, vol. 2 (Amsterdam: North-Holland Publishing Co., 1992) at 599, http://anthonydamato.law.northwestern.edu/encyclopedia/good-faith.pdf; and John Burroughs, "Good Faith: A Fundamental Principle of International Law," the Lawyers Committee on Nuclear Policy Inc. website, http://lcnp.org/wcourt/BurroughsNiRarticle_May2008.htm.

solely on common law or international definitions of good faith are not enough. Good faith negotiations must be reflective of the dispute resolution practices of *all* the parties involved, including the Indigenous participants, if true reconciliation is going to be achieved. How can Indigenous participants, like the Hul'qumi'num First Nations, have faith in a process that does not take into account practices and standards of "good faith" flowing from their own legal traditions?

As the dispute over the E&N land grant has demonstrated, some of the most intense political and legal disputes in multicultural societies centre not only on struggles over scarce resources, but also on deep conflicts about cultural values and understandings.[37] Therefore, defining just procedures to deal with such conflicts requires that one come to terms with the implications of cultural differences. Conflict resolution processes should be designed to meet the needs, capacities, and sensibility of those they serve, rather than as a one-size-fits-all depot like the current British Columbia treaty process.

The first step into developing an alternative to the current treaty-making process is to jettison the adversarial and imperial premises that went into constructing the process in the first place. There must be a renewal of the process of reconciliation – one that respects the practices, customs, traditions, and principles of the Indigenous peoples, like the Hul'qumi'num people, themselves. Although I am not suggesting that the Hul'qumi'num legal tradition holds all the answers to the resolution of this conflict, I am suggesting that the incorporation of their principles of dispute resolution could prove to be very fruitful, especially given the pluralistic nature of their own legal traditions.[38] As the next section illustrates, Hul'qumi'num dispute resolution practices share a commitment to some of the basic values articulated in both the Canadian common law and international law in relation to the promotion of just relationships. Aspects of these basic values can be seen in the Hul'qumi'num teachings related to (1) defining the relationship, (2) restitution, (3) consensus, and (4) neutral third-party decision-makers.

---

37 David Kahane, "What Is Culture? Generalizing about Aboriginal and Newcomer Perspectives" in Catherine Bell and David Kahane, eds., *Intercultural Dispute Resolution in Aboriginal Contexts* (Vancouver: UBC Press, 2004) 28 at 28.

38 See generally, Morales, *supra* note 2.

I). DEFINING THE RELATIONSHIP

An important consideration in the development of a conflict resolution process is that of defining the relationship – both the current relationship and the future relationship of the parties involved in the dispute. Many scholars have noted that a significant failing of the modern treaty process is the inconsistency in the future visions of Indigenous and non-Indigenous negotiators and constituents. Where the Indigenous groups interpret negotiations as nation-to-nation discussions between equals, governments enter negotiations as representatives of the Crown with the perspective that it is meeting with minority groups within Canada.[39] Similarly, others have explained that the key difference separating Indigenous governments from non-Indigenous governments is that the former have visions of justice that are rooted in the past and concentrated on redressing historical wrongs, whereas the latter focus on using the process to guide the future.[40] Finally, the state has expressed that certainty is one of its main goals in participating in this process. However, some Indigenous groups, like the Hul'qumi'num First Nations are fundamentally opposed to any process that aims to circumscribe their rights. For them, extinguishment, modification, or diminishment of their inherent rights are unacceptable.

The Hul'qumi'num dispute resolution principle of respect supports the idea that parties must come to a common understanding of the issue(s) at the outset of the dispute resolution process.[41] This process should be based on the recognition that no two disputes are the same. As such, parties should be given an opportunity to explain their positions at the outset of a dispute.[42] This is a common practice within Hul'qumi'num communities. At the outset of every gathering, individuals are provided an opportunity to share their feelings, positions, history, connection, and so on. They can either do so themselves, or they can hire a speaker to represent their and their family's interests.

---

39 See generally James Tully, "Reconsidering the B.C. Treaty Process," in *Speaking Truth to Power: A Treaty Forum* (Ottawa: Law Commission of Canada, 2001) and Frances Abele and Michael J. Prince, "Aboriginal Governance and Canadian Federalism: A To-Do List for Canada," in Francois Rocher and Miriam Smith, eds., *New Trends in Canadian Federalism* (Peterborough, ON: Broadview Press, 2003).

40 Peter Russell, review of *Between Justice and Certainty: Treaty Making in British Columbia*, by Andrew Woolford (2007) 76:4 *Pacific Historical Review* at 650.

41 See generally Morales, *supra* note 2.

42 *Ibid* at 285.

This process is witnessed in order to prevent future conflicts related to the understanding of the event or decisions made at the event. It was described to me in the following way:

> So you have to think things through before you say it. And you have to make sure that once it is said, everyone has accepted it. And that is the basic component to why you have witnesses.
>
> So when you call a witness and you pay them to be there; you have invited them, and that is going to be your witness. Witness all the people you name – they are going to stand by you and say this is the way it was said. And if anything comes up from it, you call your witnesses back and they are going to stand up and say this is what happened; this is the way it was done ... This is why you have a witness in the house. They help you to know and stand up and say this is how I seen it. And if there is any conflict, you can resolve it there.
>
> Your witnesses can stand up and say we thank you for the respect you are using and the way you did that and usually that is how they would say it if there is a conflict. Or even if there was a conflict in the territory we would call you and say "We want to address that and come to a resolution." They would all speak about it and have a say. It's not just one person making a decision. Decision-making is what you are going to do – you come together and each one has to have a say about it ... and everyone will come to a decision about it. That is how you can help your conflict get solved – not just by you, but by your Elders or your witnesses.[43]

As this passage demonstrates, the practice of defining the relationship helps to foster a mutual understanding between parties who oftentimes enter these types of processes with preconceived notions about the other party's position and/or interests. It also helps to build a shared vocabulary to be drawn upon throughout the process. As the example above illustrates, words and the use of words are very important to conflict resolution within the Hul'qumi'num communities.[44] It is recognized that they can either exacerbate or help to diminish disputes. As such, agreeing upon shared terms or building vocabularies of comparison is vital to defining the issue within a dispute resolution process.

---

43 Florence James, interview by Sarah Morales, 19 July 2010.

44 Morales, *supra* note 2 at 298.

Ironically, the British Columbia treaty process is not only causing disputes between Indigenous peoples and the government but also among Indigenous peoples. A lot of this has to do with the manner in which rights are being defined within this process. In describing a dispute between the Hul'qumi'num communities and the Tsawwassen First Nation, one of the few First Nations to sign a modern-day treaty, respected Elder Wes Modeste noted,

> … What Tsawwassen did was take advantage of the treaty process because it allowed them to create their boundaries within our territory. We have attempted to meet with them to remove the boundary line but they wouldn't. They chose not to remove the boundary line back. But they didn't come from those islands, the Cowichan people had rights to those islands – from South Pender, Maine, and Galiano Island – that was known as the Cowichan archipelago.
>
> … This is what I don't understand about the process and law in general. How can it allow such a small community to encompass such a large land base that traditionally was held by the Cowichan? So in effect, they would have more rights to this through treaty than the Cowichan and that is not acceptable.
>
> So we went to court … We went to Washington, DC, and pulled the early records of the commission to establish the 49th parallel through the Gulf Islands in the mid-1800s … The boundary line was supposed to come straight across the Georgia Strait, and the UK said, "The Cowichan are here. There is no reason why their land should be in your waters." So they went to those islands and there is substantial evidence of occupation of those islands by the Cowichan. So those islands remained in Canada. So it is because of our presence there that their location is in Canada. But we don't enjoy ownership of it.
>
> With that evidence Tsawwassen said, "Oh, we can see that it's yours." And then they had the gall to come to our meeting and tell us how they would manage the resources in our islands.[45]

The British Columbia treaty process is transforming the way First Nations in British Columbia conceive of their land and territories. In the example above, one can sense the frustration Wes felt because of the unwillingness of Tsawwassen First Nation to respect the rights and

45 Wes Modeste, interview by Sarah Morales, 23 June 2010.

presence of the Hul'qumi'num Mustimuhw within the boundary lines of their treaty lands. Although the treaty process was established to help resolve Indigenous land rights in British Columbia, it has not done so in a manner that reflects traditional Indigenous dispute resolution processes. As a result, it is creating more conflicts than resolutions. As explained to me by Willie Seymour:

> You just look at the Tsawwassen Treaty – how it overlaps us. You know, they had no respect for us, to come over and explain their knowledge of the islands. They didn't do that.
>
> Now Luchiim and them went out to the island to take care of some uncovered remains and we had to write to Tsawwassen to get permission to go to that island because that is their claim.
>
> … How can we right that wrong? The treaty commissioners didn't do their job. They were supposed to help everybody and remain neutral. The government's supposed to allow First Nation, First Nation negotiations, but they stepped in and said, "No, we aren't going to change this boundary." They aren't supposed to say that. They are supposed to allow HTG and Tsawwassen to sit down and have a productive discussion on that.
>
> But yes, I do say that today's modern thinking has changed us. What Tsawwassen don't have is affecting their decision-making. It's always up here – *snuw'uyulh*.[46]

In the kin-oriented social world of the Hul'qumi'num Mustimuhw, these seemingly arbitrary boundaries, such as treaty lines, are creating conflicts and hard feelings between kinship groups. They "offend the kin- and ancestor-centred senses of place, and have the potential, if empowered with the institutions of the state, of limiting many of the other kinds of associations with land in the Coast Salish world."[47] As Willie's statement suggests, the failure to recognize and account for Indigenous systems of dispute resolution within the modern-day treaty process is weakening the legal traditions of the Coast Salish people, rather than reconciling their position within Canada's legal system.

---

46 Willie Seymour, interview by Sarah Morales, 23 June 2010.

47 Brian Thom, "Coast Salish Senses of Place: Dwelling, Meaning, Power, Property and Territory in the Coast Salish World" (PhD diss., McGill University, 2005) [unpublished] at 402.

II). RESTITUTION

The Hul'qumi'num teaching of restitution is related to defining the relationship between the parties involved in the conflict – in particular, their future relationship. Because Hul'qumi'num dispute resolution processes aim to restore balance within the community, many of the processes and measures used to resolve disputes mirror those ceremonies used by the Hul'qumi'num people to strengthen bonds within the community, both kin and non-kin.[48] Frank Malloway gave this description on how families might settle problems between members:

> I think most of it was done through the head of the family. The head of the families would meet and they would discuss the crime, or whatever it was, and they'd reach a consensus. I've never really heard about what the sentences were. They'd say, "Well, we had a family meeting with this family, and they decided on what had to be done," but you never really hear about the punishment itself and how the families reach that verdict, or whatever you'd call it ... If you did something wrong the family would take the responsibility and make an offering. They call it an offering. Some of the things in the old days were canoes, because they were like cars today, "Ah, I'll give you my car if you forget about this." But it was canoes in those days. I don't think it was really food because food was so plentiful that it wasn't expensive. Later on, my dad was saying, when it was settlement time, it was horses. They took the place of canoes. He talked about bringing horses right into the longhouse to distribute to somebody.[49]

This exchange of gifts, or restitution, creates a situation where the families are brought together and their relationship strengthened. It works to foster community relations. I have heard it referred to as an exchange of "good feelings" and it can be thought of as conforming to the larger cultural pattern of interchange that occurs within Coast Salish communities.[50] As such, it may be appropriate in some instances to utilize practices, such as a feast or a gift exchange, to symbolize the conclusion of a dispute. Such procedures could allow for the traditional

48 Morales, *supra* note 2 at 271.

49 Bruce Miller, *The Problem of Justice: Tradition and Law in the Coast Salish World* (Lincoln: University of Nebraska Press, 2001) at 146.

50 *Ibid.*

recitation of the offence that resulted in the conflict, storytelling, sharing of oral history, acceptance of gifts (which represent the acknowledgment of wrongdoing and subsequent forgiveness), and a celebration. Such a process serves to foster a new relationship and new history for those in conflict; however, as the section on international law has demonstrated, the state is not prepared to discuss restitution, even symbolically, at the treaty negotiations.

III). CONSENSUS

Any process designed to resolve the land rights question in British Columbia must begin with the goal of achieving consensus. Consensus is a key aspect of the Hul'qumi'num dispute resolution process because it is viewed as fostering harmony within the community.[51] In traditional dispute resolution processes among the Hul'qumi'num people, it was explained to me that parties would meet continuously, sometimes for days, until an understanding was reached that was acceptable to all:

> The leaders got together from the different communities and whatever time it took, one day, two days, three days, of deliberations and then they would decide. They decided, well, you can go … and my community will go … and someone else will sometimes volunteer, I will go … But the leaders deliberated and then the communities were brought together and this is what I'm talking about – reconciliation.
>
> If one community was offended, they never allowed that to go by. Somebody would step in, even somebody that is in the background would step in, and then they would blanket the ones that are victims … they will have a ceremony, mask dance, or sometimes they will just stand them up … and honour them with gifts.
>
> ... blanketing them. You shield them from the hurt. You shield them from the harm and at the same time you are embracing them back their strength. You are picking up their soul and putting it back into their being. So it serves more than one purpose.[52]

Once the decision was made, they would go around asking everyone present *"nil ow' stuhthi' ni' 'utun shqualuwun"* ("Is this okay with you personally?"). As this understanding suggests, reconciliation or

51 Morales, *supra* note 2 at 305.

52 Seymour interview, *supra* note 46.

restoring harmony between communities was considered just as important as resolving disputes within communities.

Contrast that view with the dispute resolution process the Hul'qumi'num people are currently engaged in – the British Columbia treaty process. When articulating to me some of the ongoing struggles of the treaty table, my father shared the following account:

> One morning of treaty negotiations one of our hereditary chiefs was asking a question of the government negotiator and he wouldn't respond. Our chief kept asking and rewording the question but the federal chief negotiator still refused to answer his question. Finally, the federal chief negotiator replied to him, "Look! This is a voluntary process. If you're not happy with our mandates, you're free to leave."[53]

Although this process is aimed at reconciling the land question within the province of British Columbia, oftentimes the process is anything but conciliatory. As the above passage demonstrates, the processes used are not reflective of a "true" negotiation. Governments come to the table with mandates in hand and refuse to negotiate away from them.

These immovable mandates are further entrenched by the power disparity between the parties involved. It is no secret that Canada's colonial history has given federal and provincial governments a patent negotiating advantage over Indigenous peoples. Scholars agree that this clear power differential has impacted land claims negotiations.[54] Because of this power imbalance, Indigenous groups, such as the Hul'qumi'num Treaty Group, who demand moral reckoning or material redistribution for past injustices such as the E&N land grant, are severely limited in the extent to which this may be reached. As such, consensus rarely seems attainable, and it is the government vision that tends to dominate negotiations, forcing participating Indigenous groups to respond accordingly.

---

53 Robert Morales (Chief Negotiator, Hul'qumi'num Treaty Group), interview by Sarah Morales, 15 January 2015.

54 See generally Christopher Alcantara, "To Treaty or Not to Treaty? Aboriginal Peoples and Comprehensive Land Claims Negotiations in Canada" (2008) 38:2 *Publius: The Journal of Federalism* 343; and Janet Ajzenstat, review of *Indigenous Difference and the Constitution of Canada*, by Patrick Macklem (2002) 35:2 *Canadian Journal of Political Science* 426.

IV). NEUTRAL THIRD-PARTY DECISION-MAKER

Although consensus was the preferred form of conflict resolution, it is acknowledged within the Hul'qumi'num legal tradition that this is not always attainable. In some instances, families simply chose to avoid the conflict.[55] However, in other circumstances, individuals or families would call upon a *si'em* to make a binding decision – acting as an arbitrator of sorts.[56] It is important to note that both parties must come to the decision that they are at an impasse and recognize that they would be unable to resolve the conflict on their own.[57] Also, both parties must agree to the *si'em* to be given the authority to decide the dispute for them.[58] The belief dominant in western contexts is that the best mediator will be an outsider, impartial and unbiased. However, is an uninvolved third party really the norm or the ideal? Certainly not for the Hul'qumi'num people, who oftentimes chose familiar, but widely recognized and respected people, as mediators within their disputes.

It is interesting to note that third party mediators, though rarely used in intra-family disputes, were often used in inter-family disputes.[59] This is in contrast to the modern British Columbia treaty process, which utilizes a negotiation style of alternative dispute resolution between participants with a very tenuous relationship. When one considers the current challenges at the Hul'qumi'num Treaty Group table, one has to question whether or not mediation would be more effective than negotiation given the legal tradition of the Hul'qumi'num people? Perhaps an option for the British Columbia treaty process, which the Hul'qumi'num people could utilize, is for the BC Treaty Commission to refer good faith disputes to voluntary or mandatory mediation either by the BC Treaty Commission or by professional mediators.

Any new process designed to resolve disputes between the Hul' qumi'num people and government must contemplate that in some instances, consensus will be unattainable. In such circumstances, a well-respected and neutral third party will be required to arbitrate. Although I am hesitant to give a neutral third party, who is not politically accountable for the solutions reached, the power to decide on these important

55 Morales, *supra* note 2 at 287.
56 *Ibid* at 269.
57 *Ibid*.
58 *Ibid* at 308.
59 *Ibid* at 308–11.

rights and title issues, I believe that an arbiter could be used to make a ruling on good faith. This finding could have a significant impact on negotiations and provide recommendations to involved parties on how to move forward through impasses. The decision-maker could take the form of an independent tribunal, or it could be a well-respected expert, perhaps from the international community, who is well-versed in Indigenous issues. However, as the recent Hul'qumi'num petition to the Inter-American Commission has demonstrated, Canada is not usually willing to submit itself to international jurisdiction or scrutiny.

5. Conclusion

As the Hul'qumi'num experience illustrates, the British Columbia treaty-making process has become a tool for governments to expedite and extinguish land claims while overlooking the deeper issues surrounding Indigenous/non-Indigenous relations in Canada. Rather than taking advantage of this opportunity to acknowledge and correct past injustices and move forward towards a new understanding, governments have entrenched themselves in their political mandates and modern-day treaty negotiations have suffered as a result. Nowhere is this any clearer, than at the Hul'qumi'num Treaty Group table, where 85 per cent of their traditional territory has been unilaterally taken off the table for negotiation.

Arguably these treaty negotiations are at a standstill because they are not being negotiated in good faith. Although the concept of good faith is difficult to define at common law, and even international law, I would argue that Indigenous legal traditions can offer greater understanding of this concept and its related practices. In fact, I believe that one of the greatest failures of the British Columbia treaty process is that the process itself fails to take account of the dispute resolution principles and practices of one of its main parties – the Indigenous peoples of British Columbia, including the Hul'qumi'num First Nations. As this chapter has illustrated, the Hul'qumi'num people have a well-established legal tradition that has developed principles and processes to resolve disputes, both within and outside of their communities.

My experience, and the experiences shared with me to date, suggest to me that the Hul'qumi'num people's and non-Hul'qumi'num people's cultures possess such completely different systems of language and understanding, that although some accommodations could be agreed to between them, this consensus may be deeply unstable because of their different world views. Through undertaking this project, however, I have come to realize that although these communities often seem completely at odds with one another, they share a history. As such, their cultures bear traces of one another and within those traces lie the roots of common understanding. The struggle, then, is to try to develop a process that builds upon these cultural traces of shared understanding. I would argue that in order to do so, one must focus on the shared traces of understanding found within the process of dispute resolution itself.

PART III

"Fitting the Forum to the Fuss" – Re-examining the Forums in which Treaty Disputes Are Addressed

11 A Treaty in Another Context: Creating Reimagined Treaty Relationships in Aotearoa New Zealand

JACINTA RURU

Should we look at other forums to implement treaties and to resolve treaty disputes? To provide a comparative perspective on treaty-remedying, this chapter discusses the forum established in Aotearoa New Zealand. In doing so the author demonstrates that the law can be used to create novel solutions for addressing treaty disputes. The new Te Urewera Act 2014 is a good example of such a law, as the Act recognizes a legal identity grounded in Maori values and traditions for a space that was once a national park.

An impetus for this book was the recognition that 2014 marked the 250th anniversary of the Treaty of Niagara – the beginning of the historic treaty-making process in Canada. On the other side of the world, as I write this chapter in my home country in 2015, this year marks the 175th anniversary of the signing of the Treaty of Waitangi between the British Crown and many Maori chiefs. Aotearoa New Zealand is marking this national milestone with government, school, and community-led events throughout the country.[1] The Treaty of Waitangi is being heralded on this anniversary as our founding nationhood document – a sentiment that has historically not always been proclaimed. There are long periods in our past during which the government and the courts dismissed the treaty as, for example, "a simple nullity."[2] Today,

1 For example, see the coordinated activities lead by the government at the Ministry for Culture and Heritage at http://www.mch.govt.nz/waitangi175 and the dedicated website for schools and organizations to share what they are doing to mark this anniversary at http://www.waitangi.tki.org.nz/.

2 *Wi Parata v Bishop of Wellington* [1877] 3 NZ Jur (NS) 72, 78.

the place of the treaty in our society has been reimagined and now has the prominent status of the document that gave birth to our nation. This chapter thus considers the history and present ramifications of the treaty in New Zealand.

At first glance, the Treaty of Waitangi 1840 looks different from the earlier friendship treaties or the later Numbered Treaties in Canada. The Treaty of Waitangi is a singular bilingual treaty written in both Maori and English; it consists of three short articles that address who has sovereignty of, and who owns the property in, New Zealand. While short, this treaty is far from simple. In brief, the Maori version records an agreement whereby the Maori chiefs cede governorship (but in the English version cede sovereignty) to the British Crown. Both language versions record that Maori would remain the owners of their property, defined in the English version to mean lands, estates, forests, fisheries, and other properties. The intent of the treaty has been controversial ever since its signing. Today, the Crown accepts that it has breached the intent of the treaty and accepts that it must remedy these breaches.

This chapter provides an insight into modern treaty-remedying in New Zealand focusing specifically on the recent treaty settlement legislated for in *Te Urewera Act 2014*.[3] This Act removes a national park from Crown ownership by declaring the land to be its own legal entity with "all the rights, powers, duties, and liabilities of a legal person."[4] This is a creative bicultural Maori/Crown settlement of a long-standing dispute that has attracted international attention. This chapter thus explores what is unique about the New Zealand contemporary treaty claims settlement process and what have been its results. In writing this chapter, I have been much stimulated in the challenges posed by the other authors in this book to think more deeply about the role treaties play in the relationships between Indigenous peoples and colonial governments. All the authors in this book have raised pertinent questions that have universal appeal. This chapter, in a nod to the strength and continuing value of comparative law,[5] considers whether some of the challenges raised exist in a similar or different fashion in New Zealand.

3 *Te Urewera Act 2014*, No 51 (NZ). New Zealand legislation can be viewed online at http://www.legislation.govt.nz/.

4 *Te Urewera Act 2014* (NZ), s. 11(1).

5 Annelise Riles, "From Comparison to Collaboration: Experiments with a New Scholarly and Political Form" (2015) 78:1–2 *Law and Contemporary Problems* 147.

1. Aotearoa New Zealand: Story and Fact

All countries have stories of nationhood. Many of the authors in this book reflect on the wrongness of Canadian imaginings of national origin. Aaron Mills, for example, provides a glimpse of the Canadian nationhood story: "[A] bunch of white folks got together and in 1867, through the exercise and upward delegation of their respective wills to a centralized, sovereign authority – the *Constitution Act, 1867* – established the political community internationally recognized today as Canada."[6] The story in New Zealand is different but by no means any better. A common nationhood story here tells of how, in the nineteenth century, the civilized Europeans rescued the native noble savages from communalism but were then forced into warfare with the thankless natives because they refused to part with land essential for the settler growth of the country, and these natives have since brought upon themselves a lifestyle of poverty and crime because they are inherently lazy and morally bad. They have a novel culture of *haka* (warfare dance) and wearing *pounamu* (greenstone) that we like especially for attracting overseas tourists. And, well, really our natives have been treated quite well – yes, the best in the world, certainly better than those in Australia.

Maori have consistently challenged this nationhood story, evidenced by local, national, and international protests and petitions.[7] The New Zealand government only began, in the latter half of the twentieth century, to deeply accept some of the fallacies of this mainstream story.[8] Specifically, in the 1970s, New Zealand commenced its commitment to the contemporary transitional justice settlements of Crown breaches of the Treaty of Waitangi.[9] These modern-day treaty settlements seek to put

6 Aaron Mills, "What Is a Treaty? On Contract and Mutual Aid," chapter 8 in this volume.

7 See, for example, Aorha Harris, *Hikoi: Forty Years of Maori* Protest (Wellington, NZ: Huia Books, 2004), and Maria Bargh, ed., *Resistance: An Indigenous Response to Neoliberalism* (Wellington, NZ: Huia Books, 2007).

8 It is important to accept that earlier the New Zealand government had attempted in part to rectify some of the wrongs it had perpetrated. For example, see *South Island Landless Natives Act 1906* (NZ). See also Waitangi Tribunal, *Ngai Tahu Report 1991* (Waitangi Tribunal, Wai 27, 1991) at chap. 20. Note Tribunal reports can be viewed at the Waitangi Tribunal website at http://www.waitangi-tribunal.govt.nz/.

9 See *Treaty of Waitangi Act 1840* (NZ).

right the stories of our nationhood, but even so components of the sanitized Pakeha (European New Zealander) account remain hard to eliminate. For example, in 2014, Prime Minister Hon. John Key dismissed a Waitangi Tribunal finding that certain Maori chiefs in Northland had not ceded their authority to make and enforce law when they signed the Treaty of Waitangi.[10] As part of this dismissal, Key declared: "In my view New Zealand was one of the very few countries in the world that were settled peacefully."[11] He was rightfully lambasted in the media for denying the reality of the thousands who were killed in the 1850s and 1860s when the government went to war against many Maori tribes because the tribes refused to alienate their land to the Crown. So what is this country Aotearoa New Zealand?

New Zealand's government system shares a similar origin with Canada. Both countries were colonies of Britain and established Westminster-type democratic parliamentary systems of government. Over the years, New Zealand has modified its system of government differently than Canada. While New Zealand dabbled with federalism in its early years as a colony, by 1876 it was very much a unitary state with the British monarch as head of state, represented by a Governor General, and with the head of government being the elected prime minister. In 1950, New Zealand abolished its upper house, the legislative assembly, leaving the House of Representatives to be New Zealand's single legislative body. Canada replaced the Privy Council with its own Supreme Court in the nineteenth century whereas New Zealand only did so in 2002.[12] In contrast to Canada, New Zealand's constitution is described as informal and not entrenched. This means that while New Zealand's constitution consists of several statutes, treaties, and conventions, under our constitutional system Parliament is supreme and has no formal limits to its law-making power.[13]

---

10 Waitangi Tribunal, *He Whakaputanga me te Tiriti/The Declaration and the Treaty: The Report on Stage 1 of the Te Paparahi o Te Raki Inquiry* (Waitangi Tribunal, Wai 1040, 2014).

11 See "New Zealand 'settled peacefully' – PM," *Stuff* [New Zealand], 20 November 2014, at http://www.stuff.co.nz/national/politics/63377474/New-Zealand-settled-peacefully-PM.

12 See *Supreme Court Act 2002* (NZ).

13 To better understand New Zealand's constitutional system, see Philip Joseph, *Constitutional and Administrative Law in New Zealand*, 4th ed. (Wellington, NZ: Thompson Brookers, 2014); Matthew Palmer, "Constitutional Realism About Constitutional Protection: Indigenous Rights Under a Judicialized and a Politicized Constitution" (2007) 29 *Dalhousie Law Journal* 1.

Of significance to this chapter, while Canada and New Zealand are homes to Indigenous peoples, the first peoples of New Zealand are one group of people known today as Maori who share a single language and similar customs and values. Also in contrast to Canada, in 1840 the British Crown sought to sign a single bilingual treaty with some Maori chiefs throughout the country who, the Crown recognized, had sovereignty and ownership of the lands. There are translation differences between the two language versions. The Maori language version, which contains the signatures of more than 500 Maori chiefs, records that Maori would retain *tino rangatiratanga* (sovereignty) over their lands and treasures but otherwise gave *kawanatanga* (governance) rights to the British Crown. The English version, in contrast, states that Maori ceded sovereignty to the British Crown but Maori retained full, exclusive, and undisturbed possession of their lands, estates, forests, fisheries, and other properties. Following the signing of the treaty, the Crown officially proclaimed sovereignty of New Zealand. The current orthodox judicial position is that the Treaty of Waitangi forms part of New Zealand's constitution but is not part of New Zealand's domestic law unless it has been specifically incorporated into domestic legislation.[14] This means that in New Zealand, the courts can only rely on the treaty as a source of law if it has been incorporated into legislation, or at least this is the conventional view.[15] New Zealand is thus different from Canada because there is no provision like section 35 of Canada's *Constitution Act, 1982* in New Zealand.

Today, Maori own an unknown quantity of general freehold land and own in fee simple about 6 per cent of the country's landmass in a Maori freehold land title. There are no reserves like those Canada created for its Aboriginal peoples. In 1840, the European settlers understood that Maori owned the land in New Zealand. Following the signing of the treaty, the British Crown began acquiring land from Maori. By the

14 *Hoani Te Heuheu Tukino v. Aotea District Maori Land Board* [1941] AC 308. To view a current example of statutory incorporation, see section 8 of the *Resource Management Act 1991* (NZ). For a discussion of the treaty in law, see Jacinta Ruru, "Constitutional Indigenous Treaty Jurisprudence in Aotearoa New Zealand," in Patrick Macklem and Douglas Sanderson, eds., *From Recognition to Reconciliations: Essays on the Constitutional Entrenchment of Aboriginal and Treaty Rights* (Toronto: University of Toronto Press, 2016) at 425–58.

15 For an alternative view, see Alex Frame, "Hoani Te Heuheu's Case in London 1940–1941: An Explosive Story" (2006) 22 *New Zealand Universities Law Review* 148.

early 1860s, the Crown had become the owner of most of the land in the South Island and the lower part of the North Island, an area constituting about 60 per cent of New Zealand's land mass and where about 10 per cent of Maori lived.[16] After this point, the Crown sold this land to the new European settlers. In the 1860s, legislation enabled the Crown acquisition of most of the remaining lands in the North Island through outright confiscation as well as the more subtle, but equally successful, waiver of the British Crown's right of pre-emption in favour of the creation of what were initially called "Native freehold" land titles.[17] A Native Land Court was established with the primary objective of encouraging Maori land owners to transfer their customary holdings into this Native freehold title, enabling them to alienate their lands as they wished.[18] This legislation encapsulated the mainstream nationhood story of the time. For example, the preamble of the *Native Lands Act 1862* states outright that the purpose of the Act is to "promote the peaceful settlement of the Colony and the advancement and civilization of the Natives" by creating freehold land titles. In reality, many owners of the newly titled Native freehold land were forced to sell their lands to pay for financial debt incurred in the transfer process (e.g. mandatory court fees and survey costs). Today, there is said to be very little if any Maori customary land remaining. The 6 per cent that is held in what are now referred to as Maori freehold titles are mostly held by multiple tenants, not inhabited, and located in rural areas with little arable value. Maori freehold land can be alienated, but legislation enacted in 1993 – *Te Ture Whenua Maori Act/Maori Land Act* – has emphasized new twin principles to help ensure that Maori *retain* ownership and *use* of the land. There are some remarkable financial success stories mostly concerning forestry, farming, and geothermal industries on Maori freehold land where annual profits are in the millions of dollars.

16 Note that many of these early sales included clauses that promised to set aside some land for reserves, but this was rarely done. Moreover, even where it was done, Maori were not forced to reside on the reserved lands. See Waitangi Tribunal, *Te Whanganui A Tara Me Ona Takiwa, Report on the Wellington District*, Wai 145 (Wellington: Legislation Direct, 2003). Note Tribunal reports can be viewed at the Waitangi Tribunal website at http://www.justice.govt.nz/tribunals/waitangi-tribunal. See also Richard Boast, *The Native Land Court, 1862–1887: A Historical Study, Cases and Commentary* (Wellington, NZ: Thomson Reuters, 2013).

17 *Native Lands Act 1865* (NZ).

18 See David V. Williams, *"Te Kooti Tango Whenua": The Native Land Court, 1864–1909* (Wellington, NZ: Huia Publishers, 1999).

Maori have a strong political national presence. Since the 1860s Maori have had guaranteed representation in the House of Representatives,[19] with four electoral seats set aside for Maori voters.[20] It was not until 1975 that Maori had the choice to enrol in either the Maori or the general roll.[21] Since the 1990s, when the country moved from a first past the post to a mixed member proportional voting system, the Maori seats have been adjusted to reflect the number of the persons enrolled in the Maori seats.[22] There are currently seven Maori seats, and an increasing number of Maori being elected to Parliament on party lists, representing the spectrum of political ideologies. The Maori Party (first established in 2004) is a party that operates with a commitment to the Maori world view. Maori ethics govern the Maori Party. The Maori Party has a Relationship Accord with the National Party that currently leads government. One of the benefits of this arrangement is that the co-leader of the Maori Party is the Minister of Maori Development.[23]

New Zealand has been fortunate to have had the Waitangi Tribunal to resolve treaty disputes. This has been our primary forum for discussing Crown breaches of the Treaty of Waitangi. It is this process, first implemented in 1975, that has paved the way for where New Zealand is now with treaty-remedying. Since 1975, Maori have had the opportunity to present arguments to the specially created permanent commission of inquiry – the Waitangi Tribunal – on alleged Crown contemporary breaches of the principles of the Treaty of Waitangi.[24] From 1985 to 2010,

---

19 The Parliament of New Zealand has two parts. One is the head of state, Queen Elizabeth II, who is represented by the Governor General. The other part is the House of Representatives, which is comprised of Members of Parliament who are elected every third year.

20 *Maori Representation Act 1867* (NZ). See Andrew Geddis, "A Dual Track Democracy? The Symbolic Role of the Maori Seats in New Zealand's Electoral System" (2006) 5:4 *Election Law Journal* 347.

21 *Electoral Amendment Act 1975* (NZ).

22 Mixed member proportional voting means that the proportion of votes a party gets will largely reflect the number of seats it has in parliament. See Andrew Geddis *Electoral Law in New Zealand: Practice and Policy*, 2nd ed. (Wellington, NZ: LexisNexis, 2013).

23 See the Maori Party website for information about this party, including this agreement, http://www.maoriparty.org/.

24 *Treaty of Waitangi Act 1975* (NZ). Paul Hamer, "A Quarter-Century of the Waitangi Tribunal: Responding to the Challenge," in Janine Hayward and Nicola Wheen, eds., *The Waitangi Tribunal: Te Roopu Whakamana i te Tiriti o Waitangi* (Wellington: Bridget Williams Books, 2004) at 3.

Maori were able to lodge arguments that Crown actions, policies, or laws between 1840 and 1992 breached the treaty principles.[25] Some of these historical claims are still being heard by the tribunal, which can still accept to hear new contemporary claims. The Waitangi Tribunal consists of both Maori and non-Maori judges from Maori Land Court and other notable appointed persons. The tribunal has released numerous reports on tribe- and region-specific claims alleging historical breaches throughout the country, and it has reported on an array of generic issues ranging from the use of the Maori language, to customary fishing rights, to the allocation of radio frequencies, petroleum, aquaculture, and water. In some instances the government has accepted the tribunal's recommendations for redress and enacted appropriate legislation (e.g., the *Maori Language Act 1987*) but denied several others (e.g., the reports on petroleum and on the foreshore and seabed).[26]

In many instances, boosted by the redress packages in the Treaty of Waitangi claim settlements, Maori are regaining control of their affairs. The modern Treaty of Waitangi claim settlement statutes provide the foundation for a new and continuing relationship between the Crown and the claimant group based on the treaty principles. Settlements contain Crown apologies of wrongs done, financial and commercial redress, and recognition of the claimant group's spiritual, cultural, historical, or traditional associations with the natural environment. Some significant examples of cultural redress include the return of all *pounamu* (greenstone) found in its natural state to Ngai Tahu ownership,[27] the co-management of the Waikato River,[28] and the recognition of the legal personality of a large national park.[29] More than twenty-five tribal groups have now received historical district treaty redress with all other tribes closely following suit.[30] In addition, there have been financially notable

25 *Treaty of Waitangi Amendment Act 1985* (NZ), s. 3(1).

26 Waitangi Tribunal, *The Petroleum Report*, Wai 796 (Wellington: Legislation Direct, 2003); Waitangi Tribunal, *Report on the Crown's Foreshore and Seabed Policy*, Wai 1071 (Wellington: Legislation Direct, 2004).

27 *Ngai Tahu (Pounamu Vesting) Act 1997* (NZ).

28 *Waikato-Tainui Raupatu Claims (Waikato River) Settlement Act 2010* (NZ).

29 *Te Urewera Act 2014* (NZ), discussed in detail later in this chapter.

30 For a current list of negotiated settlements, see "Progress of Claims," Office of Treaty Settlements at https://www.govt.nz/organisations/office-of-treaty-settlements/. For discussion, see Nicola R. Wheen and Janine Hayward, eds. *Treaty of Waitangi Settlements* (Wellington, NZ: Bridget Williams Books, 2012).

pan-tribal settlements regarding commercial fisheries, aquaculture, and forestry.[31] The increased wealth of the tribes has enabled Maori to have more national political clout[32] as well as the means to work with members of their tribes to grow their tribal assets and provide many social benefits. Nonetheless, despite many modern successes, Maori still constitute a high proportion of the wrong side of statistics on health, education, imprisonment, and unemployment.[33]

This overall account is similar in some ways to the general experiences of Aboriginal peoples in Canada. Aboriginal peoples have similarly been dispossessed of much of their lands and treasures, lost many of their languages and much of their cultural histories, but have retained collective strength in who they are and what they desire. There are of course differences arising in part from the different colonial tools used. For instance, Canada has the *Indian Act* and reserves, a history of residential Native schooling, no single treaty, and no judicial institutions similar to the Maori Land Court or the Waitangi Tribunal. In thinking about many of the questions raised in this book, as well as my desire to provide insight into modern treaty-remedying in New Zealand, the next section presents a close consideration of a recent treaty settlement.

2. A Recent Treaty Settlement: *Te Uruwera Act 2014*

One recent settlement shows that dreams are possible even in an imperfect legal and political matrix. A new dawn for conservation management in New Zealand has arrived with the enactment of *Te Urewera Act 2014*. Te Urewera was named a national park in 1954 and managed as Crown land by the Department of Conservation pursuant to the *National Parks Act 1980* and the *Conservation Act 1987*. This place became simply Te Urewera on 27 July 2014: "a legal entity" with "all the

31 *Treaty of Waitangi (Fisheries Claims) Settlement Act 1992* (NZ); *Maori Fisheries Act 2004* (NZ); *Maori Commercial Aquaculture Claims Settlement Act 2004* (NZ); *Central North Island Forests Land Collective Settlement Act 2008* (NZ).

32 For example, in 2005 the Iwi Chairs Forum was established. See "Kaupapa," Iwi Chairs Forum at http://iwichairs.maori.nz/our-kaupapa/.

33 See "Browse for Statistics," Statistics New Zealand, at http://www.stats.govt.nz/browse_for_stats.aspx.

rights, powers, duties, and liabilities of a legal person."[34] *Te Urewera Act* is undoubtedly legally revolutionary here in New Zealand and on a global scale.

Te Urewera contains remote and deeply forested lands in the North Island.[35] It is a place with a long and fraught history between the government and the Maori tribe of the area – Ngai Tuhoe. The government perpetrated wrong after wrong in this area: Tuhoe lands were confiscated, Tuhoe villages and crops were burned, Tuhoe families were killed, and Tuhoe men were executed.[36] Crown representatives did not travel to the remote lands of Tuhoe in 1840 to seek Tuhoe chiefs' signatures for the Treaty of Waitangi. No Tuhoe signed the treaty and the Crown's assertion of sovereignty of New Zealand in 1840 had no impact in Te Urewera. The first recorded government visitor to Te Urewera district was in 1862.[37] Following that visit, Ngai Tuhoe lives changed immediately. The government wreaked long-standing havoc on Ngai Tuhoe with many brutal invasions and large-scale land confiscations.

Up until very recently, relationships between government and Ngai Tuhoe have been consistently strained. A recent extreme low point was the "Tuhoe raids" in 2007 during which about 300 armed police and members of the Armed Offenders Squad and Special Tactics Groups raided the small rural Ngai Tuhoe township Ruatoki at dawn in response to an alleged paramilitary training camp. Armed searchers terrorized the town with raids of family homes and full searches of all vehicles that passed through established barricades, including the school bus carrying children. In 2014, the police commissioner formally

---

34 *Te Urewera Act 2014* (NZ), s. 11(1). Note that this writing draws on Jacinta Ruru, "Tuhoe-Crown settlement – Te Urewera Act 2014" (October 2014) *Maori Law Review* 16, http://maorilawreview.co.nz/2014/10/tuhoe-crown-settlement-te-urewera-act-2014/.

35 To understand the importance of this land to Ngai Tuhoe, see Simon Day, "Healing Our Dark Heart" *Stuff*, 13 April 2014, http://www.stuff.co.nz/national/9936055/Healing-our-dark-heart.

36 See, for example, Judith Binney, *Encircled Lands: Te Urewera, 1820–1921* (Wellington, NZ: Bridget Williams Books, 2009); Waitangi Tribunal, *Te Urewera* (Waitangi Triubnal, Wai 894, pre-publication 2014).

37 See Vincent O'Malley, "Tuhoe-Crown Settlement – Historical Background" (October 2014) *Maori Law Review*, available at http://maorilawreview.co.nz/2014/10/tuhoe-crown-settlement-historical-background/.

apologized to the Ruatoki community and Ngai Tuhoe for the wrongdoings committed during those raids in 2007.[38]

Reaching agreements about settling sustained Crown treaty breaches was not straightforward. As with many treaty settlements, this one raised several complex issues, requiring, for example, decisions about mandate (who is the tribe and who is speaking for the tribe) and cross-boundary disputes (what is the tribal boundary).[39]

The *Tuhoe Claims Settlement Act 2014* is the broader anchor of the *Te Urewera Act 2014* and provides the overall framework to settle the historical claims of Tuhoe. The *Tuhoe Claims Settlement Act* provides cultural, commercial, and financial redress. It records the history of the claim and acknowledges and apologies for Crown wrongdoings. These sections should be read by all who seek to understand the depth of New Zealand's treaty-remedying legislation. The statements are extensive, factual and emotional. For example, this *Settlement Act* states:

> The Crown acknowledges that the impacts of these actions on Tūhoe included widespread starvation and extensive loss of life. The Crown's actions had an enduring and devastating effect on the mana, social structure, and well-being of the iwi. The Crown acknowledges that its conduct showed reckless disregard for Tūhoe, went far beyond what was necessary or appropriate in the circumstances, and was in breach of the Treaty of Waitangi and its principles.[40]

And the apology is equally extensive. The Crown states that this is "a long-overdue apology," that it "unreservedly apologises," and it is "deeply sorry" for its actions and failures.[41] The apology concludes with these words:

---

38 For media coverage of the apology see for example James Ihaka, "Apology over Urewera raids," *NZ Herald*, 27 July 2014 at http://www.nzherald.co.nz/nz/news/article.cfm?c_id=1&objectid=11299914.

39 See Rawinia Higgins, "Tuhoe-Crown Settlement – Te Wharehou o Tuhoe: The House that 'We' Built" (October 2014) *Maori Law Review* 7 at http://maorilawreview.co.nz/2014/10/tuhoe-crown-settlement-te-wharehou-o-tuhoe-the-house-that-we-built/.

40 *Tuhoe Claims Settlement Act 2014* (NZ), s. 5.

41 See *ibid*, s. 10.

> Despite the hardship Tūhoe and Tūhoetanga endure, your culture, your language, and identity that is Te Urewera are inextinguishable. The Crown acknowledges you and te mana motuhake o Tūhoe.
>
> Through this apology and settlement the Crown hopes to honestly confront the past and seeks to atone for its wrongs. The Crown hopes to build afresh its relationship with Tūhoe and that this new relationship will endure for current and future generations.
>
> Let these words guide our way to a greenstone door – tatau pounamu – which looks back on the past and closes it, which looks forward to the future and opens it. [42]

The *Te Urewera Act* sits alongside the *Tuhoe Claims Settlement Act*. The *Te Urewera Act* is specifically about land that the Crown had deemed a national park in 1954. The *Te Urewera Act* makes it clear that this land ceases to be Crown land and ceases to be a national park.[43] Te Urewera is now freehold land, but unlike other freehold land, it is inalienable except in accordance with the *Te Urewera Act*.[44] Te Urewera is now not managed by the Department of Conservation but by a new Te Urewera board. This board has the responsibility "to act on behalf of, and in the name of, Te Urewera."[45] Te Urewera will still have a management plan like other national parks in New Zealand, but the board, rather than the Department of Conservation, will approve these plans.[46] For the first three years, the board has a 50/50 membership of Tuhoe and Crown-appointed persons, with four persons from each group. Thereafter, the board will increase by one and the ratio will change to six persons Tuhoe-appointed to three persons Crown-appointed.[47]

The board, in contrast to nearly any other statutorily created body, including the Department of Conservation, is mandated to reflect Maori customary values and law. Section 3(6) of the *Te Urewera Act* states: "Te Urewera expresses and gives meaning to Tūhoe culture, language, customs, and identity. There Tūhoe hold mana by ahikāroa; they are tangata whenua and kaitiaki of Te Urewera." The Act does not define these

---

42 See *ibid*, s. 10(6)–10(8).
43 *Te Urewera Act 2014* (NZ), s. 12.
44 See *ibid*, s. 13.
45 *Ibid*, s. 17(a).
46 *Ibid*, s. 18.
47 *Ibid*, s. 21.

Maori values in English because they need to be understood within the Maori language. But for the international reader a simplistic translation is *mana* (authority), *ahikāroa* (continuous occupation), *tangata whenua* (people of the land), and *kaitiaki* (guardian). Section 18(2) reinforces this commitment to Indigenous values and traditions. It states that the board may "consider and give expression to … Tūhoetanga" and "Tūhoe concepts of management such as – (i) rāhui: (ii) tapu me noa: (iii) mana me mauri: (iv) tohu." These are Maori management concepts that respect the balance and life force in the environment.

Section 20 makes it clear that the board "must consider and provide appropriately for the relationship of Maori and their culture and traditions with Te Urewera when making decisions" and that the purpose of this is to "recognise and reflect" Tuhoetanga and the Crown's responsibility under the Treaty of Waitangi. The Act mandates that the board must strive to make some decisions by unanimous agreement (such as the approval of Te Urewera management plan) and some decisions by consensus.[48]

The chief executive of Tūhoe Te Uru Taumatua and the Director-General of conservation are responsible for the operational management of Te Urewera[49] and must prepare an annual operational plan.[50] The Director-General and every other person who performs functions and exercises powers and duties under the *Conservation Act 1987* has the powers that are necessary or expedient for the performance of the functions and exercise of the powers and duties under *Te Urewera Act*.[51]

The *Te Urewera Act* stipulates which activities are permitted in Te Urewera, which activities require authorization, and what form of authorization is acceptable.[52] The *National Parks Act* does something similar for national parks. Section 58 of the *Te Urewera Act* lists activities that require an activity permit. These include taking any plant; disturbing or hunting any animal (other than sports fish); possessing dead protected wildlife for any cultural or other purpose; entering specially protected areas; making a road; establishing accommodation; farming; and recreational hunting. This is a comprehensive list and demonstrates that the

48 See *ibid* ss. 33–4.
49 *Ibid*, s. 50.
50 *Ibid*, s. 53.
51 *Ibid*, s. 52.
52 See *ibid*, s. 55.

tight rules for preserving national park land have been transported to Te Urewera.

Throughout the *Te Urewera Act* it is clear that Te Urewera may still be mined. Section 64(1) is one example of this and states clearly: "Despite anything in this Act, Te Urewera land is to be treated as if it were Crown land described in Schedule 4 of the Crown Minerals Act 1991."[53]

Section 3 of *Te Urewera Act* is so beautifully expressed that I have copied it in full here:

Te Urewera

(1) Te Urewera is ancient and enduring, a fortress of nature, alive with history; its scenery is abundant with mystery, adventure, and remote beauty.
(2) Te Urewera is a place of spiritual value, with its own mana and mauri.
(3) Te Urewera has an identity in and of itself, inspiring people to commit to its care.

Te Urewera and Tūhoe

(4) For Tūhoe, Te Urewera is Te Manawa o te Ika a Māui; it is the heart of the great fish of Maui, its name being derived from Murakareke, the son of the ancestor Tūhoe.
(5) For Tūhoe, Te Urewera is their ewe whenua, their place of origin and return, their homeland.
(6) Te Urewera expresses and gives meaning to Tūhoe culture, language, customs, and identity. There Tūhoe hold mana by ahikāroa; they are tangata whenua and kaitiaki of Te Urewera.

Te Urewera and all New Zealanders

(7) Te Urewera is prized by other iwi and hapū who have acknowledged special associations with, and customary interests in, parts of Te Urewera.
(8) Te Urewera is also prized by all New Zealanders as a place of outstanding national value and intrinsic worth; it is treasured by all for the distinctive natural values of its vast and rugged prime-

53 See also *ibid* section 56(b) where a mining activity authorized by the *Crown Minerals Act* can be undertaken without authorization from the board.

val forest, and for the integrity of those values; for its indigenous ecological systems and biodiversity, its historical and cultural heritage, its scientific importance, and as a place for outdoor recreation and spiritual reflection.

The *Te Urewera Act* is significant in a comparative domestic and international context. First, *Te Urewera Act* marks for the first time in New Zealand's history a national park that has been permanently removed from the national park legislation. It had been long-standing Crown policy that conservation land should not be returned to tribal ownership.[54] The creation of Te Urewera as its own entity has provided a win-win solution for Tūhoe and the Crown. The only other treaty claims settlement that contemplates removal of land from the *National Parks Act 1980* is land in the South Island. This provision is found in the *Ngāi Tahu Claims Settlement Act 1998* that provides that the Crown will vest the title of Aoraki/Mount Cook in Te Rūnanga o Ngāi Tahu for a period of seven days.[55] After seven days, Ngāi Tahu will gift the mountain back to the nation as the centre piece of the Aoraki/Mount Cook National Park. Te Rūnanga o Ngāi Tahu have yet to action this temporary vestment.

Second, while there are similarities between *Te Urewera Act* and the *National Parks Act* (such as the requirement to have a management plan and ensure these lands are available for public use and enjoyment), the purpose of setting aside the land is subtly but importantly different. The *National Parks Act* is premised on preserving national parks in perpetuity "for their intrinsic worth and for the benefit, use, and enjoyment of the public, areas of New Zealand that contain scenery of such distinctive quality, ecological systems, or natural features so beautiful, unique, or scientifically important that their preservation is in the national interest."[56]

The *National Parks Act* does not recognize the importance of lands encased in national park boundaries as being culturally and spiritually important to *iwi*. The *National Parks Act* is a monocultural statute based

---

54 See discussion in Jacinta Ruru, "Settling Indigenous Place: Reconciling Legal Fictions in Governing Canada and Aotearoa New Zealand's National Parks" (PhD diss., University of Victoria, Canada, 2012) [unpublished].

55 *Ngāi Tahu Claims Settlement Act 1998* (NZ), ss. 15–16.

56 *National Parks Act 1980* (NZ), s. 4.

on Western values for preserving land. The *Te Urewera Act* demonstrates a new bicultural way of articulating the importance of national park lands for multiple reasons that range from scientific to cultural. This is apparent in section 4 of the *Te Urewera Act*, which reads:

> The purpose of this Act is to establish and preserve in perpetuity a legal identity and protected status for Te Urewera for its intrinsic worth, its distinctive natural and cultural values, the integrity of those values, and for its national importance, and in particular to –
>
> - (a) strengthen and maintain the connection between Tūhoe and Te Urewera; and
> - (b) preserve as far as possible the natural features and beauty of Te Urewera, the integrity of its indigenous ecological systems and biodiversity, and its historical and cultural heritage; and
> - (c) provide for Te Urewera as a place for public use and enjoyment, for recreation, learning, and spiritual reflection, and as an inspiration for all.

Third, the *Te Urewera Act* will be of interest internationally for its treatment of ownership, management, and purpose. For example, the Canadian national park legislation states that the Crown has "clear title to or an unencumbered right of ownership in the lands to be included in the park."[57] In the late nineteenth century and early twentieth century, at times, Canada forcibly removed Aboriginal groups from lands intended for national parks in order to assert clear title. In the 1970s, as Canada sought to create new national parks in the remote northern territories of Canada, a new solution to mitigating the ownership issue was initiated. Canada introduced a novel legislative tool: the national park reserve label. The legal definition of a national park reserve is an area or a portion of an area proposed for a park that is subject to a claim in respect of Aboriginal rights that has been accepted for negotiation by the Government of Canada.[58] The idea is that Canada can set land aside as a national park reserve and manage it as if it were a national park, even if there is an accepted Aboriginal rights claim to the land in

57 *Canada National Parks Act 2000*, s. 5(1)(a).
58 *Canada National Parks Act 2000*, s. 4(2).

question. After negotiating with the relevant Aboriginal peoples, the Crown can confirm the land as a national park. There are several instances in the northern territories where the Aboriginal peoples are acquiescing to national parks and thus Crown ownership of these lands.[59] But in the southern and more heavily populated provinces, the ownership issue is more contentious. No national park reserves in the south have been reclassified as national parks. In fact, national parks created since the 1970s in the south have rarely used this temporary national park reserve label. Ownership and management of many of the southern national parks remains heated.[60]

All treaty settlements are important for the retelling of the nationhood story in New Zealand. The *Te Urewera Act* is no exception. The comments by some of our Members of Parliament during the final third reading of the *Te Urewera Act* capture the importance of this statute. For example, the then Minister for Conservation, Hon. Dr. Nick Smith stated,

> … It is surprising for me, as a Minister of Conservation in the 1990s who was involved under the leadership of the Rt Hon Jim Bolger – who is in the House – in the huge debate that occurred around the provisions of the Ngāi Tahu settlement in respect of conservation land, how far this country and this Parliament have come when we now get to this Tūhoe settlement in respect of the treasured Te Urewera National Park. If you had told me 15 years ago that Parliament would almost unanimously be able to agree to this bill, I would have said "You're dreaming mate." It has been a real journey for New Zealand, iwi, and Parliament to get used to the idea that Māori are perfectly capable of conserving New Zealand treasures at least as well as Pākehā and departments of State …[61]

59 For example, see *Nunavut Land Claims Agreement, Inuit Impact and Benefit Agreement, Vuntut Gwitchin First Nation Final Agreement, Champagne and Aishihik First Nation Final Agreement, Inuvialuit Final Agreement, Western Artic (Inuvialuit) Claim Settlement Act 1984,* and *An Act Creating One of the World's Largest National Park Reserves 2000* SC 2009.

60 See discussion in Ruru, *supra* note 54.

61 New Zealand Parliament, "Tūhoe Claims Settlement Bill, Te Urewera Bill – Third Readings," 23 July 2014, at http://www.parliament.nz/en-nz/pb/debates/debates/50HansD_20140726_00000128/t%C5%ABhoe-claims-settlement-bill-te-urewera-bill-%E2%80%94-third-readings.

The then Minister for Maori Affairs, Hon. Dr. Pita Sharples, stated:

> … The settlement is a profound alternative to the human presumption of sovereignty over the natural world. It restores to Tūhoe their role as kaitiaki and it embodies their hopes of self-determination – Tūhoe autonomy for the 21st century, Tūhoe services for Tūhoe, benefit on Tūhoe terms, and Tūhoe living by Tūhoe traditions and Tūhoe aspirations …[62]

I agree. This is a profound settlement that was not thought possible fifteen years ago, or even seven years ago. Even in my own writing on national parks in 2012, I concluded my comparative New Zealand/ Canada national park-focused thesis with this statement:

> National park lands encase the lived homes of Indigenous peoples. Today, the law reflects a new societal goal that seeks to reconcile with Indigenous peoples for the past wrongs of taking their lands and denying them the very means to be true to themselves, their ancestors, and their grandchildren. National parks have the potential to play an instrumental role in committing to this reconciliation journey. National parks are symbolic of our national identity and our future, and the parks contain Crown lands that thus enable the Crown to lead in implementing a new way of thinking about owning and managing lands including national parks.[63]

While I dreamed for radical legislative reform when writing that conclusion to my thesis, I did not know that the horizon for change was so near. The enactment of the *Te Urewera Act* makes me immensely proud to be a New Zealander. It offers hope and inspiration that legislative change is possible. And it gives us heart and courage in New Zealand as we consider the future of our historical Treaty of Waitangi. While we face many challenges in building relationships and creating true restitution, there are some glimmers of hope that come from our brave Maori communities and Maori leaders who continue to push the Crown's boundaries for justice and for what is right, as they have always done.

62 *Ibid.*

63 Ruru, *supra* note 54 at 367.

3. Concluding Comments

In New Zealand, the historical promises recorded in 1840 in the Treaty of Waitangi remain of utmost importance.[64] As stated at the outset of this chapter, the Treaty of Waitangi is being heralded now as our nation's founding document. The modern-day treaty claim settlement statutes are not premised on replacing this 1840 treaty, but are instead an attempt by Maori chiefs and the Crown "to start afresh." The modern-day settlements contain extensive Crown apologies for wrongs done and provide a small fraction of recompense in the form of cultural, commercial, and financial redress. Nonetheless, like the famous Magna Carta (which celebrated its anniversary of 800 years in 2015), the contemporary reading of the Treaty of Waitangi tends to emphasize "the principles" of the treaty, rather than the text. The New Zealand Parliament has been at the forefront of this by incorporating "the principles of the Treaty" into specific statutes. For the most part, however, Maori are more enamoured with the actual text, specifically the Maori language text. At the bequest of a Northland tribe, the Waitangi Tribunal has recently focused on the "sovereignty" text of the treaty, declaring,

> Our essential conclusion, therefore, is that the rangatira [chiefs] did not cede their sovereignty in February 1840; that is they did not cede their authority to make and enforce law over their people and within their territories. Rather, they agreed to share power and authority with the Governor. They and Hobson were to be equal, although of course they had different roles and different spheres of influence.[65]

The tribunal stressed that while "this conclusion may seem radical [i]t is not."[66] As the tribunal explained, many of New Zealand's leading scholars have been saying this for a long time and of course such a conclusion is not new to tribes. It is interesting to note that leading

64 On the specifics of the role of history in treaty settlements and the law see, for example, Carwyn Jones, *New Treaty, New Tradition: Reconciling New Zealand and Maori Law* (Vancouver, UBC Press, 2016) and Matthew Palmer, *The Treaty of Waitangi in New Zealand's Law and Constitution* (Wellington, NZ: Victoria University Press, 2008).

65 Waitangi Tribunal, *He Whakaputanga me te Tiriti/The Declaration and The Treaty: The Report on Stage 1 of the Te Paparahi o Te Raki Inquiry* (Waitangi Tribunal, Wai 1040, 2014) at 526–7.

66 *Ibid* at 527.

Canadian scholars have reached the same conclusion. Michael Asch and Kent McNeil, for example, have both concluded that the historical treaty-making process in Canada did not lead to Aboriginal peoples giving up their jurisdiction to govern themselves.[67] This thinking may have real currency in New Zealand as it could explain the insertion of "sovereignty" in the English version and "governance" in the Maori version – perhaps the two versions are in fact saying something similar? This issue deserves a lot more consideration and illustrates the potential power of comparative dialogue.

To conclude, I go to the question Michael Coyle poses in his chapter in this volume: What is the significance today of Canada's historical treaties? My answer, in a different context, is that New Zealand's 1840 Treaty of Waitangi is our nation's most prominent contract. It is our commitment to one another for respect and compromise. And it is more than this for it provides the foundation for our story of nationhood. While our story is far from idyllic, containing many horrendous government crimes against Maori, the treaty-remedying process instituted in 1975 is producing a new way forward – one slightly more aligned to the vision our Maori chiefs had back in 1840 when they signed the treaty. Even though this modern-day process is flawed too, there are strengths that have the capacity to provide the basis for long-lasting transitional justice. The Crown has apologized and returned a smidgen of stolen property and money. Maori can and will make what they want of this. Tribes throughout the country have dreams of, and now some means to actualize, the flourishing health and well-being of Maori communities. It is for all of us as New Zealanders to embrace the new visions for reconciliation and build stronger and more valued relationships in order to create a more just future for our descendants.

67 See Michael Asch, *On Being Here to Stay: Treaties and Aboriginal Rights in Canada* (Toronto: University of Toronto Press, 2014) at 59–72, 100–15, and Kent McNeil, "Sovereignty on the Northern Plains: Indian, European, American and Canadian Claims," (2000) 39:3 *Journal of the West* at 10–18.

12 Nanabush, Lon Fuller, and Historical Treaties: The Potentialities and Limits of Adjudication

JEAN LECLAIR*

[J]ustice is a quality, rather than a result …

– Roderick A. Macdonald[1]

This chapter addresses the role of courts in resolving treaty disputes and the part that legal traditions should play in such a process. It stresses that, in discussing the role of state law or Indigenous law in these matters, one must start by acknowledging that all lawmaking processes – whether state or Indigenous sponsored – are, in some way or other, the product of power structures, because all such mechanisms involve an inevitable peremptory dimension. The morality and legitimacy of a legal order's lawmaking mechanisms will thus be assessed according to the measure of freedom to participate in, and therefore to choose, that such mechanisms afford to affected parties. Applied to the treaty context, this perspective calls for greater resort to Indigenous laws and Indigenous legal theories in the adjudication of historical treaties. In fact, it

* This chapter formed the basis of a conference paper delivered at the 25th Annual Indigenous Bar Association Fall Conference entitled "Peace, Friendship & Respect: A Critical Examination of the Honour of the Crown on the 250th Anniversary of the Royal Proclamation and the Treaty of Niagara," 7–9 October 2013, Casino Rama, Chippewas of Rama First Nation, Ontario. I wish to thank my dear friends Jeremy Webber, Grégoire Webber, Kent Roach, and two young and brilliant scholars, Sébastien Brodeur-Girard and Aaron Mills, for their comments on a preliminary version of this chapter. Finally, I want to acknowledge my debt to Roderick A. Macdonald, my friend and mentor, who, although bedridden with a terminal cancer, took the time to comment extensively on my manuscript.

1 Roderick A. Macdonald, "Access to Justice and Law Reform" (1990) 10 *Windsor Yearbook of Access to Justice* 287 at 311 [Macdonald, "Access"].

argues for the establishment of alternative lawmaking processes where Indigenous representatives would be part of the decision-making process, ensuring a greater role for Indigenous laws in the development of the "intersocietal" normativity the "law of Aboriginal rights" is said to embody.

The judicial implementation of historical treaties raises such complex issues that one often feels a sense of helplessness when reflecting upon these. I believe that part of the answer to the question of what courts may contribute to the implementation of historical treaties lies in the manner in which one assesses the purpose of law in general and of adjudication in particular and, more deeply, on which grounds one appraises their moral quality.[2] After a brief examination of these issues in

---

2 Having been specifically asked to examine what remedies *courts* should or could provide where Indigenous historical treaties are concerned, I leave for another time an inquiry as to which other lawmaking process would be appropriate for solving differences over such matters. Because adjudication is premised on the belief that "justice is about the resolution of disputes" and that "disagreements must become disputes before an issue of justice arises" (*ibid* at 310), a less confrontational means of providing justice might prove more suitable. Indeed, courts might not be the best social institutions to respond to treaty injustices because of the heavy burdens the adjudicative process places on the plaintiffs, especially Indigenous plaintiffs (*ibid* at 330): "[Among other things,] [t]he very formality of legal recourses demands a degree of intellectual sophistication, a fund of personal and familial emotional resources, an ability to restate often diffuse and inarticulable hurts and grievances as legal claims, and a capacity to transform a sense of powerlessness about external events in the world – such as shoes that fall apart or rental accommodation that is in disrepair – into a belief that something can be done. Most citizens (even in the middle class) cannot easily marshall such resources, and even when they are obliged to do so by the state (as criminal defendants or in matrimonial disputes) their reaction is often simply one of wishing to get the process over as quickly as possible. Except where the resources of one's family, community, friends, religion, or employment setting provide (or except where one has the economic resources to purchase on the marketplace) vehicles for dealing with life's setbacks, these simply go unremedied as part of the fate (like death) which all human beings must endure" (*ibid* at 330).

However, as demonstrated by Michael Coyle in various articles, negotiation leading to some form of contractual solution is also fraught with difficulties and plagued by power imbalances: "Transcending Colonialism? Power and the Resolution of Indigenous Treaty Claims in Canada and New Zealand" (2011) 24:4 *New Zealand Universities Law Review* 596; "Les négociations sur la gouvernance autochtone au Canada: pouvoir, culture et imagination," (2009) 15:3 *Téléscope* 14; "Marginalized by Sui Generis? Duress, Undue Influence and Crown-Aboriginal Treaties" (2007) 32:2 *Manitoba Law Journal* 34.

the first part of my presentation, I will try, in the second part, to analyse how these preliminary considerations impact one's understanding of the limits and potentialities of adjudication in matters involving historical treaty implementation.

1. What is Law? What is Specific to Adjudication?

Some – I will call them the apriorists[3] – will try to assess the moral quality of court action from an external perspective, from a foothold resting outside social practices, and therefore, outside the field of human interaction. They will claim, for instance, that a close analysis of the wording of legal texts and historical treaties, conjoined with the mobilization of supposedly universal *a priori* abstract legal standards, such as the concepts of contract, sovereignty, or rights, will lead to just interpretations and therefore to just remedies. But these notions and interpretative methodologies are for the most part the product of the Western legal tradition. In that perspective, the implementation of officially recognized – written – *rules* is implicitly thought of as leading to morally valid outcomes. Therefore, the morality of law is not understood as resting on the quality of the *processes* by which law-making is made possible.

Adjudication, in the apriorist perspective, is thus envisaged as an exercise of authority for the purpose of effecting social control. It is not conceived, to quote legal theorist Lon Fuller, as "a form of social ordering, as a way in which the relations of men to one another are governed and regulated,"[4] as a law-making mechanism "serving the purpose of putting in order and facilitating human interaction."[5]

3 I use the terms "apriorists" and "culturalists" as Weberian ideal types. However, Tom Flanagan's approach to legal issues in his book *First Nations? Second Thought* (Montreal: McGill-Queen's University Press, 2000) certainly fits the apriorist perspective, whereas James Sa'ke'j Youngblood Henderson and Marie Battiste's depiction of both Western law and Indigenous law in *Protecting Indigenous Knowledge and Heritage: A Global Challenge* (Saskatoon: Purich, 2000) bears very close resemblance to the "culturalist" paradigm.

4 Lon L. Fuller, "Forms and Limits of Adjudication," in Kenneth I. Winston, ed., *The Principles of Social Order: Selected Essays of Lon L. Fuller*, rev. ed. (Portland, OR: Hart Publishing, 2001) 101 at 105.

5 Lon L. Fuller, "Human Interaction and the Law," in Kenneth I. Winston, ed., *The Principles of Social Order: Selected Essays of Lon L. Fuller*, rev. ed. (Portland, OR: Hart Publishing, 2001) 231 at 256.

In opposition to the apriorists' view, others – I will call them the culturalists – will claim that whatever a Canadian court does, the morality of its actions will be tainted by the inherently imperialistic content of Western legal culture. Their perspective is premised on the existence of an unbridgeable cultural divide between Indigenous and non-Indigenous peoples. From such a perspective, adjudication by a Canadian tribunal cannot but be conceived as an illegitimate act of authority, if not as the manifestation of a blatantly abusive form of power. But there is more to such a perspective. Its proponents often claim that there is an artificial quality to state law, one that is said to contrast with the presumed openness, spontaneity, and naturalness of Indigenous legal orders. Whereas state law would stem solely from the exercise of power, Indigenous legal orders would somehow naturally burst forth from social practices "without any form of decision or imposition," Indigenous norms being mere "projection[s] from the practices themselves."[6] Indigenous social practices are therefore conceptualized as unperturbed by any disagreements. If and when such disagreements are acknowledged, they are said to be rare and quickly resolved by Indigenous justice processes emphasizing social harmony. One is left with the feeling that all Indigenous members of a particular community are in accord with each and every norm of that community. Seen through the eyes of such authors, Western and Indigenous legal orders face each other in their own self-contained and self-referential universes.

Again, from such a perspective, we stand outside the field of human interaction, at least where Indigenous and non-Indigenous peoples are concerned. Or rather, interaction between the two groups is seen as confined to what for a long time has been – and still is, in many instances – the state's undeniably brutal imperial attitude towards the Indigenous peoples. One also senses that, from that perspective, for Indigenous peoples to stray from some sort of cultural nodal point would be tantamount to undermining the moral quality of their actions.

In both intellectual postures described above, there seems to be a presumption that there exists a single, just, normative answer to a particular question. Consequently, for the apriorists, adjudication is capable of providing such an answer, whatever the issue at hand may be, a

6 Jeremy Webber, "Legal Pluralism and Human Agency" (2006) 44 *Osgoode Hall Law Journal* 167 at 180.

rule always being available in Canadian law to authoritatively solve the problem. Conversely, for the culturalists, adjudication can never provide an entirely satisfying answer, in view of the cultural gulf separating Indigenous and non-Indigenous peoples.

Both perspectives, it seems to me, reify law, more particularly state law, to the level of an exercise of authority pure and simple. They tend to leave unanswered the question of the purpose for which such authority is exercised. In fact, their top-down understanding of Canadian law renders the need to answer such a question academic. Paraphrasing John Borrows, I would say that there are other stories lying at the heart of law.[7]

For instance, if, along with Lon L. Fuller, we admit that law, be it Indigenous or non-Indigenous, is an interactional phenomenon[8] and that it is never "simply a chart of do's and don'ts" but aims rather at providing "a program for living together,"[9] it then becomes obvious, from such a bottom-up perspective, that law serves "the purpose of ordering and facilitating the interactions of citizens with one another."[10] Social control is not its primary function. The purpose of law is not so much to provide definite and substantial answers to problems, but rather to "furnish [an individual] with baselines against which to organize his life with his fellows."[11] But then, how might a legal order provide for these *common* baselines?

The answer to this question requires, first, that we accept, as Jeremy Webber rightly observes, that "[l]aw is never simply given"; rather, "[i]t is always made against a background of disagreement."[12] If such is the case, it follows that, "[f]or a legal order to exist, disagreement has to be brought to a close, at least provisionally, and a common normative outcome established."[13] Hence, *all* legal orders, Indigenous as well as

---

7 See John Borrows, this volume.

8 Lon L. Fuller, "A Reply to Professors Cohen and Dworkin" (1965) 10 *Villanova Law Review* 655 at 661 [Fuller, "Reply"]: "[A]ll we need do to accept the idea of an internal morality of the law is to see the law, not as a one-way projection of power downward, but as lying in an interaction between law-giver and law-subject, in which each has responsibilities toward the other."

9 Fuller, "Human Interaction," *supra* note 5 at 242.

10 *Ibid* at 251.

11 *Ibid* at 254.

12 Webber, *supra* note 6 at 195.

13 *Ibid*.

non-Indigenous, face the same problem: How and by which mechanisms does a legal order provide for the formulation of a common normative outcome? And from what basis will the moral quality of this outcome flow?[14]

The success or failure of a particular legal order will depend on its ability to establish "stable interactional expectancies."[15] In short, the legal system will function only if the affected parties accept as law and willingly observe the rules generated by the legal system's law-making mechanisms.[16] Now, if normative diversity is the rule in any society, then choices will have to be made by its individual members. And if such is the case, the morality of the decisions arrived at by the system's law-making mechanisms will hinge upon the manner in which these allow the affected parties to participate in the decisions reached, even though disagreement will never be entirely wiped away.[17] The morality of a legal order's law-making mechanisms will thus be assessed according to the measure of freedom to participate in, and therefore to choose, that such mechanisms afford to affected parties. Furthermore, establishing stable interactional expectancies not only implies allowing parties to participate. It also requires of law-making processes that they be receptive and respectful of the response generated. Law's morality in this perspective is internal to itself and does not rest solely upon the conformity of the adopted rules with any external notion, such as an abstract principle. As I said, it is the quality of participation allowed by a process aimed at formulating a common normative outcome that will determine the internal morality of a legal order. As demonstrated by Roderick A. Macdonald,[18] Fuller's point is that the particular form of participation implied by each type of law-making process is essential to the morality of the outcome. The *outcome of a decision* may be morally

---

14 This should not be understood to mean that all rules are constantly negotiated against a background of disagreement. Acknowledging that determinate norms are always interactionally achieved is not incompatible with recognizing that, over time, some "normative outcomes" become quite settled and stable.

15 Fuller, "Human Interaction," *supra* note 5 at 244.

16 *Ibid* at 254–5.

17 Fuller, "Forms and Limits," *supra* note 4 at 106–7. For a "pragmatic" philosophical understanding of law similar to the one defended here, see David Dyzenhaus, "The Legitimacy of Legality" (1996) 46 *University of Toronto Law Journal* 129 at 178–80.

18 Macdonald, "Access," *supra* note 1. See also Roderick A. Macdonald, "A Theory of Procedural Fairness" (1980) 10 *Windsor Yearbook for Access to Justice*.

justified according to some external moral conception, but the *moral legitimacy of the decision* will be compromised if the process leading to it does not respect the mode of participation that is inherent to it.[19]

These law-making mechanisms or processes must be understood as sources of social order and justice. However, since they do not all allow for the same kind of participation, law-making mechanisms do not all establish moral relationships between citizens in the same way. Customary law, for instance, is itself the product of a "coordination of expectations and actions that arises tacitly out of interaction."[20] In a

---

19 Fuller was of the opinion that respect for the internal morality of law will incline the lawmaker, for instance the legislator, toward making rules that are just in their substantive aims: "[A]ll the ordering forms by which human beings are united – language, conceptual thought, law, morals, custom, the rules of games – work most effectively when there is mutual respect. Language is a social product, but it receives its forms in an interaction between communicating individuals. Each of us has his own special ways of using the forms of language. If we are to communicate successfully, we must be able to conform our minds to the ways others have of expressing themselves. If we understand them in the sense we would have intended had we used their language, misunderstanding is inevitable. Understanding depends on respect and a capacity for transcending self. So in law and morals, we cannot project our views upon others without giving them some opportunity to understand those views – we cannot condemn them for violating rules that are left unpublished or could not be known to them, nor punish them for occurrences that came about without their fault or intent. *There is, therefore, in an ordered system of law, formulated and administered conscientiously, a certain built-in respect for human dignity, and I think it is reasonable to suppose that this respect will tend to carry over into the substantive ends of law*" [my emphasis] (Fuller, "Reply," *supra* note 8 at 665–6). In "Positivism and Fidelity to Law: A Reply to Professor Hart" (1958) 71 *Harvard Law Review* 630 at 636, Fuller also says, "I shall have to rest on an assertion of a belief that may seem naive, namely that coherence and goodness have more affinity than coherence and evil. Accepting this belief, I also believe that when men are compelled to explain and justify their decisions, the effect will generally be to pull those decisions towards goodness, by whatever ultimate standards of goodness there are." Finally, in *The Morality of Law*, rev. ed. (New Haven, CT: Yale University Press, 1969) at 162, he also makes the following comment: "I have repeatedly observed that legal morality can be said to be neutral over a wide range of ethical issues. It cannot be neutral in its view of man himself. To embark on the enterprise of subjecting human conduct to the governance of rules involves of necessity a commitment to the view that man is, or can become, a responsible agent, capable of understanding and following rules, and answerable for his defaults."

20 Lon L. Fuller, "The Role of Contract" in Kenneth I. Winston, ed., *The Principles of Social Order: Selected Essays of Lon L. Fuller*, rev. ed. (Portland, OR: Hart Publishing, 2001) 187 at 188.

sense, customary law also allows for the participation of our forebears. Contract, on the other hand, allows the parties to negotiate, and elections allow one to exercise the right to vote. As for adjudication, its distinguishing characteristic "lies in the fact that it confers on the affected party a peculiar form of participation in the decision, that of presenting proofs and reasoned arguments for a decision in his [or her] favor."[21]

Furthermore, different social contexts will call for different forms of social ordering, including different forms of law-making processes.[22] For instance, elections and voting are more appropriate for deciding issues in large, impersonal contexts. Mediation, a process analogous but not identical to adjudication,[23] is, on the contrary, more suitable to "relationships[s] of heavy dependence"[24] such as those characteristic of families or small Indigenous face-to-face societies. Customary law, on the other hand, would fit any sort of social context: families, small communities as well as the international community itself.

Nanabush would have understood such distinctions, for although he had the power to morph himself into the shape of any corporal being whatsoever – a raven, a tree, a hare, a cloud – he well knew that his power was circumscribed, and therefore limited, by the form he espoused. As a raven, he could surge up in the air but could not leap and caper about like a hare, and vice versa.[25] So it is with law-making processes. And the distinctions between the latter as well as the different social contexts within which they can best operate must be kept in mind when we reflect upon the question of what courts may contribute to the implementation of historical treaties. Such a question brings us back to an examination of adjudication's specificity. Court decisions are

21 Fuller, "Forms and Limits," *supra* note 4 at 107. The next sentence reads, "Whatever heightens the significance of this participation lifts adjudication toward its optimum expression. Whatever destroys the meaning of that participation destroys the integrity of adjudication itself."

22 Fuller, "Human Interaction," *supra* note 5 at 257; see also Macdonald, "Procedural Fairness," *supra* note 18.

23 Fuller, "Forms and Limits," *supra* note 4 at 112; see also the excerpts of Fuller's letter written to a colleague in 1972 reproduced in Lon L. Fuller, "Mediation – Its Forms and Functions," editor's note, in Kenneth I. Winston, ed., *The Principles of Social Order: Selected Essays of Lon L. Fuller*, rev. ed. (Portland, OR: Hart Publishing, 2001) 141 at 141.

24 Fuller, "Mediation," *supra* note 23 at 148.

25 Basil Johnston, *Ojibway Heritage* (Toronto: McClelland and Stewart, 1976) 159 at 160.

different in that they are "reached within an institutional framework that is intended to assure to the disputants an opportunity for the presentation of proofs and reasoned arguments."[26]

Contrary to decisions resulting from an election or a contract, adjudication is expected to allow the expression of *reasoned* arguments by all parties involved, and the detached consideration of those by the judge or arbiter. A hockey referee is not a judge in that deeper sense, because he is not expected to listen to and assess reasoned arguments. Furthermore, in the absence of reasoned argument, meaningful participation would be impossible. The simple affirmation of something does not qualify as reasoned argument. The latter can be so only if some principle or principles are asserted upon which its soundness and relevancy rest.[27] That is why, in the words of Lon Fuller, "[t]he proper province of adjudication is to make an authoritative determination of questions raised by claims of right and accusations of guilt."[28]

2. What Can One Expect of Adjudication in Matters Involving Historical Treaty Implementation?

What can we make out of all the above for the adjudication of Indigenous issues? First, the positions of apriorists and culturalists alike are deficient. The apriorists do not allow any significant space for Indigenous laws and understandings in the process of adjudication, and if so, only interstitially. They might allow for the integration within state law of certain well-identified Indigenous norms. However, they would still envisage law as a body of *norms*, and not as an enterprise characterized, above all, by *mechanisms and processes* enabling the identification of one provisional normative proposition out of the many diverse normative propositions – some of them of Indigenous origins – existing prior to a decision being made. The same goes for culturalists, who tend to discard decisions emanating from Canadian courts as products of structures of brute power. In so doing, they fail to recognize that Indigenous norms themselves are the product of processes of norm selection

26 Fuller, "Forms and Limits," *supra* note 4 at 108.

27 *Ibid* at 111: "The litigant must therefore, if his participation is to be meaningful, assert some principle or principles by which his arguments are sound and his proofs relevant."

28 *Ibid*.

enabling the identification of one proposition out of the many potential normative propositions circulating within Indigenous communities. However participatory a particular law-making process can be, all such mechanisms involve an inevitable peremptory dimension.[29] That is so because there will always remain a certain amount of disagreement over the normative standards eventually chosen. So, claiming that state law is the product of power structures is not, in itself, sufficient to disavow it. All law-making processes are, in some way or other, the product of power structures.[30]

Second, as it insists on the participation of the affected Indigenous parties in the adjudication process, the vision of law advocated here requires a greater resort to Indigenous laws and Indigenous legal theories in the adjudication of historical treaties.[31] If law, as I said, emanates from social interactions, both sides of the normative equations must be taken into account. Meaningful participation also presumes an ability to communicate and to persuade. Therefore, a common standard of decision, "some shared context of principle,"[32] must exist for participation to be real. A blunt imposition of Euro-Canadian norms will not be sufficient if the result of adjudication is to be imbued with a moral quality. In fact, and I will come back to this later, the best solution would entail Indigenous representatives taking an active part in the law-making mechanism that will eventually select the one provisional normative proposition out of the many possible ones.

Third, even though these common normative propositions might not yet have definitively emerged in Canadian law, adjudication enables their gradual discovery and articulation. True, change is slow to come, and we are still far from a recognition of Indigenous legal traditions or legal theories in Canadian law or from the development of truly common standards. However, there is progress. As an example, I will examine the recent *Manitoba Metis Federation* case,[33] which might eventually,

---

29 Webber, "Legal Pluralism," *supra* note 6 at 179.

30 However, as the rest of this chapter will try to demonstrate, this should not be understood as a claim that the state courts provide the most appropriate mechanism to achieve a truly intersocietal justice.

31 On Indigenous legal theories, see Gordon Christie, "Indigenous Legal Theory: Some Initial Considerations" in Benjamin Richardson, Shin Imai, and Kent McNeil, eds., *Indigenous Peoples and the Law: Comparative and Critical Perspectives* (Portland, OR: Hart Publishing, 2009) 195.

32 Fuller, "Forms and Limits," *supra* note 4 at 114.

as I will try to show, provide a means of impelling the Crown to diligently fulfil its treaty obligations.

In that case, a majority of the Supreme Court[34] concluded that, since limitations of actions statutes "cannot prevent the courts, as guardians of the Constitution, from issuing declarations on the constitutionality of legislation," "[b]y extension, [they] cannot prevent the courts from issuing a declaration on the constitutionality of the Crown's conduct."[35] In that case, the Metis were seeking a declaration that "a provision of the *Manitoba Act* – given constitutional authority by the *Constitution Act, 1871* – [had] not [been] implemented in accordance with the honour of the Crown, itself a 'constitutional principle.'"[36] According to the majority, a declaration of unconstitutionality was a judicial remedy of a "limited nature,"[37] distinct from an action for breach of fiduciary duty, and thus not subject to the application of limitations of actions statutes. The majority emphasized that constitutional grievances that still remained outstanding could not be barred by statute. Deciding otherwise would fly in the face of the necessary reconciliation of the Metis people with Canadian sovereignty.[38]

This approach is not without appeal for Indigenous claimants. As underlined by the dissenting judges in the case,[39] "[w]here the parties ask for a declaration only and link it to some constitutional principle, the courts will now be empowered to decide those cases no matter how long ago the actions and facts that gave rise to the claim occurred."[40] In so doing, courts are preventing the use of law as a means of shutting out from the judicial arena the tragic consequences flowing from the fate suffered by generations of Indigenous peoples at the hands of the Canadian state. Moreover, once a governmental action has been declared incompatible with the honour of the Crown, how could the latter not satisfy the claims of the affected Indigenous party? How could the

33 *Manitoba Metis Federation Inc. v Canada (Attorney General)*, 2013 SCC 14, [2013] 1 SCR 623 (CanLII) [*Manitoba Metis Federation*].
34 Chief Justice McLachlin and Justice Karakatsanis (Justices LeBel, Fish, Abella, and Cromwell concurring).
35 *Manitoba Metis Federation*, *supra* note 33 at para 135.
36 *Ibid* at para 136.
37 *Ibid* at para 143.
38 *Ibid* at paras 140, 143.
39 Justice Rothstein (Justice Moldaver concurring).
40 *Manitoba Metis Federation*, *supra* note 33 at para 265.

Crown morally elude its duty to grant a remedy when a majority of the Supreme Court has declared that many of the policy rationales underlying limitations statutes could not be invoked to prevent the claim of the Metis?[41] In fact, the majority in the *Manitoba Metis Federation* case candidly asserted that the latter sought "this declaratory relief in order to assist them in extra-judicial negotiations with the Crown in pursuit of the overarching constitutional goal of reconciliation that is reflected in s. 35 of the Constitution."[42]

In addition, this decision is interesting because the majority of the Court also decided that a new duty sprang from the Crown's obligation to act honourably. To the already known requirement that the Crown take a broad purposive approach to the interpretation of a constitutionally entrenched promise made to an Indigenous group is now added a duty to fulfil the latter diligently.[43] It follows, in the words of the majority, "that the honour of the Crown requires the Crown to endeavour to ensure its obligations are fulfilled."[44] This is much more onerous for the Crown than a simple obligation not to give too legalistic an interpretation to an entrenched promise. To satisfy this obligation to act diligently, "Crown servants must seek to perform the obligation in a way that pursues the purpose behind the promise."[45]

Although the promise in that case was enshrined in a constitutional provision – section 31 of the *Manitoba Act* – rather than set in a historical treaty, the mobilization of the obligation to act diligently might also be possible in the case of treaties.[46] Indeed, they share many of the attributes recognized by the majority judges as belonging to section 31 of the *Manitoba Act*. First, the majority underlined that the obligation to act diligently "ha[d] arisen largely in the treaty context, where the Crown's honour is pledged to diligently carrying out its promises."[47]

41 *Ibid* at para 141.
42 *Ibid* at para 137.
43 *Ibid* at para 75.
44 *Ibid* at para 79.
45 *Ibid* at para 80.
46 The dissenting judges remarked upon the imprecise nature of this obligation: "[…] the majority reasons are unclear as to what types of legal documents will give rise to solemn obligations: Is it only provisions in the Constitution or does it also include treaties?" (*ibid* at para 205). In *ibid* at para 75, the majority appears to restrict its conclusion on diligence to *constitutional* obligations to Aboriginal peoples. But, in *ibid* at para 79, it opines that the duty applies whether the obligation arises in a treaty or in the Constitution.
47 *Ibid* at para 79.

Second, the judges insisted on the fact that only constitutional obligations analogous to solemn treaty promises could trigger this duty.[48] Finally, if, in the words of the majority, the objective pursued by section 31 of the *Manitoba Act* was "to reconcile the Métis community with the sovereignty of the Crown and to permit the creation of the province of Manitoba,"[49] one could certainly affirm that, at the very least, the objective pursued by historical treaties was to reconcile Indian communities with the sovereignty of the Crown.

In deciding as it did, the Court chose to play an active role in the enterprise of articulating the kind of interaction that should prevail between Indigenous peoples and the Crown. Indeed, one should remember that, strangely enough, the majority did not simply conclude, as it could have done, that the Crown had violated a constitutional provision, that is, section 31 of the *Manitoba Act*. Instead, after underlining the fact that this provision enshrined an explicit and solemn obligation to the Metis akin to that found in a treaty, the majority resorted to the principle of the honour of the Crown to impose upon the latter a duty to act diligently. Two reasons justify the taking of such a long route. First, the normative impact of a decision based on the Crown's violation of its duty to act honourably and to diligently fulfil a solemn promise made to the Metis is infinitely superior to a simple acknowledgment of the Crown having violated a 142-year-old technical constitutional provision. In short, it is much more damaging for the Crown to be draped in the mantle of dishonour than it would have been for it to be accused of failing to abide by a constitutional provision. Second, if the Court had contented itself with a simple acknowledgment of a violation of section 31 without resorting to the principle of the honour of the Crown, it would have been very difficult, even if a broad purposive interpretation of that provision had been used, to engraft on it a duty to act diligently. Hence, it could be said that the *Manitoba Metis Federation* case opens up new avenues to Indigenous litigants.

Be that as it may, some might still deplore the timidity of the Court in its prescription of remedies to treaty violations. However, one may ask: How far can a court go in dealing with the implementation of historical treaties? The latter often raises what Lon L. Fuller referred to as "polycentric"[50] issues – that is, issues involving many affected parties,

48 *Ibid* at paras 71, 78–9.
49 *Ibid* at para 98.
50 Fuller, "Forms and Limits," *supra* note 4 at 126–36.

not all of them represented before the court – whose complex ramifications make it difficult to measure the repercussion a particular award could have on the political dynamics between different Indigenous nations and between these and the Crown.[51] Furthermore, adjudication, concerned as it is with claims of rights, has an "I win/you lose" dimension that is not always favourable to fruitful interactions. Prudence is thus required if the internal morality of adjudication is to be preserved. In the words of Fuller, "[a]djudication is not a proper form of social ordering in those areas where the effectiveness of human association would be destroyed if it were organized about formally defined rights and wrongs."[52] The majority of the Court evidently felt that it had made the most out of the adjudicative process. Going any further would have compromised the legitimacy of its decision. However, the decision opened the door for recourse to a different law-making process.[53]

The various forms of law-making processes are not isolated from each other but rather interact with one another. In the *Manitoba Metis Federation* case, the specific mode of participation characteristic of adjudication provided the Court with the facts and reasoned arguments necessary to formulate a decision that would enable the parties to proceed with another form of social ordering – negotiation of a contract (agreement or treaty) – which has its own special mode of participatory interaction.[54]

---

51 Fuller stresses that the majority principle is also not appropriate for solving polycentric problems (*ibid* at 132).

52 *Ibid* at 113.

53 Although written nearly forty years ago, Abram Chayes' "The Role of the Judge in Public Law Litigation" (1976) 89 *Harvard Law Review* 1281 remains a very stimulating analysis of the advantages and disadvantages of judicial involvement in public law litigation. Also interesting is his description of the progressive phasing-out of the traditional understanding of the lawsuit as a vehicle for settling disputes between private parties about private rights, in favour of an understanding of civil litigation as a less bipolar, less self-contained episode.

54 See Fuller, *Morality of Law*, *supra* note 19 at 91. Lon Fuller gives a good example of the reciprocal dependence of the various lawmaking processes: "With all its subtleties, the problem of interpretation occupies a sensitive, central position in the internal morality of the law. It reveals, as no other problem can, the cooperative nature of the task of maintaining legality. If the interpreting agent is to preserve a sense of useful mission, the legislature must not impose on him senseless tasks. If the legislative draftsman is to discharge his responsibilities he, in turn, must be able to anticipate rational and relatively stable modes of interpretation. This reciprocal dependence permeates in less immediately obvious ways the whole legal order.

Notwithstanding the need for deference I have just mentioned, I do believe that more could be done and that the Supreme Court should seek more adamantly to nourish its understanding of historical treaties from an Indigenous perspective. This task will become easier as, with the passing of time, more Indigenous scholars explore the normative understanding of specific signatories to such treaties. For instance, two recent books, one by Harold Johnson dealing with Treaty 6[55] and the other by Aimée Craft studying Treaty 1,[56] as well as Aaron Mills' contribution to this volume, now offer to the uninitiated the possibility of peering into the treaty vision of specific Indigenous nations, as opposed to a more general understanding of this issue.[57]

Many contributions to this volume also provide avenues that the Court could, or rather should, follow.[58] Mark Walters and John Borrows

No single concentration of intelligence, insight, and good will, however strategically located, can insure the success of the enterprise of subjecting human conduct to the governance of rules." Macdonald underlines that problems can be transformed or converted into a form that makes them amenable to resolution under a different ordering process (Macdonald, "Procedural Fairness," *supra* note 18 at 28n7, 30).

55 Harold Johnson, *Two Families: Treaties and Government* (Saskatoon: Purich Publishing, 2007).

56 Aimée Craft, *Breathing Life into the Stone Fort Treaty: An Anishinabe Understanding of Treaty One* (Saskatoon: Purich Publishing, 2013).

57 John Borrows pioneered such research in his memorable article "Wampum at Niagara: The Royal Proclamation, Canadian Legal History, and Self-Government" in Michael Asch, ed., *Aboriginal and Treaty Rights in Canada: Essays on Law, Equity, and Respect for Difference* (Vancouver: UBC Press, 1997) 155.

58 I have argued elsewhere for a solution emphasizing the manner in which a federal spirit could infuse a new dynamic to the relationships of Indigenous and non-Indigenous people, both as individuals and as members of political communities: "Le fédéralisme: un terreau fertile pour gérer un monde incertain," in Ghislain Otis and Martin Papillon, eds., *Fédéralisme et gouvernance autochtone/ Federalism and Aboriginal Governance* (Quebec: Les Presses de l'Université Laval, 2013) 21, at http://papers.ssrn.com/sol3/papers.cfm?abstract_id=2321331); Jean Leclair, "Military Historiography, Warriors and Soldiers: The Normative Impact of Epistemological Choices" in Patrick Macklem and Douglas Sanderson, eds., *Essays on the Constitutional Entrenchment of Aboriginal and Treaty Rights* (Toronto: University of Toronto Press, 2016) at 179, http://papers.ssrn.com/sol3/papers.cfm?abstract_id=2326486; Jean Leclair, "Federal Constitutionalism and Aboriginal Difference" (2006) 31 *Queen's Law Journal* 521, at http://papers.ssrn.com/sol3/papers.cfm?abstract_id=1678795http://ssrn.com/abstract=1678795; Jean Leclair, "Envisaging Canada in a Disenchanted World: Reflections on Federalism, Nationalism, and Distinctive Indigenous Identity" (2016) 25 *Constitutional Forum constitutionnel* 15, at http://papers.ssrn.com/sol3/papers.cfm?abstract_id=2797880.

both insist on the importance for courts of embracing what the latter calls "the Treaty Story," a narrative requiring that the ongoing formation of the Canadian state be understood as having been "forged through seeking continual consensus between Indigenous peoples and the Crown,"[59] rather than being the unavowed product of the doctrine of *terra nullius* and consequent acts of imperialism.[60] Mark Walters further emphasizes that when the Treaty Story itself is interpreted according to an Indigenous legal perspective (in this case, the Anishinaabe's), we are forced "to shift the focus of our analysis from the idea of *rights* that flow from the treaty back to the idea of *right* manifested through the activity of participating in the special form of discourse contemplated by the treaty."[61] And such participation should also nourish our understanding of Canadian sovereignty. The latter can no longer be conceived as the "property," so to speak, of "an absolute political authority vested in a single entity," in this case Canada.[62] Rather, one has to admit that it was born out of the acknowledgment of "the existence of multiple and interlocking centres or nodes of normativity,"[63] Indigenous as well as non-Indigenous.

In the same vein, if we accept that historical treaty-making in Canada was aimed at "establish[ing] a new structure of relationships between the parties that would endure indefinitely,"[64] and if we presume that Indigenous peoples participating in this endeavour were rational agents, then, as argued forcefully by Michael Coyle, we are compelled to admit that generic principles ensue from these assumptions – principles that have the great advantage of not "depend[ing] for their validity on the evidentiary details of a particular treaty negotiation."[65] Furthermore, as opposed to the "honour of the Crown" concept often

59 John Borrows, this volume.

60 As underlined by Borrows, although the Supreme Court has officially denied that the doctrine of *terra nullius* had ever applied in Canada (*Tsilhqot'in Nation v British Columbia*, 2014 SCC 44 (CanLII) at 69), and even though "it [...] presents an alternative view," nevertheless this "overstatement [...] conceals how *terra nullius* continues to operate in Canada."

61 Mark D. Walters, this volume.

62 *Ibid.*

63 *Ibid.* Although the sentence quoted is a description of sovereignty as imagined under the Covenant Chain, if the Treaty Story is embraced, this description should also nourish our understanding of Canadian sovereignty.

64 Michael Coyle, this volume.

65 *Ibid.*

invoked in the context of treaty litigation, these principles do not invest one party with a hierarchical superiority nor do they lay all the obligations on the shoulders of a single partner.

Julie Jai, for her part, argues that mechanisms such as the creation of co-management bodies and dispute resolution processes, and the recognition of the most-favoured-nation concept, mechanisms that are all part and parcel of modern treaties, should be "read into historic treaties as implied terms based on the obligation of the Crown to act honourably and based on the oral promises which were made at the time."[66] She reaches this conclusion by drawing on the idea that Indigenous peoples are rational agents and that, therefore, absent fraud and duress, the signatories of historical treaties would never have agreed to the terms of those *ententes*. As she claims, justice demands that these treaties be "polished" anew. On what basis can we justify the double standard presently existing according to which Indigenous peoples unlucky enough to have signed a treaty between 1871 and 1921 are deprived of the advantages afforded to other Indigenous groups entering into agreements after 1974?[67]

Kent McNeil, instead of focusing on Indigenous law or on the specific issue of historical treaties, reminds us that the potentialities of the common law tradition itself should not be stultified by an overly positivistic interpretation. Rights, he rightly stresses, can have a legal existence without being justiciable.[68] Furthermore, "[j]ust because a legal issue has not yet been resolved by a court does not mean there is no law in relation thereto."[69] The common law tradition entertains a much richer understanding of normativity, one that distinguishes between "positive laws, consisting of rules laid down by statute or stemming from particular cases, from the reason of the law and fundamental principles (sometimes stated as legal maxims)."[70] Forgetting the possible reach of common law normativity could diminish our chances of making state law more amenable to Indigenous perspectives. As

66 Julie Jai, this volume.

67 The first modern treaty, the *James Bay and Northern Quebec Agreement*, was signed in 1975.

68 Kent McNeil, this volume.

69 *Ibid.*

70 *Ibid.*

for Sara Seck, she advocates that "the search for 'appropriate remedy' should also include insights from international law," including private international law. More specifically, she questions whether Indigenous peoples "could or should 'aspire' to similar international legal personality as that of transnational corporations."[71] In one of the most interesting parts of her chapter, she demonstrates that major achievements for the cause of Indigenous peoples at the international level have been the product of Indigenous peoples' opposition and resistance movements.

The Court might also eventually deepen its description of the limits inherent in the adjudicative process, and thus explain in greater detail the reasons for its reticence in matters of treaty implementation. It might go so far as recommending the establishment of alternative law-making processes. Without delving into the nature and jurisdiction that should be attributed to such processes, it might underline the manner in which the latter could provide for greater participation by Indigenous parties and explain how they might thus produce decisions bearing a much stronger moral quality. For instance, the Court could stress the fact that if Indigenous representatives were themselves part of the decision-making process, Indigenous laws and legal theories could stand a much better chance of playing an important role in the development of the "intersocietal" normativity the "law of aboriginal rights" is said to embody.[72] The presence of Indigenous representatives would also honour the idea common to Indigenous peoples that treaties are not just contracts dealing with territory *as property*, but, on the contrary, a means of establishing rules as to *how human beings interrelate where territory is concerned*. Furthermore, such involvement in the process would lead Indigenous representatives to participate in not only the definition of their own rights and responsibilities but also the delicate task of articulating these rights in our complex contemporary

71 Sara Seck, this volume.

72 *R v Van der Peet*, [1996] 2 SCR 507, 1996 CanLII 216 (SCC) at para 42 (Lamer CJ): "Professor Slattery has suggested that the law of aboriginal rights is 'neither English nor aboriginal in origin: it is a form of intersocietal law that evolved from long-standing practices linking the various communities' (Brian Slattery, 'The Legal Basis of Aboriginal Title,' in Frank Cassidy, ed., *Aboriginal Title in British Columbia: Delgamuukw v. The Queen* (1992), at pp. 120–21 [...])."

contexts.[73] It would require interaction and accommodation from both sides, not unidirectional top-down projections of authority and interpretative monopolies. This might even entail setting limits on rights. Finally, because an Indigenous people's sense of *injustice* is grounded in its own notion of what is right and wrong, allowing some space for Indigenous normativity is a sure step towards greater justice.[74] Such various modes of Indigenous participation would undoubtedly heighten the appeal of the decisions for the affected Indigenous peoples and therefore enhance the decisions' legitimacy.[75]

The road is still long before a community of purpose is built between signatories of historical treaties and the Crown, or rather the non-Indigenous population of Canada too often subsumed in the disincarnated fiction of "the Crown." But then again, achieving one's vision has always been an arduous task. Nanabush himself failed many times before fulfilling his quest. However, once he attained his vision, he found that it called upon him to help all beings, and not just the Anishnabeg.[76] And so, in Basil Johnston's poetic prose: "Nanabush failed, yet he succeeded."[77]

---

73 John Borrows, "Let Obligations Be Done" in Hamar Foster, Heather Raven, and Jeremy Webber, eds., *Let Right Be Done: Aboriginal Title, the Calder Case, and the Future of Indigenous Rights* (Vancouver: UBC Press, 2007) 201 at 211: "Aboriginal peoples also have obligations under their [own] laws. The use of indigenous law would particularize and strengthen the content of obligations the Aboriginal peoples have to the Crown. The mutuality of rights/obligations should remain the constitutional touchstone underlying this analysis. Aboriginal people can have obligations towards the Crown flowing from the parties' relationships that incorporate principles from indigenous law. Aboriginal peoples can also have obligations that are determined through treaties. [...] These laws can be referenced to construe past and present obligations. It is important that Aboriginal obligations are stressed when Crown obligations are discussed to avoid an inflated sense of personal entitlement. A number of Aboriginal people claim rights without responsibilities and this is harmful to a balanced outlook. If everyone acts as if they only have rights and do not affirm their obligations, society is in danger of coming apart at its seams."

74 Macdonald, "Access," *supra* note 1 at 332: "[A] precondition of rendering justice accessible is to recognize how each person lives various systems of justice in daily interaction, and develops a keen sense of injustice based on expectations flowing from that system."

75 Processes such as mediation might be more apropos than adjudicative ones. On the distinction between adjudication and mediation, see Macdonald, "Procedural Fairness," *supra* note 18 at 17–18.

76 Johnston, *Ojibway Heritage*, *supra* note 25 at 160.

77 *Ibid* at 161.

13 Treaties and the Emancipatory Potential of International Law

SARA L. SECK[1]

This contribution seeks to respond to two questions posed in this volume. First, what role should be played by Indigenous values and legal traditions in treaty implementation? Second, should we look to other forums to implement treaties and resolve treaty disputes? This chapter explores whether explicit embrace of international norms by Indigenous peoples that are consistent with Indigenous law could contribute to the resolution of disputes relating to resource extraction on Indigenous lands.

1. Introduction

The 250th anniversary of the Royal Proclamation of 1763 and the Treaty of Niagara is a fitting time to revisit the relationship between Aboriginal peoples and international law. One task assigned to contributors to this volume was to seek "appropriate legal remedies for treaty implementation" in light of the historic nature of many Indigenous/Crown treaties and the unfulfilled promises they hold. At one time, implicit in the notion that legal remedies must be sought would have been the unquestioned assumption that the legal system within which to seek remedies was the Canadian judicial system, and the law to be applied was Canadian Aboriginal law. Increasingly, however, these colonial assumptions have been challenged as existing Indigenous laws and legal

1 The author would like to thank Michael Coyle and John Borrows for including her in this project, and participants in the two conferences held to discuss the ideas in this book for their thoughtful reflections.

traditions have been recognized.[2] Accordingly, as documented by John Borrows, even the Royal Proclamation cannot be understood on its own as a unilateral declaration of the British Crown. Rather, it must be understood as "part of a treaty into which First Nations had considerable input" and, in this light, "must be interpreted as it would be 'naturally understood' by them" including promises made at Niagara of "respect for the sovereignty of First Nations."[3]

The Treaty of Niagara, entered into with approximately two thousand chiefs in July and August of 1764, included the exchange of gifts and wampum belts, which recorded the promises made in accordance with First Nations diplomatic and legal understandings.[4] The Two Row Wampum is described by Borrows as "illustrat[ing] a First Nation/Crown relationship that is founded on peace, friendship, and respect, where each nation will not interfere with the internal affairs of the other."[5] Although, when read alone, the language of the Royal Proclamation claims Crown "dominion" and "sovereignty" over territories occupied by First Nations,[6] the meeting at Niagara affirmed the Covenant Chain of Friendship, "a multinational alliance in which no member gave up their sovereignty."[7]

It can thus be said that the history of the First Nations–Crown relationship is one founded on agreements among sovereign nations, as evidenced in sources drawn from both Crown and Indigenous legal traditions. The challenge, then, as framed by Borrows, has been for Canadian lawyers and courts to recognize, affirm, and clarify the relationship between legal traditions that together contribute to a "multi-juridical legal culture."[8] This has been a slow process, yet one with promise due to the increasing articulation of sources and examples

2 See generally John Borrows, *Canada's Indigenous Constitution* (Toronto: University of Toronto Press, 2010).

3 John Borrows, "Wampum at Niagara: The Royal Proclamation, Canadian Legal History, and Self-Government" in Michael Asch, ed., *Aboriginal and Treaty Rights in Canada: Essays in Law, Equality and Respect for Difference* (Vancouver: UBC Press, 1997) 155 at 168–9.

4 *Ibid* at 158, 161–5.

5 *Ibid* at 164.

6 *Ibid* at 160.

7 *Ibid* at 161.

8 See chap. 5, "Recognizing a Multi-Juridical Legal Culture" in Borrows, *Canada's Indigenous Constitution, supra* note 2.

of Indigenous law,[9] as well as examples of and potential for entrenchment of Indigenous legal traditions by the Canadian government and Canadian courts.[10]

The purpose of this chapter, however, is to propose something different: that the search for "appropriate remedy" should also include insights from international law. Notably, public international law, or the law of nations, has not been welcoming of Indigenous peoples as nations equal in sovereignty to the European colonial powers.[11] Indeed, it is precisely because of public international law's historic failure to recognize Indigenous peoples as nation states exercising sovereignty over their lands that this search for appropriate remedy is necessary. This is curious, given that a natural law tradition underlays classical international law,[12] a tradition that would seemingly fit well with the view held by Elders and leaders that treaties are sacred, "blessed by the Creator," and part of a higher law.[13] Yet, as documented by Antony Anghie, international law emerged out of the "civilizing mission" of the colonial encounter; thus, colonialism may be said to be deeply embedded within the very structure of international law.[14] As a result, neither traditional understandings of the accepted sources of international law, nor the tools of dispute resolution available in the international legal system are available to interpret historic Indigenous/Crown treaties.[15] Other international instruments and institutions linked with international

9 See chap. 2, "Sources and Scope of Indigenous Legal Traditions," and chap. 3, "Indigenous Law Examples" in Borrows, *Canada's Indigenous Constitution, supra* note 2.

10 See chap. 7, "The Role of Governments and Courts in Entrenching Indigenous Legal Traditions" in Borrows, *Canada's Indigenous Constitution, supra* note 2.

11 See generally S. James Anaya, *Indigenous Peoples in International Law* (New York: Oxford University Press, 1996).

12 Antony Anghie, *Imperialism, Sovereignty and the Making of International Law* (Cambridge: Cambridge University Press, 2005) at 21.

13 John Borrows, "Canada's Colonial Constitution," chap. 1 in this volume.

14 Anghie, *supra* note 12 at 3–4. See also Anaya, *Indigenous Peoples in International Law, supra* note 11 at 23–6 (on the civilizing mission of the trusteeship doctrine).

15 Claire Charters, "Indigenous Peoples and International Law and Policy" in Benjamin J. Richardson, Shin Imai, and Kent McNeil, eds., *Indigenous Peoples and the Law: Comparative and Critical Perspectives* (Portland, OR: Hart Publishing, 2009) 161 at 165–7. See also Articles 34, 35, and 38, *Statute of the International Court of Justice, 1945*, annexed to the United Nations Charter. Having said this, analysis of the sources of international law can create space for Indigenous voices, depending upon the methodology chosen, as will be seen below.

human rights law have emerged to provide space for claims of reparations for state violations of the rights of Indigenous peoples, yet these "have rarely gone beyond broad suggestions that states and indigenous peoples negotiate appropriate remedies."[16]

Identifying the appropriate site for the resolution of disputes arising over the interpretation of Indigenous/Crown treaties might also be informed by doctrines of private international law, according to which courts of one nation state routinely apply the laws of another in transnational disputes between private parties.[17] Private international law or conflict of laws first asks whether a court has jurisdiction over a claim brought before it, and if so, what law or combination of domestic and foreign laws should apply. Notably, private international law doctrines also provide that courts of one nation may recognize and enforce a judgment emanating from the courts of another nation.[18] Yet a traditional private international law analysis is generally not applied to the interpretation of Indigenous/Crown treaties, which are understood as nation-to-nation agreements. If it were, then seeking remedy in the courts of one nation (Canada) but never in the other (First Nation) would appear clearly inappropriate, no matter how determined the judiciary of the chosen nation is to seek reconciliation,[19] assuming this is even a

---

16 Claire Charters, "Reparations for Indigenous Peoples: Global International Instruments and Institutions," in Federico Lenzerini, ed., *Reparations for Indigenous Peoples: International and Comparative Perspectives* (Oxford: Oxford University Press, 2008) 163 at 195.

17 Sara L. Seck, "Environmental Harm in Developing Countries Caused by Subsidiaries of Canadian Mining Corporations: The Interface of Public and Private International Law" (1999) 37 *Canadian Yearbook of International Law* 139 at 174–8 (discussing choice of law). On private international law as the private side of citizenship, see Karen Knop, "Citizenship, Public and Private" (2008) 71 *Law & Contemporary Problems* 309 at 319.

18 Seck, "Environmental Harm," *supra* note 17 at 178–87 (on recognition and enforcement of foreign judgments, noting certain limitations when it comes to the enforcement of public laws, such as criminal and tax laws).

19 In this light, it is worth noting that while one state might seek justice in another's courts in relation to commercial matters, the doctrines of state immunity, act of state, and non-justiciability prevent the national courts of one state from deciding disputes in relation to the internal affairs of another state. See generally Hazel Fox, "International Law and Restraints on the Exercise of Jurisdiction by National Courts of States" in Malcolm D. Evans, ed., *International Law*, 2nd ed. (Oxford: Oxford University Press, 2006) at 361.

worthy goal.[20] Similarly, the application of Canadian Aboriginal law, but never Indigenous law, would be puzzling. Moreover, if Indigenous legal traditions are understood to include methods of dispute resolution that present an alternative to Canadian courts,[21] then these methods should equally be recognized as appropriate for the interpretation of Indigenous/Crown treaties, just as they are understood to be appropriate for issues arising within Aboriginal communities.[22]

Crucially, the proposal to consider the possibility of international law is not being brought forward here with a blind faith in the purity of (public) international law as a reflection of universal goals of a united global community. Rather, the analysis in this chapter will clearly recognize how deeply colonialism is embedded within the very structure of international law. Indeed, it is precisely because of public international law doctrines that treated Indigenous peoples as the "uncivilized other" and their lands as *terra nullius* to be "discovered" by the colonial settlers that Aboriginal lands have been understood from the perspective of public international law as having been colonized by the Crown.[23] Yet despite this bleak history, this chapter takes the position that international law is redeemable – it has an emancipatory potential that can and must be uncovered and exploited.[24] Indeed,

---

20 John Borrows, "Canada's Colonial Constitution" in this volume: "Reconciliation is a flawed metaphor in this field. Any compromise *with* colonialism causes us to be compromised *by* colonialism."

21 Borrows, *Canada's Indigenous Constitution*, *supra* note 2 at 178–9 (issuing a caution against focusing on formal state institutions and thus discounting "the role of non-governmental organizations, families or individuals in creating, interpreting, and enforcing Indigenous law. There is a tremendous danger that official state organs can overwhelm other institutions of civil society if they are regarded as exclusive legal agents in Canada. This would be a mistake and would undermine the vitality of Indigenous law.")

22 See Borrows, *Canada's Indigenous Constitution*, *supra* note 2 at 207–14 ("Indigenous Bodies and Dispute Resolution").

23 Robert J. Miller, Jacinta Ruru, Larissa Behrendt, and Tracey Lindberg, eds., *Discovering Indigenous Lands: The Doctrine of Discovery in the English Colonies* (Oxford: Oxford University Press, 2010); Jérémie Gilbert, "Means of Acquisition," chap. 1 and "Means of Extinguishment," chap. 2 in *Indigenous Peoples' Land Rights Under International Law: From Victims to Actors* (Ardsley, NY: Transnational Publishers, 2006).

24 On the emancipatory potential of international law, see Sara L. Seck, "Unilateral Home State Regulation: Imperialism or Tool for Subaltern Resistance?" (2008) 46 *Osgoode Hall Law Journal* 565 at 589–97.

however reluctantly, international law has already evolved to recognize rights claimed by Indigenous peoples, most notably in the 2007 United Nations Declaration on the Rights of Indigenous Peoples.[25]

In this spirit, this chapter will first ground its analysis in a familiar Canadian context – that of resource extraction on Indigenous lands. Noted here will be the increasingly common phenomena of agreements between Aboriginal peoples and mining companies which go beyond requirements mandated under applicable domestic laws.[26] The chapter will then explore how to understand these agreements from the perspective of public international law. To do this, it will be necessary to unpack how public international law treats non-state actors (NSAs), a broad category that can only be discovered by moving beyond the idolatry of the state found within the traditional positivist state-centric analysis of public international law.[27] The primary question that will be explored is whether Indigenous peoples, as NSAs, could or should "aspire" to similar international legal personality as that of transnational corporations (TNCs).[28] Specifically, how might better understanding of degrees of international legal personality inform strategies for Indigenous peoples seeking "appropriate remedy" for violations of historic treaties when mining is proposed on historic Indigenous lands? How might this understanding inform strategies for the negotiation of modern treaties with governments, and the negotiation of agreements with resource extraction companies?

---

25 United Nations Declaration on the Rights of Indigenous Peoples, UNGA Res 61/295 (13 September 2007) [UNDRIP]. See further below.

26 See, for example, Government of Canada, "The Atlas of Canada – Indigenous Mining Agreements," http://atlas.gc.ca/imaema/en/. See also Natasha Affolder, "Rethinking Environmental Contracting" (2010) 12 *Journal of Environmental Law and Practice* 155; Brad Gilmour and Bruce Mellett, "The Role of Impact and Benefit Agreements in the Resolution of Project Issues with First Nations" (2013) 51:2 *Alberta Law Review* 385.

27 See generally the work of the International Law Association, "Non-State Actors" at http://www.ila-hq.org/en/committees/index.cfm/cid/1023; Math Noortmann and Cedric Ryngaert, eds., *Non-State Actor Dynamics in International Law: From Law-Takers to Law-Makers* (Farnham, UK: Ashgate, 2010); Jean d'Aspremont, ed., *Participants in the International Legal System: Multiple Perspectives on Non-State Actors in International Law* (New York: Routledge, 2011).

28 Janne Elisabeth Nijman, *The Concept of International Legal Personality: An Inquiry Into the History and Theory of International Law* (The Hague, NL: T.M.C. Asser Press, 2004).

2. Canada, Indigenous Peoples, and Resource Extraction

Canada is a nation that prides itself as a leader in natural resource extraction. As a leader, Canada believes that it has much to teach the world about how to "do it right," including, in particular, mining on Indigenous lands. Canada has played a lead role in international sustainable mineral development initiatives, including the intergovernmental Forum (IGF) on Mining, Minerals, Metals and Sustainable Development.[29] IGF's "Mining Policy Framework" identifies the need to make "consultation with affected stakeholders a requirement of the permitting process and at every stage of the mining cycle"[30] and highlights the "importance of respecting human rights, indigenous peoples, and cultural heritage" by "[e]nsuring that domestic policies and law are (at a minimum) consistent with international law and norms."[31]

Indeed, Canadian laws do increasingly include requirements that Aboriginal peoples be consulted at the early stages of resource development, including exploration, on historic Indigenous lands.[32] These

---

29 "Introduction," Intergovernmental Forum on Mining, Minerals, Metals and Sustainable Development (IGF), http://globaldialogue.info/wn_e.htm. The IGF was launched by Canada and South Africa as the Global Dialogue on Mining/Metals and Sustainable Development at the 2002 World Summit on Sustainable Development in Johannesburg.

30 Intergovernmental Forum on Mining, Minerals, Metals and Sustainable Development, *A Mining Policy Framework: Mining and Sustainable Development* (revised October 2013) at 30, http://globaldialogue.info/MPFOct2013.pdf.

31 *Ibid* at 34. In order to manage "in a progressive manner" issues that fall "under the general rhetoric of human rights" such as "land acquisition and involuntary resettlement, indigenous peoples, cultural heritage and labour and working conditions" reference should be made to a number of instruments in order to develop "policies and laws or, more expediently, by governments insisting that individual instruments be applied, in whole or in part, by entities within their jurisdiction" (*ibid* at 35). These instruments include: UNDRIP, *supra* note 25; Convention Concerning Indigenous and Tribal Peoples in Independent Countries (ILO No 169), 28 ILM 1382 (1989); Universal Declaration of Human Rights, (1948) GA Res 217A(III), UN Doc A/810 (1948); UNESCO Convention Concerning the Protection of the World Cultural and Natural Heritage (1972, in force 1975); as well as international CSR standards discussed below, and related regional instruments.

32 See for example Penelope Simons and Lynda Collins, "Participatory Rights in the Ontario Mining Sector: An International Human Rights Perspective" (2010) 6:2 *McGill International Journal of Sustainable Development Law and Policy* 177.

legislated requirements are not evidence of Canadian benevolence when it comes to relationships with Aboriginal peoples, however, but rather are evidence of legislatures responding to Canadian court decisions that respond to the constitutional recognition given to the pre-existing rights of Aboriginal peoples in Canada in section 35 of the *Constitution Act, 1982*.[33] Perhaps as a result of this constitutional protection within Canadian law, it is easier to make a case that the path to dispute resolution should, for pragmatic reasons, be one-way through Canadian courts. However, these decisions are open to criticism, including the argument that they have "frozen" Aboriginal rights in time.[34] Moreover, at least until very recently, neither the Canadian government nor Canadian courts have explicitly endorsed the increasingly accepted international legal understanding that Indigenous peoples have rights to free, prior, and informed consent, rather than merely consultation.[35]

The existence of legislative consultation requirements embedded within domestic law is complemented by the increasing prevalence of domestic and international corporate social responsibility (CSR) standards that highlight the importance of consulting Indigenous peoples, if not obtaining their consent, in the natural resource extraction context. These standards, whether originating from initiatives of industry,[36]

---

33 *Constitution Act, 1982*, s. 35(1)–(3), being Schedule B to the *Canada Act 1982* (UK), 1982, c 11.

34 John Borrows, "Frozen Rights in Canada: Constitutional Interpretation and the Trickster," chap. 3 and "Nanabush Goes West: Title, Treaties and the Trickster in British Columbia," chap. 4 in *Recovering Canada: The Resurgence of Indigenous Law* (Toronto: University of Toronto Press, 2002).

35 See generally Shin Imai, "Consult, Consent and Veto: International Norms and Canadian Treaties" (research paper, Osgoode Legal Studies Research Paper Series, Osgoode Hall Law School, York University, Toronto, 2016) at 5, noting the Canadian government's initial vote against UNDRIP in 2007, and its explicit rejection of the consent standard at the World Conference on Indigenous Peoples in 2014; and at 15–17, observing the "Crown-centric" approach taken by the Supreme Court of Canada in 2014 that "requires consultation and accommodation, but allows the Crown to justify any taking up of lands except for a protected sphere of destructive activity that cannot be authorized either by the Crown or by the Indigenous people." In May 2016, the federal government officially removed its objector status to UNDRIP.

36 International Council on Mining and Metals (ICMM), *Sustainable Development Framework* (2003), http://www.icmm.com/our-work/sustainable-development-framework, and related position statements, including ICMM, *Indigenous Peoples and Mining, Position Statement* (May 2013), http://www.icmm.com/publications/pdfs/5433.pdf; Prospectors and Developers Association of Canada, *e3 Plus: A Framework for Responsible Exploration*, http://www.pdac.ca/programs/e3-plus.

multi-stakeholders,[37] or international institutions,[38] highlight the essential importance for companies of seeking their "social license to operate" in order to successfully develop mining projects.[39] These standards are informed by developments relating to Indigenous rights under international human rights law including the United Nations Declaration on the Rights of Indigenous Peoples (UNDRIP).[40] Despite positivist international legal analysis that contests the status of UNDRIP as "hard" law that is binding upon all states, the increasing recognition of Indigenous rights under international law is impossible to understate.[41] This recognition permeates international CSR standards, informing the development of implementation guidance tools for business[42] that are increasingly recommended by governments.[43]

37 Voluntary Principles on Security and Human Rights, "Voluntary Principles on Security and Human Rights," http://www.voluntaryprinciples.org/files/voluntary_principles_english.pdf; Global Reporting Initiative, *Sustainability Reporting Guidelines & Mining and Metals Sector Supplement*, Version 3.0 MMSS at 37–8, https://www.globalreporting.org/resourcelibrary/MMSS-Complete.pdf.

38 International Finance Corporation, World Bank Group, "Performance Standards on Environmental and Social *Sustainability* (1 January 2012), especially Performance Standard 7, "Indigenous Peoples," http://www1.ifc.org/wps/wcm/connect/115482804a0255db96fbffd1a5d13d27/PS_English_2012_Full-Document.pdf?MOD=AJPERES; Organisation for Economic Co-operation and Development (OECD), "OECD Guidelines for Multinational Enterprises" (Paris: OECD Publishing, 2011) at 31–4, http://www.oecd-ilibrary.org/governance/oecd-guidelines-for-multinational-enterprises_9789264115415-en.

39 First Peoples Worldwide, "Indigenous Rights Risk Report for the Extractive Industry (U.S.): Preliminary Findings" (28 October 2013), http://www.firstpeoples.org/images/uploads/R1K%20Report(2).pdf; James Anaya, *Report of the Special Rapporteur on the Rights of Indigenous Peoples*, UNHRC 21st Sess, UN Doc A/HRC/21/47 (6 July 2012) at para 72.

40 Charters, "Reparations for Indigenous Peoples," *supra* note 16; Charters, "Indigenous Peoples and International Law and Policy," *supra* note 15; Gilbert, *supra* note 23.

41 Stephen Allen and Alexandra Xanthaki, eds., *Reflections on the UN Declaration on the Rights of Indigenous Peoples* (Portland, OR: Hart Publishing, 2011).

42 See, for example, United Nations Global Compact, *A Business Reference Guide: United Nations Declaration on the Rights of Indigenous Peoples* (December 2013), https://www.unglobalcompact.org/docs/issues_doc/human_rights/IndigenousPeoples/BusinessGuide.pdf.

43 Mining Policy Framework, *supra* note 30; see also Sara L. Seck, "Canadian Mining Internationally and the UN Guiding Principles for Business and Human Rights" (2011) 49 *Canadian Yearbook of International Law* 51 at 75–85, which describes Canada's CSR strategy and CSR counsellor mechanism for the extractive industries

This combination of forces has contributed to a proliferation of Aboriginal community/mining company agreements concerning resource extraction in Canada and beyond.[44] This recent phenomena is evident in the multitude of agreements now documented throughout Canada, including impact benefit agreements, socio-economic agreements, memoranda of understanding, cooperation agreements, exploration agreements,[45] and environmental agreements.[46] However, the content of most of these agreements is secret.[47] More importantly for the purpose of this chapter, what exactly are these agreements? Are they purely domestic contracts between private parties? Or is it useful to consider whether they might (also or instead) be understood as having a certain status under international law?

3. Non-State Actors and International Law

If one were to ask a mining lawyer or a Canadian government official about the status of these agreements, it would be reasonable to speculate that they would be viewed as domestic private contracts.[48] This is because the exclusive domain of international law from a positivist viewpoint is as a system of rules made by and for states. Therefore, the argument would be that, if community/company agreements are entered into, it is either because domestic law requires such an agreement,

---

operating internationally. See also Government of Canada, "Doing Business the Canadian Way: A Strategy to Advance Corporate Social Responsibility in Canada's Extractive Sector Abroad" (November 2014), : http://www.international.gc.ca/trade-agreements-accords-commerciaux/assets/pdfs/Enhanced_CS_Strategy_ENG.pdf.

44 Governments may be party to these agreements, but often are not. On the difference in Canada between impact benefit agreements in the mining context (where they may be legislatively required) and the energy context (where they are not), see Gilmour and Mellett, "The Role of Impact," *supra* note 26 at 387.

45 Government of Canada, "The Atlas of Canada," *supra* note 26.

46 Affolder, "Rethinking Environmental Contracting," *supra* note 26.

47 Gilmour and Mellett, "The Role of Impact," *supra* note 26 at paras 53–8; see also Courthey Fidler and Michael Hitch, "Impact and Benefit Agreements: A Contentious Issue for Environmental and Aboriginal Justice" (2007) 35:2 *Environments Journal* 49, at http://www.impactandbenefit.com/kr/One.aspx?objectId=10486948&contextId=677979&lastCat=10486919.

48 See Affolder, "Rethinking Environmental Contracting," *supra* note 26 at 159 for a description of the perspective of Indian and Northern Affairs Canada (INAC) on environmental agreements, as well as Gilmour and Mellett, *supra* note 26 at 385 (paras 7–9) for an industry lawyer perspective on impact benefit agreements.

or because, from a strategic business perspective, the mining process would run less smoothly without such agreements. An agreement is simply the price that must be paid for peaceful relations between communities and companies going forward.

The idea that international law might directly impose upon mining companies the requirement to consult and seek the consent of local Indigenous communities without going through the intermediary of the state, would be, for many, a fantasy. While international law might impose obligations upon states to consult and seek the consent of Indigenous peoples, a positivist state-centric view of international law could not conceive of such an obligation being placed upon a transnational corporation. According to this view, there is simply no alternative to seeing the agreements as purely domestic, being neither required by nor recognizable under international law, as would be a treaty or convention between states.[49] In this way, community/company agreements are distinct even from investment agreements between a transnational corporation and a state, where the status of the agreement from the perspective of international law is contested – if viewed as a mere contract, the international status of the (usually Third World) state is reduced to the level of a private actor, whereas if understood as an international agreement, the status of the private-actor transnational corporation is elevated to that of the state.[50]

Yet the reality is that the power of non-state actors, both transnational corporations and Indigenous peoples, is strong. The power today of TNCs is well recognized, with questions only arising as to whether, and if so, where, to draw the line between powerful economic actors and small-scale players that might similarly adopt the for-profit corporate form, but have far less power in both domestic and global circles. International human rights lawyers commonly complain that while TNCs have "rights" under international investment law, they do not have a corresponding set of international human rights law duties or responsibilities.[51] These rights include the right to sue host states and

49 United Nations, Vienna Convention on the Law of Treaties, 23 May 1969, 1155 UNTS 331, entered into force 17 January 1980, Article 2(a), Article 3.

50 See generally Anghie, *supra* note 12 at 231–6.

51 See generally Peter Muchlinski, "Multinational Enterprises as Actors in International Law: Creating 'Soft Law' Obligations and 'Hard Law' Rights" in Math Noortmann and Cedric Ryngaert, eds., *Non-State Actor Dynamics in International Law: From Law-Takers to Law-Makers* (Surrey, UK: Ashgate, 2010) at 9.

seek compensation for regulatory expropriation under investment treaties when local communities force state governments to pay attention to their Indigenous and/or environmental rights. Moreover, while the rights of TNCs as foreign investors are enforceable under binding international arbitration proceedings held behind closed doors and heard by investment law experts,[52] there is no equivalent mechanism to enforce TNC responsibilities under international human rights law, assuming for a moment that there is agreement that these responsibilities exist in a legally cognizable form.[53]

Despite this, it cannot be said that international law has nothing to say about TNC responsibilities; indeed recent developments suggest there is something that goes beyond the international CSR standards discussed above. In 2011, the United Nations Human Rights Council endorsed Guiding Principles on Business and Human Rights which provide that states have a duty to protect against human rights violations by businesses and to provide access to judicial and non-judicial remedy for victims.[54] In addition, businesses themselves have a "responsibility to respect" all human rights, as this is what society expects of businesses that seek to acquire and retain their social licence to operate.[55] To meet the responsibility to respect human rights, businesses must have a policy that addresses all human rights at risk of being impacted by business operations; engage in human rights due diligence to "know and show" human rights compliance;[56] and provide victims

52 See generally Kyla Tienhaara, *The Expropriation of Environmental Governance: Protecting Foreign Investors at the Expense of Public Policy* (Cambridge: Cambridge University Press, 2009); and Gus van Harten, *Investment Treaty Arbitration and Public Law* (Oxford: Oxford University Press, 2007).

53 Muchlinski, *supra* note 51 at 17–28.

54 John Ruggie, *Report of the Special Representative of the Secretary-General on the Issues of Human Rights and Transnational Corporations and Other Business Enterprises: Guiding Principles on Business and Human Rights: Implementing the United Nations "Protect, Respect and Remedy" Framework*, UNHRC, 17th Sess, UN Doc A/HRC/17/31 (2011). See especially Principles 1–10 and Principles 25–7.

55 *Ibid* at Principles 11–24; John Ruggie, *Report of the Special Representative of the Secretary-General on the Issues of Human Rights and Transnational Corporations and Other Business Enterprises: Protect, Respect and Remedy: A Framework for Business and Human Rights*, UNHRC 8th Sess, UN Doc A/HRC/8/5 (2008) at para 54 (linking responsibility to "social licence to operate").

56 Ruggie, *Guiding Principles*, *supra* note 54, principles 16–21.

with access to remedy if business actions have harmed them, including through the implementation of company-level grievance mechanisms.[57] Importantly, the corporate responsibility to respect applies whether or not host states are in compliance with their own duty to protect human rights. The responsibility also extends to relationships with contractors and supply chains, although the need to provide a remedy in cases of harm does not extend so far.[58] While the Guiding Principles are frequently described as a "polycentric governance" framework,[59] and the responsibility to respect is not clearly stated as rooted in existing international law (unlike the state duty to protect),[60] the Guiding Principles nevertheless suggest that the business responsibility to respect is to be treated as a "legal compliance issue."[61]

Importantly, businesses did not stand by in the wings while state members of the UN Human Rights Council debated whether or not to accord them responsibilities. Rather, the process that led to the creation of the UN's Guiding Principles was an explicitly multi-stakeholder process in which (at least large) businesses were very much present, through individual participation, industry associations, and the participation of corporate lawyers.[62] Thus, it can be said that while state endorsement of the Guiding Principles is an important measure for the purpose of a state-centric positivist international legal analysis, it is equally crucial to note that (many? some?) businesses themselves embraced the process and the outcome of the Guiding Principles.[63]

---

57 *Ibid*, principles 22 and 29.

58 *Ibid*, principles 19 and 22.

59 Larry Cata Backer, "On the Evolution of the United Nations' 'Protect-Respect-Remedy' Project: The State, the Corporation and Human Rights in a Global Governance Context" (2011) 9 *Santa Clara Journal of International Law* 37.

60 Ruggie, *Guiding Principles, supra* note 54, general principles, principle 1, and principle 11: "The responsibility to expect is a global standard of expected conduct for all businesses wherever they operate."

61 *Ibid*, principle 23 (c): "In all contexts, business enterprises should: (c) Treat the risk of causing or contributing to gross human rights abuses as a legal compliance issue wherever they operate."

62 Sara L. Seck, "Corporate Law Tools and the Guiding Principles for Business and Human Rights" in Manoj Kumar Sinha, ed., *Business and Human Rights* (Thousand Oaks, CA: Sage, 2013) at 93.

63 Whether many TNCs in fact embrace implementation of the UN Guiding Principles remains to be seen, although implementation must also take into account the extent to which the UN Guiding Principles have influenced the content of other

While the exact nature of the business responsibility to respect human rights under international law is contested by scholars,[64] international lawyers who move beyond the narrow confines of the land of state-centric legal positivism claim that other non-state actors, beyond transnational corporations, may also at times exhibit elements of international legal personality that merit attention. For example, the Committee on Non-State Actors of the International Law Association (ILA) has suggested that there are five categories of NSAs that are of interest to international lawyers. These are TNCs; non-government organizations; *sui generis* entities like the International Committee of the Red Cross and the Holy See; certain organized armed opposition groups; and organized Indigenous peoples' groups.[65] ILA committee reports have to date examined the various methods by which NSAs contribute to the making of international law, whether directly or as participants,[66] as well as the obligations and responsibilities of NSAs under international law.[67]

Yet the ILA committee appears to have been challenged by the inclusion of Indigenous peoples on this list, with significantly more materials being developed in relation to several other NSAs, and Indigenous peoples essentially dropping out of the committee work as it has progressed.[68] Thus, while the 2010 and 2012 reports specifically

---

international standards, including those referenced above, which have been updated since the UN Guiding Principles to reflect their content. Seck, "Canadian Mining," *supra* note 43 at 104–5.

64 See generally Surya Deva and David Bilchitz, eds., *Human Rights Obligations of Business: Beyond the Corporate Responsibility to Respect?* (Cambridge: Cambridge University Press, 2013).

65 First Report of the ILA Committee, "Non-State Actors in International Law: Aims, Approach and Scope of Project and Legal Issues" (The Hague Conference, 2010) at "2. Working Definitions *a. 'Non-State Actor,'*" http://www.ila-hq.org/download.cfm/docid/7EFF9EAA-D573-441E-A40C8D2FB7740C6A.

66 Second Report of the ILA Committee, "Non-State Actors in International Law: Lawmaking and Participation Rights" (Sofia Conference, 2012), http://www.ila-hq.org/download.cfm/docid/E1B513C8-FCFF-4F8D-8C047815E1FDF8AE.

67 Third Report of the ILA Committee, "Non-State Actors" (Washington Conference, 2014), http://www.ila-hq.org/download.cfm/docid/9B5612DF-6DEF-4AFD-BB8A408EAB402DBE.

68 At least, this is the author's impression, having participated in the Vancouver conference on responsibility of NSAs in June 2013, and in light of the 2014 report. Joint International Conference of the Kwantlen Institute for Transborder Studies (ITS) and Political Science Department; the Non-State Actor Committee of

identify Indigenous peoples as one of the five NSA categories to be examined, by the 2014 report, Indigenous peoples are mentioned only once in order to note that they are included within a wide definition of "Non-Governmental Organizations"[69] that comprise one of three actors discussed in the report, "Armed Opposition Groups" and "Corporations" being the other two.[70]

The example of the ILA committee experience may be explained by a number of possible factors. First, there appears to have been a sense that while Indigenous peoples clearly have a claim to *rights*, they are too disempowered for it to make any sense for international law to place *obligations* upon them.[71] Another factor may be related to the problem of fragmentation in international law, as increasing specialization in discrete areas of international law leads to inconsistency overall.[72] Fragmentation also contributes to a practical capacity challenge for those with relevant expertise.[73] The ILA, for example, has recently established another committee on the "Implementation of the Rights

---

the International Law Association, International Law Association – Canada; the Leuven Centre for Global Governance Studies; and the Flemish Fund for Scientific Research Belgium, "Non-State Actor Responsibilities: Empirical Findings and Theoretical Considerations," Vancouver, 26–8 June 2013. See Vancouver conference program, http://www.ila-hq.org/download.cfm/docid/13993DD6-6941-45CA-BC14374504EECB0D.

69 ILA NSA Committee 2014 Report, *supra* note 67 at "3. Non-Governmental Organizations." The report states: "This report adopts a rather broad understanding of NGO as, for the sake of this discussion, it includes a wide range of interest groups, including business and industry groups and organized indigenous peoples' groups. The huge number of such entities active in the international realm makes it an important category for examination albeit their diversity makes it difficult to draw general conclusions."

70 *Ibid.*

71 This is my impression from a casual conversation with some ILA committee members at a conference held to contribute to the work of the committee.

72 Martti Koskenniemi and Päivi Leino, "Fragmentation of International Law? Postmodern Anxieties" (2002) 15 *Leiden Journal of International Law* 553; International Law Commission, *Fragmentation of International Law: Difficulties Arising from the Diversification and Expansion of International Law*, Int'l Law Comm'n, UN Doc. A/CN.4/L.682 (13 April 2006), as corrected UN Doc. A/CN.4/L.682/Corr.1 (11 August 2006) (by Martti Koskenniemi).

73 See also Math Noortmann, "The International Law Association and Non-State Actors: Professional Network, Public Interest Group, or Epistemic Community?" in Aspremont, *supra* note 27, 233 at 242.

of Indigenous Peoples."[74] Beyond the ILA, there are a multitude of arguably much more important opportunities for Aboriginal peoples to contribute to the development of international law relating specifically to Indigenous peoples.[75]

Yet, arguably, the consequence of this has troubling implications for how one views Aboriginal/mining company agreements, as well as for the interpretation of the historic treaties, with which this chapter began, and the negotiation of new treaties. TNCs, through participation in international legal processes including those leading to the formation of the UN guiding principles discussed above, appear to be proactively contributing to the *strengthening* of the international legal personality of businesses under international law. If Indigenous peoples are not similarly present – that is, if they participate only to declare their rights, but not to embrace responsibilities, even in a soft law or polycentric governance form – does this diminish the nature of the international legal personality of Indigenous peoples? If so, does or should this matter to First Nations in Canada?

To answer these questions, it is necessary to first turn to alternatives to positivist state-centric international law for insights.

4. Third and Fourth World Approaches to International Law

Indigenous peoples have clearly embraced participation in the international legal process. Indeed, the very existence and recognition of the identity of Indigenous peoples under international law, culminating in UNDRIP, is the result of global Indigenous peoples movements within the UN system.[76] While initial attempts by Indigenous peoples to seek recognition under international law in international institutions were unsuccessful,[77] international law "has developed and continues to

74 International Law Association, Committees, "Implementation of the Rights of Indigenous Peoples," http://www.ila-hq.org/en/committees/index.cfm/cid/1048.

75 See generally Lillian Aponte Miranda, "Indigenous Peoples as International Lawmakers" (2010) 32 *University of Pennsylvania Journal of International Law* 210.

76 *Ibid.*

77 Ronald Niezen, *The Origins of Indigenism: Human Rights and the Politics of Identity* (Berkeley: University of California Press, 2003) at 31–6, describing the unsuccessful attempt by Levi General Deskaheh, Chief of the Younger Bear Clan of the Cayuga Nation and spokesman of the Six Nations of the Grand River land near Brantford, Ontario, to seek a hearing at the League of Nations in the 1920s over a dispute

develop, however imperfectly, to support indigenous peoples' demands."[78] This has been the direct result of the participation of Indigenous peoples in various transnational networks and movements where knowledge has been generated and consensus reached over relevant international norms. It is also due to Indigenous peoples' participation in formal institutions and institutionalized advocacy before international and regional human rights bodies and mechanisms, further contributing to the development of relevant norms.[79]

Yet, despite this, neither historic nor contemporary treaties between Indigenous peoples and the Crown appear in the UN treaty database, nor can disputes between Indigenous peoples or between Indigenous peoples and the state be brought before the International Court of Justice. Indigenous peoples are not now nor have they ever been considered under international law as equivalent to nation states. Historically, international law conceptualized Indigenous peoples as the "uncivilized other" rather than as nations equal to the European sovereign states. Indigenous peoples were not alone in this classification, as is evident in the history of colonialism of the Third World. Because the experience of Indigenous peoples as peoples of the Fourth World bears some similarity to those of the Third World, it is useful at this point to turn to the work of scholars who adopt Third World Approaches to International Law (TWAIL).[80]

While it is beyond the scope of this chapter to offer a detailed overview of the work of TWAIL scholars,[81] a key theme of TWAIL is the

---

with Canada over self-government. See also Amar Bhatia, "The South of the North: Building on Critical Approaches to International Law with Lessons from the Fourth World" (2012) 14 *Oregon Review of International Law* 131 at 159–71.

78 Anaya, *Indigenous Peoples in International Law*, *supra* note 11 at 5.

79 Miranda, *supra* note 76 at 228, 229–52. It is beyond the scope of this paper to describe the extent of networks, movements, and institutions that have included Indigenous peoples' participation. See generally S. James Anaya, *International Human Rights and Indigenous Peoples* (New York: Aspen Publishers, 2009); Charters, *supra* notes 15 and 14.

80 On Indigenous peoples as the Fourth World, see Bhatia, *supra* note 77.

81 Obiora Okafor, "Critical Third World Approaches to International Law (TWAIL): Theory, Methodology, or Both?" (2008) 10 *International Community Law Review* 371; Makau Mutua, "What is TWAIL?" (2000) 94 *American Society of International Law Proceedings* 31; Sara L. Seck, "Transnational Business and Environmental Harm: A TWAIL Analysis of Home State Obligations" (2011) 3:1 *Trade, Law and Development* 173.

recognition that sovereign equality, a cornerstone of international law, has never been a true sovereign equality for Third World states who had to give up their economic sovereignty to international institutions like the World Bank and International Monetary Fund.[82] Sovereignty, the reward for emerging from the colonial period as a newly recognized state, was thus a bitter pill to swallow as statehood meant embracing the developmental state. In this way, the state became the enforcer that dispossessed local communities of land and livelihood in the interest of large-scale development and nation-state-building.[83] Accordingly, colonialism and imperialism are not only part of the early history of international law, but rather, neocolonialism remains embedded within contemporary international law as well.

For the purpose of this chapter, Balakrishnan Rajagopal's book *International Law from Below: Development, Social Movements and Third World Resistance* is particularly noteworthy.[84] Rajagopal challenges international lawyers to learn to "write resistance" into international law by paying attention to the power of the voices of those traditionally viewed as having no power, including the subaltern and social movements. Among other insights from Rajagopal is that the institutions of the World Bank, key international institutions of the global economic agenda, were designed with a "purely" economic purpose, not as institutions preoccupied with "good governance" and "democracy-building" or "sustainability" as they currently appear to be. Instead, the World Bank adopted a sustainable development agenda after being *forced to respond* to the resistance of social movements.[85] This may be described as a "counter-hegemonic" manoeuvre, for integration of some of the concerns of those engaging in resistance dilutes the power of the resistance, without deviating from the key economic purposes and

82 Anghie, *supra* note 12 at 191–2, 198, 207–8.

83 *Ibid* at 205–7.

84 Balakrishnan Rajagopal, *International Law from Below: Development, Social Movements, and Third World Resistance* (Cambridge: Cambridge University Press, 2003).

85 *Ibid* at 49. See also Balarishnan Rajagopal, "From Modernization to Democratization: The Political Economy of the 'New' International Law" in Richard Falk, Lester Edwin J. Ruiz, and R.B.J. Walker, eds., *Reframing the International: Law, Culture, Politics* (New York: Routledge, 2002) 136 at 149–51.

structures of the institution.[86] So, for example, the International Finance Corporation (IFC)'s Sustainability Performance Standards came into existence as a result of the need to respond to the power of resistance movements opposing private sector development projects imposed by the developmental state and supported by the IFC, but which lacked the participation or consent of local communities.

Similarly, the emergence of international corporate social responsibility standards beyond the requirements of state law may also be said to be the result of international institutions, including those that are examples of transnational private law,[87] responding to the resistance of social movements and subaltern groups, such as Indigenous peoples. If these insights are applied to the development of the UN Guiding Principles on Business and Human Rights, it may be said that the embracing by business of human rights responsibilities in a soft polycentric governance form can be interpreted as a sign of the *success* of the disempowered whose rights have been violated, for it is as a result of their resistance that business' embrace of human rights language has emerged. This dynamic is evident at the new United Nations Annual Forum on Business and Human Rights, with Indigenous peoples increasingly participating as rights-holders claiming violations against businesses, especially extractive companies.[88]

The implications of this embrace are evident in the extractive industries context. Recent reports to the UN Human Rights Council clearly express that the responsibility to consult – if not seek the consent of – Indigenous peoples when resource extraction is proposed on

86 Rajagopal, *International Law from Below*, *supra* note 84 at 161, 133–4; Rajagopal, "Political Economy," *supra* note 85 at 155. See also Balakrishnan Rajagopal, "Counter-Hegemonic International Law: Rethinking Human Rights and Development as a Third World Strategy" (2006) 27 *Third World Quarterly* 767.

87 On transnational private law, see generally Gralf-Peter Calliess and Peer Zumbansen, *Rough Consensus and Running Code: A Theory of Transnational Private Law* (Oxford: Hart Publishing, 2010).

88 See program of the 2014 United Nations Forum on Business and Human Rights, "Advancing Business and Human Rights Globally: Alignment, Adherence, and Accountability," Geneva, 13 December 2014, http://www.ohchr.org/Documents/Issues/Business/ForumSession3/Programme.pdf.

Indigenous lands rests with both states and corporate actors.[89] For example, according to James Anaya, the former Special Rapporteur on the Rights of Indigenous Peoples, the "Guiding Principles for Business and Human Rights specify that business enterprises have a responsibility to respect human rights and this responsibility is independent of State obligations."[90] Moreover, this responsibility "extends to compliance with international standards concerning the rights of indigenous peoples, in particular those set forth in the [UNDRIP]."[91] Consequently, business enterprises "should perform due diligence to ensure that their actions will not violate or be complicit in violating indigenous peoples' rights, identifying and assessing any actual or potential adverse human rights impacts of a resource extraction project."[92] Moreover, Anaya clearly affirms that Indigenous "individuals and peoples have the right to oppose and actively express opposition to extractive projects promoted by the State or third party business interests" and "indigenous peoples should be able to oppose or withhold consent to extractive projects free from reprisals or acts of violence, or from undue pressure to accept or enter into consultations about extractive projects."[93]

Yet the Anaya report also clearly states that the best way to move forward in the extractive industries context is for Aboriginal peoples themselves to play the lead role in mining development.[94] According to Anaya, the right of Indigenous peoples to self-determination "necessarily implies a right of indigenous peoples to pursue their own initiatives for resource extraction within their own territories if they so choose" and this applies "even where the State claims ownership of subsurface

89 James Anaya, *Report of the Special Rapporteur on the Rights of Indigenous Peoples: Extractive Industries and Indigenous Peoples*, UNHRC 24th Sess, UN Doc A/HRC/21/41 (1 July 2013); Margaret Sekaggya, *Note by the Secretary-General: Report of the Special Rapporteur on the Situation of Human Rights Defenders*, UNGA 68th Sess, UN Doc A/68/262 (5 August 2013); *Report of the Working Group on the Issue of Human Rights and Transnational Corporations and Other Business Enterprises*, UNHRC, UN Doc A/HRC/68/279 (6 August 2013).

90 Anaya, 2013 *Report*, *supra* note 89 at para 52; Anaya, 2012 *Report*, *supra* note 39 at paras 55–6.

91 Anaya, 2013 *Report*, *supra* note 89 at para 52.

92 *Ibid* at para 53, paras 54–7, para 89.

93 *Ibid* at para 83.

94 *Ibid* at paras 8–17.

or other resources under domestic law."[95] Notably, Anaya explicitly recognizes that "even resource extraction by indigenous peoples' own enterprises may pose certain risks to the enjoyment of human rights of members of indigenous communities, particularly in relation to the natural environment."[96]

5. Implications and Conclusions

Ultimately, then, what does this analysis have to offer for Aboriginal peoples in Canada and, in particular, for their need to seek appropriate remedies for the implementation of historic treaties and the negotiation of new treaties? First, it is clear that when it comes to resource extraction on lands subject to historic treaties or unresolved land claims, mining companies have a responsibility to consult Aboriginal peoples and seek their consent, irrespective of whether or not the Canadian state is in compliance with its own duties. As the Canadian state can act through executive, legislative, and judicial organs, the assessment of Canada's compliance with its duties must include consideration of judicial decisions emanating from Canadian courts.[97]

Second, and as established above, it is important for the analysis not only to highlight the nature of the responsibilities owed to Aboriginal peoples by NSAs like business enterprises, but also to recognize that it is in part due to the power and effectiveness of resistance by Aboriginal peoples that these corporate responsibilities have been embraced.

95 *Ibid* at para 9. Anaya notes that Indigenous peoples may at the same time "under their own customs or laws" "lay claim to all the resources, including subsurface resources, within their territories" (*ibid* at para 16).

96 *Ibid* at para 11. However, Anaya suggests that "these risks may be minimized, and the enjoyment of self-determination and related rights enhanced, when indigenous peoples freely choose to develop their own resources extraction enterprises backed by adequate capacity and internal governance institutions" (*ibid* at para 11). States, accordingly, "should have programmes in place to assist indigenous peoples to develop the capacity and means to pursue, if they so choose, their own initiatives for natural resource management and development, including extraction" (*ibid* at 12–17).

97 International Law Commission, *Draft Articles on Responsibility of States for Internationally Wrongful Acts*, in Report of the International Law Commission to the General Assembly, 56 UNGAOR, Supp No 10, UN Doc A/56/10 (2001), Article 4; Sara L. Seck, "Conceptualizing the Home State Duty to Protect Human Rights" in Karin Buhman, Mette Morsing, and Lynn Roseberry, eds., *Corporate Social and Human Rights Responsibilities: Global Legal and Management Perspectives* (New York: Palgrave Macmillan, 2010) 25 at 45–6.

Clearly, then, those who are stereotypically categorized as powerless do indeed have power, even if it can also be said that the business embrace is imperfect and the balance of power clearly rests with companies and the state. Still, this recognition leads to a different but important question: Might Aboriginal peoples wish to choose to embrace *responsibilities* under international law as Indigenous peoples, thereby enhancing their own international legal personality? This question is posed with an awareness of its implicit irony, given the state-centric history of international law and the historic position of settler states like Canada on the norm of free, prior, and informed consent.[98] It is therefore important to understand this project either as a proposal to consider "*use* of the language of the other in effectively communicating one's own concepts,"[99] or, alternately, as a proposal to express one's own concepts in one's own language: an Indigenous language that is simultaneously Indigenous international law.

There are several situations in which Indigenous peoples might choose such an embrace. First, due to pressure from both internal community members and external stakeholders, including governments, it may be that some Aboriginal peoples will decide to embrace the emerging international norm of resource payment transparency[100] and publicly disclose payments made to them by mining companies in impact benefit agreements or through similar arrangements.[101] While

98 H. Patrick Glenn, "The Three Ironies of the UN Declaration on the Rights of Indigenous Peoples" in Stephen Allen and Alexandra Xanthaki, eds., *Reflections on the UN Declaration on the Rights of Indigenous Peoples* (Oxford: Hart Publishing, 2011) at 171–82.

99 *Ibid* at 177, referring to the work of James Tully. See for example James Tully, *Strange Multiplicity: Constitutionalism in an Age of Diversity* (Cambridge: Cambridge University Press, 1995).

100 See, for example, the Extractive Industries Transparency Initiative (EITI), https://eiti.org/; Natural Resource Governance Institute, http://www.resourcegovernance.org/.

101 Since the writing of this chapter, legislation has been passed that will require resource companies to disclose payments made to Aboriginal governments, with relevant provisions coming into force in June 2017. See *Extractive Sector Transparency Measures Act*, SC 2014, c 39, s 376 (in force 1 June 2015) at s 29. Resource Revenue Transparency Working Group, "Recommendations on Mandatory Disclosure of Payments from Canadian Mining Companies to Governments" (16 January 2014), http://www.resourcegovernance.org/sites/default/files/working_group_transparency_recommendations_eng20140116.pdf.

some Aboriginal peoples may choose to resist this pressure, embracing such a responsibility under international law could reinforce the status of an Indigenous people as a sovereign power exercising its right to self-determination and, as such, exercising its sovereignty over natural resource extraction in the public interest of the nation, even if it is not a nation state.[102] This would be particularly appropriate if such a norm could be found pre-existing within the applicable Indigenous law. Curiously, though, those who have embraced – or been obliged to embrace – this responsibility have tended to be states of the Third World,[103] or business enterprises of the First World and Third.[104] Nation states of the First World have for the most part not, or at least not yet, chosen to sign up as disclosing countries.[105] This would, of course, be in keeping with the analysis earlier in this chapter highlighting the neocolonialist nature of international law and associated norms.

A second quite different example might be for Aboriginal peoples to choose to contribute to international law relating to ecological responsibilities in resource exploitation. As documented by John Borrows among others, the fact that many Indigenous peoples have a different understanding of property rights and responsibilities than those commonly said to underlie English common law property traditions has implications for environmental stewardship.[106] While Borrows argues convincingly on the need to incorporate these legal traditions as equal into legal decision-making in Canada when decisions are made that impact Aboriginal peoples who hold these beliefs,[107] it would be a mistake

---

102 See, for example, Articles 3 and 4 of UNDRIP, *supra* note 25. According to Article 4, "Indigenous peoples, in exercising their right to self-determination, have the right to autonomy or self-government in matters relating to their internal and local affairs, as well as ways and means for financing their autonomous functions."

103 See list of EITI compliant countries at https://eiti.org/countries. Norway is a clear exception.

104 See list of EITI companies at https://eiti.org/supporters/companies.

105 See list of EITI supporting countries at https://eiti.org/supporters/countries.

106 Borrows, *Canada's Indigenous Constitution*, *supra* note 2 at "Anishinabek Law and the Earth" at 244–8; See also Benjamin J. Richardson, "The Ties that Bind: Indigenous Peoples and Environmental Governance" in Benjamin J. Richardson, Shin Imai, and Kent McNeil, eds., *Indigenous Peoples and the Law: Comparative and Critical Perspectives* (Oxford: Hart Publishing, 2009) at 337; C.F. Black, *The Land Is the Source of the Law: A Dialogic Encounter with Indigenous Jurisprudence* (London: Routledge, 2011).

107 Borrows, *Canada's Indigenous Constitution*, *supra* note 2 at 248–70.

to assume that consequently non-Aboriginals are somehow "stuck" with ecologically destructive understandings of property and the environment from which they can never move away.[108] Indeed, there is an increasing amount of scholarly work and corresponding jurisprudential developments that suggest there is a more complex story to be told. A common theme of this work is the claim that Earth-relational and stewardship notions found commonly in Indigenous legal traditions are essential grounding for every society on planet Earth if we and future generations hope to continue to live together in the Anthropocene.[109] Moreover, many argue that these understandings are part of the history as well as the future of "settler" law. These concerns are increasingly reflected in international instruments as well as domestic constitutional developments that link environmental protection with human rights, along with explicit recognition of the rights of nature.[110]

The question for the purpose of this chapter is whether these developments suggest that there are emerging international norms relating to global and local environmental stewardship that could be embraced by Indigenous peoples as a responsibility, and thus reinforced for all, while simultaneously contributing to the strengthening of the international legal personality of Indigenous peoples, and reflecting Indigenous laws themselves. This is particularly important in the resource extraction context where pressure to exploit oil, gas, and mineral resources on Indigenous lands is intense. While as James Anaya notes, the potential for Indigenous peoples to play a leadership role in

---

108 D. Grinlinton and P.E. Taylor, eds., *Property Rights and Sustainability: The Evolution of Property Rights to Meet Ecological Challenges* (Netherlands: Martinus Nijhoff/Brill Publishers, 2011).

109 For a small sample of academic work, see Mary Christina Wood, *Nature's Trust: Environmental Law for a New Ecological Age* (New York: Cambridge University Press, 2014); Christina Voigt, ed., *Rule of Law for Nature: New Dimensions and Ideas in Environmental Law* (Cambridge: Cambridge University Press, 2013); Vandana Shiva, *Earth Democracy: Justice, Sustainability and Peace* (Cambridge, MA: South End Press, 2005); Jan G. Laitos, *The Right of Nonuse* (Oxford: Oxford University Press, 2012). On the Anthropocene, see http://www.anthropocene.info/en/home.

110 For a very small sample of work in this area, see David R. Boyd, *The Environmental Rights Revolution: A Global Study of Constitutions, Human Rights, and the Environment* (Vancouver: UBC Press, 2012); Donald K. Anton and Dinah L. Shelton, *Environmental Protection and Human Rights* (New York: Cambridge University Press, 2011); John H. Knox, *Report of the Independent Expert on the Issue of Human Rights Obligations Relating to the Enjoyment of a Safe, Clean, Healthy and Sustainable Environment*, UNHRC, 22d Sess, A/HRC/22/43 (24 December 2012).

mineral exploitation rather than taking a back seat is increasing, there are potential risks associated with these self-determination opportunities, risks to the human rights of community members and the natural environment. Moreover, as John Borrows worries in this volume, the danger in the Canadian context of First Nations' reliance on the section 35(1) framework against infringement by provinces hungry to develop natural resources is that even a victory in which First Nations receive profits and jobs is a failure if the result is destruction of "ancient food, social, and ceremonial sites."[111] Reinforcement of international norms obligating all nations and governments to embrace global and local environmental stewardship is crucial for the transformation of this destructive narrative of reconciliation and colonialism.

What might this mean in practice? Proactively, this could mean that endorsement by Indigenous peoples of international norms relating to transparency and environmental stewardship should feature prominently in the negotiation of new treaties with governments and agreements with resource extraction companies. Yet this is not enough. As Jean Leclair argues, drawing upon Lon L. Fuller, law is an "interactional phenomenon" that aims to provide "a program for living together."[112] Interpretation by Canadian courts of historic treaties and rights to consultation or consent should thus recognize the limits of adjudication by Canadian courts and recommend alternative processes that are better able to include Indigenous representatives in the process of law-making.[113] Among other benefits, this would facilitate respect for Indigenous laws embracing Earth-relational epistemologies,[114] and open the door to recognition of overlapping sovereignties and a re-imagining of the relationship between sovereignty, territory, and jurisdiction.[115]

---

111 John Borrows, "Canada's Colonial Constitution," chap. 1 in this volume.

112 Jean Leclair, "Nanabush, Lon Fuller, and Historical Treaties: The Potentialities and Limits of Adjudication," chap. 12 in this volume at 329.

113 *Ibid* at 342. See also Michael Coyle, "As Long as the Sun Shines: Recognizing That Treaties Were Intended to Last," chap. 2 in this volume (proposing the necessity of recognition of an institutional normative order).

114 See, for example, Aaron Mills, "What Is a Treaty? On Contract and Mutual Aid," chap. 8 in this volume (reframing the idea of "right relations" in secular language as "shared membership in a unified ecological order").

115 See, for example, Mark Walters, "Rights and Remedies within Common Law and Indigenous Legal Traditions: Can the Covenant Chain Be Judicially Enforced Today?" chap. 7 in this volume, at 195, noting that for the Indigenous peoples of

Indigenous peoples know only too well that local environments cannot be adequately protected by a single legal system in an ecologically interconnected world where caribou species at risk migrate outside protected areas, contaminants gravitate to polar regions and the breast milk of Inuit women, and traditional First Nation communities including the Anishinabek are divided by the imposed political borders of nation states. In such a world, the role of international law is inescapable. Despite its imperialist history, the emancipatory potential of international law should be embraced and enriched through Indigenous law.

---

the Great Lakes, "jurisdiction over homeland was not territorial in the European sense" but rather "territory was manifested through constant negotiation of good relations with the shifting normative domains that bound people to each other and to the world around them."

14 Consult, Consent, and Veto: International Norms and Canadian Treaties

SHIN IMAI[1]

This chapter outlines a path for Canadian courts to build on existing jurisprudence to provide a more robust recognition of the spirit and intent of historical treaties, particularly the "numbered treaties" signed between 1871 and 1929. At present, by focusing on the duty to "consult and accommodate," Canadian courts are lagging behind international and private industry standards as well as practice on the ground, all of which are moving towards the "free, prior, informed consent" standard.

In 2007, the United Nations Declaration on the Rights of Indigenous Peoples validated the necessity of obtaining free, prior, and informed consent before instituting significant extractive industry projects on Indigenous lands. The most surprising development since the declaration's adoption is the take-up of the standard by non-state private sector actors. International institutions such as the International Finance Corporation, the financial institutions that have adopted the Equator Principles, and the International Council on Mining and Metals have published policies accepting the necessity of obtaining free, prior, informed consent. In Canada, private sector actors have also recognized the consent standard, including the Prospectors and Developers Association of Canada and a grouping of industry, financial institutions, and First Nation organizations called the Boreal Leadership Council. Obviously, adopting some version of the consent standard makes practical and financial sense to the industry.

1 I would like to thank Sally Kang for research assistance and Kent McNeil and Jesse McCormick for making suggestions on the text.

The courts in Canada have dealt with extractive projects on traditional Indigenous land using a different framework. Rather than requiring consent, Canadian courts require that the Crown consult and accommodate the interests of Indigenous groups. Where treaty rights or Aboriginal rights are infringed, the courts require that the Crown justify the infringement through a test developed in *R v Sparrow*, which will be described in part two. Judges have said repeatedly that Indigenous groups in Canada do not have a "veto" over development.

In this chapter I will look at the international consent standard with a view to developing a conceptual framework for its adoption in interpreting the "numbered treaties." Eleven such treaties were signed between 1871 and 1929, and they cover a great deal of our country, spanning First Nation territories from Ontario to parts of British Columbia and north to the Northwest Territories. These treaties provide for the creation of small reserves for the Indians and the "surrender" of the remaining tracts of land to the Crown. The land that is "surrendered" continues to be available for Indigenous hunting, fishing, and harvesting activities. However, once the land is "taken up" by the provincial Crown for activities such as mining, lumbering, and settlement, the treaty rights to hunt, fish, and harvest are suppressed. I will argue that the provincial Crown does not have a unilateral right to "take up" lands; rather, the Crown should obtain the consent of the First Nations concerned before authorizing extractive activity on traditional territories.

In the argument that follows, I refer to documents created at the international level. However, I do not use these in the same way as my colleague Sara Seck. In her chapter, she places these instruments in a transnational governance context and looks at the treaties between First Nations and the Crown in the international sphere. By contrast, I am looking at how these international instruments can be used by courts in Canada to benchmark Crown and private company conduct in relation to the use of traditional Indigenous territory. My argument is not that the international instruments are binding or persuasive *qua* international law but rather that they are evidence of best practices in industry that should be incorporated into the development of the common law here. Sara Seck's approach and my approach are different but complementary.

1. Consent and the "Numbered Treaties"

The Crown entered into the numbered treaties with Indigenous peoples in order to ensure peace and goodwill with settlers who wished to enter the "tract of country" inhabited by the Indians. The treaties clearly state that the objective was "to obtain consent" of the Indians.[2] The necessary implication is that the Crown recognized that there was an Indigenous party to the treaty that could, through internal deliberations, decide to give – or withhold – consent. The three elements to the legal framework at the time, then, were that there was an Indigenous collectivity, that it had an interest in the land, and that consent of that collectivity was necessary in order for the Crown to access their territory.[3]

Unfortunately, as the treaties were being rolled out between 1871 and 1929, Canada entered into a century-long Dark Ages in its relations with Indigenous peoples. Through the policy of assimilation, legislation was drafted that legalized the theft of regalia, the destruction of totem poles, the forbidding of ceremonies, the taking of children to residential schools, and the appropriation of Indigenous lands. During this period, the legal framework for treaties and its foundation on consent were ignored. The prevailing attitude was articulated in 1929 by a judge in Nova Scotia who found that a 1752 treaty between the British and the Mi'kmaq was not enforceable:

> A civilized nation first discovering a country of uncivilized people or savages held such country as its own until such time as by treaty it was transferred to some other civilized nation. The savages' rights of sovereignty, even of ownership, were never recognized. Nova Scotia had passed to Great Britain not by gift or purchase from, or even by conquest of, the Indians but by treaty with France, which had acquired it by priority of discovery and ancient possession; and the Indians passed with it.[4]

So instead of Indigenous nations capable of making treaties, there was a new legal framework based on "savages" who were not capable of land ownership and therefore had nothing to give consent to. It is based on this legal framework that Prime Minister Pierre Trudeau released his

---

2 The James Bay Treaty – Treaty No. 9 (Made in 1905 and 1906) and Adhesions Made in 1929 and 1930 (1931; repr., Ottawa: Queen's Printer and Controller of Stationery, 1964), http://www.aadnc-aandc.gc.ca/eng/1100100028863/1100100028864#chp5.

3 I am not implying that the legal framework corresponded to the actual practice on the ground. For a general discussion of problems with treaty implementation, see Royal Commission on Aboriginal Peoples, *Looking Forward, Looking Back*, vol. 1 of the *Final Report of the Royal Commission on Aboriginal Peoples* (Ottawa: Supply and Services Canada, 1996) at 176–9.

4 *R v Syliboy*, [1929] 1 D.L.R. 307 (N.S. Co. Ct.).

White Paper on Indian Policy in 1969.[5] He proposed to convert reserves into private property and get rid of Indian status, thereby removing legal space for Indigenous collectivities and Indigenous lands.

2. Consultation, Accommodation, and Veto

A powerful blowback from First Nations against the White Paper policy, and a Supreme Court of Canada decision in 1973 that opened the possibility of Aboriginal title,[6] started to roll back this policy of legal annihilation. Judicial recognition of Indigenous peoples was propelled by the enactment of section 35(1) of the *Constitution Act, 1982*: "The existing aboriginal and treaty rights of the aboriginal peoples of Canada are hereby recognized and affirmed."[7]

In 1985 the Supreme Court of Canada said that Canada should honour the promises made by the Crown in the written versions of the treaties,[8] then went further in 1999 to reinterpret the written versions of a treaty to take into account Indigenous perspectives.[9] In 2005, the Supreme Court of Canada turned its attention to the interpretation of one of the most important clauses in the numbered treaties, and the clause that is central to the argument in this chapter:

> And Her Majesty the Queen HEREBY AGREES with the said Indians that they shall have right to pursue their usual vocations of hunting, trapping and fishing throughout the tract surrendered as heretofore described, subject to such regulations as may from time to time be made by the Government of the country, acting under the authority of Her Majesty, and saving and excepting such tracts as may be required or taken up from time to time for settlement, mining, lumbering, trading or other purposes.[10]

---

5 Minister of Indian Affairs and Northern Development, *Statement of the Government of Canada on Indian Policy (The White Paper,1969)* (Ottawa: Queen's Printer, 1969), http://www.aadnc-aandc.gc.ca/eng/1100100010189/1100100010191.

6 *Calder v British Columbia (Attorney General)*, [1973] SCR 313.

7 Part II of the *Constitution Act, 1982*, being Schedule B to the *Canada Act 1982* (U.K.), 1982 c. 11.

8 *R v Simon*, [1985] 2 SCR 387.

9 *R v Marshall*, [1999] 3 SCR 456.

10 Treaty No. 8 Made June 21, 1899 and Adhesions, Reports, Etc. (1899; repr., Ottawa: Queen's Printer and Controller of Stationery, 1966), http://www.aadnc-aandc.gc.ca/eng/1100100028813/1100100028853#chp4.

In *Mikisew Cree Nation v Canada (Minister of Canadian Heritage)*,[11] the Canadian government approved the construction of a winter road through the Wood Buffalo National Park, which would cross the trap lines of over a dozen families and would affect up to 100 Cree hunters. The First Nation argued that the road infringed its hunting and fishing rights under Treaty No. 8 and relied on the part of the clause that said that Indians could "pursue their usual vocations of hunting, trapping and fishing through the tract surrendered."

The Crown, on the other hand, relied on a different part of the same clause – the part that says that lands could be "taken up" for settlement, mining, lumbering, trading or other purposes. They argued that the text of the treaty did not say that the Crown needed to ask permission to take up the lands and did not put any limits on how much land could be taken up. Therefore, Indians had the right to hunt and fish only until the Crown exercised its unilateral right to take up the lands. The Court did not accept the Crown's interpretation of the clause. Rather, the Court incorporated Aboriginal understandings and found that the Crown did not have an unlimited, unilateral right to take up lands. This approach brought the Court to look at how the lands taken up clause would evolve over time, and divided the taking up of land into two stages. At the first stage, only consultation and accommodation would be required for taking up lands.[12] At the second stage, when so much land was taken up that "no meaningful right to hunt exists over its traditional territories,"[13] the Crown would have to do more than consult: it would have to justify its actions using the test developed in *R v Sparrow* in 1990.[14]

The "*Sparrow* test" came to be when Ronald Sparrow went fishing for food in an area traditionally used by his First Nation. He was charged under the federal *Fisheries Act* for using a net that was longer than that permitted by fisheries regulations. The Supreme Court of Canada found that the regulation could not be permitted to interfere with Sparrow's Aboriginal right to fish for food and ceremonial purposes. In the course of the decision, the Court set out the connection between Aboriginal rights and Crown regulation in a two-part test.

11 *Mikisew Cree Nation v Canada (Minister of Canadian Heritage)*, [2005] 3 SCR 388.

12 *Ibid*, para 55.

13 *Ibid*, para 48. See also, *Keewatin v Ontario (Natural Resources)*, 2014 SCC 48, para 52.

14 *R v Sparrow*, [1990] 1 SCR 1075.

First, if the Crown law infringed an existing Aboriginal right, the law would have to have a "compelling and substantial purpose." The example used in *Sparrow* for an appropriate law would be a regulation aimed at conservation of a resource used by the First Nation. Second, the Crown needed to act honourably and justify the infringement by consulting with the First Nation about the legislation, infringing the Aboriginal right as little as possible and, where appropriate, providing compensation. This "infringe-and-justify" framework has been applied in hundreds of cases at various levels of court that have addressed the duty to consult and accommodate, both in the context of Aboriginal rights and treaty rights. To summarize broadly, the cases say that the Crown must engage with Indigenous groups and try to address concerns that they raise. Indigenous parties must participate in the process and exchange information. Whether the process of consultation and the substantive accommodations proposed by the Crown or project proponents is sufficient to meet the legal standard is up to the courts. If a court finds that the Crown has met the standard to consult and accommodate, then the project can proceed. If the standard is not met, the Court may impose conditions or may require further consultation and accommodation. Many of these cases mention that the First Nation does not have a veto.[15] In this context, "no veto" means that the final decision on whether the project proceeds does not lie in the hands of the Indigenous group, but rather in the hands of the Court. To look at the issue from the Crown or project proponent perspective, the fact that Indigenous groups have "no veto" does not mean that the project will necessary go ahead. The Court will determine whether the procedural and substantive standards have been met.

I will return to the discussion of "no veto" in the next section, where I discuss the relationship between the concept of veto and the concept of consent.

3. Consent and the United Nations Declaration on the Rights of Indigenous Peoples

At the international level, developments on relations between states and Indigenous peoples began with an assimilationist approach evident in the Indigenous and Tribal Populations Convention ("ILO

15 For example, see *Behn v Moulton, Contracting Ltd.*, 2013 SCC 26, para 29.

107") of the International Labour Organization (ILO), adopted in 1957.[16] ILO 107 was aimed at "integration" of Indigenous people into the majority population and focused on individual equality rights. By the mid-1980s, it became clear that Indigenous peoples themselves did not favour such an approach, and the ILO drafted another convention, ILO 169, named the Indigenous and Tribal Peoples Convention, 1989.[17] The change from "populations" to "peoples" signalled a change in direction: explicitly recognizing the existence of Indigenous collectivities. ILO 169 went further, requiring that Indigenous people be consulted:

> [G]overnments shall establish or maintain procedures through which they shall consult these peoples, with a view to ascertaining whether and to what degree their interests would be prejudiced, before undertaking or permitting any programmes for the exploration or exploitation of such resources pertaining to their lands.[18]

The growing international movement for Indigenous rights, led by Indigenous people, resulted in the enactment of the United Nations Declaration on the Rights of Indigenous People in 2007 (UNDRIP).[19] This declaration recognized the right of Indigenous peoples to self-determination, the preservation of their cultures, and rights to land in their territories. The provision that is most relevant for this chapter is found in Article 32, which provides that Indigenous people must give their free prior and informed consent (FPIC):

---

16 International Labour Organization, Indigenous and Tribal Populations Convention, 1957 (No. 107), http://www.ilo.org/dyn/normlex/en/f?p=NORMLEXPUB:12100:0::NO::P12100_INSTRUMENT_ID:312252. The ILO is a specialized body of the United Nations, made up of representatives of workers, employers, and governments. It was the first organization to have an instrument directed specifically at Indigenous people.

17 International Labour Organization, Indigenous and Tribal Peoples Convention, 1989 (No. 169), http://www.ilo.org/dyn/normlex/en/f?p=NORMLEXPUB:12100:0::NO:12100:P12100_INSTRUMENT_ID:312314:NO. The requirement to consult in ILO 169 came a year before the Supreme Court of Canada released *R v Sparrow*, which said that consultation was necessary before infringing Aboriginal rights. Canada has not signed ILO 169, so it has no legal applicability in Canada.

18 *Ibid*, Article 15.2.

19 United Nations Declaration on the Rights of Indigenous Peoples [UNDRIP] UNGA Res 61/295 (13 September 2007), http://www.un.org/esa/socdev/unpfii/documents/DRIPS_en.pdf.

> States shall consult and cooperate in good faith with the indigenous peoples concerned through their own representative institutions in order to obtain their free and informed consent prior to the approval of any project affecting their lands or territories and other resources, particularly in connection with the development, utilization or exploitation of mineral, water or other resources.[20]

The Government of Canada's reaction to these provisions was baffling. Canada was one of only four countries in the world to vote *against* the adoption of UNDRIP in 2007, and in 2014 at the World Conference on Indigenous Peoples, when every nation in the General Assembly endorsed the principles of UNDRIP, Canada stood alone to raise an objection to the consent standard, because in its view, requiring consent would mean that Indigenous people would have a veto over projects on their traditional lands.[21]

The Government of Canada was sharply out of step with international developments and even domestic developments in the private sector.[22] In the sections below, I outline the adoption of some sort of consent standard by a number of international and Canadian institutions to illustrate the depth and diversity of support for FPIC.[23]

---

20 *Ibid*, Article 32.

21 "Canada's Statement on the World Conference on Indigenous Peoples Outcome Document" (New York, 22 September 2014), http://www.canadainternational.gc.ca/prmny-mponu/canada_un-canada_onu/statements-declarations/other-autres/2014-09-22_WCIPD-PADD.aspx?lang=eng.

22 In October, 2015, a new Liberal government under Prime Minister Justin Trudeau came into power and promised to create more positive policies for Indigenous peoples. At the time of writing, there has not been any clear statement on whether the new government will accept the consent standard.

23 I am not providing an exhaustive list of relevant instruments, some of which do not mention free, prior, informed consent. For example, the Organisation for Economic and Cooperative Development's Guidelines for Multinational Enterprises have not been updated since 2011 and do not set out any standards specifically for Indigenous peoples. See http://mneguidelines.oecd.org/text/. As well, I am not going to focus on different iterations of the consent standard or address the effectiveness (or lack of effectiveness) of the voluntary standards themselves. This chapter outlines the conceptual framework for incorporating consent into the implementation of treaties and is not meant to be an analysis of the standards themselves. For an overall review and critique of these voluntary standards, see Penelope Simons and Audrey Macklin, *The Governance Gap* (London: Routledge, 2014).

A. The International Finance Corporation

The International Finance Corporation (IFC) was established in 1956 to offer investment, advisory, and asset management services with the aim of encouraging private sector development in developing countries. A member of the World Bank Group headquartered in Washington, DC, the IFC is owned, and its policies are determined by, its 184 member countries. Its current work in over 100 developing countries is meant to create jobs, generate tax revenues, improve corporate governance, and improve environmental performance by providing loans to private sector companies active in emerging markets.[24]

The IFC has published performance standards that loan recipients must follow. These standards provide guidance on how to identify and manage risks and impacts. Performance Standard 7 requires that IFC clients identify adverse impacts on affected Indigenous communities and develop action plans to address these impacts with the participation of those communities. The 2006 version of the performance standards mentioned "free, prior, informed *consultation*" with Indigenous peoples, but the 2012 version requires free, prior and informed *consent*.[25]

According to the IFC, the client company must procure FPIC through good-faith negotiation with the affected Indigenous community as well as document (1) the mutually accepted process between the parties for obtaining consent, and (2) evidence of agreement between the parties on the outcome of the negotiations.[26] The performance standard also directs companies to involve Indigenous peoples' representative bodies and members of the affected communities, including vulnerable groups such as women and youth, and to provide sufficient time for decision-making.[27]

B. The Equator Principles

The Equator Principles provide a risk management framework for determining, evaluating, and managing environmental and social risk in

24 International Finance Corporation (IFC), "About IFC: Overview," http://www.ifc.org/wps/wcm/connect/corp_ext_content/ifc_external_corporate_site/about+ifc.

25 International Finance Corporation (IFC), "Performance Standard 7: Indigenous Peoples," http:/www.ifc.org/wps/wcm/connect/1ee7038049a79139b845faa8c6a8312a/PS7_English_2012.pdf?MOD=AJPERES.

26 *Ibid*, para 12.

27 *Ibid*, para 18.

projects. They primarily function to "provide a minimum standard for due diligence to support responsible risk decision-making"[28] and are designed to assist member institutions in their decisions to disburse loans to finance particular projects. Member institutions commit to implementing and honouring the Equator Principles within their internal environmental and social policies, procedures, and standards for financing projects and must not provide project financing or project-related corporate loans where the client/project either will not or cannot comply with the Principles.

The establishment of the Equator Principles has brought social/community standards and responsibility – such as those regarding Indigenous peoples, labour/employment, and consultation with affected local communities – to the forefront within the project finance market. In doing so, they have helped rally support for the convergence and consensus around common environmental and social standards. For instance, multilateral development banks and export credit agencies are increasingly drawing on and applying the same standards as the Equator Principles.[29]

Currently, there are eighty-four members in thirty-five countries. They are among the most important financial institutions in the world, including Banco Santander, Bank of America, JP Morgan Bank, Barclays, and all five of the major banks in Canada. These institutions cover more than 70 per cent of international project finance debt in emerging markets.[30]

The requirement for "free, prior, informed *consent*" was instituted in 2013 in "Equator Principles III," a change from the preceding requirement for "free, prior, informed *consultation*" found in "Equator Principles II."[31]

C. The International Council on Mining and Metals

The International Council of Mining and Metals (ICMM) was established in 2001 to improve sustainable development performance in the

28 Equator Principles, "About the Equator Principles," http://www.equator-principles.com/index.php/ep3/ep3/38-about/about/195.

29 *Ibid.*

30 *Ibid.*

31 Equator Principles, "The Equator Principles III – 2013," http://www.equator-principles.com/index.php/ep3.

mining and metals industry. It brings together twenty-two mining and metals companies, as well as thirty-three national and regional mining associations and global commodity associations, to address core sustainable development challenges.[32] Canadian members are Barrick Gold, Goldcorp, Teck, the Mining Association of Canada, and the Prospectors and Developers Association of Canada.

The council's May 2013 position statement, "Indigenous Peoples and Mining," explicitly requires its member companies to "work to obtain the consent of indigenous communities for new projects (and changes to existing projects) that are located on lands traditionally owned by or under customary use of Indigenous Peoples and are likely to have significant adverse impacts on Indigenous Peoples."[33] This is a significant shift from the prior position, which required only consultation.[34]

D. Akwé: Kon Guidelines

The United Nations Convention on Biological Diversity came into force in December 1993. It promotes "the conservation of biological diversity, the sustainable use of its components, and the fair and equitable sharing of benefits arising from the use of genetic resources."[35] One part of the Convention addresses traditional knowledge of Indigenous people. In order to ensure that traditional knowledge was included in cultural, environmental, and social impact assessments, the members of the Convention developed the Akwé: Kon Guidelines in 2012. These guidelines state that consultations with Indigenous groups should include a way for the local and Indigenous communities to "have the option to accept or oppose a proposed development that may impact on their community."[36]

---

32 International Council on Mining and Metals, "About Us," http://www.icmm.com/about-us/about-us.

33 International Council of Mining and Metals (ICMM), "Indigenous Peoples and Mining: Position Statement" (May 2013), http://www.icmm.com/document/5433.

34 Sarah A. Altschuller, "ICMM Releases Position Statement on Indigenous Peoples Establishing Commitment to FPIC," *Corporate Social Responsibility and the Law* (30 May 2013), http://www.csrandthelaw.com/2013/05/30/icmm-releases-position-statement-on-indigenous-peoples-establishing-commitment-to-fpic/.

35 Convention on Biological Diversity, "History of the Convention," https://www.cbd.int/history/.

36 Convention on Biological Diversity, Article 8(e) in "Akwé: Kon Guidelines," at https://www.cbd.int/doc/publications/akwe-brochure-en.pdf.

E. The Boreal Leadership Council

The purpose of this Canadian organization is to establish "a network of large interconnected protected areas covering about half of the country's Boreal Forest and the use of leading-edge sustainable development practices in remaining areas."[37] The seventeen members of the Canadian Boreal Leadership Council come from the finance sector, Indigenous groups, non-governmental organizations, and the forestry industry.[38]

The council believes that the development of the boreal forest requires the free, prior, informed consent of the Indigenous peoples concerned. In September 2012, the council released "Free Prior Informed Consent in Canada," a guidebook that provides information on best practices for implementing FPIC.[39] and in 2015 the Council reinforced this policy in "Understanding Successful Approaches to Free, Prior, and Informed Consent in Canada"[40]

F. Prospectors and Developers Association of Canada

The Prospectors and Developers Association of Canada (PDAC) is the largest mining body in Canada, with more than 1,200 corporate and 9,000 individual members. It published *e3 Plus – A Framework for Responsible Exploration* in order to help resource exploration companies improve their social, environmental, health, and safety performance and to comprehensively integrate these three aspects into all their exploration programs. e3 Plus is a voluntary guideline designed to help explorers in their decision-making for exploration projects around the world.[41]

The e3 Plus guidelines say that "the concept of free, prior, and informed consent (FPIC) provides a standard for interaction with indigenous

---

37 Boreal Leadership Council, at http://borealcouncil.ca/.

38 Boreal Leadership Council, "Members," at http://borealcouncil.ca/members/.

39 Boreal Leadership Council, "Free Prior Informed Consent in Canada," September 2012, http://borealcouncil.ca/wp-content/uploads/2013/09/FPICReport-English-web.pdf.

40 Boreal Leadership Council, "Understanding Successful Approaches to Free, Prior, and Informed Consent in Canada," http://borealcouncil.ca/wp-content/uploads/2013/09/FPICReport-English-web.pdf.

41 Prospectors and Developers Association of Canada, "About Us," http://www.pdac.ca/about-pdac/about-pdac.

communities."[42] As a member of the International Council on Mining and Metals, PDAC has subscribed to the consent requirement as articulated by that organization.

Having reviewed five examples of the use of the consent standard, I turn to reasons why the standard makes sense for such a diverse group of institutions.

4. Why Does It Make Sense for Financial Institutions and Industry to Require the Consent of Indigenous Peoples?

Because *consult* is a lower standard, it would seem to make it easier to go forward with development projects, because the Indigenous party can never say "no." Getting *consent* from the community would present another barrier for projects to overcome and would appear to make it more difficult for projects to go ahead. Why would the private sector be in favour of consent?

Part of the answer lies in the fact that the costs of community conflict are significant and can result in serious impacts on companies, including suspensions and closures of projects. The degree of opposition has resulted in violent confrontations across the globe, with thousands of people killed, injured, and raped, and huge losses to companies.[43] For example, Newmont's U.S.$4.8 billion Conga project in Peru faced massive opposition, including general strikes and road blockades. Newmont was forced to "voluntarily" suspend operation of the mine, with losses in the hundreds of millions of dollars.[44] Opposing the mine has come at a heavy price for community members, with five farmers killed during one of the protests and many community leaders injured and beaten.

---

42 Prospectors and Developers Association of Canada, *e3 Plus Principles and Guidance Notes*, at 80, http://www.pdac.ca/docs/default-source/e3-plus---principles/e3-plus-principles-amp-guidance-notes---update-2014.pdf.

43 For examples of case studies of twenty-two conflicts involving Canadian companies in Latin America, see Working Group on Mining and Human Rights in Latin America, *The Impact of Canadian Mining in Latin America and Canada's Responsibility* (March 2014), http://www.dplf.org/sites/default/files/report_canadian_mining_executive_summary.pdf.

44 Mining.com, "Peru Abandons Newmont's $4.8 Billion Conga Project," 28 August 2012, http://www.mining.com/peru-abandons-newmonts-4-8-billion-conga-project-66180/; Earthworks, "Mining Giant Newmont Urged to Obtain Community Consent," 25 April 2013, https://www.earthworksaction.org/media/detail/mining_giant_newmont_urged_to_obtain_community_consent#.VJXxiP8OjA.

Another example is the Canadian company HudBay Minerals, which purchased a Guatemalan mine that had been riddled with conflict and assassinations throughout its history. The conflicts continued under HudBay's ownership as it tried to evict Indigenous people from the mine site. During one confrontation, a community leader was murdered and others injured. The head of security of the mining company was charged and jailed. HudBay ended up selling the mine for CAD$176 million in 2011, shortly after it was sued in Canada for the murder and for the alleged gang rapes of women that had occurred during an earlier eviction carried out by the mine's previous owners.[45] HudBay had bought the mine three years before, for CAD$446 million.

In Northern Ontario, Canada, a conflict between the Kitchenuhmaykoosib Inninuwug First Nation and a junior mining company called Platinex would have turned out better for all parties concerned had consent been the standard.[46] In this case, the First Nation had been asking for a moratorium on mining activity in the area since 2001 and insisted that drilling not commence until there had been compliance with the First Nation's Development Protocol, which included a referendum in the community. In August 2005, when Platinex announced its plan to begin exploration, the First Nation sent a strong letter of objection. In October 2005, Platinex began raising $1 million by selling shares – not mentioning the August letter of objection and, instead, telling investors that the First Nation had given verbal consent. In February 2006, Platinex sent in a drilling team without informing the First Nation. A confrontation occurred with members of the First Nation, and the drilling team left. Platinex then launched a law suit for $10 billion against the Kitchenuhmaykoosib Inninuwug. This was approximately $10 million for every man, woman, and child on the reserve. The First Nation asked for an injunction to stop drilling.

In July 2006,[47] Justice G.P. Smith ordered that drilling be halted in order to permit consultation and negotiations to take place. Over the next

45 For a history of the El Estor mine, see Shin Imai, Bernadette Maheandiran, and Valerie Crystal, "Access to Justice and Corporate Accountability: A Legal Case Study of HudBay in Guatemala" (2014) 35 (2) *Canadian Journal of Development Studies* 286–303.

46 For a description of this case, see Rachel Ariss and John Cutfeet, *Keeping the Land: Kitchenuhmaykoosib Inninuwug, Reconciliation and Canadian Law* (Blackpoint, NS: Fernwood, 2012).

47 *Platinex Inc. v Kitchenuhmaykoosib Inninuwug* [2006] OJ No. 3140. *[Platinex 2006]*.

few months, the Ontario Ministry of Mines and Northern Development joined in the negotiations and appeared at subsequent hearings to support Platinex. Various proposals were made to the First Nation with respect to employment, future consultation, a community fund, and fees for negotiation and litigation. The First Nation refused consent and objected to the fact that Platinex and the ministry demanded that the First Nation agree to the drilling before they would enter into substantive consultations. A year passed by, and by 1 May 2007,[48] the judge decided that the balance of convenience had shifted and phase one was allowed to proceed.

At a hearing on 18 May 2007,[49] the judge decided that an agreement reached between the ministry and Platinex, without the consent of the First Nation, was satisfactory and should be imposed on the First Nation. When the First Nation continued to block exploration activity, the judge found that the chief and the majority of the members of the elected council were guilty of contempt of court. At the urging of a lawyer for the Ontario government, who asked that the penalty be harsh enough "to make it hurt," the judge sentenced them to six months in jail. The matter went up to the Ontario Court of Appeal, and the chief and councillors were released after spending two months in jail.[50]

Platinex was still determined to proceed, and in August 2009 another attempt was made to land a floatplane to begin exploration. The plane was prevented from landing by the chief. Platinex then began negotiating with the Ontario Ministry of Northern Development, Mines and Forestry and settled for a payment of $5 million from the government, far short of the $10 billion originally demanded.[51]

Analysing this situation, we can see that all parties suffered: Platinex lost access to its property. Its investors lost – in December 2014, the stock was trading at one cent.[52] Ontario taxpayers had to pay $5 million,

---

48 *Platinex Inc. v Kitchenuhmaykoosib Inninuwug* [2007] 3 CNLR 181.

49 *Platinex Inc. v Kitchenuhmaykoosib Inninuwug* [2007] OJ No. 2214.

50 *Platinex Inc. v Kitchenuhmaykoosib Inninuwug*, (2008), 91 OR (3d) 18 (Ont. C.A.).

51 Republic of Mining, "K.I. vs. Platinex: A 'Worst Case' Example of Community Relations" (22 September 2011), http://www.republicofmining.com/2011/09/22/k-i-vs-platinex-a-%E2%80%98worst-case%E2%80%99-example-of-community-relations-canadian-business-ethics-research-network/.

52 The *Globe and Mail, Stock Quote*, at http://www.theglobeandmail.com/globe-investor/markets/stocks/summary/?q=PTX-X#.

and probably more to cover legal fees, to compensate Platinex. The members of the First Nation spent time in jail.[53]

The Platinex case is but one example of a generalized problem. A Harvard University report on company-community conflicts, based on case studies from around the world, found that the absence of opportunity to consent to projects that affect the community was one of the two major issues that precipitate conflict.[54]

The reality of community opposition provides practical reasons to consider obtaining consent, but there is also a theoretical basis for favouring consent in the thinking of those in the Harvard Negotiation Project. For them, power imbalance is counterproductive. In the words of Lawrence Susskind and Jeffrey Cruikshank, "The potential parties to a consensus-building effort cannot participate in a relationship in which one party holds all the power."[55] This imbalance may be a disincentive for weaker parties to engage in negotiation because they may believe they have more effective extra-legal options or they may believe there is more built-in protection in the adjudicative system. If there is no true consensus, and the more powerful party imposes a solution, even if the solution makes some accommodation for the weaker party, the weaker party will not have made a commitment to the solution. This means that the solution will not be as durable nor proceed with the cooperation of the weaker party. In situations where there is conflict over a mine, it will mean continued conflict.

The problem with the *consult* standard is that the community feels powerless, because they *are* powerless. It is difficult for people to trust a process of discussion when they know that no matter what happens,

---

53 Another exploration company, God's Lake Resources, attempted to explore on the territory of the Kitchenuhmaykoosib. In this case, the province accepted that the First Nation would not consent to the exploration and paid the company $3.5 million to give up its right to explore. "Ontario Reaches Agreement with Gods Lake Resources," 29 March 2012, https://news.ontario.ca/mndmf/en/2012/03/ontario-reaches-agreement-with-gods-lake-resources.html.

54 Rachel Davis and Daniel Franks, *Costs of Community-Company Conflict in the Extractive Sector* (Cambridge: CSR Initiative at the Harvard Kennedy School, 2014) at 16. See also Ciaran O'Faircheallaigh, "International Recognition of Indigenous Rights, Indigenous Control of Development and Domestic Political Mobilisation" (2012) 47 *Australian Journal of Political Science* 531–45 at 542 where he describes Rio Tinto's promise to seek consent from an Indigenous group in Australia.

55 Lawrence Susskind and Jeffrey Cruikshank, *Breaking the Impasse: Consensual Approaches to Resolving Public Disputes* (New York: Basic Books, 1987).

the final decision is not in their hands. It is through recognition of the necessity of *consent* that the Indigenous community will have power that can be a balance to the superior economic power of the mining company and the superior political power of government.

5. What Is the Difference between Consent and Veto?

I have indicated above that Canadian courts have said that Indigenous people do not have a veto and that Canada raised objections to the consent provisions in the United Nations Declaration on Indigenous Peoples at the 2014 World Conference on Indigenous Peoples. Canada said that these provisions would give Aboriginal groups the right to a veto, and it would be incompatible with Canadian law.

A. The International Level and Veto

A group of First Nations attending the World Conference expressed outrage at Canada's position and pointed out that the word "veto" does not appear in the UN document. Grand Chief Matthew Coon Come of the Grand Council of the Crees stated bluntly, "The government has never explained what it means by 'veto.' Is a 'veto' absolute? If so, then a 'veto' isn't the same thing as 'consent.'"[56] James Anaya, United Nations Special Rapporteur on the Rights of Indigenous Peoples, takes the same position as Coon Come. He says that there is no right to a veto if it means that Indigenous communities can reject any project whatsoever:

> When the Special Rapporteur affirms that Indigenous people do not enjoy a right to have a veto in the context of consultation processes, he refers to the proposition that there is absolute power to unilaterally prohibit or impede all proposals and decisions of the state that could affect them, based on whatever justification or no justification at all. In his view, such a proposition is not supportable. To speak of a right to a veto in that sense, in relation to matters that can be in the legitimate interests of not only the Indigenous party but also national society in general is not consistent with

56 Jenny Uechi, "First Nation Groups Condemn Federal Government's 'Indefensible Attack' on Indigenous Rights at UN Meeting," *Vancouver Observer*, 25 September 2014, http://www.vancouverobserver.com/news/first-nation-groups-condemn-federal-governments-indefensible-attack-indigenous-rights-un.

the standard of participatory consultation that is incorporated into international norms.[57]

Although Anaya does not think that there exists an absolute veto, he goes on to say that Indigenous communities can refuse to grant their consent when a project would have a significant impact.

> In those cases in which the impact of a proposal or initiative on the well-being and rights of an Indigenous people is significant, the consent of the Indigenous party, through an agreement, is not only the objective of consultation, but also a necessary precondition for carrying out the proposed measures.[58]

At the international level, then, the debate is not over whether there is a veto or not but over the circumstances in which consent is required. The consent issue was addressed by the Inter-American Court of Human Rights in the case of *Pueblo Saramaka v Suriname*.[59] The Saramaka are descendants of escaped slaves and have lived in the rainforest since the seventeenth century. They carved out their own territory, which they were able to protect from intruders until the mid-twentieth century. At that time, the Government of Suriname began displacing the Saramaka for logging and mining. The Saramaka brought a complaint to the Inter-American Court of Human Rights, which released its decision on 28 November 2007. The Court referred to the United Nations Declaration on the Rights of Indigenous People to find that the Saramaka had the right to be consulted and to consent before mineral and forestry development in their territory:

---

57 Declaración pública del Relator Especial sobre los derechos humanos y libertades fundamentales de los indígenas, James Anaya, sobre la "Ley del derecho a la consulta previa a los pueblos indígenas u originarios reconocido en el Convenio No. 169 de la Organización Internacional de Trabajo" aprobada por el Congreso de la República del Perú, 7 de julio de 2010, punto 1 (Public Declaration of the Special Rapporteur on the human rights and fundamental freedoms of indigenous peoples on the "Law on the right to prior consultation of indigenous and original peoples recognized in ILO 169 of the International Labour Organization," 7 July 2010), unofficial translation by author, http://www.ohchr.org/SP/NewsEvents/Pages/DisplayNews.aspx?NewsID=10194&LangID=S.

58 *Ibid*, point 4.

59 Inter-American Court of Human Rights, *Case of the Saramaka People v Suriname* (Merits, Reparations and Costs) (27 November 2007) Series C No 82.

> ... the Court considers that, regarding large-scale development or investment projects that would have a major impact within Saramaka territory, the State has a duty, not only to consult with the Saramakas, but also to obtain their free, prior, and informed consent, according to their customs and traditions.[60]

It is fair to say that the precise parameters for identifying when consent is required are still in development. The Inter-American Court itself provides three iterations of the test. The above quote from the 2007 judgment mentions "large-scale development or investment projects" that would have a "major impact within Saramaka territory." Three paragraphs later in the judgment, the court describes the required impact as "a profound impact on the property rights of the members of the Saramaka people to a large part of their territory."[61] In an Interpretive Judgment from 2008, the Court says that consent is necessary when the impact "could affect the integrity of the Saramaka people's lands and natural resources."[62]

UNDRIP provides specific examples of instances when consent is required from Indigenous peoples: relocation from their lands and territories;[63] the taking of their cultural, intellectual, religious, or spiritual property;[64] the taking of "lands, territories and resources which they have traditionally owned or otherwise occupied or used";[65] and the storage of hazardous materials on Indigenous lands.[66]

The International Financial Corporation's Performance Standard 7 sets out four similar circumstances to trigger free prior informed consent: adverse impacts on lands and natural resources that are subject to traditional ownership or customary use;[67] relocation from communally held lands;[68] significant project impacts on critical cultural

---

60 *Ibid*, para 134.
61 *Ibid*, para 137.
62 Inter-American Court of Human Rights, *Interpretation of Saramaka Judgment* (12 August 2008), Ser C, No 185, 6 [17] (emphasis added). I wish to thank Jackie Hartley, PhD candidate, University of New South Wales, for bringing these differences in wording to my attention.
63 UNDRIP, *supra* note 19, Article 10.
64 *Ibid*, Article 11.
65 *Ibid*, Article 28.2.
66 *Ibid*, Article 29.2.
67 IFC, *supra* note 25, paras 13 and 14.
68 *Ibid*, para 15.

heritage;[69] use of cultural heritage, including knowledge, innovations, and practices, for commercial purposes.[70]

In 2012, the Expert Mechanism on the Rights of Indigenous Peoples, an advisory body to the United Nations Human Rights Council, provided a more comprehensive description:

> The Declaration on the Rights of Indigenous Peoples requires that the free, prior and informed consent of indigenous peoples be obtained in matters of fundamental importance to their rights, survival, dignity and well-being. In assessing whether a matter is of importance to the indigenous peoples concerned, relevant factors include the perspective and priorities of the indigenous peoples concerned, the nature of the matter or proposed activity and its potential impact on the indigenous peoples concerned, taking into account, inter alia, the cumulative effects of previous encroachments or activities and historical inequities faced by the indigenous peoples concerned.[71]

We can see that a number of formulations for the circumstances when consent is required are being developed at the international level. I do not intend to parse the differences in wording nor analyse the specific circumstances that have been highlighted, as in this chapter, I focus more on the larger trajectory of the need to obtain consent.

B. Canadian Courts and Consent

We can now turn to decisions of the Supreme Court of Canada, where the focus has been on the duty to consult and accommodate. The cases below discuss Aboriginal title claims in situations where there are no treaties. I apply these principles to the treaty context in part seven.

In *Delgamuukw v British Columbia*,[72] the Supreme Court of Canada approached the concept of consent in the context of Aboriginal title. Chief Justice Lamer noted that arising from the Crown's fiduciary duty

---

69 *Ibid*, para 16.

70 *Ibid*, para 17.

71 Human Rights Council, Expert Mechanism, *Follow-up Report on Indigenous Peoples and the Right to Participate in Decision-Making, with a Focus on Extractive Industries* A/HRC/21/55 (16 August 2012), para 22, http://www.ohchr.org/Documents/HRBodies/HRCouncil/RegularSession/Session21/A-HRC-21-55_en.pdf.

72 *Delgamuukw v British Columbia*, [1997] 3 SCR 1010.

towards Aboriginal peoples, "[t]here is always a duty of consultation." He further noted,

> The nature and scope of the duty of consultation will vary within the circumstances. In occasional cases, when the breach is less serious or relatively minor, it will be no more than a duty to discuss important decisions that will be taken with respect to lands held pursuant to aboriginal title ... In most cases, it will be significantly deeper than mere consultation. Some cases may even require the full consent of an aboriginal nation, particularly when provinces enact hunting and fishing regulations in relation to aboriginal lands.[73]

So *Delgamuuk* tentatively identifies a sphere of activity where consent is required. However, this case also provides limits on how the First Nation uses Aboriginal title lands because of the special bond that exists between the nation and the land:

> ... if occupation is established with reference to the use of the land as a hunting ground, then the group that successfully claims aboriginal title to that land may not use it in such a fashion as to destroy its value for such a use (e.g., by strip mining it). Similarly, if a group claims a special bond with the land because of its ceremonial or cultural significance, it may not use the land in such a way as to destroy that relationship (e.g. by developing it in such a way that the bond is destroyed, perhaps by turning it into a parking lot).[74]

In 2014, the Supreme Court of Canada released its decision in *Xeni Gwet'in v British Columbia*.[75] The Court found that the Tsilhqot'in First Nation had Aboriginal title over 1,750 square kilometres (675 square miles) of land in British Columbia, which gave them the right to decide how the land would be used; the right of enjoyment and occupancy of the land; the right to possess the land; the right to the economic benefits of the land; and the right to proactively use and manage the land.[76] As a general proposition, then, consent of the First Nation would be

73 *Ibid*, para 168.
74 *Ibid*, para 128.
75 *Xeni Gwet'in v British Columbia*, 2014 SCC 44.
76 *Ibid*, para 73.

necessary for government or a company to use Aboriginal title land. However, in a somewhat puzzling move, the Court decided the Crown could dispense with consent if the land was needed for agriculture, mining, lumbering, building of infrastructure, or settlement. In order to override the lack of consent, the Crown would have to comply with the *Sparrow* test and show, among other things, that there was a "compelling and substantial" purpose for dispensing with consent and that the Crown had consulted with the First Nation.[77] However, in another puzzling move, although the Crown could override lack of consent from the Tsilhqot'in, it could not do so if it would "substantially deprive future generations of the benefit of the land."[78]

To summarize where we are so far, we see that the *Xeni Gwet'in* case established that the Tsilhqot'in have Aboriginal title and that consent is necessary for using their lands, but that the requirement for consent could not necessarily prevent agriculture, mining, lumbering, building of infrastructure, or settlement, because the Crown could override the lack of consent using the *Sparrow* test. However, the Crown override does not apply to projects that would deprive future generations of the benefit of the land, so that the Crown's authority has an outer limit. Does this mean that the Tsilhqot'in themselves can consent to uses that would deprive future generations of the use of the land? Apparently not. Although the Court finds that the Tsilhqot'in can put their lands to use in "modern ways," the Tsilhqot'ins' land cannot "be developed or misused in a way that would substantially deprive future generations of the benefit of the land."[79] Consequently, it appears that Aboriginal title provides absolute protection of the land for the future. This is starting to look like a Russian doll, with exceptions buried within exceptions.

This Canadian framework is different from the international approach, which protects the sphere of detrimental impact by requiring free, prior, and informed consent by Indigenous people. Both the international and Canadian approaches recognize that there is something special about the link between the land and Indigenous people that needs to be protected. However, the Canadian approach to date fails to provide sufficient agency and recognition to the role of the Indigenous group. The Canadian approach is Crown-centric and primarily concerned with

77 *Ibid*, para 76.
78 *Ibid*, para 86.
79 *Ibid*, para 74.

Crown conduct in relation to Indigenous people. This is obvious from the questions in the *Sparrow* test: Is the Crown infringing Aboriginal rights? Is the Crown consulting? Is the Crown acting honourably? The international consent standard, on the other hand, adds a focus on the Indigenous group as well. States have obligations to consult and ensure that there is free, prior, informed consent, and this requirement puts Indigenous groups at the centre of the process in a way that the *Sparrow* test's infringe-and-justify test for the Crown does not.

In the next section, I will provide some preliminary ideas on how the consent standard could be applied to implement treaties in Canada.

6. Court Adoption of Best Practices Standards

While private-sector corporate social responsibility initiatives have helped to bring discussions on consent into the mainstream, these voluntary initiatives generally do not provide any form of redress for individual complaints, and are unenforceable against the companies themselves. As such, in cases where there is an allegation of a breach by one of the signing institutions, the complainant is left with little or no recourse.

For instance, the Equator Principles simply oblige member institutions to require any company with whom they deal to establish a grievance mechanism designed to receive and facilitate resolution of concerns about a project's environmental and social performance within the company or project itself. However, the Equator Principles do not impose a duty on its members to adopt grievance mechanisms of their own. Consequently, if someone feels that a member bank has lent money for a project that does not have Indigenous consent, there is no avenue for complaining to the bank or the Equator Principles organization.[80]

There are similar problems with the other standards. The e3 Plus guidelines from the Prospectors and Developers Association of Canada are not mandatory for members, and there is no way to determine which, if any, companies have adopted them. The International Council on Mining and Metals (ICMM) makes its guidelines mandatory to its members, but there is no way of complaining if there is a breach. The ICMM website states that if the ICMM office receives a complaint, it will

80 For general commentary on the Equator Principles, see Simons and Macklin, *supra* note 23, 142–50.

be referred directly to the company; the ICMM itself does not address or mediate issues between a third party and a member.[81] The Boreal Leadership Council developed its guidelines on free, prior, informed consent to "encourage and contribute to a solutions-based dialogue,"[82] but the council does not police adherence to the guidelines. Similarly, the Secretariat on the UN Convention on Biological Diversity does not police implementation of its Akwé: Kon Guidelines.

Of the organizations whose performance standards are studied in this chapter, only the International Finance Corporation is equipped with a grievance mechanism: the Compliance Advisor Ombudsman (CAO), an independent recourse mechanism for projects supported by the private-sector agencies of the World Bank Group. Indigenous groups can make a direct complaint to this agency rather than the company against whom they are making the complaint. However, the CAO merely "responds to complaints from project-affected communities" by "help[ing] parties identify alternatives for resolving the issues of concern." The CAO has explicitly stated that it does not "impose solutions or find fault,"[83] so remedies to individuals or enforcement against the company are not within its mandate.[84]

While the consent standards described above do not provide any direct remedies to Indigenous communities, they do give an indication of what some bodies consider to be "best practices" for the industry. The actions of particular government or industry players can be judged against the best practices suggested for the industry in judicial proceedings.

For example, the Akwé: Kon Guidelines of the Convention on Biological Diversity are not directly binding on anyone, but the Inter-American Court of Human Rights took note of the guidelines as a standard for assessing the behaviour of the Government of Suriname in the consultation process in the *Saramaka* case. The Court called the Guidelines "[o]ne of the most comprehensive and used standards for

---

81 ICMM, *FAQs on Membership Requirements*, http://www.icmm.com/our-work/sustainable-development-framework/faqs-on-membership-requirements.

82 Boreal Leadership Council, *supra* note 37.

83 Office of the Compliance Advisor/Ombudsman, *How We Work: Ombudsman*, http://www.cao-ombudsman.org/howwework/ombudsman/.

84 Although the IFC could technically withdraw funding from a project for failing to comply with the Performance Standards, this has happened only rarely. See Simons and Macklin, *supra* note 23, 130–42.

[Environmental and Social Impact Assessments] in the context of indigenous and tribal Peoples."[85] Other bodies have referenced, recognized, or adopted the Akwé: Kon Guidelines as well, including the Kenya Industrial Property Institute,[86] the UK National Contact Point for the Organization for Economic Cooperation and Development,[87] the Government of Finland,[88] and the Supreme Court of India.[89]

In Ontario, the decisions in two cases referred to the e3 Plus Aboriginal engagement guidelines published by the Prospectors and developers Association of Canada, although, as I have already indicated, these guidelines are voluntary and even PDAC members are not

---

85 *Case of the Saramaka People v Suriname* (Interpretation of the Judgment on Preliminary Objection, Merits, Repartions, and Costs) 12 August 2008, Series C No. 185, fn 23.

86 The Traditional Knowledge and Genetic Resources Unit of the Kenya Industrial Property Institute was established in March 2009 to address issues of intellectual property rights relating to traditional knowledge associated with genetic resources for Indigenous and local communities practising traditional lifestyles. In this context, the unit's work was to also address the Akwé: Kon Guidelines. See Kenya Industrial Property Institute, "Traditional Knowledge," www.kipi.go.ke/index.php/traditional-knowledge.

87 In its final statement respecting a complaint brought by Survival International against Vedanta Resources under the OECD Guidelines for Multinational Enterprises, the UK National Contact Point for the OECD Guidelines for Multinational Enterprises included a list of recommendations. Among these was the recommendation that Vedanta immediately and adequately engage with the Indigenous group Dongria Kondh regarding, among other things, the construction of Vedanta's proposed mine. As a guide to pursue the consultation process, the UK National Contact Point recommended that Vedanta refer to the consultation process outlined in the Akwé: Kon Guidelines. See "Follow Up to Final Statement by the UK National Contact Point for the OECD Guidelines for Multinational Enterprises," www.oecd.org/corporate/mne/46085980.pdf.

88 The Government of Finland applied the Akwé: Kon Guidelines in connection with the management and land use planning for the Hammastunturi Wilderness Area, which involved the participation of the Saami people. Finland is the first country to have applied these guidelines in practice. See *Fifth National Report to the Convention on Biological Diversity, Finland*, 99, www.cbd.int/doc/world/fi/fi-nr-05-en/pdf.

89 The Akwé: Kon Guidelines were discussed extensively before the Supreme Court of India in the Sethusamudram case. This case concerned the validity of an environmental impact assessment for the Sethusamudram Shipping Canal Project, which would create a shipping route between Indian and Sri Lanka. The petitioner raised the question of the Akwé: Kon Guidelines. In the end result, the Supreme Court directed the Government of India to consider an alternate shipping route for the project.

obliged to follow them. Nonetheless, two courts in Ontario have used them as a touchstone for company behaviour. In *Wahgoshig First Nation v Solid Gold Resources Corp*,[90] Solid Gold, a small exploratory company headquartered in Sudbury, refused to consult with the Wahgoshig First Nation, in spite of its being advised to do so by the Ontario government. When Solid Gold attempted to continue exploring, the First Nation took the matter to court. In granting an injunction against further exploration, Justice Carole Brown wrote, "[I]t ... appears that Solid Gold has failed to meet industry standards for responsible exploration as set forth by the Prospectors and Developers Association of Canada with respect to First Nations engagement."[91]

Another example is the *Platinex Inc. v Kitchenuhmaykoosib Inninuwug First Nation* described above.[92] Justice G.P. Smith, the judge in this case, noted that Platinex did not follow the Prospectors and Developers Association of Canada's Best Practices Exploration and Environmental Excellence Standards, which state that before drilling is to commence on lands under an Aboriginal claim, the drilling company should sign a memorandum of understanding.[93] This was one of the factors that led the judge to suspend drilling until consultations had taken place.

We see here that some of these voluntary standards have been given life in both international and domestic courts. In the next section, I argue that the consent standard from non-binding international and domestic instruments should inform judicial thinking. Why should courts shy away from requiring best practices for resource extraction on Indigenous lands?

7. Application of Consent Standard to Numbered Treaties

As I stated at the beginning of this chapter, I am going to sketch out some preliminary thoughts on a legal framework for consent, building on existing case law. The two elements of the numbered treaties that are relevant to this discussion are the clause dealing with the "surrendering" of traditional territories; and the hunting and fishing "lands

90 *Wahgoshig First Nation v Ontario*, 2011 ONSC 7708.
91 *Ibid*, para 59.
92 *Platinex 2006*, *supra* note 47
93 *Ibid*, para 41–3.

taken up" clause. The treaties also created reserves – small pieces of land, perhaps fifty square kilometres (twenty square miles), which are under a separate *Indian Act* legal regime that does not apply here. The lands that are the subject of the analysis in this chapter are large tracts that are covered by the treaty but are outside of the reserves. I refer to these as "treaty lands." The fact pattern I have proposed for exploring the legal framework is for extractive industry access to treaty lands (that is, off reserve), not covered by a land claims agreement, not patented (that is, Crown lands), in a rural area.

There are three building blocks to my analysis:

(i) Courts have found that there is an Indian interest in treaty lands in spite of the "surrender clause" and that the Crown has neither unilateral nor unlimited power to take up lands for extractive industry, in spite of the "lands taken up clause." There is a duty to consult and accommodate for any taking up of lands, but in cases where the taking up will impact the meaningful right to harvest, the Crown must justify its actions using the *Sparrow* test.
(ii) I argue that there should be negotiations to identify how much land is needed to maintain a meaningful right to harvest. Until there are such negotiations, the courts need to provide a forum for identifying the point in time when the right is threatened.
(iii) The *Mikisew Cree* case, discussed in part two, dealt with the "taking up" of lands and said that "compelling and substantial" purposes could justify taking away the meaningful right to harvest. I argue that further "taking up of lands" should require Indigenous consent.

A. The Surrender Clause and Continuing Indigenous Interest in Traditional Lands

The fact that the written versions of "numbered treaties" say that the land was "surrendered" to the Crown raises the question of the nature of the Indian interest on lands that are covered by the treaty but are outside of the reserves. The "surrender" clause in Treaty No. 8, for example, reads like an absolute transfer of title from First Nations to the Crown:

> ... the said Indians DO HEREBY CEDE, RELEASE, SURRENDER AND YIELD UP to the Government of the Dominion of Canada, for Her Majesty

> the Queen and Her successors for ever, all their rights, titles and privileges whatsoever, to the lands included within the following limits ... [94]

First Nations say that they never considered the treaties to be real estate deals – rather, they were meant to create relationships with the Crown. There is plenty of evidence that in various negotiations, the Indians were told that their livelihoods would not change. In his chapter in this book, Michael Coyle explains the problems arising from the different understandings of the treaties. Although there is some judicial support for questioning the validity of the surrender clause as it is set out in the written version of the treaty,[95] most courts assume that the surrender is valid, and that rights to the land have been alienated. If the surrender is valid, can consent from Indigenous groups be required for the use of land that belongs to the Crown?

For our purposes, I do not think that we need to answer the question of who "owns" the land. Whether or not there was a total surrender of the land, it is not disputed that treaty First Nations have an *interest* in their traditional lands arising from their traditional use and occupancy of the land. The right to continue to use the land for harvesting purposes is written into the treaty through the "lands taken up" clause. As indicated earlier in this chapter, this clause, if read literally, gives the Crown unlimited unilateral authority to take up lands until there is nothing left for the harvesting activities. The Supreme Court of Canada, however, in *Mikisew Cree* and in *Keewatin* recognized that the Crown's authority was not unlimited – the First Nation needs enough land to "meaningfully" exercise harvesting rights. Nor could the Crown exercise its authority unilaterally, as the Court imposed a requirement to consult and accommodate the First Nation before taking up the lands.

Canadian law is consistent with the thinking on the nature of Indigenous interest in land at the international level. The United Nations Declaration on the Rights of Indigenous Peoples refers to "lands, territories and resources which they have *traditionally owned* or *otherwise occupied or used*."[96] The International Finance Corporation Performance Standard 7, which is incorporated into both the Equator Principles

94 Treaty No. 8, *supra* note 10.

95 See *Ka'a'Gee Tu First Nation v Canada (Minister of Indian and Northern Affairs)*, 2007 F.C. 764.

96 UNDRIP, *supra* note 19, Article 28.2, emphasis added.

and the International Council on Mining and Metals standards, specifically provides for the requirement of consent on lands that are "*traditionally owned or under customary use.*" Legal title or demarcation is not necessary:

> Indigenous peoples are often closely tied to their lands and related natural resources. Frequently, these lands are traditionally owned or under customary use. While Indigenous peoples may not possess legal title to these lands as defined by national law, their use of these lands, including seasonal or cyclical use, for their livelihoods, or cultural, ceremonial, and spiritual purposes that define their identity and community, can often be substantiated and documented.[97]

B. The Lack of a Forum to Discuss the "Meaningful Right to Harvest"

As we have seen, the Crown is required to consult on, but not justify, taking up lands until the point where there is no longer enough land to "meaningfully" exercise harvesting rights. One of the practical challenges, then, is trying to decide when that point in time is reached. How do we know when a particular project will send us over the edge? Is anyone keeping track?

Individual decisions based on the rights of individuals to hunt or fish, or judicial review of the adequacy of consultations in individual project proposals, do not provide the overview necessary for decision-making bodies to determine whether the taking up of land in a particular treaty area is approaching the point in time when the "meaningful right" disappears. For example, in 2004, the Saulteau First Nations argued that there needed to be a study of the cumulative impacts of development because "if approvals are not considered broadly in context, small incremental infringements may threaten treaty rights by 'death by a thousand cuts.'"[98] This anxiety is not misplaced, because almost every square centimetre of land in Canada is subject to some type of non-Indigenous interest, ranging from mining concessions and water rights for private companies to rights of way for recreational snowmobilers. Furthermore, there is legislation in the provinces that will permit

97 IFC, *supra* note 25, para 13, emphasis added.

98 *Saulteau First Nations v British Columbia (Oil & Gas Commission)*, 2004 BCSC 92, para 4.

an automatic "taking up" of treaty lands with no scrutiny or notice whatsoever. For example, the free-entry system for mines in British Columbia allows company to stake claims without obtaining any prior approval from government,[99] and the Ontario Court of Appeal has upheld provincial legislation that dedicates highways for public use by the passage of time, without requiring any decision on anyone's part.[100]

In spite of these continual creeping encroachments, there is at present no systematic process for gathering information on what rights need to be "meaningfully" protected or how much land needs to be set aside to protect those rights. Ideally, there would be a political negotiation process to address this problem. In an article in 2001, I argued that the treaty lands problem can be resolved only through a process that will set aside enough lands to preserve the meaningful right to hunt, fish, and trap.[101] Such comprehensive negotiations on treaties as a whole were recommended by the Royal Commission on Aboriginal Peoples as far back as in 1985,[102] and by Michael Coyle in his chapter in this book. Without a political framework, however, matters end up in court, and the courts are struggling.

Four cases illustrate how difficult it is to find an appropriate judicial forum to discuss the meaningful right to harvest and operationalize the test in *Mikisew Cree*.

In the first case, *Buffalo River Dene Nation v Saskatchewan (Minister of Energy and Resources)*,[103] the question of timing for raising an objection to

---

99 For a description of the free entry system in Ontario as it existed at the time of the dispute between Platinex and the Kitchenuhmaykoosib Inninuwug, see Rachel Ariss and John Cutfeet, "Kitchenuhmaykoosib Inninuwug First Nation: Mining, Consultation, Reconciliation and Law" (2011) 10 *Indigenous Law Journal* 1. In *Ross River Dena Council v Yukon*, 2012 YKCA 14, the court found that the free-entry system in the Yukon was unconstitutional because it did not provide for consultation with affected First Nations.

100 *R v Jacob* (2009), 245 OAC 381.

101 Shin Imai, "Treaty Lands and Crown Obligations: The 'Tracts Taken Up' Provision" (2001) 27 *Queen's Law Journal* 1.

102 Canada, *Report of the Royal Commission on Aboriginal Peoples: Restructuring the Relationship*, vol. 2 (Ottawa: Supply and Services Canada, 1996), 46–54.

103 *Buffalo River Dene Nation v Saskatchewan (Minister of Energy and Resources)*, [2015] 2 C.N.L.R. 81 (Sask. C.A.). This decision runs counter to a decision by the Yukon Court of Appeal, which decided that the Crown's duty to consult was triggered when a mining claim was registered: *Ross River Dena Council v Yukon*, 2012 YKCA 14 at para 56.

exploration is the issue. In this case, the Saskatchewan Court of Appeal held that consultation was not required before the issuing of an exploration permit, because there would be no actual impact until a second permit for exploitation was issued. The court reasoned as follows:

> To trigger [the duty to consult], actual foreseeable adverse impacts on an identified treaty or Aboriginal right or claim must flow from the impugned Crown conduct. While the test [for consultation] admits *possible* adverse impacts, there must be a direct link between the adverse impacts and the impugned Crown conduct. If adverse impacts are not possible until after a later-in-time, independent decision, then it is that later decision that triggers the duty to consult.[104]

However, the Court failed to appreciate that the exploration stage is not benign. It sets in motion a set of expectations and financial relationships. The court itself notes that the exploration companies must raise money from investors. These investors should know what interests the First Nations will assert if exploitation begins. It is not fair to allow exploration companies to keep investors in the dark. If a First Nation has a strong position against development of resources on a particular part of their territory, investors should know before speculating on the exploration company. Unfortunately, the *Buffalo River Dene Nation* case does nothing but punt the problem into the future, where the Crown, First Nation and mining company will find themselves deadlocked in the same way that the parties in *Platinex* were deadlocked: the mining company and investors have made financial commitments and need to move ahead with the project; the First Nation continues to block access to its land; and the Crown must buy themselves out of a political bind using public funds. It is a lose-lose-lose proposition.

The second case deals with the process appropriate for raising the issue of the meaningful right to harvest. In *Yahey v British Columbia*,[105] the Blueberry River First Nations (BRFN), which are protected by Treaty No. 8, commissioned a study that showed development in their traditional territory has resulted in two-thirds of their territory being used for industry or located within 250 metres of an industrial location. At this rate, by 2060 there would be no land left for hunting and

104 *Ibid* para 104.

105 *Yahey v British Columbia*, 2015 BCSC 1302 (B.C.S.C.).

fishing activities guaranteed by the treaty. The First Nation asked for an injunction on the sale of certain timber licences. The court denied the injunction on the basis that stopping the particular timber licences would only affect a small portion of the treaty territory, and that the First Nation should seek a general moratorium on all development in the area.

> BRFN may be able to persuade the court that a more general and wide-ranging hold on industrial activity is needed to protect its treaty rights until trial. However, if the court is to consider such a far-reaching order, it should be on an application that frankly seeks that result and allows the court to fully appreciate the implications and effects of what it is being asked to do. The public interest will not be served by dealing with the matter on a piecemeal, project-by-project basis.[106]

Prophet River First Nation v British Columbia (Minister of Environment)[107] raises the issue of which bodies are obliged to consider whether the meaningful right to harvest is in play. Four Treaty No. 8 First Nations challenged the approval of an environmental assessment for a dam on the Peace River that would have created a reservoir of 9,330 hectares. The First Nation argued that development in the Peace River basin would take away the meaningful right to hunt and therefore infringe the rights in the treaty. The British Columbia Supreme Court decided that the ministers, in approving the environmental assessment, did not have to take into consideration whether the impact on treaty lands would take away the meaningful right to hunt. Rather, the only obligation was to ensure that there was deep consultation. The court suggested that the larger issues on treaty infringement needed to be raised in an action that would address the issue for the whole territory.

The problem with the "piecemeal" approach for First Nations is that each development, taken in isolation, will not likely constitute treaty infringement. But if First Nations cannot raise these issues in specific cases, they will be left to do what the judge suggests – initiate actions for moratoria on *all* development in treaty territories. One could imagine that courts would be hard pressed to impose such wide-ranging moratoria on development, and one would anticipate a significant

---

106 *Ibid* para 64.

107 *Prophet River First Nation v British Columbia (Minister of Environment)*, [2015] B.C.J. 2026.

backlash from the non-Native population. No such case has ever succeeded in Canada.[108]

In the fourth case that I want to highlight here, the issue was whether consultation was enough to override treaty rights. In *Athabasca Chipewyan First Nation v Canada (Minister of the Environment),*[109] an environmental panel found that the Shell Canada Energy Jackpine Mine Expansion in northern Alberta would have extensive irreversible adverse impacts on the land and culture of the First Nation covered by Treaty No. 8. Nonetheless, the governments decided to proceed with the project after a six-year study that included "deep consultation" with the First Nation. To the extent that this case suggests that a project which will have irreversible impacts on treaty rights can be countenanced simply because there has been "deep consultation," I would suggest the court is applying the wrong test. When there is an infringement of a treaty right, as appears to be the case here, whether the consultation is adequate is the wrong test. It seems to me that in this case, we are dealing not with a consultation problem but, rather, with a problem relating to the infringement of the treaty that would have required the application of the *Sparrow* test.

At the risk of repeating myself, let me explain where I think that courts have taken us. First, the *Buffalo River Dene Nation* case suggests that First Nations cannot object if the exploratory activity does not have an impact on the First Nation. The First Nation must wait until the resource extraction company and its investors have made financial commitments to the project and plan to exploit the resource. Second, the *Yahey* case makes it impossible to raise the larger issues relating to a meaningful right to hunt in an injunction for specific licences, and *Prophet River* suggests that the issue cannot be addressed in the environmental assessment process. Third, the *Athabasca Chipewyan First Nation* case shows that even if the First Nation were able to show treaty infringement, deep consultation would be enough to permit the project to go ahead. So none of these cases permits a discussion of the big picture relating to the meaningful right to harvest. The only option suggested by the

---

108 See *Ontario (Attorney General) v. Bear Island Foundation* [1991] 2 SCR 570, where the Court lifted a caution placed on the provincial registry for all land in the traditional area of the Bear Island First Nation.

109 *Athabasca Chipewyan First Nation v Canada (Minister of the Environment),* 14 FC 1185 (FC).

courts is for First Nations to bring a court case to stop *all* development on their treaty lands. As I have already indicated, this is not a realistic proposition, and judges themselves would likely be taken aback should such a claim ever be made. Certainly, forcing First Nations to make such broad claims would not facilitate reconciliation between Indigenous and non-Indigenous people but rather invite a harsh backlash.

If these four cases articulate the present law, the courts have closed off a substantive consideration of whether the "meaningful right" described in *Mikisew Cree* has been infringed. These cases have not attempted to construct a viable framework for assessing when the "meaningful right" to hunt has disappeared. It is clear that a political process is needed to resolve these issues, but is there anything that courts could be doing differently until there are broad negotiations on treaty lands? In my view, courts can make an important contribution.

I suggest that courts should look at development on treaty lands, not as issues relating to consultation but as issues relating to treaty infringement. In other words, new licences for resource extraction would not be subject to the consultation and accommodation test set out in *Haida Nation* but, rather, the infringement and justification test set out in *Sparrow* and *Mikisew Cree*. By applying the *Sparrow* test, the courts would look for the Crown to do more than consult. The Crown would have to justify the objectives of the legislation and show that it acted honourably in infringing treaty rights. It is here that the consent standard could be applied. As mentioned above, the Supreme Court of Canada suggested in 1997, in *Delgamuukw v British Columbia*, that consent may be necessary where the proposed development would infringe harvesting rights. While courts have not expanded on the concept of consent, I have argued above that international standards and industry practice have overtaken judicial and governmental reluctance to recognize the consent standard. So part of the justification would involve determining whether there was consultation, and determining whether the infringement was significant enough to require consent.

If the default position were that any resource exploration on treaty lands could potentially take away the meaningful right to harvest, and thereby infringe treaty rights, then the Crown would be forced to enter discussions early with the First Nation to obtain their consent. It may be that some accommodation could be reached for exploratory activities and eventual exploitation. But if no accommodation were possible, then the mining company and its investors would know before they made irrevocable financial commitments.

Does this mean that First Nations would have a "veto" on all resource extraction on their lands? Under the present law, the answer would be "no," because courts decide on a case-by-case basis whether the Crown has justified the infringement of the treaty right and whether consent has been obtained. Courts must do this analysis sooner or later, and it is manifestly better to face the problem earlier rather than later, when the parties have more at stake and the losses will be more impactful.

C. Adoption of the Consent Standard Should Not Be Difficult

I began by describing the three elements of the original legal framework for the numbered treaties: recognition of an Indigenous collectivity; recognition of an interest of the collectivity in their lands; and recognition of the necessity of obtaining consent to access those lands.

After a dark century, where neither government nor courts recognized any of the three elements of the framework, reconstruction began towards the end of the twentieth century. Today, almost two decades into the twenty-first century, recognition of Indigenous collectivities and their interest in their lands is well settled. However, Canadian courts have not yet explicitly started developing a law around consent. Instead, courts in Canada have been focusing on consultation and accommodation embedded in an overall lack of a "veto" by Indigenous people. I argue in part five that an advantage of the consent standard being developed internationally is that it puts Indigenous people at the centre of the decision on land in a way that the infringe-and-justify framework does not. In this part, I argue that we are on the precipice of losing the meaningful right to harvest, and that there is a legal and moral imperative to require consent of First Nations for further taking up of lands. I also point out that in *Delgumuukw*, the Supreme Court of Canada contemplated the necessity of consent when hunting, fishing, and trapping rights would be taken away.

But my views are also informed by the fact that consent is already the "best practice" for the extractive industries. International state-sponsored institutions such as the United Nations, the Convention on Biological Diversity, the Inter-American Commission of Human Rights, and the International Finance Corporation as well private-sector bodies such as the Equator Principles, the International Council on Mining and Metals, and the Boreal Leadership Council have already adopted the consent standard. The adoption of this standard makes sense, both practically and theoretically. For the practical utility of the standard, I have given the examples of the high cost of conflict in the multi-billion-dollar Conga project in Peru, now suspended by Newmont, and in Canada, the halting of Platinex's exploratory activities on the treaty lands of the Kitchenuhmaykoosib Inninuwug. For the theoretical advantage of respecting the consent standard, I have pointed to negotiating theory, which suggests that the greater equality of bargaining power that comes with the recognition of the necessity of consent will more likely lead to better and more durable outcomes.

In Canada, recognizing consent is more a conceptual barrier for governments and the courts than an actual practical concern. Industry practice has largely moved to the consent standard in the form of Impact Benefit Agreements (IBAs) – agreements that are negotiated directly between companies and Indigenous communities. In return for a promise from the community not to oppose the project, the company will provide monetary benefits, some training, and perhaps some form of environmental monitoring.[110] In spite of some highly publicized conflicts, like that of the Kitchenuhmaykoosib, the majority of projects in Canada are able to proceed after IBAs have been signed.

Government, as well, has largely moved to seeking agreements with First Nations on large land claims. The federal and provincial governments were first forced into negotiations with the Cree and Inuit of Quebec in 1973, when an ambitious hydroelectric project was temporarily halted by a Quebec court that recognized an Aboriginal interest in land.[111] Although the initial case was overturned a few days later,[112] the governments and the Indigenous parties signed the first modern treaty in 1977.[113] Since then there have been about a dozen

110 For a discussion of impact benefits agreements, see IBA Research Network, www.impactandbenefit.com/. The Impact Benefit Agreements are not without problems, including issues related to power imbalance and lack of transparency; see Ken J. Caine and Naomi Krogman, "Powerful or Just Plain Power-Full? A Power Analysis of Impact and Benefit Agreements in Canada's North," 2010 *Organization & Environment* 23(1): 76–98.

111 *Gros-Louis v Société de développement de la Baie James* (1973), 8 C.N.L.C. 188.

112 *James Bay Development Corp. v Kanatewat* (1973), 8 C.N.L.C. 414; and *Société de développement de la Baie James v Kanatewat* (1974), 8 C.N.L.C. 373.

113 James Bay and Northern Quebec Agreement, 1977, www.gcc.ca/pdf/LEG000000006.pdf. For a general description of this agreement, see Shin Imai, "Land Claims in Canada" in *Handbook of the North American Indians*, vol. 2 (Washington, DC, Smithsonian Institute, 2007), 177–84.

other treaties signed in British Columbia, the Yukon, the Northwest Territories, Nunavut, and Labrador, covering, in total, 40 per cent of Canada's lands, waters, and resources.[114] In other words, the Crown has embarked on a modern treaty-making exercise that, like the historic treaties, recognizes the existence of an Indigenous collectivity, recognizes their interest in their land, and recognizes the necessity of obtaining consent to access their territory.

Until the Crown institutes comprehensive negotiations on treaty lands, the issues relating to a meaningful right to harvest will continue to be presented in the courtroom. At the present time, courts have developed neither a framework nor a forum for discussing this issue. It cannot be raised before the exploration phase because there are not yet any impacts. It cannot be raised during the assessment phase or the exploration phase because only the impacts of the specific project can be considered. And even if treaty infringement is proved, deep consultation is sufficient to allow the project to proceed.

I argue that courts can find a way out of this morass using the existing framework developed in *Sparrow* and recognizing that new resource extraction activities on treaty lands could result in treaty infringement. In analysing justification for Crown conduct, courts could start developing the concept of consent first mentioned by the Supreme Court of Canada in *Delgamuukw v British Columbia.* By doing this, courts will encourage the Crown to negotiate early and perhaps push the Crown to develop a broad process for setting aside treaty lands to fulfill the treaty promises.

8. Concluding Thoughts

Having argued for the adoption of the consent standard, I realize that these preliminary ideas cannot be implemented without a great deal of refinement. I will point out four important policy issues that need further consideration.

114 For a listing and description of agreements see Aboriginal Affairs and Northern Development Canada, Final Agreements and Related Implementation Matters, https://www.aadnc-aandc.gc.ca/eng/1100100030583/1100100030584. For a perspective from the First Nations parties to these agreements, see Land Claims Coalition, www.landclaimscoalition.ca/.

First, the contemporary status of the land may have an impact on the implementation of the consent standard. Unoccupied Crown land would be relatively straightforward to bring into the consent framework, but lands that have already been "taken up" for extractive industries, or lands that have already been alienated to third parties, would raise complicated discussions on the interests of non-Indigenous parties.

Second, the precise *circumstances* that would trigger the necessity of consent would have to be worked out in the Canadian context. Opinion at the international level suggests that consent would not have to be sought on every decision that could affect Indigenous land interests. However, the articulation of what "significant" impact would attract the requirement for consent should be developed through the consideration of specific cases.

Third, there would have to be some thought put into what "hunting, fishing, and trapping" means in the context of the land as *a source of livelihood* today. Are these words to be read narrowly, to encompass only subsistence harvesting activities? In my 2001 article, I argued that the harvesting rights recognized in treaties should not be seen as rights of individual Indians, but rather as a guarantee of collective survival.[115] That is, the Crown must ensure that there are sufficient resources on treaty lands to provide for the survival of the collective as a whole. Although the words in the treaty seem to be limited to individual rights to harvest from the land, a more historically accurate reading would see that the harvesting rights were a recognition that the Indigenous parties relied on the land for their economic survival. This economic survival approach is supported in the Supreme Court of Canada's decision in *R v Marshall*.[116] In this case Donald Marshall, a Mi'kmaq in Nova Scotia, was acquitted of fishing and selling eels without a licence. The Court interpreted a 1760 treaty, which did not mention fishing at all but had a clause providing for commercial relations between the British and the Mi'kmaq. As there was evidence that fish were traded at the time of the treaty, the Court found that the trading clause meant to protect "access to the things that were to be traded." In other words, the Court took into account the larger economic context of the Indigenous relation to the land.

115 *Supra* note 101.
116 *R v Marshall*, [1999] 3 SCR 456.

Fourth, would the consent standard permit a First Nation to authorize hazardous activities, such as nuclear waste dump on its lands? In other words, does the ability to *prevent* deleterious activity also provide the Indigenous group an ability to *authorize* activity that would have a significant impact on its lands? I would say "no," because the ability of a First Nation to *authorize* activities on its lands involves governance issues that are addressed in the self-government and land claims agreements mentioned above.[117] The consent standard does not itself address governance issues. It has been applied at the international level as a shield against detrimental extractive projects on Indigenous lands, not as a sword that can give authority to Indigenous groups. Both *Delgamuukw* and *Xeni Gwet'in* say that Indigenous people may not permit uses on their lands that would be inconsistent with the foundation of the Indigenous connection to the land and the interests of future generations. It seems to me, then, that in Canada, adopting the free, prior, informed consent standard will not open the way for unregulated deleterious uses of Indigenous lands.

If there were treaty negotiations, these four questions would be an important part of the discussions. Absent such negotiations, the issues will be addressed in the courtroom. At the present time, courts in Canada are lagging behind international and private industry standards, as well as practice on the ground. Rather than focusing on the fact that Indigenous parties do not have a veto, courts should focus on the development of the concept of consent.

117 See text at note 114.

Contributors

Francesca Allodi-Ross

Francesca Allodi-Ross received her Honours BA from McGill University in political science and her JD from Osgoode Hall Law School. She has volunteered with a number of organizations that work on Indigenous issues, including Dare to Dream in Rama First Nation, the Justice and Corporate Accountability Project, and the Miguel Agustin Pro Juarez Human Rights Centre in Mexico City. She is a staff lawyer at Community Legal Clinic – Simcoe, Haliburton, Kawartha Lakes, where she supervises the Aboriginal Justice Outreach Program.

John Borrows

John Borrows is the Robina Chair in Law, Public Policy and Society at the Faculty of Law, University of Victoria. Holding law degrees from the University of Toronto and Osgoode Hall Law School, he is a leading scholar and teacher in Indigenous, constitutional, and environmental law. A member of Ontario's Chippewas of Nawash First Nation and Anishinaabe, he has worked with and for Indigenous peoples in many countries. Supreme Court of Canada Justices have cited his work when ruling on Aboriginal cases. Professor Borrows is a recipient of the Aboriginal Achievement Award in Law and Justice; a Fellow of the Trudeau Foundation; a Fellow of the Academy of Arts, Humanities and Sciences of Canada (FRSC) (Canada's highest academic honour); and a 2012 recipient of the Indigenous Peoples Counsel (IPC) from the Indigenous Bar Association for honour and integrity in service to Indigenous communities. His publications include *Recovering Canada:*

The Resurgence of Indigenous Law (Donald Smiley Award for the best book in Canadian Political Science, 2002), *Canada's Indigenous Constitution* (Canadian Law and Society Best Book Award 2011), and *Drawing Out Law: A Spirit's Guide.*

Michael Coyle

Michael Coyle is an Associate Professor at the Faculty of Law, University of Western Ontario. His research and writing focus on the adequacy of legal mechanisms aimed at resolving Aboriginal rights claims and facilitating the reconciliation of Aboriginal rights and the assertion of Crown sovereignty. His research flows in part from more than a decade of experience as a mediator appointed to assist the Crown and First Nations to resolve disputes over historic treaty and governance rights. A particular focus of his research is the role of power relations in the alternative dispute resolution processes established by the Crown to address Aboriginal claims. His recent publications include "Transcending Colonialism? Power and the Resolution of Indigenous Treaty Claims in Canada and New Zealand" (2011) 24:4 *New Zealand Universities Law Review*; "Establishing Indigenous Governance: The Challenge of Confronting Mainstream Cultural Norms" in G. Otis and M. Papillon, eds., *The Relational Dimension of Indigenous Governance and Federalism: Theories and Practices* (Quebec City: Presses de l'Université Laval, 2013); and "Negotiating Indigenous Peoples' Exit from Colonialism: The Case for an Integrative Approach Discourse and Negotiations across the Indigenous/Non-Indigenous Divide" (2014) 27 *Canadian Journal of Law and Jurisprudence* 283.

Sari Graben

Sari Graben is Assistant Professor, Law and Business, Ryerson University. Professor Graben's primary theoretical interests are in the field of Indigenous law and development, with a special focus on regulatory institutions, emergent property systems, and governance. Her research analyses key challenges that arise from the regulation of Indigenous rights and engages with critical theories that deepen comparative frameworks used for pragmatic experimentation. Her published works on contemporary treaties address their legal interpretation as constitutional documents but also as frameworks that regulate resource use through co-management and property ownership. She publishes widely in the field and is currently co-editing a book (with Angela Cameron and Val Napoleon) entitled *Indigenous Peoples and Real Property: Beyond Privatization*. Professor Graben obtained her doctorate from Osgoode Hall Law School, held a SSHRC postdoctoral fellowship at the University of California – Berkeley Law, and held the Canada–US Fulbright Visiting Research Chair at the University of Washington (Seattle).

Shin Imai

Shin Imai is an Associate Professor at Osgoode Hall Law School where he co-directs the Intensive Program in Aboriginal Lands, Resources, and Governments and directs the Justice and Corporate Accountability Project. His research interests include Aboriginal law in Canada, the role of courts in negotiations, and Indigenous rights in Latin America. With law degrees from the University of Toronto and Osgoode Hall Law School, Professor Imai became a lawyer in 1980, practising at Keewaytinok Native Legal Services in Moosonee and later opening his own practice in the areas of human rights, refugee law, and Indigenous rights. In 1989, Professor Imai joined the Ontario Ministry of the Attorney General to work on developing alternative dispute resolution programs and initiating justice projects in Indigenous communities. Professor Imai's publications include the *Aboriginal Law Handbook*, "Breaching Indigenous Law: Canadian Mining in Guatemala" with Ladan Mehranvar and Jennifer Sander, and "Counter-pedagogy for Social Justice."

Julie Jai

Julie Jai is an Associate Fellow with the Caledon Institute. She holds an LLB from Osgoode Hall Law School and an LLM from the University of Toronto. With her impressive public service career, Jai is a recognized expert on public policy and the law, with special interests in Aboriginal law and human rights law. Jai was the chief negotiator for the Yukon government on negotiations leading to the ground-breaking Teslin Tlingit Council Administration of Justice Agreement which created a First-Nation-run justice system. She is an experienced lawyer, negotiator, mediator, policy adviser, director, and mentor who believes in working collaboratively with others to bring about positive change. Her publications include *The Journey of Reconciliation: Understanding our Treaty Past, Present and Future* (Caledon Institute of Social Policy, 2014);

"The Interpretation of Modern Treaties and the Honour of the Crown" (2009) 26:1 *National Journal of Constitutional Law*; and "The Invisibility of Race in Section 15: Why Section 15 of the Charter Has Not Done More to Promote Racial Equality," with Joseph Cheng, (2006) 5:1 *Journal of Law and Equality* 125.

Jean Leclair

Jean Leclair is a 2013 Trudeau Foundation Fellow and a law professor at Université de Montréal. Following the completion of his law degree from the Univeristé de Montréal in 1985 and his admission to the Quebec Bar in 1986, Professor Leclair clerked for the Honourable Justice Alice Desjardins at the Federal Court of Appeal. For more than ten years, his research has focused on the (re)configuration of political relationships between governments and Aboriginal peoples and the reconfiguration of relationships within Aboriginal communities. The structuring effects of law on the evolution of these relationships are the main focus of his research. Professor Leclair is working on a theory of federalism that would satisfy Aboriginal communities without requiring their members to adhere to a monistic concept of their identity.

Kent McNeil

Kent McNeil has been a law professor at Osgoode Hall Law School since 1987, and was formerly the Research Director of the University of Saskatchewan Native Law Centre. Holding degrees from the University of Saskatchewan and Oxford, Professor McNeil is a member of the Bar of Saskatchewan. In 2006, he was awarded a prestigious Killam Fellowship to pursue research on the legality of European assertions of sovereignty in North America. Professor McNeil's research focuses on the rights of Indigenous peoples. Aspects of his work include land rights, treaty rights, and self-government. He has written a book, *Common Law Aboriginal Title*, and numerous monographs and articles, some of which are collected in *Emerging Justice? Essays on Indigenous Rights in Canada and Australia*.

Matthew Mehaffey

Matthew Mehaffey is a consultant and negotiator specializing in modern Aboriginal treaties and self-government. Since studying law at the

University of British Columbia, his work has included negotiating some of the first Aboriginal tax-sharing agreements in Canada, negotiating fiscal transfer agreements and administration of justice agreements, as well as representing clients in treaty-based dispute resolution processes related to fiscal and program matters. He has participated in the development and drafting of reports related to the implementation of Yukon Final and Self-Government Agreements, Yukon Self-Government Financial Transfer Agreements, and the Tlicho Financing Agreement, as well as the Land Claims Agreements Coalition implementation policy. He currently represents Aboriginal groups in the Yukon, Northwest Territories, and British Columbia.

Aaron Mills

Aaron Mills is a bear clan Anishinaabe from Couchiching First Nation, Treaty #3 Territory, and from North Bay, Robinson-Huron Treaty Territory. He's a lawyer (JD Toronto, LLM Yale) and doctoral candidate at the University of Victoria. His graduate work on Anishinaabe constitutionalism has garnered numerous academic awards: Aaron is a SSHRC Talent Award winner, a Trudeau Foundation Scholar, a Vanier Canada Scholar, and a Fulbright Canada Scholar. Aaron sat on the Indigenous Bar Association's board of directors from 2013 to 2016. During his JD he sat on the board of directors of Aboriginal Legal Services of Toronto and served as editor-in-chief of the *Indigenous Law Journal*.

Sarah Morales

Sarah Morales, a Cowichan Tribes member, is an Assistant Professor at the University of Ottawa Faculty of Law. She completed an LLB from the University of Victoria in 2004 and an LLM from the University of Arizona in 2006. Professor Morales was the Department of Justice Congressional Fellow at the University of Arizona, clerked for the Pasqua Yaqui Tribal Appellate Court, and worked on a petition to the Organization of American States. She has worked for numerous First Nation organizations in British Columbia, including the Hul'qumi'num Treaty Group, the National Centre for First Nations Governance and Cowichan Tribes. Professor Morales received her PhD from the University of Victoria in 2015. Her research focuses on Coast Salish legal traditions and the development of a process to reconcile conflicts between these and outside legal traditions.

Jacinta Ruru

Jacinta Ruru (of Maori descent – Ngati Raukawa and Ngati Ranginui) is Professor of Law at the University of Otago, New Zealand, Co-Director of Nga Pae o te Maramatanga (New Zealand's Maori Centre of Research Excellence), and a centre associate at the Indigenous Law Centre, University of New South Wales, Australia. Jacinta holds a PhD from the University of Victoria, Canada. Her research focuses on exploring Indigenous peoples' legal interests to own, manage, and govern land and water. Some of her work is interdisciplinary with the social sciences and comparative with Australia, Canada, United States, and the Nordic countries. Jacinta has published widely, including co-authoring *Discovering Indigenous Lands: The Doctrine of Discovery in the English Colonies* (Oxford University Press, 2010). She holds editorial responsibilities on many journals, including editor of New Zealand's leading resource management journal, *Resource Management Theory & Practice*, consultative editor for *Maori Law Review*, and book review editor of the *Journal of Human Rights and the Environment*. Jacinta has won awards for her research, teaching of undergraduate students, and supervision of post-graduate students.

Sara L. Seck

Sara L. Seck is an Associate Professor at the Faculty of Law, Western University. With law degrees from the University of Toronto and Osgoode Hall Law School, her PhD research concerned home state obligations to regulate transnational mining companies under international environmental and human rights law. In 2015, she received the Emerging Scholarship award from the IUCN's Academy of Environmental Law. Seck's publications include "Canadian Mining Internationally and the UN Guiding Principles for Business and Human Rights" (2011) 49 *Canadian Yearbook of International Law* 51; "Transnational Business and Environmental Harm: A TWAIL Analysis of Home State Obligations" (2011) 3:1 *Trade, Law & Development* 164; and, "Home State Responsibility and Local Communities: The Case of Global Mining" (2008) 11 *Yale Human Rights and Development Law Journal* 177.

Heidi Kiiwetinepinesiik Stark

Heidi Kiiwetinepinesiik Stark (Turtle Mountain Ojibwe) is an Assistant Professor of Political Science at the University of Victoria. She has a

PhD in American Studies from the University of Minnesota. Her research interests include Aboriginal and treaty rights and Indigenous politics in the United States and Canada. She is the co-editor of *Centering Anishinaabeg Studies: Understanding the World through Stories* with Jill Doerfler and Niigaanwewidam Sinclair and is the co-author of the third edition of *American Indian Politics and the American Political System* with Dr. David E. Wilkins. Her other publications include "Respect, Responsibility, and Renewal: The Foundations of Anishinaabe Treaty-Making with the United States and Canada" (2010) 34:2 *American Indian Culture and Research Journal* 145, and "Marked by Fire: Anishinaabe Articulations of Nationhood in Treaty Making with the United States and Canada" (2012) 36:2 *American Indian Quarterly* 119.

Mark D. Walters

Mark D. Walters is the F.R. Scott Professor of Public and Constitutional Law at McGill University. He received a BA (Political Science) from the University of Western Ontario in 1986, an LLB from Queen's University in 1989, and a DPhil (in Law) from Oxford University in 1996. In 1999, he joined the Faculty of Law at Queen's where he taught until he took up his present position at McGill in 2016. Walters researches and publishes in two related legal fields: the rights of Indigenous peoples, with a particular emphasis on historical perspectives, and theories of legality in common law jurisdictions, also with an emphasis on history and the history of ideas. He has published articles in leading peer-reviewed journals in Canada and in the United Kingdom, as well as book chapters in volumes published by leading university presses. In 2013, he was an HLA Hart Fellow at University College, Oxford, and a Herbert Smith Visitor in the Faculty of Law at Cambridge University. His research in the area of Aboriginal rights has been funded by grants from the Social Sciences and Humanities Research Council of Canada, and in 2006, he was awarded the Canadian Association of Law Teachers Award for Academic Excellence.

Index